Government Spending on the Elderly

Also by Dimitri B. Papadimitriou

THE DISTRIBUTIONAL EFFECTS OF GOVERNMENT SPENDING AND TAXATION *(editor)*

INDUCED INVESTMENT AND BUSINESS CYCLES *(with Hyman P. Minsky)*

MODERNIZING FINANCIAL SYSTEMS *(editor)*

STABILITY IN THE FINANCIAL SYSTEM *(editor)*

ASPECTS OF DISTRIBUTION OF WEALTH AND INCOME *(editor)*

POVERTY AND PROSPERITY IN THE US IN THE LATE TWENTIETH CENTURY *(Co-editor with Edward N. Wolff)*

PROFITS, DEFICITS AND INSTABILITY *(editor)*

FINANCIAL CONDITIONS AND MACROECONOMIC PERFORMANCE: Essays in Honor of Hyman P. Minsky *(Co-editor with Steven M. Fazzari)*

Government Spending on the Elderly

Edited by

Dimitri B. Papadimitriou
President, The Levy Economics Institute
Jerome Levy Professor of Economics, Bard College,
Annandale-on-Hudson, New York

Selection and editorial matter © Dimitri B. Papadimitriou 2007
Individual chapters © their respective authors 2007

All rights reserved. No reproduction, copy or transmission of this publication may be made without written permission.

No paragraph of this publication may be reproduced, copied or transmitted save with written permission or in accordance with the provisions of the Copyright, Designs and Patents Act 1988, or under the terms of any licence permitting limited copying issued by the Copyright Licensing Agency, 90 Tottenham Court Road, London W1T 4LP.

Any person who does any unauthorised act in relation to this publication may be liable to criminal prosecution and civil claims for damages.

The authors have asserted their rights to be identified as the authors of this work in accordance with the Copyright, Designs and Patents Act 1988.

First published in 2007 by
PALGRAVE MACMILLAN
Houndmills, Basingstoke, Hampshire RG21 6XS and
175 Fifth Avenue, New York, N.Y. 10010
Companies and representatives throughout the world.

PALGRAVE MACMILLAN is the global academic imprint of the Palgrave Macmillan division of St. Martin's Press, LLC and of Palgrave Macmillan Ltd. Macmillan® is a registered trademark in the United States, United Kingdom and other countries. Palgrave is a registered trademark in the European Union and other countries.

ISBN-13: 978–0–230–50061–7 hardback
ISBN-10: 0–230–50061–7 hardback

This book is printed on paper suitable for recycling and made from fully managed and sustained forest sources. Logging, pulping and manufacturing processes are expected to conform to the environmental regulations of the country of origin.

A catalogue record for this book is available from the British Library.

Library of Congress Cataloging-in-Publication Data

   Government spending on the elderly / edited by Dimitri B. Papadimitriou.
     p. cm.
   Includes bibliographical references and index.
   ISBN 0–230–50061–7 (alk. paper)
     1. Older people – Government policy – United States. 2. Social security – United States. 3. Old age assistance – United States. 4. Older people – United States – Social conditions. 5. Age distribution (Demography) – Economic aspects – United States. I. Papadimitriou, Dimitri B.

HQ1064.U5G566 2007
362.6—dc22   2007022500

10 9 8 7 6 5 4 3 2 1
16 15 14 13 12 11 10 09 08 07

Printed and bound in Great Britain by
Antony Rowe Ltd, Chippenham and Eastbourne

Contents

List of Tables	viii
List of Figures	xii
List of Abbreviations and Acronyms	xvi
The Levy Economics Institute of Bard College	xviii
Acknowledgements	xix
Notes on Contributors	xx

1 Economic Perspectives on Aging: An Overview 1
  Dimitri B. Papadimitriou

Part I Welfare State and the Incentives to Retire

2 European Welfare State Regimes and Their Generosity toward
  the Elderly 23
  Axel Boersch-Supan

  Comments to Chapter 2 48
  Sergio Nisticò

3 Global Demographic Trends and Provisioning for the Future 53
  L. Randall Wray

  Comments to Chapter 3 73
  Richard Startz

Part II Aspects of Economic Well-being and Gender Disparities among the Elderly

4 Net Government Expenditures and the Economic Well-being
  of the Elderly in the United States, 1989–2001 81
  Edward N. Wolff, Ajit Zacharias, and Hyunsub Kum

  Comments to Chapter 4 118
  Robert Haveman

5 Differing Prospects for Women and Men: Young Old-Age,
  Old Old-Age, and Eldercare 123
  Lois B. Shaw

  Comments to Chapter 5 137
  Rania Antonopoulos

v

Part III Changing Patterns of Retirement Behavior

6 Working for a Good Retirement 141
Barbara A. Butrica, Karen E. Smith, and C. Eugene Steuerle

   Comments to Chapter 6 175
   Lucie G. Schmidt

7 Net Intergenerational Transfers from an Increase in Social Security Benefits 178
Li Gan, Guan Gong, and Michael Hurd

   Comments to Chapter 7 189
   Daniel L. Thornton

Part IV Interaction between Private and Public Provisioning

8 The Changing Role of Employer Pensions: Tax Expenditures, Costs, and Implications for Middle-class Elderly 193
Teresa Ghilarducci

   Comments to Chapter 8 218
   Zvi Bodie

9 Retiree Health Benefit Coverage and Retirement 220
James Marton and Stephen A. Woodbury

   Comments to Chapter 9 243
   Barbara Wolfe

Part V Budgetary and Macroeconomic Implications of Aging

10 Population Forecasts, Fiscal Policy, and Risk 249
Shripad Tuljapurkar

   Comments to Chapter 10 266
   Clark Burdick

11 Wage Growth and the Measurement of Social Security's Financial Condition 272
Andrew G. Biggs and Jagadeesh Gokhale

   Comments to Chapter 11 306
   Stephanie A. Kelton

Part VI Retirement Security: Problems and Prospects

12 The Adequacy of Retirement Resources among the
Soon-to-Retire, 1983–2001   315
Edward N. Wolff

   Comments to Chapter 12   343
   Brooke Harrington

13 Minimum Benefits in Social Security   347
*Melissa M. Favreault, Gordon B. T. Mermin, and
C. Eugene Steuerle*

   Comments to Chapter 13   389
   Robert K. Triest

Author Index   393

Subject Index   398

List of Tables

2.1	Income inequality, leisure time, and life expectancy at birth	25
2.2	Time-series regressions of social expenditure share devoted to the elderly on social expenditure share devoted to the young (percentage of GDP)	32
2.3	Distribution of income, consumption, and wealth among the elderly (GINI coefficients)	34
2.4	Life expectancy at birth, 2003	37
2.5	Pooled time-series cross-section regressions of social expenditures for the elderly as percent of GDP	39
2.6	Preferences about size and redistribution of welfare state	41
2.7	Incentive effects and retirement behavior	44
4.1	A comparison of the LIMEW and Extended Income (EI)	83
4.2	Household money income (2005 dollars)	86
4.3	Household base income (2005 dollars)	89
4.4	Income from home wealth (2005 dollars)	90
4.5	Income from nonhome wealth (2005 dollars)	92
4.6	Government cash transfers (2005 dollars)	93
4.7	Government noncash transfers (2005 dollars)	93
4.8	Public consumption (2005 dollars)	94
4.9	Taxes (2005 dollars)	96
4.10	Net government expenditures (2005 dollars)	97
4.11	Government expenditures and taxes: nonelderly and elderly households (mean values, 2005 dollars)	99
4.12	Household production (2005 dollars)	100
4.13	LIMEW (2005 dollars)	102
4.14	Composition of LIMEW and Extended Income: nonelderly and the elderly	104
4.15	Inequality among the elderly and nonelderly by measure of well-being (Gini ratios)	110
5.1	Percent married, probability of surviving to next age, and percent female by age	124
5.2	Disabilities and nursing home residence by age and gender	128
6.1	Summary of policy simulations	146
6.2	Mean baseline respondent wealth and change from additional work (2006 $)	149
6.3	Mean respondent wealth and annuity income in 2049 under current law and estimated change under alternate reform scenarios (2006 $)	151

6.4	Total Social Security income, cost, Social Security deficit in 2045 by reform scenario (dollars in billions)	155
6.5	Total change in income tax, Social Security deficit, and unified deficit in 2045 by reform scenario (dollars in billions)	158
6.A.1	Summary of core processes modeled in DYNASIM	162
6.A.2	Mean respondent wealth and annuity income in 2049 under current law and estimated change under alternate reform scenarios (2006 $)	167
6.A.3	Aggregate impact of working one and five years longer on Social Security and general revenues (population in millions and amounts in billions)	169
7.1	Interest rate and utility function parameters	182
7.2	Bequeathable wealth, Social Security benefits, expected present value of consumption and bequests (thousands) 65-year-old male	185
7.3	Bequeathable wealth, Social Security benefits, expected present value of consumption and bequests (thousands) 65-year-old female	186
7.4	Bequeathable wealth, Social Security benefits, expected present value of consumption and bequests (thousands) 65-year-old male	186
7.5	Bequeathable wealth, Social Security benefits, expected present value of consumption and bequests (thousands) 65-year-old female	186
8.1	Selected tax expenditures for the US budget	195
8.2	Pension participation and growth rates of all private sector workers by selected category and ranked by participation rates in 2005	197
8.3	DB pension spending has increased faster than cash compensation and medical insurance for all workers (production and salary expressed in dollars per hour)	199
8.4	Changes in job tenure for industries with the largest job growth	203
8.5	Pension benefit simulations: of a 401(k) and typical DB plan under ideal and probable conditions	205
8.A.1	Selected characteristics of job as reported by people working age 55–60 in 2002	211
9.1	Summary statistics of samples used in estimation (sample proportions except where noted)	232
9.2	Probit estimates of retirement probability between 1992–1994, 1994–1996, and 1992–1996, full-time older male workers in the HRS (probit betas, with P-values and marginal effects)	235
11.1	Actuarial balance and change in response to change in real wage growth and discount rates	286

11.2	Infinite term actuarial balance under alternative horizons for continued decline in the worker-to-beneficiary ratio	291
11.3	Social Security trustees' sensitivity analysis of real wage growth on 75-year actuarial balance	293
11.4	Impact of productivity growth on infinite term income, cost, and payrolls	294
12.1	Mean and median household wealth and income, 1983, 1989, and 2001 (in thousands of 2001 dollars)	325
12.2	Household net worth and income, ages 47–64, 1983, 1989, and 2001 (in thousands of 2001 dollars)	326
12.3	Percentage of households with retirement wealth ages 47–64, 1983, 1989, and 2001 (in percentage points)	327
12.4	Mean retirement and augmented wealth, ages 47–64, 1983, 1989, and 2001 (in thousands of 2001 dollars)	328
12.5	Mean income and wealth, middle three income quintiles, ages 47–64, 1989 and 2001 (in thousands of 2001 dollars)	329
12.6	Retirement wealth by race/ethnicity, ages 47–64, 1983, 1989, and 2001 (in thousands, 2001 dollars)	330
12.7	Income and wealth by race/ethnicity, ages 47–64, 1983, 1989, and 2001 (in thousands, 2001 dollars)	330
12.8	Retirement wealth by family status, ages 47–64, 1983, 1989, and 2001 (in thousands, 2001 dollars)	331
12.9	Income and wealth by family status, ages 47–64, 1983, 1989, and 2001 (in thousands, 2001 dollars)	332
12.10	Expected mean retirement income based on wealth holdings and expected retirement benefits, 1989 and 2001 (in thousands, 2001 dollars)	335
12.11	Percent of households with expected retirement income less than twice the poverty line, 1989 and 2001	336
12.12	Percent of households with expected replacement income more than one half of projected income at retirement, 1989 and 2001	338
12.13	Distribution of households in age group 47–64 by expected replacement rates, based on wealth holdings and expected pension and Social Security benefits, 1989 and 2001 (in percentage points)	339
13.1	Selected minimum benefit proposals for Social Security	353
13.2	Combined Social Security and SSI benefits as a percentage of poverty under current law for never married low-wage workers from the 1943 birth cohort	357
13.3	Percentage of retired worker beneficiaries with OASDI benefits of less than 99 percent of poverty under current law, December 2004	359

13.4	Years of Social Security – covered earnings in 2000 for the 1936–1940 cohort, by sex	362
13.5	Options Simulated	365
13.6	Percentage of OASDI beneficiaries age 62 and older receiving a minimum benefit under four alternative specifications, 2025 and 2050	369
13.7	Share of OASDI benefits received by different groups at age 62 and older under four alternative minimum benefit specifications, 2050	371
13.8	Share of OASDI benefits received by different groups at age 62 and older under wage-indexed standard minimum benefit specification and three alternatives, 2050	375
13.9	Share and number of Social Security beneficiaries in poverty under the options at age 62 and older, 2050	379
13.10	Time paths of the alternatives: expenditures as a percentage of current law benefits under each of the options, 2010–2050	381

List of Figures

2.1	GDP per capita (EU25 = 100)	24
2.2	Population aging in Europe and the US: percentage age 65 and older	24
2.3	Size of the welfare state (social expenditures per GDP, in percentages)	26
2.4	Size of the welfare state (social expenditures per capita, in Euro PPP)	26
2.5	Social expenditures dedicated to the elderly (per capita, in Euro PPP)	27
2.6	Share of social expenditures dedicated to the elderly (percentages of total)	28
2.7	Share of social expenditures dedicated to the young (percentages of total)	29
2.8	Social expenditures dedicated to the young (per capita, in Euro PPP)	29
2.9	Relative generosity to the elderly versus the young (social expenditure shares to the elderly divided by social expenditure shares to the young)	30
2.10	Relative generosity to the elderly versus the young (expenditure per capita devoted to the elderly versus per capita spending devoted to the young, Euro PPP)	31
2.11	Relative generosity to the elderly vs. the young (social expenditures devoted to the elderly versus social expenditures devoted to the young; percentage of GDP)	32
2.12	Income level of retirees (age 72 and less/age 73 and more) relative to income of working persons aged 50–65	33
2.13	Percentage of youths aged between 15 and 19 who are not in education nor in employment, 2003	35
2.14	Employment rate of individuals aged 55–64, 1992–2004	36
2.15	Walking speed and grip strength of individuals aged 50 and older	36
2.16	Comprehensive health index of individuals aged 50 and older	37
2.17	Age structure of European countries	40
2.18	Preferences about pension reform options (in percentage)	42
2.19	Employment and retirement rates conditional on good health	42
2.20	Disability insurance prevalence, by correction for health status	43
3.1	Working-age population shares	58
3.2	World population pyramids	60

3.3	US population pyramids, selected years	61
3.4	US death probabilities by age (2001, updated April 22, 2005)	62
3.5	OASDI expenditures as a percent of GDP	64
3.6	US productivity, historical and projected	66
3.C.1	Old age dependency – United States	74
3.C.2	Dependency rates – United States	74
3.C.3	Weighted dependency rates – United States	75
3.C.4	Old age dependency	76
4.1	Relative well-being of elderly subgroups: money income (ratio of subgroup to overall elderly mean values)	87
4.2	Relative well-being of elderly subgroups: equivalent money income (ratio of subgroup to overall elderly mean values)	88
4.3	Differentials in base income among elderly subgroups (ratio of subgroup to overall elderly mean values)	89
4.4	Differentials in income from home wealth among elderly subgroups (ratio of subgroup to overall elderly mean values)	91
4.5	Differentials in income from nonhome wealth among elderly subgroups (ratio of subgroup to overall elderly mean values)	91
4.6	Differentials in cash transfers among elderly subgroups (ratio of subgroup to overall elderly mean values)	93
4.7	Differentials in noncash transfers among elderly subgroups (ratio of subgroup to overall elderly mean values)	94
4.8	Differentials in public consumption among elderly subgroups (ratio of subgroup to overall elderly mean values)	95
4.9	Differentials in taxes among elderly subgroups (ratio of subgroup to overall elderly mean values)	96
4.10	Differentials in net government expenditures among elderly subgroups (ratio of subgroup to overall elderly mean values)	97
4.11	Differentials in household production among elderly subgroups (ratio of subgroup to overall elderly mean values)	101
4.12a	Relative well-being of elderly groups by money income and LIMEW, 1989 (ratio of subgroup to overall elderly mean values)	106
4.12b	Relative well-being of elderly groups by money income and LIMEW, 2001 (ratio of subgroup to overall elderly mean values)	107
4.13	Lorenz curve for Extended Income and LIMEW: 1989, 2001	110
4.14	Decomposition of inequality in LIMEW, 2001	111
4.15	Decomposition of EI, 2001	111
4.16	Contribution to the change in the Gini ratio of the elderly, 1989–2001	113
4.17	Contribution to the change in Gini ratio of the nonelderly, 1989–2001	113

6.1	Net income of a hypothetical worker by age and employment status	144
6.2	Percent change from baseline in average annuity income at retirement by lifetime earnings quintile and additional work effort	153
6.3	Aggregate income and costs to the Social Security system, under the baseline, 2000–2050	154
6.4	Social Security cost to income ratio under various working five more years reform scenarios, 2000–2049	156
6.5	Social Security cost to income ratio under various working five more years reform scenarios including additional income tax, 2000–2049	159
7.1	Consumption path	181
7.2	Consumption and wealth paths	183
7.3	Response to increase in Social Security	184
9.1	Percentage of private-sector establishments offering health insurance to retirees, 1997–2003	222
9.2	Percentage of private-sector establishments with > 1,000 employees offering health insurance to retirees, 1997–2003	222
9.3	Percentage of public-sector establishments offering health insurance to retirees, 1997–2003	223
9.4	Percentage of state government establishments offering health insurance to retirees, 1997–2003	223
9.5	Transitions of employed full-time workers ages 51–61 with and without retiree health benefits, 1992–1994	225
9.6	Transitions of employed full-time workers ages 51–61 with and without retiree health benefits, 1992–1996	226
9.7	HRS analysis samples illustrated	231
9.C.1	Provision of Retiree Health Benefits by Employers with 1,000+ Employees, 1991–2003	244
10.1	Sexes-combined life expectancy, historical and forecast	252
10.2	Total fertility rate, historical and forecast	254
10.3	Total population forecasts ($\times 10^8$)	255
10.4	Old age dependency ratio $(65+)/(20–64)$	256
10.5	Projected US population 2010; uncertainty is 95 percentile range	257
10.6	Projected US population 2025; uncertainty is 95 percentile range	258
10.7	Projected US population 2050; uncertainty is 95 percentile range	259
10.8	75-year summarized actuarial balance	261
10.9	Chance of solvency until 2052: tax increase and investment	262
10.10	Chance of solvency until 2052, tax and NRA	263

11.1	Effect of faster real wage growth on actuarial balance under a constant versus a declining worker-to-beneficiary ratio	279
11.2	Locus of $dAB/dG = 0$ when current benefits depend on current wages and wages in 35 past periods – declining weights	283
11.3	Projected worker-beneficiary ratio and its rate of change (b) in the United States	284
11.4	Projected US worker-beneficiary ratio, worker population, and total population	285
11.5	Actuarial balance for alternative rates of decline in the worker-beneficiary ratio and real wage growth	287
11.6	Annual balance ratios under alternative wage growth rates (1.1% and 1.6%) – stylized model under US calibration	289
11.7	Present valued weights under alternative wage growth rates (1.1% and 1.6%) – stylized model under US calibration	289
11.8	Weighted annual balance ratios under alternative wage growth rates (1.1% and 1.6%) (SSASIM model; $b > 0$; wage-price indexing)	295
11.C.1	Historic and projected growth of US economy	307
11.C.2	Percent of wages subject to Social Security tax	309
13.1	Design of simulation with additional bend point (in the context of reduced benefits), compared with current law and current law with scalar reductions	367

List of Abbreviations and Acronyms

AARP	American Association of Retired Persons
ADEA	Age Discrimination in Employment Act
ADL	Activities of daily living
AHEAD	Asset and health dynamics study
AIME	Average indexed monthly earnings
AMT	Alternative minimum tax
AW	Augmented wealth
CBO	Congressional Budget Office
CCRC	Continuing care retirement community
CPI	Consumer Price Index
CPS	Current Population Survey
CREF	College retirement equities fund
CSSS	Commission to strengthen Social Security
DB	Defined benefit
DC	Defined contribution
DYNASIM	Dynamic simulation of income model
EEA	Early entitlement age
ECCLI	Extended Care Career Ladder Initiative
EGTRRA	Economic Growth and Tax Relief Reconciliation Act of 2001
EI	Extended income
EPHI	Employer Provided Health Insurance
ERISA	Employee Retirement Income Security Act of 1974
EU	European Union
EUROSTAT	Statistical office of the European communities
FAS	Financial accounting statement
FE	Financial education
FI	Full income
GDP	Gross Domestic Product
HI	Health insurance
HRS	Health and retirement survey
IADL	Instrumental activities of daily living
IBONDS	Inflation-indexed bonds
IRA	Individual Retirement Account
JGTRRA	Jobs and Growth Tax Relief Reconciliation Act of 2003
LIMEW	Levy Institute Measure of Economic Well-being
MEPS-IC	Medical expenditure panel survey – insurance component
MESP	Measurement of economic and social performance

List of Abbreviations and Acronyms xvii

MI	Money income
NBDS	New beneficiary data system
NCRP	National commission on retirement policy
NCS	National compensation survey
NDC	National defined contribution
NIPA	National Income and Product Accounts
NLSY	National longitudinal survey of youth
NRA	Normal retirement age
NW	Net worth
NWX	New worth excluding DC pensions
OASDI	Old-age, survivors, and disability insurance
OASI	Old-age and survivors insurance
OCACT	Office of the chief actuary
OECD	Organisation for Economic Co-operation and Development
PB	Pension benefit
PBGC	Pension benefit guarantee corporation
PDV	Present discounted value
PIA	Primary insurance amount
PIMS	Pension insurance modeling system
PSID	Panel study of income dynamics
RHB	Retiree health benefits
RW	Retirement wealth
SCF	Survey of Consumer Finances
SHARE	Survey of health, aging, and retirement in Europe
SIG	Senior income guarantee
SIPP	Survey of Income and Program Participation
SSA	Social Security Administration
SSASIM	Social Security and accounts simulator
SSW	Social Security wealth
TFR	Total fertility rate
TIAA	Teachers insurance and annuity association
TIPS	Treasury inflation-protected securities
UN	United Nations

The Levy Economics Institute of Bard College

Founded in 1986, The Levy Economics Institute of Bard College is an autonomous nonprofit public policy research organization. It is nonpartisan, open to the examination of diverse points of view, and dedicated to public service.

The Institute believes in the potential for economic study to improve the human condition. Its purpose is to generate viable, effective public policy responses to important economic problems. It is concerned with issues that profoundly affect the quality of life in the United States, in other highly industrialized nations, and in countries with developing economies.

The Institute's present research programs include such issues as financial instability, economic growth and employment, international trade, problems associated with the distribution of income and wealth, the measurement of economic well-being, and gender, globalization, and poverty.

The opinions expressed in this volume are those of the authors and do not necessarily represent those of the Institute, its Board of Governors or the Trustees of Bard College.

Board of Governors

Lakshman Achuthan
Leon Botstein
Martin L. Leibowitz
J. Ezra Merkin
Dimitri B. Papadimitriou, President
Joseph Stiglitz
William Julius Wilson

Acknowledgements

I would like to thank the Board of Trustees of Bard College for sponsoring the Levy Economics Institute's ongoing research project on the *Distribution of Income, Wealth and Well-being* and the Smith Richardson Foundation for its support of the conference on "Government Spending on the Elderly" from which the chapters of this book are drawn. As part of this research project, many distinguished scholars, policy makers, and business leaders participate in seminars and conferences aimed at finding policy options to pressing economic problems. I am grateful to the authors for their cooperation in carrying out revisions, and to my assistant Deborah C. Treadway for copyediting the entire volume, managing the final details of collating the changes by the authors and commentators, and overseeing all tasks of proofreading.

To her, my warm and sincere thanks.

DIMITRI B. PAPADIMITRIOU

Notes on Contributors

Rania Antonopoulos is a Research Scholar at the Levy Economics Institute. Prior to her present position, she taught economics at New York University for 10 years. She specializes and teaches courses in macroeconomics, international trade and globalization, feminist economics, and history of economic thought. Since 2002, she has been a coprincipal investigator and cocoordinator for GEM-IWG, an international network that promotes capacity building and knowledge sharing on Gender, Macroeconomics, and International Economics. Her current research focuses on the macroeconomics of full employment policies and on gender-aware economic modeling. Antonopoulos received a PhD in economics from New School for Social Research, New York.

Andrew G. Biggs is Associate Commissioner for Retirement Policy at the Social Security Administration, where his office focuses on the use of microsimulation modeling to analyze the distributional effects of current-law Social Security as well potential policy reforms. Previously he has worked as a staffer on the House Banking and Financial Services Committee and as a Social Security Analyst at the Cato Institute. In 2001 he served on the staff of the President's Commission to Strengthen Social Security, and in 2005 on the staff of the White House National Economic Council. Andrew holds a Bachelor's Degree from the Queen's University of Belfast, Northern Ireland; a Master's Degree from Cambridge University; and a PhD from the London School of Economics and Political Science.

Zvi Bodie is the Norman and Adele Barron Professor of Management at Boston University. He holds a PhD from the Massachusetts Institute of Technology and has served on the finance faculty at the Harvard Business School and MIT's Sloan School of Management. Professor Bodie has published widely on pension finance and investment strategy in leading professional journals. His books include *Foundations of Pension Finance, Pensions in the US Economy, Issues in Pension Economics, and Financial Aspects of the US Pension System*. His textbook, *Investments*, is the market leader and is used in the certification programs of the Financial Planning Association and the Society of Actuaries. His textbook *Finance* is coauthored by Nobel Prize winning economist, Robert C. Merton. His latest book is *Worry Free Investing: A Safe Approach to Achieving Your Lifetime Financial Goals*.

Axel Boersch-Supan is Director of the Mannheim Research Institute for the Economics of Aging (MEA), which he founded, and Professor for Macroeconomics and Public Policy at the University of Mannheim, Germany.

He holds a diploma in mathematics from the University of Bonn, Germany. He received his PhD in economics from the Massachusetts Institute of Technology and taught at Harvard's Kennedy School of Government and at Dortmund University before joining Mannheim. Boersch-Supan chairs the Council of Advisors to the German Economics Ministry and the Pension Reform Unit of the German Social Security Reform Commission. He is member of the German Presidents' Commission on Demographic Change, of the German Academy of Sciences at Berlin-Brandenburg, and of the German Academy of Natural Sciences Leopoldina.

Clark Burdick has been an Economist in Social Security's Office of Policy since 1999. Prior to joining SSA, he worked in the research department of the Federal Reserve Bank of Atlanta and taught economics at Georgia Tech and Indiana Universities. He attended graduate school at Stanford University earning a PhD in economics and a MS degree in statistics. Clark specializes in macroeconomics and time series econometrics. His research at SSA has been primarily focused on the development of stochastic models of the economic and demographic variables affecting the OASDI trust funds. He is currently using stochastic modeling techniques to study the potential costs of offering benefit guarantees in a mixed system of traditional benefits and Personal Retirement Accounts.

Barbara A. Butrica is a labor economist with research interests in aging and income dynamics. Dr. Butrica is currently a Senior Research Associate at the Urban Institute where she studies issues related to the economic security of the boomer generation, Social Security, and the engagement of older adults. She previously served as an analyst at Mercer Human Resource Consulting, and as an economist at the Social Security Administration. She holds a PhD from Syracuse University and a BA from Wellesley College.

Melissa M. Favreault is a Senior Research Associate in the Urban Institute's Income and Benefits Policy Center. She has written extensively about the distributional effects of proposed changes to Social Security. Her work in this area has focused on how changes in family structure and work/earnings patterns impact economic well-being in retirement, with a special emphasis on impacts for women, low-wage workers, and persons with disabilities. She earned her BA from Amherst College, and her MA and PhD in Sociology from Cornell University.

Li Gan is currently an Associate Professor of Economics at Texas A&M University, College Station, and a Faculty Research Fellow at the National Bureau of Economic Research. He obtained his PhD in economics from the University of California, Berkeley, in 1998. His research interest is applied microeconomics.

Teresa Ghilarducci is a Professor of Economics at the University of Notre Dame and director of the Higgins Labor Research Center at the University.

Her new book, under way, *The End of Retirement*, for Princeton University Press, investigates the effect of pension losses on older Americans. She served on the Pension Benefit Guaranty Corporation's Advisory Board from 1995 to 2002, and on the Board of Trustees of the State of Indiana Public Employees' Retirement Fund from 1997 to 2002.

Jagadeesh Gokhale is a Senior Fellow at the Cato Institute. His research focuses on US entitlement policies, national saving, wealth distribution, and intergenerational transfers. Jagadeesh is coauthor of *Fiscal and Generational Imbalances: New Budget Measures for New Budget Priorities*. Jagadeesh has published many papers in top-tier academic journals and he is a cocreator of ESPlanner, a widely acclaimed financial planning software package.

Guan Gong is an Associate Professor at the Shanghai University of Finance and Economics. He earned a PhD in Economics from the University of Texas at Austin and his research interests include aging, labor, and applied econometrics.

Brooke Harrington is Assistant Professor of Sociology and Public Policy at Brown University and is currently a visiting scholar at the Max Planck Institute for the Study of Societies in Cologne, Germany. Her interests include investor behavior in the stock market, and its implications for retirement funding. She is the recipient of grants from the National Science Foundation, the Russell Sage Foundation, and the Center for Retirement Research. Her forthcoming book, *Pop Finance: Investment Clubs and Stock Market Populism*, will be published by Princeton University Press in Fall 2007.

Robert Haveman is John Bascom Emeritus Professor, Department of Economics and La Follette School of Public Affairs, University of Wisconsin-Madison, and Research Affiliate of the Institute for Research on Poverty. He has published widely in the economics of poverty and social policy, including *Succeeding Generations: On the Effects of Investments in Children* (1994) (with B. Wolfe) and papers in the *American Economic Review, Quarterly Journal of Economics*, and *Journal of the American Statistical Association*.

Michael Hurd is the Director of the RAND Center for the Study of Aging and a Research Associate at the National Bureau of Economic Research. He specializes in the economics of aging, particularly saving behavior and retirement.

Stephanie A. Kelton is an Associate Professor of Economics at the University of Missouri, Kansas City, and a Research Scholar at the Center for Full Employment and Price Stability (C-FEPS). Her primary research interests include monetary theory, international economics, employment policy, social security, and European monetary integration. She has published widely in the *Journal of Economic Issues*, the *Cambridge Journal of Economics*, the *Journal of Post Keynesian Economics*, the *Review of Social Economy* and *Challenge Magazine*. Her book (edited with Edward J. Nell), *The State, The Market, and the Euro: Metallism versus Chartalism in the Theory of Money*, is available through Edward Elgar Press.

Hyunsub Kum is a Research Scholar at the Levy Economics Institute and working on the Levy Institute Measure of Economic Well-being (LIMEW) within the distribution of income and wealth program. His research interests are mostly placed on the measurement of inequality, inequality and economic growth, the distributional effects of public spending, including cross-country comparisons, statistical matching, and microsimulation. He recently published articles with James K. Galbraith in *CESifo Economic Studies* and *Review of Income and Wealth*. Kum received a PhD in public policy from the University of Texas at Austin; an MPP from the University of Michigan, Ann Arbor; and an MPA and BA from Seoul National University, Korea.

James Marton is an Associate Professor in the Andrew Young School of Policy Studies at Georgia State University. He was previously a faculty member at the Martin School of Public Policy and Administration at the University of Kentucky and a visiting post-doctoral research fellow at the Taubman Center for Public Policy at Brown University. He received his undergraduate degree in Mathematics from St. Louis University and his MA and PhD in economics from Washington University in St. Louis, graduating in 2002. Jim's research focuses on public policy issues in health insurance markets. His work on Medicaid and SCHIP financing has appeared in the *Journal of Policy Analysis and Management*, the *Journal of Urban Economics*, and *Inquiry*.

Gordon B. T. Mermin is a Research Associate at the Urban Institute specializing in retirement and aging. He has written on the potential distributional impacts of Social Security reform options, work impediments at older ages, and the impact of health and employment shocks on the accumulation of retirement savings. Prior to joining the Urban Institute, Mermin worked on retirement issues as a Senior Analyst at the Government Accountability Office (GAO). He received his MA in economics from the University of Michigan in 1999 and his BA in economics from Stanford University in 1994.

Sergio Nisticò graduated (1986) in Political Sciences and earned a PhD in Economics (1991) at "La Sapienza" University of Rome where, in 1992, he was hired as Assistant Professor of Economics. In 1995 and 1996 he was elected Member of the Commission for the Italian Transportation Plan at the Ministry of Transports. Since 2001 he has been an Associate Professor of Economics at the Faculty of Economics of the University of Cassino, where he teaches microeconomics, history of economic thought, and social security economics. His recent publications include "Classical-type Temporary Positions: a Cost-plus Model," *Journal of Post-Keynesian Economics* (2002);

Competing Economic Theories (ed. with D. Tosato), Routledge (2002); "Consumption and Time in Economics: Prices and Quantities in a Temporary Equilibrium Perspective," *Cambridge Journal of Economics*, (2005); "Implementing the NDC theroretical model: a comparison of Italy and Sweden," (with S. Gronchi) in Holzmann R. and Palmer E. (eds) *Pension Reform: Issues and Prospects for Non-Financial Defined Contribution (NDC) Scheme*, World Bank (2006); "The Theoretical Foundations of NDC Pension Schemes" (with S. Gronchi), *Metroeconomica*, forthcoming.

Dimitri B. Papadimitriou is President of The Levy Economics Institute, and Executive Vice President and Jerome Levy Professor of Economics at Bard College. His areas of special interest are macroeconomics and modeling, employment policy, community development banking, financial structure, the federal reserve, monetary and fiscal policy, and the distribution of income and wealth in the United States and other countries. He has served as vice chairman of the congressional US Trade Deficit Review Commission. Papadimitriou is general editor of the Levy Institute's book series, a member of the editorial board of *Challenge* and the author of many articles and books. He received his BA from Columbia University and a PhD in economics from the New School for Social Research.

Lucie G. Schmidt is an Assistant Professor in the Department of Economics at Williams College. She received her PhD and MA degrees in Economics from the University of Michigan, and received an AB in Government from Smith College. Professor Schmidt's research to date has concentrated on two primary areas: (1) the economics of marriage and fertility decisions, and (2) examining costs and benefits of various social insurance programs. She has also written on the relationship between gender, marriage, and asset accumulation in the United States, and is currently examining the effects of demographic changes on private saving.

Lois B. Shaw is a semiretired economist who occasionally consults on social insurance, pensions, and other women's issues at the Institute for Women's Policy Research in Washington, DC. She previously held research positions at the US General Accounting Office and at the Ohio State University's Center for Human Resource Research. She has written numerous journal articles and monographs on women's employment, retirement, and poverty and recently served as one of the guest editors of a special issue of *Feminist Economics* on gender and aging. She received her PhD from the University of Michigan.

Karen E. Smith is a Senior Research Associate at The Urban Institute. She has designed and developed microsimulation models for Social Security, taxation, wealth and savings, labor-supply, charitable giving, health expenditure, student aid, and welfare reform. She received her BA from the University of Michigan and has done graduate work in statistics and econometrics at George Washington University. Prior to joining the Urban

Institute, she was a manager in the Health Policy Economics Group at Price Waterhouse. She has also worked as a microsimulation modeling consultant to the New Zealand Treasury and as a Principal Analyst at the Congressional Budget Office.

Richard Startz is Castor Professor of Economics at the University of Washington, where he has taught since 1984. He received his BA from Yale University in 1974 and his PhD from the Massachusetts Institute of Technology in 1978. He is coauthor of the textbook *Macroeconomics* and author of three books on computing, as well as numerous academic articles. His research interests include macroeconomics, econometrics, finance, and the economics of race. Articles from his op-ed pieces, which appear regularly in newspapers in Washington State can be found at http://www.uwnews.org/startz/

C. Eugene Steuerle is a Senior Fellow at the Urban Institute, codirector of the Urban-Brookings Tax Policy Center, and a columnist for Tax Notes Magazine. Among other positions, he has served as Deputy Assistant Secretary of the Treasury for Tax Analysis (1987–1989), President of the National Tax Association (2001–2002), Chair of the 1999 Technical Panel advising Social Security on its methods and assumptions, Economic Coordinator and original organizer of the 1984 Treasury study that led to the Tax Reform Act of 1986, and a columnist for the Financial Times. He is the author, coauthor, or coeditor of over 150 articles, reports, and testimonies, 650 briefs, and 11 books.

Daniel L. Thornton is Vice President and Economic Advisor at the Federal Reserve Bank of St. Louis. He has published numerous articles in the Federal Reserve Bank of St. Louis *Review* and in professional journals, and is an Associate Editor of the *Journal of Banking and Finance*, the *Journal of International Financial Markets Institutions and Money*, *Applied Economics*, and *Finance Letters*.

Robert K. Triest is a Senior Economist and Policy Advisor in the Research Department of the Federal Reserve Bank of Boston. Triest's research has focused on topics in public sector economics and labor economics. He is a coeditor of *Seismic Shifts: The Economic Impact of Demographic Change* (with Jane Little), *Social Security Reform: Links to Saving, Investment and Growth* (with Steven Sass), and *The Macroeconomics of Fiscal Policy* (with Richard Kopcke and Geoffrey Tootell), and is a coauthor of *Job Creation, Job Destruction and International Competition* (with Michael Klein and Scott Schuh). Triest earned his PhD degree in economics from the University of Wisconsin at Madison.

Shripad Tuljapurkar is the Morrison Professor of Population Studies and Professor of Biological Sciences at Stanford University. He has written extensively on the probabilistic analysis of population change, with applications to demography, the economy, and ecology.

Barbara Wolfe is Director, LaFollette School of Public Affairs and Professor of Economics and Population Health Sciences at the University of Wisconsin-Madison. Her interests focus on health economics, labor, and social insurance. She has written extensively including recent articles on national health insurance, child care and the role of subsidies, determinants of choices made by teens, evaluation of welfare reform and especially, expansions of publicly financed insurance and on the adequacy of resources at retirement. She is a member of the Institute of Medicine and has been a visiting scholar at the Russell Sage Foundation and a Fellow at the Netherlands Institute of Advanced Study.

Edward N. Wolff received his PhD from Yale University in 1974 and is Professor of Economics at New York University, where he has taught since 1974, and a Senior Scholar at the Levy Economics Institute of Bard College. He is also a Research Associate at the National Bureau of Economic Research. He served as Managing Editor of the *Review of Income and Wealth* from 1987 to 2004 and was a Visiting Scholar at the Russell Sage Foundation in New York (2003–2004), President of the Eastern Economics Association (2002–2003), a council member of the International Input-Output Association (1995–2003), and a council member of the International Association for Research in Income and Wealth (1987–2004).

Stephen A. Woodbury is a Professor of Economics at Michigan State University and a Senior Economist at the W. E. Upjohn Institute in Kalamazoo, Michigan. He was Deputy Director of the Advisory Council on Unemployment Compensation (US Department of Labor) during 1993–1994 and has worked on policies to assist unemployed workers and on issues in employee benefits. His books include *Search Theory and Unemployment* (coedited with Carl Davidson, 2002), *Employee Benefits and Labor Markets in Canada and the United States* (coedited with William Alpert, 2000), and *The Tax Treatment of Fringe Benefits* (coauthored with Wei-Jang Huang, 1991). He received his PhD in Economics from the University of Wisconsin–Madison in 1981.

L. Randall Wray is a Professor of Economics and Research Director, the Center for Full Employment and Price Stability at the University of Missouri–Kansas City, and Senior Scholar at the Levy Economics Institute of Bard College, NY. He is the author of Understanding Modern Money: The Key to Full Employment and Price Stability (Elgar, 1998) and Money and Credit in Capitalist Economies (Elgar 1990) and the editor of Credit and State Theories of Money (Edward Elgar 2004). Wray is also the author of numerous scholarly articles in edited books and academic journals, including the *Journal of Economic Issues, Cambridge Journal of Economics, Review of*

Political Economy, Journal of Post Keynesian Economics, Economic and Labour Relations Review, Economie Appliquée, and *the Eastern Economic Journal.*

Ajit Zacharias is a Senior Scholar at the Levy Economics Institute. His research interests include concepts and measurement of economic well-being, effects of taxes and government spending on well-being, valuation of noncash transfers, and time use. In addition to his several Institute publications, Zacharias has also published in the *Cambridge Journal of Economics* and the *Review of Radical Political Economics*. Zacharias received an MA from the University of Bombay, and a PhD from New School for Social Research.

1
Economic Perspectives on Aging: An Overview

Dimitri B. Papadimitriou

The aging of the US population, over the decades ahead, will affect our society and economy and be one of the primary domestic public policy issues. The US Census Bureau projects the fraction of the elderly in the total population to increase from its 2002 level of 12.5 per cent to 16.3 percent by 2020. Concomitantly, the fraction of working age population (20–64) is projected to decline from its current level of 59 to 57.2 percent in 2020. Alternatively, as Kotlikoff and Burns (2005) prefer to put it, in 2030 there will be as many as 77 million baby-boomers hobbling into old age – twice as many retirees as there are currently – but only 18 percent more of potential workers. What this means is that the ratio of the number of people eligible to retire to the entire population and to the projected workforce would both be higher (Bernanke, 2007). These trends are in sharp contrast to those observed during 1970–2002 when the proportion of the working age population in the US actually grew by about 5 percentage points. These demographic changes certainly imply a significant growth in the federal entitlement programs. Apart from the growth in the number of beneficiaries, existing benefit rules and rapidly escalating health care costs are expected to lead to fiscal pressures on the federal budget and pose challenges for economic growth. Federal expenditures for Social Security, Medicare, and Medicaid (via payments for long-term care) together represented almost 40 percent of the federal budget, or about 8.5 percent of GDP, in fiscal year 2006. The Congressional Budget Office's (CBO) long-term projections suggest that by 2015, Social Security, Medicare, and Medicaid (for long-term care payments) will increase by about 2 percentage points of GDP, totaling 10.5 percent, while by 2030, according to CBO, these expenditures will be as high as 15 percent of GDP.[1] This, pundits warn, will create a "generational storm" and a "fiscal crisis" as the United States, unable to afford the expense for caring for its aged, will be forced to institute "skyrocketing taxes, drastically lower retirement and health benefits" and experience "high inflation, a rapidly depreciating dollar, unemployment, political instability" and be, all in all, in "desperate trouble".[2]

The impending demographic change is due to the post World War II decreasing rates of fertility and the increasing life expectancies. Moreover, demographers project stability of the current rates of fertility into the foreseeable future, while forecasts on life expectancy show a positive trend (Bernanke, 2006). The anticipated growth of the aged (65 and older) is not only due to the simple fact that they would retire, but also due to the fact that over the next several decades America's population is expected to progressively grow older and remain so, even as the baby-boomers disappear from the scene (Bernanke, 2006).

The United States is not alone in confronting this demographic transition – the aging baby-boomers with higher life expectancies and low fertility rates – and facing the challenges posed by it. In fact, in most countries with advanced economies, the problem is far more severe (Papadimitriou, 2006). In Germany, for example, the share of the elderly in the total population was already 16 percent in 2000, the level that the United States is expected to reach in 2020. Most western European countries, including Australia and Japan, have more generous government programs for the elderly, and most already have higher rates of taxation, especially payroll taxation, as compared to the United States, leaving them with harder choices. A detailed study of nine industrialized countries[3] showed that, as a percentage of GDP, old-age pension spending in the United States (4.4 percent) was the lowest among these countries (OECD, 2001). In Italy, Germany, Sweden, Finland, and Japan, the ratio of old-age pension spending to GDP is at least twice as much as that in the United States.

However, this favorable international comparison does not suggest complacency in the United States, and the challenges of coping with an aging population require action in the near term to forestall more difficult choices in the long term. Thus, an assessment of the forces that are driving and will continue to drive government spending on the elderly is absolutely essential. Such assessment will need to examine how the retirement and health care for the elderly might be financed and measure the potential impact of different proposals for reform. Even though the coming demographic change is real, its effects on each entitlement program is different. The Social Security problem, if there is one, appears to be of manageable size, and a number of commentators have suggested that as a program, it has been run responsibly, has made adjustments[4] to prepare for an aging population, and is a sustainable system (Baker and Weisbrot, 1999; Papadimitriou and Wray, 1999a; Krugman, 2005). Medicare and Medicaid spending, however, is neither a function of the demographic problem nor is it driven by rising prices for existing medical procedures; instead, and to a much larger extent, its level of expenditures reflects advances in medical innovation that dramatically increase the opportunity to extend and save lives (Krugman, 2005).

Every adult irrespective of the country of residence has heard cries of alarm that the country's retirement systems are poised on the brink of a financial crisis precipitating by the swelling numbers of retirees relative to workers. However, there are marked differences in the forecasts. To set priorities and form strategies, policy makers need to have a set of clear ideas about the dimensions of the emerging problem and the uncertainties surrounding the projections. In the United States the Trustees of Social Security and Medicare, for example, are required to report the financial health of the programs in purely accounting terms that need not reflect the economic costs, that is, the proportion of future GDP required for public spending on the elderly (Centers for Medicare and Medicaid Services, 2003; Social Security Administration, 2003). The forecasting of the costs in accounting and economic terms involves making assumptions about crucial variables such as future earnings growth, productivity growth, inflation (including the price of medical care), and the age profile of the overall population and the working population (Papadimitriou and Wray, 1999a). It is important for policy makers to have an assessment of the reasonable range of available forecasts (for example, is government spending for the elderly likely to grow to be 10 percent or 15 percent of GDP in 2030?) and the relative importance of the various sources of uncertainty (for example, is the uncertainty about the growth of immigration more important than that about fertility rate?).

The natural inclination to be conservative when making projections over periods of 75 years or even longer is understandable, but relatively minor adjustments to the assumptions lead to very different assessments that are especially important for Social Security's long-term financial soundness. These adjustments and their impact on the trustees calculations have been analyzed in detail elsewhere (Papadimitriou and Wray, 1999a, 1999b); suffice it to say, however, that small changes in the values of variables included in the projections such as fertility rates, growth of the labor force, increased longevity, net immigration flows, growth of real wages, proportion of taxable wages, real interest rate, the disability incidence rate, and the disability termination rate can yield significant changes in the actuarial results. The uncertainty of the future trends of these variables casts doubt on the trustees' calculation of actuarial balance 75 years later. Consequently, one must be cognizant about proposing major reforms to correct problems that may never unfold.

Most analyses, including the ones conducted by the trustees and CBO, confuse the difference between *financial* provisioning and *real* provisioning for retirees in the future (ibid., p. 7; Wray in Chapter 3, this book). If the problem is the financial soundness of the Social Security Trust Funds, its resolution may require only relatively simple adjustments in accounting procedures (Friedman, 1999) instead of raising taxes now or lowering benefits in the near future or even running budget surpluses now (Papadimitriou and Wray, 1999a). If the problem is the real provisioning for retirees with sufficient quantities of resources in the future, this can only be resolved by increasing productive capacity in the future, thus ensuring that a sufficient share of resources will be transferred to the elderly of the future. These can be achieved by increasing the rate of private and public investment together with revisions in taxation at the time the baby-boom generation is well into retirement.

There remains, then, the question whether there is, in fact a looming crisis or whether the economy can "grow itself out of the problem" (ibid.). As it was mentioned earlier, if the problem is *real*, it requires a fiscal policy stance to be biased toward increasing productive capacity. If, on the other hand, the problem is *financial*, the options to be considered may include the following: (1) changing the composition of the budget to meet the spending for the elderly while keeping the overall size of the budget (relative to GDP) within specified limits necessitating reductions in the share of discretionary spending, (2) decreasing benefits by means testing or altering the benefit formulas, (3) raising payroll and/or income taxes. Clearly, the implications of the various options for long-run macroeconomic performance and the political feasibility of the options are to be very carefully considered.

While the impact of aging on fiscal balances has been investigated frequently, an equally important, but less-studied issue is whether future retirees will be able to maintain a decent standard of living (OECD, 2001; Wolff, 2002). This turns out to be dependent on the assets they can accumulate during their working life, the type of private pensions available to workers, and the adequacy of public pension and medical benefits. Recent trends in the United States raise concerns as to whether the soon-to-retire population (those aged 47–64) might face resource-inadequacy crisis when they retire. Estimates by the Federal Reserve showed that during the 1990s, debt burden faced by the elderly had grown substantially, and that the percentage of elderly that owned their homes (the main asset for an average family) outright had declined (Aizcorbe, Kennickell and Moore, 2003). Anecdotal evidence also points to the elderly being increasingly mired in debt, often as a result of soaring medical bills and providing financial assistance for their grown-up children (Bayott, 2004). While the majority of workers in the soon-to-retire age group are covered by employer-provided pension plans, the structure of such plans has changed most dramatically: defined-contribution plans have overtaken defined-benefit plans and pension wealth has become increasingly concentrated at the top, favoring better-paid workers among the soon-to-retire (Wolff, 2003). The shortfall of resources available to the elderly can, apart from aggravating their material hardship, also increase strains on the Medicaid program (for long-term care) and other means-tested assistance programs.

There is general consensus that government spending on retirees reduces overall inequality in annual income because it reduces the incomes of the working population via payroll taxes and increases the incomes of the elderly via transfer payments (Danziger and Weinberg, 1994). For example, recent analysis undertaken at the Levy Economics Institute shows that nearly two-thirds of the inequality-reducing incremental effect of government transfers was due to Social Security and Medicare in 2000 (Wolff and Zacharias, 2006).[5] Indeed, the progressivity of government spending for the elderly in this sense is a welcome side effect that contributes significantly to public policies aimed at social cohesion and reducing the marginalization of vulnerable social groups.

Several recent studies have examined progressivity from a lifetime perspective (Caldwell et al., 1999; Coronado, Fullerton and Glass, 2000; Gustman and Steinmeier, 2000; Liebman, 2002). However, in the comparisons of lifetime benefits and lifetime contributions, and with respect to the effect of *net benefit* (benefits less contributions) on overall income distribution, studies sometimes arrive at conflicting results. For example, Cohen, Steuerle and Carasso (2003) find, using a sample based on Social Security Administration (SSA) records, that the Old Age and Survivors and Disability Insurance (OASDI) system produces internal rates of return[6] that are relatively higher for those at the bottom of lifetime earnings distribution, while Coronado, Fullerton and Glass (2000) argue, using a Panel Study of Income Dynamics (PSID)-based sample, that Social Security is slightly regressive under certain conditions. The methods and findings from this strand of research are highly relevant for evaluating the equity aspects of reform proposals such as that recommended by President Bush's Commission to Strengthen Social Security involving the creation of individual retirement accounts (USGAO, 2004) or that reportedly favored by the former Fed Chairman Alan Greenspan involving benefit reductions and raising eligibility age for Social Security and Medicare (Henderson, 2004).

Another area of research that is important for the evaluation of reform proposals and their implications for public finances is research on retirement behavior. It has been argued that microeconometric models built using individual-level data on crucial labor market and demographic variables in conjunction with detailed modeling of the pension and tax rules can provide valuable insights on why and when individuals retire (for example, Whitehouse, 2001). The steep decline in the labor force participation rates for men aged from 60 to 64 – it fell by about 30 percentage points from 82 percent to 53 percent during 1960 to 1996 – is probably hard to understand without some discussion of the changing trade-off between retirement and work (Gruber and Wise, 2002). While there is fairly large literature on estimating incentives to retire, often these models suffered from not being able to separate the effects of Social Security from private pensions, lack of sufficient data and a host of other specification problems (most importantly, given the nonlinear relationship between Social Security benefits and earnings, not being able to account separately for the effects of earnings and Social Security benefits on the decision to retire; see Krueger and Pischke, 1992).

The availability of rich microdata from the Health and Retirement study (HRS) starting in the early 1990s has given rise to a new generation of studies on retirement behavior. Recent research based on the HRS and using modeling techniques that overcome some of the limitations of the earlier research has shown that increasing the delayed retirement credit is likely to have as large an effect on postponing retirement as raising the normal retirement age (Coile and Gruber, 2000). Admittedly, this result may be substantially modified if the effects of changing social norms regarding the "appropriate" retirement age are taken into account. A challenge for future retirement behavior research is to assess the policy implications of the effects stemming from the interaction between the formation of social norms and institutional environment.

Most discussions about the potential fiscal imbalances that result from population aging focus on how changes in benefits or taxes on workers can contribute to alleviate the situation, with almost no mention of how changes in employment contracts and global competitive pressures contribute to this process. Just as the gradual substitution of defined-contribution plans for defined-benefit plans has greatly reduced the employers' liability of paying pensions, a similar shift towards reduced employer liability for health care also appears to be under way. According to the HRS data, about 66 percent of male and 50 percent of female full-time workers in the age group 51–61 are covered under some type of employer-provided retiree health benefits (Johnson, et al., 2003). Indeed, since Medicare covers only about half of the medical expenses of the elderly, employer-provided benefits are a crucial part of the safety net for them. It is estimated that for the nondisabled, nonindigent retired elderly in the age group 65–67 covered by Medicare, 85 percent have supplementary coverage; the majority (56 percent) obtain such coverage via employer or union (Finkelstein, 2004).

However, soaring health care costs over the past decade have brought about a substantial decline in the percentage of employers who are offering these benefits to new retirees. At the same time, the employers are also passing on an increasing proportion of the cost increases to the retirees. Both trends are likely to accelerate in the near future, putting pressures on the physical and economic well-being of the elderly. It appears that the new Medicare prescription drug plan might offer some relief to those who have no supplementary coverage, but the existing drug plans available under most existing retiree health plans are superior to the Medicare plan (Kaiser-Hewitt Survey, 2004). While there is plenty of anecdotal evidence about how soaring health care costs in the United States are hurting the competitiveness of US based production, there is need for more systematic study.[7] It is also worth exploring the potential of innovative types of employment contracts that will lower the costs to business in the long run and maintain a reasonable level of benefits for employees (for example, Ghilarducci, 2003).

An adequate examination of policy options has to be based on a sound assessment of the economic well-being of the elderly. The most widely used measure of economic well-being in considering the gaps in economic well-being between elderly and nonelderly households and the deprivation of the elderly is gross money income. However, as several studies have pointed out, noncash transfers (for example, Medicare) and wealth play a crucial role in shaping the economic well-being of the elderly (for example, OECD, 2001). Additionally, the US Census Bureau, the publisher of the official scoreboard on the level and distribution of economic well-being of American households, has recently started publishing what it previously used to call "experimental measures" on par with the standard gross money income measure (DeNavas-Walt et al., 2003). Noncash transfers, crucial for the well-being and making up at least 40 percent of government transfer payments, are excluded from the official measure of gross money income. The economic advantage from wealth ownership is reckoned in the money income measure as actual property income (dividends, rent, and interest). A more complete measure of income from wealth has to take into account the advantages of home ownership (either in the form of imputed rental cost or annuity on home equity) and the long-run benefits from the ownership of nonhome wealth (for example, in the form of an imputed annuity; see Moon, 1977; Caner and Wolff, 2004). By means of such a comprehensive measure, policy makers gain better insights into the relative importance of different income sources in sustaining the economic well-being of the elderly and forces shaping inequality among the elderly.

The equity considerations mentioned previously regarding the distribution of benefits from social insurance programs were confined to individuals differentiated solely according to their earnings. Among other things, differentials in mortality rates among demographic groups, variation in family types (for example, single retiree vs. elderly couple), and gender differences in the number of years of earnings contribute to the observed patterns of redistribution. The differences in economic security among population subgroups are also of interest in themselves. A crucial demographic feature of the elderly population, due to gender differences in life expectancies, is that 60 percent of that population is women (as compared to 50 percent in the nonelderly population), and women's share increases as we move to higher age groups among the elderly. There are huge gaps in living arrangements (40 percent of elderly women live alone, compared with only 16 percent of elderly men), which has a negative impact on resource availability, and women rely to a much greater extent on social insurance than men to sustain their economic well-being (Lee and Shaw, 2003). The growth in female-headed households and relatively high divorce rates among the baby-boom generation imply that a greater percentage of women will be entering retirement in the coming years without being eligible for the spousal benefits under Social Security (Smeeding, et al., 1999). Research also indicates that a significant proportion of women with low lifetime earnings will not be able to take advantage of provisions to protect low-wage workers because they will not have a sufficient number of years with covered earnings (Hungerford, 2004). The implicit model of the typical family that existed at the conception of the Social Security program was the "male breadwinner model". Reform proposals must be evaluated in light of the changes that have taken place in women's relation with paid work and changes in household structure and composition.

The generosity of each country's welfare system toward the elderly has profound implications for the composition of government budgets. We can distinguish three types of generosity of social security schemes: average generosity, generosity toward early retirement, and generosity toward the poor. On the basis of some theoretical predictions, an examination of the statistical correlations among those types of generosity can be observed. In Europe, for example, the statistical findings can be interpreted in relation to the evolution of the process of integration (Lefèbvre and Pestieau, 2006). The cross-country differences in the composition of government budgets beg the important question whether spending on the elderly crowds out spending on the young. Has spending on the nonelderly declined in major public programs (for example, education) and/or have tax rates on the nonelderly increased as a result of the increasing expenditure burden of entitlement programs devoted to the elderly? These are some of the questions that Boersch-Supan attempts to answer in Chapter 2. Given the more pronounced trends of population aging and lower fertility rates across the countries the implications are clearly a dramatic growth of expenditures toward the elderly (pensions, health care, long-term care) and *a fortiori* toward the young and/or employed. How would this affect the longevity of the welfare state and what are the consequences of its survival? Boersch-Supan's analysis, using aggregate statistical data from Eurostat and Organization for Economic Co-operation and Development (OECD) and individual data from Survey of Health, Aging and Retirement in Europe (SHARE), determines the correlations among the different dimensions of welfare state generosity. He compares the respective generosities between the aged and nonaged, and assesses policy outcomes – economic (unemployment, poverty, and inequality in wealth, income, and consumption) and noneconomic (health and longevity). The author's main focus of research is in determining the correlation between the spending share for the elderly and the young, which he finds to be positive for the EU15 countries. In addition, he examines the evidence for convergence among the EU15 in light of the accelerated integration and the adoption of a single currency and whether a new "European welfare state model" can be created and concludes that no such case can be made. The commentary that follows Chapter 2 by Nisticò suggests, however, that there are many reasons to expect that "a new European welfare state model" may become a reality so as to ensure that expenditures toward the elderly will not endanger its continuation and survival.

An interesting perspective that can inform public policy toward the elderly is to examine demographic trends of past, current, and future periods as these relate to age and gender distributions, employment/population ratios, labor-participation ratios and dependency ratios (aged, youth, total). This is precisely the focus of Chapter 3 by Wray who links global demographic trends with mostly what he calls *real* provisioning to the elderly at the time it will be needed. Wray provides detailed demographic transitions for the United States and other developed, developing, and emerging economies and the world as a whole. By paying particular attention to the dependency ratios for all these countries, he suggests that the demographic alarm for the global economy may be exaggerated. He returns on the topic of previous research (Papadimitriou and Wray 1999a, 1999b) reaffirming the crucial importance of dependency ratios – especially for social security systems, as well as the distinction between financial and real provisioning for the elderly both playing significant role in policy design. He insists that the primary concern of policy makers that would alleviate the aging burden should be increasing productivity and employment for those that are able and willing to work in most countries, but especially in Europe. Other suggestions for policy options, that Wray proposes, include changing immigration laws that can help forestall a country's workers rising burdens, childcare support systems that encourage mothers to enter and continue in the formal labor markets, and further advances for efficient health care delivery. Startz's commentary following Chapter 3, reinforces Wray's findings and brings to the fore the role of saving in the further development of a nation's capital stock – a theme that echoes the words of the current Federal Reserve Chairman (Bernanke, 2007).

Government expenditure and taxes are known to have an equalizing effect on economic well-being between the aged and the nonaged. The gap in well-being between the two groups is then dependent on the types of expenditures and taxes that are considered as well as the income concept used to calculate economic well-being. The recently developed Levy Institute Measure of Economic Well-being (LIMEW) and its associated microdatasets offer a comprehensive view of the level and distribution of economic well-being in the United States during the period 1989–2000 (Wolff and Zacharias, 2006). The main components of the LIMEW are earnings, pensions, and income from wealth, transfers, public consumption, taxes, and household production. In Chapter 4, using the database developed for the LIMEW, Wolff, Zacharias, and Kum determine the disparities between retirees and nonretirees, the structure of inequality among the elderly, and the extent to which government spending on the aged has an equalizing effect on the overall distribution of economic well-being. They carefully document the relative importance of various sources of income in sustaining the living standards of the elderly and then, contrast their results with the "experimental" measure of extended income published by the US Census Bureau. Their results differ significantly from those of the Census Bureau in that, based on the LIMEW, the elderly appear to be better off in relation to the nonelderly, contrary to the official measures. The difference in the measures, they explain, is mainly due to much higher calculated values of income from wealth together with higher net government spending toward the elderly. Wolff, Zacharias, and Kum offer other measures among population subgroups within the elderly – male/female, white/nonwhite, and single/married – noting again the differences from those of the Census Bureau. Haveman commenting on Wolff, Zacharias, and Kum accepts the importance of the comprehensive nature of the LIMEW measures, but raises valuable and constructive questions relating to imputation procedures included in the LIMEW datasets.

A substantial body of research has been carried out of late in studying gender gaps in earnings and working conditions. Gender disparities in economic security during old age are, in contrast, a relatively new area of research that has yielded some valuable insights. Higher life expectancy combined with disadvantaged earnings histories might make the net lifetime benefits for women higher relative to that for men, yet a much larger fraction of older single women (age 75 and over) live in poverty as compared to men. Moreover, the relatively higher lifetime benefits for women also reflect gender disparity in earnings as well as women's greater role in caring for the family – unpaid work. Shaw's Chapter 5 makes an invaluable contribution in the economics of aging by examining government spending toward the elderly women. Shaw offers detailed demographic data pertaining to women, paid and unpaid work and the limited options available during old age. She reports, for example, that in the United States, 60 percent of wives at ages over 55 are caregivers to spouses and almost 25 percent of daughter caregivers are over 60 years of age, and many of them are employed. Women are to a much larger extent than men confronted with the conflict between paid and unpaid care giving work to children, spouses and elderly parents. Finally, she assesses the implications of the strategies for major policy reforms regarding Social Security, Medicare, and especially Medicaid for longer-care, and offers her own proposals for effective policies that address the particular concerns of elderly women. Rania Antonopoulos comments positively about what Shaw writes in the chapter, but encourages that one should consider the recommendations for policy reforms by recounting Eaton's (2005) perceptive contributions to the existing debate on elderly care in the United States.

The solvency of the US Social Security System is the focus of the modeling exercises offered by Butrica, Smith, and Steuerle in Chapter 6. Using the Urban Institute's Dynamic Simulation of Income Model (DYNASIM3 model), they explore a number of scenarios of delaying retirement and/or benefit cuts to assess the impact on the solvency of the Social Security Trust Funds. The model's simulations in delaying retirement by one to five years improve the solvency problem but do not completely eliminate the Trust Funds' deficit. The simulated options of delayed retirement also impact individual-level outcomes in terms of total net wealth, consumption, and retirement (annuitized value) benefits. The five scenarios derived from the DYNASIM3 model offer "a useful and informative comparison of outcomes," but it is a rather open question if any of them can be considered "a Good Retirement." In the commentary that follows the chapter, Schmidt raises a number of thoughtful procedural questions for improving the simulations and clarifying the results.

An important area of inquiry relating to the economics of aging is the relationship of a benefit increase in Social Security with the level of bequeathable wealth, whether planned or accidental. This line of inquiry is based on the assumption that at times of retirement an increase in retirement benefits does not necessarily cause an equivalent increase in consumption and thus it may lead to augmenting net wealth. This, then, leads to some fraction of the benefit increase being bequeathed back to the younger generations. Gan, Gong, and Hurd look at this relationship in Chapter 7 and attempt to quantify this intergenerational transfer via an estimation of a life-cycle model about consumption by singles. The simulation results for several instances reveal that the relationship does not hold or at least not substantially. Thornton in the commentary that follows Chapter 7 brings up a number of the life-cycle model's limitations. He raises questions whether such models can lead to effective policy responses and concludes that they most likely cannot.

Employers have been substantially involved in shaping the structure of old-age benefits to their workers. Several studies have documented dramatic changes in employer-provided plans over the recent years. The erosion of unionized employment has affected the retirement security of workers. Assessing and designing realistic policy options that promote a more active involvement by employers for old-age benefits is paramount since these can in turn reduce fiscal pressures. The evolution of employer pensions, the relative merits of the socialization of costs of providing for retirees, and the combination of public and employer provisioning of benefits form the theme of Ghilarducci's contribution in Chapter 8. In it, Ghilarducci analyzes the changing role of employers pension plans and their impact on retirees especially those belonging in the lower end of the income distribution. Her findings can be simply stated: (1) There is tax favoritism and tax expenditures in the current US employer-pension system. (2) The shift from Defined Benefit (DB) plans to Defined Contribution (DC) apart from its heavy subsidization has not improved coverage, has not increased participation, besides its claims to the contrary, but, has made participants in the DC plans more insecure by subjecting them to substantial risks they are not qualified to assume and manage. (3) Only 50 percent of the labor force is covered. (4) The participation and coverage are skewed to higher income workers and not toward the middle- class workers, (5) Younger workers are most likely to be worse off with DC (401(k)) plans than the DB plans because 401(k) plans are used as severance plans rather than pension plans. (6) Employer-based pension plans should be maintained for many good reasons. Ghilarducci covers a lot of ground in this chapter. She successfully documents the evolving structure/shift of employer-provided pensions, the resultant utility to employers and disutility to workers, and participation rates and cites a number of well-known firms that pioneered the transformation of pensions from DB to DC plans. The message of this analysis is that appropriate government pension policy should be implemented so that the goals of adequacy, efficiency, horizontal and vertical equity, voluntary working, and contribution to economic growth can be attained. This can only come to pass by expanding pension coverage to lower income workers and ensuring retirement income security. The commentary by Bodie supplements Ghilarducci's suggested policy prescriptions by encouraging a larger role of the government to further augment the efficiency of a pension system. His policy proposals include, among others, truthful advertising in investment vehicles and introduction of lesser risk-burden assets offered by strong financial institutions employing state-of-the art financial technology.

Most of the research on the potential fiscal burden imposed by retirees has not paid enough attention to how much of the burden can be relieved by government and/or employers in providing health insurance coverage for retirees, especially those taking early retirement. While for a large number of retirees the main source of health care coverage is from the public sector private coverage offered by the employer, union is also an important element in ensuring access to quality care and meeting costs for many retirees. Trends in the private provisioning of retiree health benefits are declining, necessitating a reconsideration of Medicare coverage which can be extended to include early retirees or creating incentives for employers to include retiree health coverage. Data from the HRS provide useful information on the availability of retiree health and pension benefits. Another important database is the Survey of Income Program Participation (SIPP) used in a recent study (Fronstin, 2005) that generated estimates confirming the declining trend of expected retiree health benefits to be offered at retirement. Marton and Woodbury, in Chapter 9, extend and qualify Fronstin's estimates using a sample drawn from HRS. Their estimates show lower levels of employer-provided retiree health benefits and are closer to the percentages or retirees who report actually receiving them. This suggests that workers expectations are unrealized. Another reason, they cite, for the declining trends in making retiree benefits available is the Financial Accounting Statement (FAS 106) requiring companies to include the expense of these benefits, other than pensions, as liabilities causing reconsideration of availability and in many cases reduction or elimination of these benefits. The Marton and Woodbury analysis provides the following key findings for workers of ages 51–61 in their sample:

- In 1992 with both employee and retiree health benefits, there was a 55 percent increase in the probability of workers retiring in the next two years than those with only employee health benefit.
- In 1994 with both employee and retiree health benefits, for the same group of workers, there was a 29 percent increase in probability of retiring in the next two years than those with only employee health benefit.
- In both cases spouse coverage is very relevant.

Marton and Woodbury draw the inference that workers with retiree health benefits are more likely to retire when they are relatively young. The implication, however, is that this helps induce experienced workers with several remaining years to retire, creating labor supply reductions. A critical assessment by Wolfe in the commentary following Chapter 9 cautions that the results may not be as robust as they appear. For the models estimations include unsatisfactory variables. She also suggests that complementary estimates be used of smaller age cohorts 55–58 and 59–61.

As we have seen before, long-run fiscal implications of the aging population are assessed on the basis of forecasts about demographic trends – mortality, fertility, and immigration – benefits, and economic performance. While traditional methods of forecasting underpinning most of the official assessments is the scenario approach, there have been new developments based on stochastic methods (Lee and Tuljapurkar, 2000). The advantage of using a probabilistic framework is that it yields estimates of the potential margin of errors in the forecasts and forces the analyst to specify the assumptions about demographic and economic processes carefully. (An example can be the use of a structural model of fertility rates based on historical data for forecasting.) Probabilistic forecasts (of expected values and probability bounds) are generated from many random sample paths that describe a large number of possible trajectories, including high and low trajectories. These high and low trajectories for the key inputs to the forecast, that is, fertility rates, low mortality, and so on, create scenarios about the future population size or growth rate, in addition to the preferred forecast. Differences between the two approaches have significant implications for the design of long-run fiscal policy. Tuljapurkar, in Chapter 10, using stochastic population forecasts shows how these can be used to test the sensitivity of various policy changes to bring government spending toward the elderly into fiscal balance in the long-run. He projects demographic rates, mortality, fertility, and immigration using probabilistic forecasts, which combined make stochastic forecast of population number and composition. Tuljapurkar's rigorous analysis provides estimates of policy proposals and their probabilities in achieving actuarial balance. For example, solvency of the Social Security Trust Fund would be improved by about 40 percent with a tax increase of 1 percent. If, in addition, 20 percent of the trust fund is also invested in the stock market, the solvency probability improves to 60 percent. There are other policy changes that are projected, including revisions in the Normal Retirement Age (NRA) that unsurprisingly improve the actuarial balance over the long range. The query still remains, however, as to how forecasts, even those with the highest degree of sophistication, can incorporate future unpredictable and uncontrollable events, increasing uncertainty in the future path of a nation's economy. This is the issue that Burdick illustrates in his thoughtful and meticulous response to the analysis articulated in Chapter 10.

Views of Social Security's long-term financial condition and the implication it might have on the economy and the government's budget vary. As was mentioned earlier, the program's long-range actuarial imbalance is based on projections of demographic and economic variables that are subject to uncertainty and very sensitive to even the smallest of errors (Papadimitriou and Wray, 1999a; Wray, Chapter 3 of this volume). Chapter 11 is yet another contribution to the growing literature of Social Security's long-term solvency. Biggs and Gokhale attempt to link economic and wage growth and the implication these parameters might have on the program's financial condition. Following the Trustees recent interest in projecting funding balances over the very long-term (perpetuity), Biggs and Gokhale test the proposition that faster economic growth improves the system's funding balance. They also assume that faster economic growth does concomitantly lead to faster wage growth that in its turn raises average wages that affect the calculation of retiree benefits. Using the Social Security and Accounts Simulator (SSASIM) actuarial model, Biggs and Gokhale show that the pay-as-you-go structure with a faster wage growth over the infinite time horizon would paradoxically worsen the actuarial balance, if the ratio of workers to beneficiaries declines sufficiently, even though the system's 75-year balance would improve. The underlined assumptions of such modeling exercise are strongly put in question by Kelton in her commentary to this chapter. She finds little usefulness, if any, in forecasts of the infinite future and also critiques Biggs and Gokhale's analysis framed within static rather than a more appropriate dynamic setting. Among the other objections she raises is the assumption of average real wage growth without regard to the differing growth rates between low and high wage earners and the effect of earnings inequality on Social Security's finances.

Another central issue of crucial importance to the soon-to-retire workers – the age group of 47–64 – is whether they will have enough resources – private and public – to maintain a reasonable standard of living in retirement. Characteristically, the adequacy of projected retirement income is contrasted to some absolute benchmark, that is, poverty line and pre-retirement income ("replacement rate"). A comprehensive study (Wolff, 2002) utilizing data up to 1998 found that among the households headed by a soon-to-retire worker, the proportion expected to be in poverty or unable to replace at least half their pre-retirement income rose during the 1990s in spite of the booming stock market and economy. Wolff, in Chapter 12, updates the findings of his earlier study utilizing the 2001 Survey of Consumer Finances and the latest annual Current Population Survey (CPS) income surveys to determine the retirement income security of the soon-to-retire. The new findings show that retirement income did improve between 1989 and 2001. The improvement accounted for 5 percent of heads of households of ages 47 to 64 who expected to have retirement incomes of twice the poverty line – from 40 percent in 1989 to 35 percent in 2001. Moreover, the number of households that hoped to replace at least half of their projected pre-retirement income at age 65 increased from 49 to 53 percent. These improvements notwithstanding, a substantial share (24 percent) of households in the same age group expected to retire with only the Social Security benefits and without a private pension – a marked cause for maintaining and strengthening Social Security. The absence of private pension plans was a major factor of the pronounced inequality in retirement wealth affecting, to a greater extent, African-American, Hispanic households, and single women. In his own words "African-American and Hispanic households made no progress in closing the large gap with respect to white households in terms of retirement wealth or total wealth … . While mean retirement wealth gained 84 percent for whites, it actually lost 1 percent for minorities." Furthermore, single women fell behind their male counterparts as well as married couples between 1983 and 2001. Wolff provides a plethora of statistics and gives many details in the profiles of the soon-to-retire. The significance of his analysis is his urging that public policy be directed in securing private pension wealth to improve retirement income adequacy for all Americans and their families. As Harrington writes in her commentary to Wolff's contribution, Social Security needs to become first and foremost secure since particularly in the absence of private retirement wealth, it helps limit economic inequality among the retirees and the soon-to-retire citizens who are the most vulnerable – women, minorities, and renters. She notes that Social Security is crucial even to homeowners with excessive levels of mortgage debt and high levels of credit card debts as the of late increasing rates of bankruptcy filings exemplify.

The final chapter, Chapter 13, returns to a similar topic as some of the previous chapters have in that it offers an analysis of the redistributive provisions of the present Social Security system as they are presently configured and contrasts them against a minimum benefit. Redistributive provisions to retirees with low lifetime earnings are based on a progressive formula of benefit rates, a limited number of years counted in the benefit formula, and spousal and survivor benefits. Favreault, Mermin, and

Steuerle offer an alternative provision that involves a minimum benefit. They contend, as many other studies have concluded, including national and presidential commissions on retirement policy, that a minimum benefit is a more efficient vehicle to effect redistribution. A minimum benefit structure can vary widely, and the most typical forms are summarized in Table 13.1. Utilizing the Urban Institute's dynamic simulation model they estimate the effects of minimum benefits for a sample of 100,000 individuals drawn from the 1990 to 1993 SIPP. The results of the authors's various simulations are encouraging in that minimum benefits appear to reduce elderly poverty framed in a system reform of cutting benefits to improve the program's financial sustainability. The minimum retirement benefit appears to be central in the current debate in reforming Social Security as Triest suggests in his commentary of Chapter 13. He cautions, however, that the trade-off of the minimum benefit for the low lifetime earners with decreasing the benefit of those with high lifetime earnings will entail a substantial welfare cost.

The contributions in this book cover an exceptionally large area of research on government expenditures for the elderly. They present conceptual and empirical studies that identify key issues dealing with various aspects profoundly affecting the aging populations. While many a reader may not agree with every argument and policy strategy made or accept every conclusion drawn, the chapters in this collection are thoughtful and perhaps some of them provocative. They need to be read and discussed, and their implications considered as we attempt to find better approaches to improve the human condition of our elderly citizens.

Notes

1. These projections represent the Congressional Budget Office's (2005) intermediate expenditure scenario, which Fed Chairman Bernanke suggested may be too optimistic especially for Medicare based on the past 25 year experience (Bernanke, 2007).
2. See Kotlikoff and Burns (2005).
3. The countries included are Canada, Finland, Germany, Italy, Japan, Netherlands, Sweden, United Kingdom, and United States.
4. Revisions in benefits and revenues were made in 1977 and 1983 that fundamentally changed the Social Security program from pay-as-you-go to advance funding or accumulation of reserves. It was believed that benefits could be supplemented from the reserves when Social Security revenues begin to fall short of expenditures.
5. The incremental effect refers to the percentage decline that would occur in overall inequality if every household's income from government transfers were to increase by 1 percent, with other things remaining the same.
6. The internal rate of return is calculated as an interest rate that workers would need to earn on their lifetime contributions to make this sum equal to the lifetime benefits they receive, in inflation-adjusted dollars.
7. In the crucial automobile industry, about half of all United Auto Workers (UAW) are expected to retire within five years. A spokesman for General Motors has

recently stated that the company is at a competitive disadvantage especially with producers in countries where health care is paid for by the government (Garsten, 2004). The combination of threat to the bottom line of major US corporations and health security of ordinary people may prove to be a potent catalyst to fundamental reform in the health care system.

References

Aizcorbe, A. M., A. B. Kennickell and K. B. Moore (2003) "Recent Changes in US Family Finances: Evidence from the 1998 and 2001 Survey of Consumer Finances," *Federal Reserve Bulletin*, vol. 89 (January 2003), pp. 1–32.

Baker, D. and M. Weisbrot (1999) *Social Security: The Phony Crisis* (Chicago, IL: University of Chicago Press).

Bayott, J. (2004) "As Bills Mount, Debts on Homes Rise for Elderly," *New York Times*, July 4.

Bernanke, B. S. (2007) "Long-Term Fiscal Challenges Facing the United States." Testimony given on January 18 before the Committee on the Budget, US Senate.

Bernanke, B. S. (2006) "The Coming Demographic Transition: Will We Treat Future Generations Fairly?" Testimony given on October 4 before The Washington Economic Club.

Caldwell, S., M. Favreault, A. Gantman, J. Gokhale, T. Johnson and L. J. Kotlikoff (1999) "Social Security's Treatment of Postwar Americans," in James M. Poterba (ed.) *Tax Policy and the Economy* (Cambridge, MA: MIT Press), Vol. 13: pp. 109–148.

Caner, A. and E. N. Wolff (2004) "Asset Poverty in the United States, 1984–1999: Evidence from the Panel Study of Income Dynamics," *Review of Income and Wealth* 50(4): 469–491.

Centers for Medicare and Medicaid Services (2003) *The 2003 Annual Report of the Board of Trustees of the Federal Hospital Insurance and Federal Supplementary Medical Insurance Trust Funds* (17 March 2003).

Cohen, L., C. E. Steuerle and A. Carasso (2003) "Redistribution under OASDI: How Much and to Whom?" Available at: http://www.urban.org/url.cfm?ID=1000596

Coile, C. and J. Gruber (2000) "Social Security and Retirement," NBER Working Paper No. 7830 (Cambridge, MA: National Bureau of Economic Research).

Coronado, J. L., D. Fullerton and T. Glass (2000) "The Progressivity of Social Security," NBER Working Paper No. 7520 (Cambridge, MA: National Bureau of Economic Research).

Danziger, S. and D. Weinberg (1994) "The Historical Record: Trends in Family Income, Inequality, and Poverty," in Sheldon Danziger, Gary Sandefur and Daniel Weinberg (eds) *Confronting Poverty: Prescriptions for Change* (Cambridge, MA: Harvard University Press), pp. 38–44.

DeNavas-Walt, C., R. Cleveland and B. H. Webster, Jr. (2003) US Census Bureau, Current Population Reports, Income in the United States (Washington, DC: US Government Printing Office), pp. 60–221.

Eaton, S. C. (2005) "Eldercare in the United States: Inadequate, Inequitable, but Not Lost Cause," *Feminist Economics* 11 (July): 37–52.

Finkelstein, A. (2004) "The Interaction of Partial Public Insurance Programs and Residual Private Insurance Markets: Evidence from the US Medicare Program," *Journal of Health Economics* 23(1): 1–24.

Friedman, M. (1999) "Social Security Chimeras," *The New York Times* (January 11).

Fronstin, P. (2005) "The Impact of the Erosion of Retiree Health Benefits on Workers and Retirees," Issue Brief No. 279 (Washington, DC: Employee Benefit Research Institute).

Garsten, E. (2004) "GM Health Care Bill Tops $60 Billion: Cost Adds $ 1,400 Per Vehicle, Hurts Competitiveness," *The Detroit News*, March 11.

Ghilarducci, T. (2003) "Delinking Benefits from a Single Employer: Alternative Multiemployer Models," in Olivia S. Mitchell, David S. Blitzstein, Michael Gordon and Judith F. Mazo (eds) *Benefits for the Workplace of the Future* (Pennsylvania: University Pennsylvania Press) and (2004) *Social Security Programs and Retirement around the World, an NBER Conference Report* (Chicago, IL: University of Chicago Press).

Gruber, J. and D. A. Wise (2002) "Social Security Programs and Retirement around the World: Micro Estimation," NBER Working Paper No. 9407 (Cambridge, MA: National Bureau of Economic Research).

Gustman, A. and T. Steinmeier (2000) "Social Security Benefits of Immigrants and US Born," in George Borjas (ed.) *Issues in the Economics of Immigration* (Chicago, IL: University of Chicago Press), pp. 309–350.

Henderson, N. (2004) "Fed Chief Urges Cut in Social Security," *Washington Post*, February 26.

Hungerford, T. (2004) "How Ignoring Fluctuations in Lifetime Earnings Affects Social Security," *Challenge* 47(2): 90–108.

Johnson, R. W., A. J. Davidoff and K. Perese (2003) "Health Insurance Cost and Early Retirement Decisions," *Industrial & Labor Relations Review* 56(4): 716–730.

Kaiser/Hewitt Survey (2004) *Retiree Health Benefits Now and in the Future* (Menlo Park, CA: The Henry J. Kaiser Family Foundation and Lincolnshire, IL: Hewitt Associates).

Kotlikoff, L. and S. Burns (2005) *The Coming Generational Storm* (Cambridge, MA: MIT Press).

Krueger, A. B. and J. S. Pischke (1992) "The Effect of Social Security on Labor Supply: A Cohort Analysis of the Notch Generation," *Journal or Labor Economics* 10(4): 412–437.

Krugman, P. (2005) "America's Senior Moment," *New York Review of Books* 52(4), March 10, pp. 6–11.

Lee, R. D. and S. Tuljapurkar (2000) "Population Forecasting for Fiscal Planning: Issues and Innovations," in A. Auerbach and R. Lee (eds) *Demography and Fiscal Policy* (New York, NY: Cambridge University Press), pp. 7–57.

Lee, S. and L. B. Shaw (2003) *Gender and Economic Security in Retirement* (Washington, DC: Institute for Women's Policy Research).

Lefèbvre, M. and P. Pestieau (2006) "The Generosity of the Welfare State towards the Elderly," in D. B. Papadimitriou (ed.) *The Distributional Effects of Government Spending and Taxation* (New York and United Kingdom: Palgrave Macmillan).

Liebman, J. B. (2002) "Redistribution in the Current US Social Security System," in M. Feldstein and B. Liebman (eds) *The Distributional Aspects of Social Security and Social Security Reform* (Chicago, IL: University of Chicago Press), pp. 11–47.

Moon, M. (1977) *The Measurement of Economic Welfare: Applications to the Aged* (New York, NY: Academic Press).

OECD (2001) *Ageing and Income: Financial resources and Retirement in 9 OECD Countries* (Paris: OECD).

Papadimitriou, D. B. (2006) "Government Effects on the Distribution of Income: An Overview," in D. B. Papadimitriou (ed.) *The Distributional Effects of Government Spending and Taxation* (New York and United Kingdom: Palgrave Macmillan).

Papadimitriou, D. B. and L. R. Wray (1999a) "Does Social Security Need Saving? Providing for Retirees throughout the Twenty-first Century," Public Policy Brief No. 55 (Annandale-on-Hudson, NY: The Levy Economics Institute of Bard College).

Papadimitriou, D. B. and L. R. Wray (1999b) "How Can We Provide for the Baby Boomers in Their Old Age?," Policy Note 1999/5 (Annandale-on-Hudson, NY: The Levy Economics Institute of Bard College).

Smeeding, T. M., C. Estes and L. Glasse (1999) "Social Security Reform and Older Women: Improving the System," Income Security Policy Series No. 22 (Syracuse, NY: Maxwell School of Citizenship and Public Affairs, Syracuse University).

Social Security Administration (2003) *The 2003 Annual Report of the Board of Trustees of the Federal Old Age and Survivors Insurance and Disability Insurance Trust Funds* (17 March 2003).

Whitehouse, E. (2000) "How Poor are the Old? A Survey of Evidence from 44 Countries," *Social Protection Discussion Papers* (Washington, DC: World Bank).

Wolff, E. N. (2003) "The Devolution of the American Pension System: Who Gained and Who Lost?" *Eastern Economic Journal* 29(4): 477–495.

Wolff, E. N. (2002) *Retirement Insecurity: The Income Shortfalls Awaiting the Soon-to-Retire* (Washington, DC: Economic Policy Institute).

Wolff, E. N. and A. Zacharias (2006) *"An Overall Assessment of the Distributional Consequences of Government Spending and Taxation in the United States, 1989 and 2000,"* in D. B. Papadimitriou (ed.) *The Distributional Effects Of Government Spending And Taxation* (New York and United Kingdom: Palgrave Macmillan) pp. 15–68.

United States General Accounting Office (2004) Social Security: Distribution of Benefits and Taxes Relative to Earnings Level (Washington, DC: US Government Printing Office).

Part I
Welfare State and the Incentives to Retire

Part I

Welfare State and the Incentives to Retire

2
European Welfare State Regimes and Their Generosity toward the Elderly

*Axel Boersch-Supan**

2.1 Introduction

Europe is known for its well-developed welfare state, particularly if seen from the US American perspective. The GDP share of social expenditures of the EU15 countries in the year 2001 was 23.9 percent vis-à-vis 14.7 percent in the United States (OECD Factbook, 2006). Some think that the European welfare state is too large because it crowds out economic activities. Indeed, GDP per capita in the United States is almost 50 percent higher than the average of the EU15 countries; see Figure 2.1.

Discomfort with this figure, however, is limited in Europe. Europeans cite their longer leisure time, their lower income inequality, and their longer life expectancy; see Table 2.1.

This balance may become upset by the demographic aging process. The European population is already much older than the US population, and population aging continues at a faster rate than in the United States due to the lower European fertility rate (Figure 2.2).

Europe now is as old (measured as share of individuals aged 65 and older) as the United States is projected to be in 2017. Even more dramatic is the aging of Europe beyond the year 2025: While Europe will continue to age, the proportion of elderly in the United States will stay relatively stable.

Aging implies more social security expenditures toward the elderly (pensions, health care, long-term care) per capita, and a forteriori per young and/or employed person. Will the expenditures for the elderly blast the welfare state? Will the welfare state disable itself because the incentive effects created by ever increasing tax and contribution rates will crowd out economic activity, thus eroding the tax base which finances the welfare state? Will spending for the elderly crowd out spending for young families and education, undermining fertility and productivity?

24 *Welfare State & the Incentives to Retire*

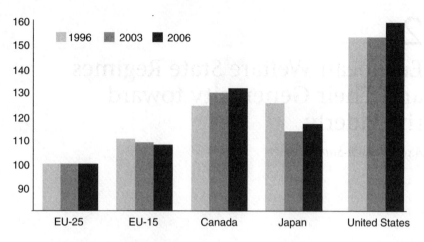

Figure 2.1 GDP per capita (EU25 = 100)
Source: Eurostat Yearbook 2005.

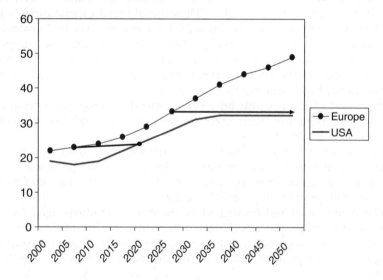

Figure 2.2 Population aging in Europe and the US: percentage age 65 and older
Source: UN population projections, 2002 Revision.

This chapter uses aggregate data (official statistics from Statistical Office of the European Communities (EUROSTAT) and Organisation for Economic Co-operation and Development (OECD)) as well as individual data (from SHARE, the new Survey of Health, Ageing, and Retirement in Europe) in order to show the statistical correlations among various dimensions of welfare state

Table 2.1 Income inequality, leisure time, and life expectancy at birth

	Annual workhours	Gini	Life expectancy at birth
EU15	1,690	30.05	79.0
US	1,920	35.67	77.2

Source: OECD Factbook 2006.

generosity. It has a simple structure: System description – Outcomes – Causes. Section 2.2 describes the European welfare states and their evolution during the European integration process. It compares their generosity to the elderly with the generosity toward the young. Section 2.3 looks at actual policy outcomes, such as unemployment and poverty rates among the young and the elderly, and the inequality in wealth, income, and consumption. We also look at noneconomic outcomes such as health and longevity. Section 2.4 makes a causal analysis of: why the generosity of the European welfare state evolved as it has done? We offer some demographic and political economy reasons, and collect some evidence on incentive effects. Section 2.5 concludes.

2.2 European Welfare States

This section describes the European welfare states and their evolution during the European integration process. We first look at the general size of the welfare states, then at their generosity toward the elderly, and finally at expenditures targeted to the young.

2.2.1 General generosity: size of the welfare states

The size of the welfare state – usually measured as the share of GDP devoted to social expenditures – varies a great deal in Europe, although almost all European countries feature the distinctively higher share than the United States that was mentioned before. The Scandinavian countries, notably Sweden, have the highest social expenditure shares, and Ireland has the lowest.

The European Union in general, and particularly the Scandinavian countries, experienced a retrenchment of the welfare states in the early 1990s. Quite interesting is the opposite development in Ireland and Portugal, the poorest countries of the EU in the 1980s. While Portugal increased the GDP share of social expenditures throughout the observation period depicted in Figure 2.3, Ireland did not increase social expenditures nearly as fast as their GDP, resulting in the only social expenditure share that is lower than the United States.

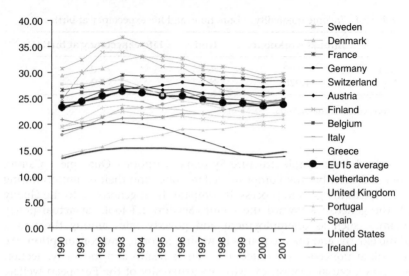

Figure 2.3 Size of the welfare state (social expenditures per GDP, in percentages)
Source: OECD Factbook 2006.

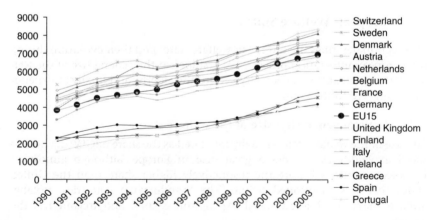

Figure 2.4 Size of the welfare state (social expenditures per capita, in Euro PPP)
Source: Eurostat Data Archive 2005.

Generosity may more appropriately be defined as per capita social spending, in purchasing power parity terms. This is depicted in Figure 2.4. According to this measure, Switzerland, Sweden, and Denmark are most generous to their citizens, and Ireland and the Mediterranean countries are the least generous welfare states. Of those five countries, however, Italy is much closer to the

EU15 average, while the other four countries feature a remarkable gap in per capita social expenditures vis-à-vis the rest of the pre-accession EU.

Figure 2.4 also reveals that the growth rates of per capita spending are almost identical for all EU15 countries. While Italy features a particularly low increase, Ireland a particularly large one, these differences are relatively small and there is little sign of convergence. European integration has not – at least not so far – led to an equalization of per capita social expenditures. There is, however, some sign of convergence in the GDP share of social expenditures, see the preceding Figure 2.3. Overall, the variety of the European welfare states is large; larger than the three or four archetypical welfare state models à la Esping-Andersen (2003) suggest.

The following subsection will deepen this point. We will split social expenditures in three parts: spending that can be reasonably clearly targeted to the elderly (mainly pensions, see the following subsection 2.2.2); spending that can be reasonably clearly targeted to the young (mainly education and family allowances, subsection 2.2.3); and spending which may go to the young and the old as well as the middle aged (for example, healthcare; this is contained in the figures of this subsection but will not be analyzed separately).

2.2.2 Generosity toward the elderly

Spending for the elderly – here defined as expenditures for old-age, disability, and survivor pensions – is actually diverging in Europe; see Figure 2.5. Sweden and Austria spend most for the elderly on a per capita basis, and Ireland spends the least, with a remarkable gap. Portugal, Spain,

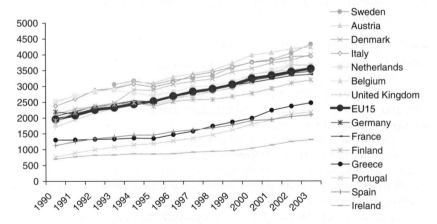

Figure 2.5 Social expenditures dedicated to the elderly (per capita, in Euro PPP)
Source: Eurostat Data Archive 2005.

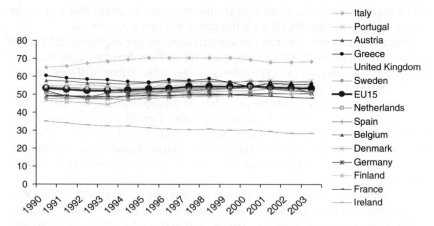

Figure 2.6 Share of social expenditures dedicated to the elderly (percentages of total)
Source: Eurostat Data Archive 2005.

and Greece have increased their spending on the elderly, but not so much as to converge with the rest of the EU15.

Holding total social spending constant, the picture is remarkably different, see Figure 2.6. Italy and Ireland stand out: Italy spends about 70 percent of the entire social budget on the elderly, 15 percentage points more than the EU15 average, while Ireland spends less than a third of its social budget on the elderly, 25 percentage points less than the EU15 average. Essentially, these expenditure shares have stayed constant over the past 15 years.

2.2.3 Generosity toward the young

Figure 2.7 corresponds to Figure 2.6 and shows the share of the social budget devoted to the young – defined as family and child support, education, and unemployment benefits. It is not the flip side of Figure 2.6 because health care and a variety of smaller social transfers that go to both young and old are not included in Figures 2.6 and 2.7.

While Italy and Ireland still stand out as extreme, at least in recent years, they do not stand out as extreme with regard to the share of the social budget devoted to the elderly. Remarkable is the great variety of spending shares to the younger generations in Europe: it ranges from about 5 percent to about 30 percent of the social budget.

Equally different are the per capita expenditures; see Figure 2.8. Here, Denmark and the other Scandinavian countries stand out.

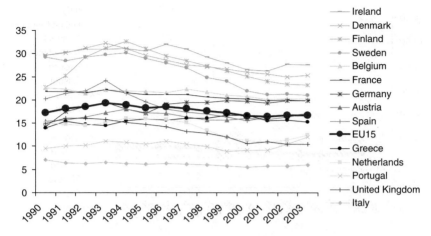

Figure 2.7 Share of social expenditures dedicated to the young (percentages of total)
Source: Eurostat Data Archive 2005.

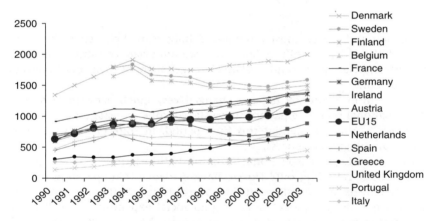

Figure 2.8 Social expenditures dedicated to the young (per capita, in Euro PPP)
Source: Eurostat Data Archive 2005.

2.2.4 Old versus young: relative generosity, crowding out

The resulting picture emerges quite clearly; see Figure 2.9. Here the share of the social budget devoted to the elderly (Figure 2.6) is divided by the share of the social budget devoted to the young (Figure 2.7). For the pre-accession EU, this ratio is about three and has not changed very much between 1990 and 2003. Relative to this benchmark, the Netherlands, Portugal, the United

30 Welfare State & the Incentives to Retire

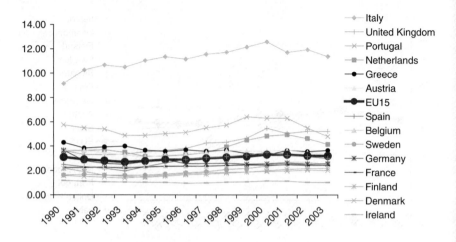

Figure 2.9 Relative generosity to the elderly versus the young (social expenditure shares to the elderly divided by social expenditure shares to the young)
Source: Eurostat Data Archive 2006.

Kingdom, and, by far most pronounced Italy, lean their generosity more toward the elderly, while Ireland, the Scandinavian countries, Belgium, France, and Germany spend a relatively larger share of their social budgets on the young.

The ratio in Figure 2.9 has not changed very much between 1990 and 2003: national spending patterns have stayed rather constant and different from each other throughout this time period, in spite of an accelerated European integration process.

Does this stark cross-sectional variation within Europe teach us something about crowding out? Do we have evidence that spending on the elderly crowds out spending on the young? Figure 2.10 sheds some light on this question. It plots the per capita social expenditures (in Euro at purchasing power parity) depicted in Figures 2.5 and 2.8 against each other.

This picture reveals no evidence for a negative correlation between the spending share for the elderly and the spending share for the young. More formally, a pooled regression through the points in Figure 2.10 yields a positively significant coefficient with an R^2 of 0.27. The time series correlation of the EU15 average has about the same slope and an R^2 of 0.85; and a cross-sectional regression for the 2003 values features a slightly smaller, but still positively significant coefficient with an R^2 of 0.12. The positive correlation can be interpreted as evidence that the welfare states have expanded without much of a trade-off between spending toward the elderly and spending toward the poor.

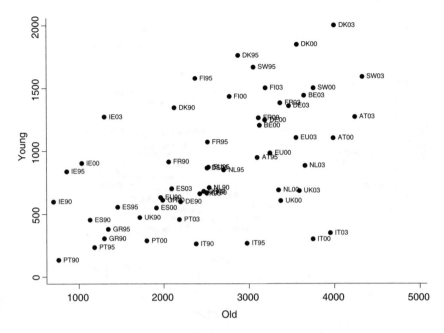

Figure 2.10 Relative generosity to the elderly versus the young (expenditure per capita devoted to the elderly versus per capita spending devoted to the young, Euro PPP)

Figure 2.11 repeats this exercise on the basis of spending shares (measured as percentage of GDP). This figure seems to show less of a positive correlation, and, in the case of Italy, maybe even a negative correlation.

More formally, Table 2.2 displays a set of time-series regressions by country based on the above data. Indeed, Italy exhibits a negative coefficient but it is insignificant. In about half of the European countries, the regression produces a significant slope. In all of these cases, the slope is a positive one. The aggregate EU15 regression also features a positive slope, although not significant at conventional levels.

We conclude that there is little evidence for a crowding out effect between being generous to the elderly and being generous to the young. Social spending for the elderly and the young expanded and contracted pretty much in sync with the overall social budget, which increased considerably in absolute terms (Figure 2.4) and consolidated relative to GDP (Figure 2.3).

2.3 Policy outcomes

Section 2.3 looks at actual policy outcomes, such as unemployment and poverty rates among the young and the elderly, and the inequality in wealth, income,

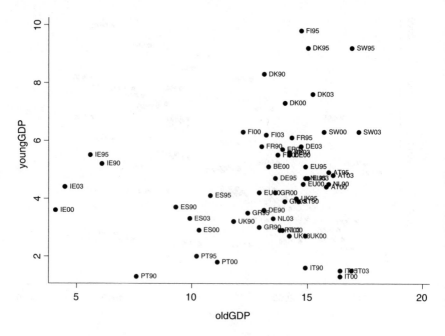

Figure 2.11 Relative generosity to the elderly vs. the young (social expenditures devoted to the elderly versus social expenditures devoted to the young; percentage of GDP)

Table 2.2 Time-series regressions of social expenditure share devoted to the elderly on social expenditure share devoted to the young (percentage of GDP)

Country	Coef.	Std. Err.	t-stat	P > |t| (%)	[95% Conf.	Interval]
European Union	0.97	0.60	1.6	13	−0.34	2.29
Italy	−2.24	2.04	−1.1	29	−6.68	2.19
Denmark	−0.13	0.23	−0.6	57	−0.63	0.36
United Kingdom	−0.02	0.39	−0.1	95	−0.87	0.82
Belgium	0.78	0.90	0.9	44	−1.72	3.27
Spain	0.27	0.17	1.5	15	−0.11	0.64
France	0.78	0.44	1.8	10	−0.18	1.74
Austria	1.17	0.37	3.1	1	0.36	1.99
Sweden	0.30	0.09	3.4	1	0.10	0.50
Germany	0.96	0.24	4.0	0	0.43	1.48
Netherlands	1.16	0.21	5.6	0	0.71	1.61
Portugal	3.60	0.62	5.8	0	2.26	4.94
Greece	1.89	0.32	5.9	0	1.19	2.58
Finland	0.64	0.06	9.9	0	0.49	0.79
Ireland	0.96	0.09	10.2	0	0.76	1.17

Source: Author's regressions based on the data depicted in Figure 2.11.

and consumption. We also look at noneconomic outcomes such as health and longevity. Most of this section is based on the SHARE data collected in 2004.

2.3.1 Income levels

Figure 2.12 examines the actual relative income level of pensioners. It distinguishes young (aged 72 and younger) and old retirees (aged 73 and older) and relates their net public and private income to the total net income of working individuals aged between 50 and 65.

Denmark and the Netherlands have Beveridgian flat base pensions, while the other countries have Bismarckian earnings-related pensions. For the younger retirees, this is reflected in the much lower relative public income levels in those two countries. In the Netherlands, this is fully compensated by private income (largely occupational pensions), but not in Denmark. The older Dutch retirees still enjoy a much higher prereform public pension. In the other countries, old-age income is dominated by public pensions.

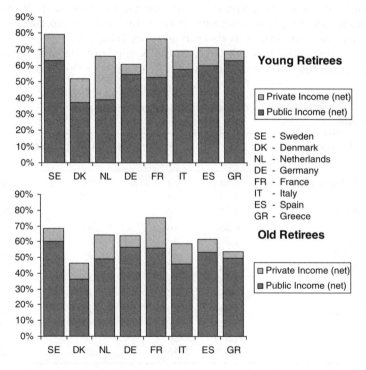

Figure 2.12 Income level of retirees (age 72 and less/age 73 and more) relative to income of working persons aged 50–65

Source: Wilke (2006), based on SHARE 2004.

The patterns in Figure 2.12, based on micro data, are somewhat different from what one might expect after having seen Figure 2.5 which was based on aggregate spending figures. The case of Denmark catches the eye. If the main goal of welfare state generosity toward the elderly is to prolong accustomed income levels also during retirement, then Denmark, which spends considerably more than the average EU15 country on social expenditures geared toward the elderly, fails.

Another feature that catches the eye in Figure 2.12 is the high income for French retirees. Most additional private incomes are occupational pensions financed pay-as-you-go, while the public pension level, relative to the middle aged, is in line with the European average.

2.3.2 Distribution of income, wealth, and consumption

One explanation lies in a different goal of social expenditures in Denmark, namely poverty reduction and income equality. Denmark, together with Sweden, has by far the lowest Gini coefficient on income inequality among the population aged 50+. Note that this is in spite of a considerable wealth inequality in Denmark, pretty much the same as everywhere in the SHARE countries. Consumption inequality, maybe the most appropriate measure for equal living conditions, is also very low (see Table 2.3).

Income inequality is much larger in the Netherlands. Figure 2.12 masks the large heterogeneity in additional private income for Dutch elderly.

Table 2.3 Distribution of income, consumption, and wealth among the elderly (GINI coefficients)

Macro-Region and Country (%)	N[a]	Income (%)	Consumption (%)	Wealth (%)
Northern Europe	2,981	33	24	60
Sweden	1,787	33	22	59
Denmark	1,194	32	28	62
Central Europe	6,867	46	35	63
Germany	1,825	42	25	62
Netherlands	1,741	49	46	65
Switzerland	743	47	38	63
Austria	1,589	51	33	58
France	969	47	45	61
Southern Europe	4,021	47	41	65
Italy	1,445	41	47	64
Spain	897	56	26	68
Greece	1,679	45	28	52

Note:
[a] N is the number of observations
Source: Bonsang, Perelman, and van den Bosch (2005), based on SHARE 2004.

2.3.3 Youth and elderly unemployment

France and Denmark are interesting cases because one of the main indicators for successful social policy to the young comes out dramatically different in both countries. While Denmark has one of the lowest youth unemployment rates of the OECD countries, France has by far the highest youth unemployment rate in Europe, topped in the OECD only by Turkey and the Slovak Republic. French social spending levels on the young are above EU15 average (see Figures 2.7 and 2.8); however, much of this goes to family and child subsidies and less to education than in other European countries. In a very broad sense, one might interpret this finding as a kind of crowding out: public attention focused on maintaining the income level of retirees has crowded out attention on the unemployment situation of the young (see Figure 2.13).

The flip side of youth unemployment is the unemployment rate among the elderly. In the age range of 55 and older, unemployment is often disguised as early retirement, often with a disability pension or similar financing mechanisms. Hence, Figure 2.14 depicts the employment rate of individuals aged 55–64.

Sweden has by far the highest labor force participation rate in this age range, exceeding that of the United States and even Japan. Denmark and the United Kingdom are also considerably above the EU15 average.

In turn, France, Italy, Belgium, and Austria have very low labor force participation rates, more than 10 percentage points below the EU15 average

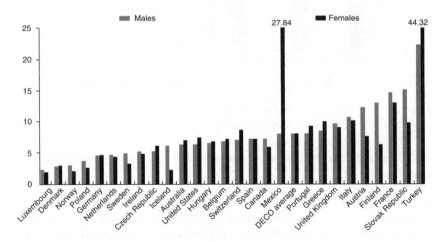

Figure 2.13 Percentage of youths aged between 15 and 19 who are not in education nor in employment, 2003
Source: OECD Factbook 2006.

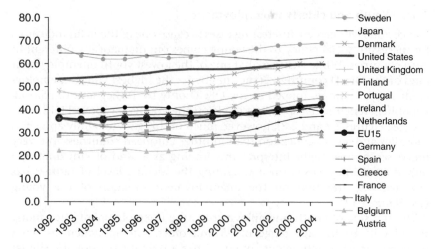

Figure 2.14 Employment rate of individuals aged 55–64, 1992–2004
Source: Eurostat Online Data Archive April 2006.

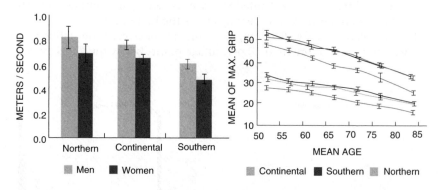

Figure 2.15 Walking speed and grip strength of individuals aged 50 and older
Source: Mackenbach, Avendano, Andersen-Ranberg, and Aro (2005), based on SHARE 2004.

and 20 percentage points below the so-called Lisbon Target of 50 percent participation.

2.3.4 Health and longevity

Arguably one of the most important social policy outcomes is health, since it is a main driver for well-being. Differences in the health status of a population are very difficult to measure. The SHARE data has a wide array of physical and mental health measures, some self-reported, others physically measured (see Figure 2.15). Two examples of a physical measurement are grip strength and walking speed. They show a remarkably consistent North–South gradient through Europe.

Using all available health data in SHARE, including several mental health and cognition tests, Jürges (2005) has developed a comprehensive health index depicted in Figure 2.16.

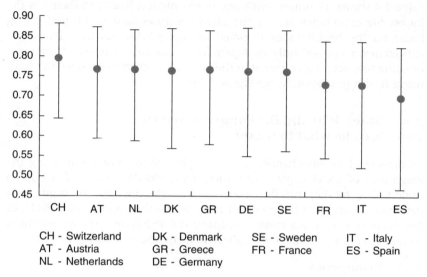

Figure 2.16 Comprehensive health index of individuals aged 50 and older
Source: Jürges (2005), based on SHARE 2004.

Table 2.4 Life expectancy at birth, 2003

Life expectancy at birth, 2003	
Denmark	77.2
United States	77.2
Portugal	77.3
Ireland	77.8
Belgium	78.1
Greece	78.1
Germany	78.4
Finland	78.5
United Kingdom	78.5
Austria	78.6
Netherlands	78.6
France	79.4
Italy	79.9
Sweden	80.2
Switzerland	80.4
Spain	80.5
Japan	81.8

Source: OECD Health Data 2005.

It paints a more detailed picture and identifies Switzerland and Spain as well-defined extremes with a health index well above and well below the SHARE countries' average. Variation in the population is, of course, very large, as shown by the brackets.

Worse health does not necessarily translate in lower life expectancy, as Table 2.4 shows. Denmark, with one of the highest health indexes has the lowest life expectancy among the EU15 countries, and Spain, performing badly on the health index depicted in Figure 2.16, has the highest life expectancy, surpassed only by Japan. This paradox is subject of intensive ongoing research; it is mirrored in the fact that women live longer, but have worse health (for example, see Figure 2.15).

2.4 Causes: Why did the European welfare states become what they are?

In the sequel of this chapter, we move a few steps toward explaining the magnitude of social expenditures toward the elderly. This is of course an undertaking far beyond the scope of a single chapter. We begin with demographic and political economy reasons, and then collect some evidence for incentive effects that create an expanded demand for social expenditures toward the elderly, particularly early retirement and disability pensions.

2.4.1 Demography

One obvious explanation for the differences in the size of the welfare state and its generosity toward the elderly is, almost a banality, their number. While all European countries are aging, more so than the United States, and all EU15 countries except Ireland have a higher share of older individuals than the United States, Europe is far from homogeneous in its current population age structure as Figure 2.17 shows.

Italy has by far the largest share of elderly in the population, explaining part of the huge ratio between spending for the elderly and spending for the young visible in Figure 2.9.

To proceed somewhat more formally, Table 2.5 shows time-series cross-section regressions on the expenditure data depicted in Figure 2.11. The first four regressions are simple pooled ordinary least squares (OLS) regressions. The last two regressions are fixed effects regressions, the first using only the cross-national variation, the second only the time-series variation. Indeed, the share of individuals age 65 and older is the key explanatory variable for the spending share on the elderly relative to GDP in almost all regression variants, the only exception being the last regression, indicating that the time-series variation of the elderly share is still very small: the aging process during the 1990–2003 time period is still very modest. As a side product, these regressions also reiterate the positive coefficient of spending for the young, rejecting the crowding-out hypothesis.

Table 2.5 Pooled time-series cross-section regressions of social expenditures for the elderly as percent of GDP

oldgdp	Coef.	t-state	Coef.	t-state	Coef.	t-state	Coef.	t-state	Coef.	t-state	Coef.	t-state
younggdp	0.252	2.6	0.197	2.0	0.263	3.6	0.129	1.9	0.057	0.8	0.733	9.8
gdpcap			0.164	3.47	0.066	1.82	0.337	7.05	0.387	7.8	0.054	2.6
share65p					1.197	12.3	1.436	15.8	1.438	15.8	0.310	4.1
year							−0.416	−7.6				
const	12.087	23.5	9.242	9.6	−7.410	−4.8	816.0	7.6	−16.181	−9.4	4.062	4.3
Adj R-squared	0.027		0.080		0.482		0.609		*Within*	0.626	*Within*	0.485
									Between	0.351	*Between*	0.150
									Overall	0.404	*Overall*	0.160

Source: Author's regressions based on the data depicted in Figure 2.11.

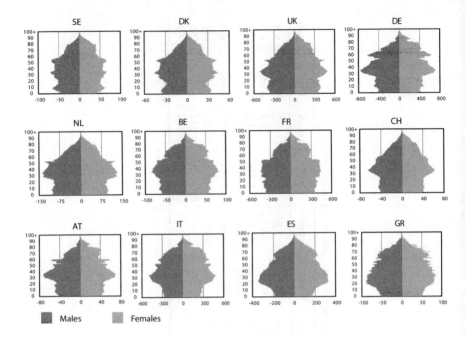

Figure 2.17 Age structure of European countries
Source: Eurostat 2003.

2.4.2 Political preferences

A second potential cause for the spending patterns observed in Section 2.2 are differences in political preferences. In some countries, a majority of voters may be in favor of more spending to the elderly, in others more to the young. This is of course most likely connected to the age structure of the populace, but there might be additional differences across countries.

Boeri, Boersch-Supan and Tabellini (2001, 2002, 2004) have conducted a series of small surveys in a few European countries to shed light on the political preferences of European citizens. Their aim was to understand resistance to structural reforms, in particular to pension reforms. A first set of surveys was conducted in the Spring of 2000 for four countries. The survey was repeated one and a half years later in Germany and Italy, and once more for Germany in the Spring of 2003. Table 2.6 summarizes results relevant for this chapter; the exact wording of the questions is quoted on top of the table.

The results show an astounding variation across the four countries. First, the status quo bias is strong in all countries, but weakest in Italy. Second, further expansion of the welfare state does not find majority, but neither its

Table 2.6 Preferences about size and redistribution of welfare state

	Larger size of welfare state?[a] (Percentages)			(ii) More generous to elderly?[b] (Percentages)		
	(+)	(0)	(−)	(+)	(0)	(−)
Germany (Spring 2000)	13	54	25	17	62	22
Germany (Fall 2001)	12	48	34	27	51	23
Germany (Spring 2003)	19	36	34	19	45	29
Italy (Spring 2000)	17	40	43	19	35	46
Italy (Fall 2001)	23	47	30	34	28	38
France (Spring 2000)	14	51	35	14	66	20
Spain (Spring 2000)	31	53	16	10	60	30

Notes:
[a] Size of welfare state: Should the state (+) increase pensions and/or transfers, thereby raising taxes and compulsory contributions to households, (0) maintain taxes and compulsory contributions at current levels, or (−) reduce pensions and/or transfers to households, thereby cutting taxes and/or compulsory contributions?
[b] Intergenerational redistribution: Should the state (+) allocate more resources to pensions and less to unemployed or young job seekers, (0) keep the current situation (−), or allocate less resources to pensions and more to unemployed and young job seekers?
Source: Boeri, Boersch-Supan, and Tabellini (2001, 2003), Boersch-Supan, Heiss, and Winter (2004).

retrenchment. Relatively speaking, the Spanish lean most toward an expansion of the welfare state. Third, except for Germany in 2001 (just after an incisive pension reform), there are more citizens who want to shift the welfare states' generosity from the old toward the young than in the reverse order. This is most pronounced in Italy, where this share even surpasses the status quo percentage. Note that this is in stark contrast to the fact that Italy has the oldest populace.

The results in Table 2.6 align with the actual spending shares (Figure 2.3) and the distribution between old and young (Figure 2.9) in a reverse pattern. Spain has the smallest welfare state and wishes to expand most. Italy has the most skewed distribution toward the elderly and wishes to change this most starkly. This may be interpreted as a desire for convergence within Europe, or simply as a tendency to give up most easily those transfers that are supplied most generously, since this is likely to hurt least. Evidence for this interpretation comes from another set of results derived from the 2001 survey by Boeri, Boersch-Supan and Tabellini (2002). Figure 2.18 shows how different Germans and Italians judge the attraction of six pension reform proposals. Italians would vote in majority for an increase in the retirement age (currently having one of the lowest average exit ages in Europe), while Germans rather reduce their pension benefits (currently having one of the highest pension benefits, measured in absolute Euro terms at purchasing power).

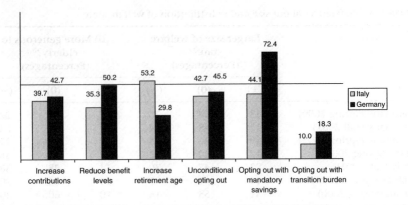

Figure 2.18 Preferences about pension reform options (in percentage)
Source: Boeri, Boersch-Supan, and Tabellini (2002, 2004), Boersch-Supan, Heiss, and Winter (2004).

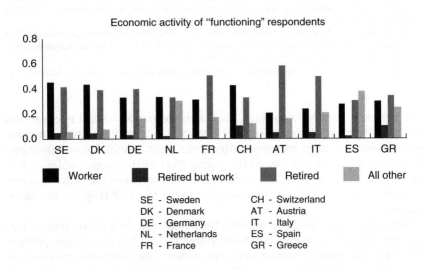

Figure 2.19 Employment and retirement rates conditional on good health
Source: Brugiavini, Croda, and Mariuzzo (2005), based on SHARE 2004.

2.4.3 Early-retirement incentives

A third reason for the large differences in the size of the welfare state and the generosity toward the elderly are incentive effects in the public transfer systems, especially toward early retirement. Early retirement is widespread in Europe, as the low labor force participation rates among individuals aged 55–64 have indicated in Figure 2.14. Most striking are the cross-national differences in economic activity vis-à-vis retirement if differential health

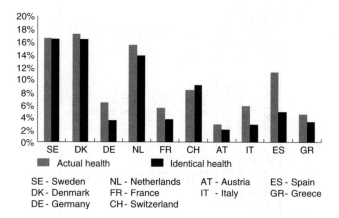

Figure 2.20 Disability insurance prevalence, by correction for health status
Source: Boersch-Supan (2006), based on SHARE 2004.

(measured as a set of functional measures, so-called activities of daily living) is taken account of; see Figure 2.19.

The cross-national differences are most evident between Sweden and France, for example, or between the Alpine neighbours Austria and Switzerland. To a large extent, these differences can be explained by incentive effects, as the International Social Security Project led by Gruber and Wise (1999) has shown. The incentive effects of early- old-age pensions measured in this project align very well with the actual early retirement behavior; see Table 2.7.

Early retirement financed by old-age pensions is only part of the incentive story in Europe. In addition, disability pensions are often a substitute for stricter old-age pensions, often paid without a medical test. Figure 2.20 shows the large cross-national variation in disability insurance prevalence, both with and without a correction for health. As it turns out, differential health cannot explain the cross-national differences. If they are regressed on variables that measure the generosity of disability pensions, together with the ease of obtaining such a pension, almost 75 percent of the cross-national variation can be explained: 22 percent by the extent of coverage, 14 and 11 percent by the minimum and maximum benefit level, 12 percent by the benefit level at full disability, and 15 percent by the stringency of a medical exam (Boersch-Supan, 2006).

Combining the results of Table 2.7 and Figure 2.20 helps to explain the large social expenditures to the elderly in Sweden, Denmark, and the Netherlands: While the public pension sector is relatively small in the Netherlands, early retirement is very frequent, and disability uptake as well. Sweden has very generous pensions (this is, for the current elderly under the

Table 2.7 Incentive effects and retirement behavior

Country	Unused Labor Capacity, 55–65	Men Out of Labor Force, Age 59	Early Retirement Age	Replacement Rate at Early Retirement Age (%)	Accrual in Next Year (%)	Implicit Tax on Earnings in Next Year (%)	Tax Force Early Retirement Age to 69	Hazard Rate at Early Retirement Age (%)
Belgium	67	58	60	77	−5.6	82	8.87	33
France	60	53	60	91	−7.0	80	7.25	65
Italy	59	53	55	75	−5.8	81	9.20	10
The Netherlands	58	47	60	91	−12.8	141	8.32	70
The United Kingdom	55	38	60	48	−10.0	75	3.77	22
Germany	48	34	60	62	−4.1	35	3.45	55
Spain	47	36	60	63	4.2	−23	2.49	20
Canada	45	37	60	20	−1.0	8	2.37	32
The United States	37	26	62	41	0.2	−1	1.57	25
Sweden	35	26	60	54	−4.1	28	2.18	5
Japan	22	13	60	54	−3.9	47	1.65	12

Source: Gruber and Wise (1999).

old pay-as-you-go system) and a generous disability insurance. Denmark spends a lot on a base pension that is generous to the poor and the middle class, plus a lot on a lenient disability insurance.

2.5 Summary and conclusions

The aim of this chapter was to examine the generosity of the European welfare states toward the elderly. We have used a mixture of aggregate data from EUROSTAT and the OECD and survey data in particular from the new SHARE.

As a first insight from this analysis, we observe that the size of the welfare state varies a great deal in Europe, as well as its relative generosity to the elderly and the young. There is no such thing as "the European welfare state model," and even the three or four archetypical welfare state models à la Esping-Andersen (1990, 1999, 2003) mask some highly relevant differences within this typology.

Second, while the size of the welfare states has changed over time – some retrenchment in the early 1990s when measured as share of GDP, but a fairly linear increase in absolute per capita expenditures – the spending patterns and the relative generosity between old and young has remained remarkably stable between 1990 and 2003. There is very little indication of a convergence in spite of the accelerated European integration through the Maastricht process and the introduction of a single currency.

Third, we did not find any convincing evidence for the hypothesis that spending for the elderly crowds out spending for the young. Rather, spending for both age groups has expanded and contracted during the 1990–2003 period with the general size of the welfare state. This does not imply, however, that crowding out might occur at higher spending levels on the elderly in the future when dependency ratios will be substantially higher than in the 1990–2003 period.

Fourth, while a causal analysis explaining the size of the various European welfare state models is of course an undertaking far beyond the scope of this single chapter, we have identified three dimensions that explain a great deal of the time-series and cross-national variation in welfare state generosity – both in general and as it relates to the elderly: the demographic forces of population aging, which differ widely across European countries; political preferences pushing politicians in directions different across Europe; and incentive effects that create an expanded demand for social expenditures toward the elderly (in particularly early retirement and disability benefits) that are more pronounced in some European countries than in others.

These incentive effects are the key mechanisms by which government spending is crowding out economic activity. In light of the accelerating demographic change during the coming decades, they need to be taken seriously because the trade-off between welfare state generosity and economic activity, by which this chapter started, is getting harsher as aging progresses. Policies which maintain spending levels but minimize incentive effects are particularly attractive. Examples are flexible retirement rules with actuarial benefit rules that strengthen labor supply, and public defined benefit plans indexed to demography that strengthen private old-age provision.

Note

* I am grateful for the comments by Sergio Nisticò, Anette Reil-Held, Christina Wilke and the participants of the Conference on Government Spending on the Elderly at the Levy Economics Institute at Bard College. Olga Novikova provided very able research assistance.

References

Boeri, T., A. Boersch-Supan and G. Tabellini (2004) "How Would You Like To Reform Your Pension System? The Opinions of German and Italian citizens," in R. Brooks and A. Razin (eds) *Politics and Finance of Social Security Reform* (Cambridge, MA: Cambridge University Press).

Boeri, T., A. Boersch-Supan and G. Tabellini (2002) "Would You Like To Reform the Pension System? The Opinions of European Citizens," American Economic Review 92: 396–401.

Boeri, T., A. Boersch-Supan and G. Tabellini (2001) "Would You Like to Shrink the Welfare State? The Opinions of European Citizens," *Economic Policy* 32: 7–50.

Bonsang, E., S. Perelman and K. van den Bosch (2005) "Income, Wealth and Consumption Inequality," in Boersch-Supan et al. (eds) *Health, Ageing and Retirement in Europe – First Results From the Survey of Health, Ageing and Retirement in Europe* (Mannheim, Germany: MEA).

Boersch-Supan, A. (2006) "Work Disability, Health and Incentive Effects" in D. Wise New Themes in the Economics of Aging (Chicago, IL: University of Chicago Press). Page: 14

Börsch-Supan, A., Heiss, F. und J. Winter, 2004, *Akzeptanzprobleme bei Rentenreformen*. Deutsches Institut für Altervorsorge, Köln 2004.

Brugiavini, A., E. Croda and F. Mariuzzo (2005) "Labour Force Participation of the Elderly: Unused Capacity?" in Boersch-Supan et al. (eds) *Health, Ageing and Retirement in Europe – First Results From the Survey of Health, Ageing and Retirement in Europe* (Mannheim, Germany: MEA).

Esping-Andersen, G. (1990) *The Three Worlds of Welfare Capitalism* (Princeton, NJ: Princeton University Press).

Esping-Andersen, G. (1999) *Social Foundations of Postindustrial Economies* (Oxford: Oxford University Press).

Esping-Andersen, G. (2003) "A Welfare State For the 21st Century," in A. Giddens (ed.) *The Global Third Way Debate* (Oxford: Polity Press), pp. 134–156.

Gruber, J. and D. Wise (1999) *Social Security and Retirement Around the World* (Chicago, IL: University of Chicago Press).

Jürges, H. (2005) "Cross-Country Differences in General Health," in Boersch-Supan, A. et al. (eds) *Health, Ageing and Retirement in Europe – First Results From the Survey of Health, Ageing and Retirement in Europe* (Mannheim, Germany: MEA).

Mackenbach, J., M. Avendano, K. Andersen-Ranberg and A. R. Aro (2005) "Socio-Economic Sparities in Physical Health in 10 European Countries," in Boersch-Supan, A. et al. (eds) *Health, Ageing and Retirement in Europe – First Results From the Survey of Health, Ageing and Retirement in Europe* (Mannheim, Germany: MEA).

OECD (2006) *OECD Factbook* (Paris: OECD). Available online at: http://caliban.sourceoecd.org/vl=3040935/cl=12/nw=1/rpsv/factbook/

Wilke, C. B. (2006) "Income Levels of Individuals Aged 50 and Older: Effective and Comprehensive Replacement Rates Based on the SHARE Data." Mimeo (Mannheim, Germany: Mannheim Research Institute for the Economics of Aging).

Comments to Chapter 2

Sergio Nisticò

How should governments respond to population aging? Advocates of the welfare state argue that it should be maintained, either in its current form, or in some revised institutional setting; their opponents propose abolition of welfare provisions as a viable alternative to increased Social Security spending (and taxes). One key point in this worldwide debate is the interpretation of Europe's long experience with a massive welfare state. Axel Boersch-Supan's paper makes an important contribution to clarifying the issues at stake.

Extracting unambiguous and meaningful information from data is not easy. On the one hand, we run the risk of "torturing" the data till it supports our own preconceptions; on the other hand it is all too easy to confirm what everybody already knows. Boersch-Supan avoids both risks, allowing the data to speak for itself and using it to find the right answers to the three crucial questions he raises in his introduction:

> Will the expenditures for the elderly blast the welfare state? Will the welfare state disable itself because the incentive effects created by ever increasing tax and contribution rates will crowd out economic activity, thus eroding the tax base which finances the welfare state? Will spending for the elderly crowd out spending for young families and education, undermining fertility and productivity?

The paper's most important argument concerns the third of these questions. According to Boersch-Supan (2006), there is no evidence that spending for elderly has reduced spending on young, families, and education. On the contrary, the data shows that "spending for both age groups has expanded and contracted during the 1990–2003 period with the general size of the welfare state." He goes on to extract another important finding from the data, namely that "there is no such thing as 'the European welfare state model'" and that "there is very little indication of a convergence, in spite of the accelerated European integration through the Maastricht process and the introduction of a single currency."

In this brief commentary, I will suggest that (1) it is no longer meaningful to talk in terms of a trade-off between spending on the elderly and spending on the young; (2) there are grounds for optimism that a new European welfare state may be on the point of becoming reality. If I am right, it is not only Boersch-Supan's third question that we can answer in the negative but also his first and second questions – at least insofar as they apply to Europe.

Young versus elderly people

There are two possible objections to the idea of a trade-off between spending for the young and spending for the elderly.

The first objection can be summarized as follows: When governments decide the level of taxes and benefits, and identify the beneficiaries of social expenditures, what they actually do is allocate property rights to a certain share of annual GDP. However, this is only the beginning of the story. After the initial allocation of property rights, social and cultural relationships between individuals in different age cohorts lead to an additional reallocation of resources through informal exchanges. This is particularly true in countries in which the tax-benefits mix favors the elderly. In these countries, intergenerational social relationships and family structures create a situation in which a (often very high) proportion of elderly people's claims on GDP (funded by taxes on the young) end up by returning to active members of the workforce – as transfers of wealth and consumption goods as well as in the form of free services such as childcare. When interpreting Italy's astonishing top ranking position in Figure 2.9, we have to bear in mind the typical structure of the Italian family. Young Italians do not receive welfare benefits directly from the government but indirectly through their elderly relatives. As a result, they are probably not much worse off (and in most instances better off) than their European peers. A more balanced transfer might well be beneficial in several different ways. But we should realize that if we spend less for the elderly and more on younger people, it is unlikely there would be a reverse transfer of resources from "kids to parents".

The second objection is that it is difficult to make a clear distinction between the two categories of beneficiary. Boersch-Supan defines spending for the elderly as the sum of old-age, disability and survivors benefits – 50 to 55 percent of welfare expenditure in the EU15 countries. Spending for the young, he defines as the sum of family and child support, education and unemployment benefits – 15 to 20 percent of the total. He cautions the reader that these definitions miss out health care and other small items, which in sum amount to some 30 percent of total expenditure. These expenditures, which benefit both the elderly and the young, together with the existence of "unusual" categories of beneficiary such as young survivors and disabled people or the elderly unemployed, make the distinction between the young and the elderly somewhat nebulous. In the near future, pension cuts and increases in the retirement age will allow increasing numbers of "elderly" workers to draw unemployment benefits[1] – further contributing to the confusion.

A more general issue is why active workers (taxpayers) should consider government spending for their parents differently from government spending for their children.

Cautious optimism

As populations grow older, per capita income is likely to fall in which case maintaining the purchasing power of non-workers would require ever increasing tax or contribution rates, both in public pay-as-you-go and in privately funded systems. Regardless of the size of welfare provisions, increases in dependency ratios raise the issue of intergenerational income redistribution. Young workers would still have to increase the share of their collective income devoted to caring for their elderly parents, even if they were exempt from Social Security contributions. Conversely, if family ties were weaker and elderly people supported themselves from accumulated wealth, they would leave lower bequests to their offspring who would thus be forced to consume less, so as to "buy" the wealth they need to support themselves later in life. Aging is aging regardless of institutional context.

An obvious alternative to increasing tax rates (intergenerational income redistribution) is to raise the "normal" or "legal" retirement age. But after many years dedicated almost entirely to work and consumption-related activities, with little time for leisure, few Europeans like the idea of putting off their retirement.[2] In fact, one of the key issues for aging societies is going to be the redistribution of the time individuals dedicate to education, consumption, work, and leisure. The real challenge is not so much the extent of welfare provisions, but the way these activities are distributed within different age groups. Many changes are possible: more work for young people in parallel with their education, more leisure and education instead of work (and consumption) for the middle-aged, some continued work and education for elderly people – on top of leisure. These are just a few examples of how it might be possible to achieve a more balanced distribution of time, enhancing individual well-being, and making later retirement more acceptable.[3] In this perspective, welfare institutions should provide individuals with a new legal framework in which they can "easily" move back and forth between leisure, education, and work. In brief, one of the biggest challenges for the future welfare state is to give individuals the feeling that they have a range of options and that the decisions they take are not irreversible.

Several European countries have already taken a first, important, step in this direction. In the mid 90s, Italy, Latvia, Poland, and Sweden adopted the so called Notional Defined Contribution (NDC) pension scheme. This scheme drops defined-benefit formulas in favor of defined-contribution rules, while maintaining a pay-as-you-go financial structure. There are two main advantages: (1) the new scheme eliminates the unfair, regressive redistributive effects typical of most European public pension plans,[4] providing beneficiaries with a uniform yearly rate of return on the (virtual) balance of their contributions; (2) as long as beneficiaries are credited with an annual rate of return equal to the rate of growth in the contribution base[5] pension expenditure is financially sustainable without raising the rate of contribution. Boersch-Supan's account brilliantly summarizes other advantages of the scheme:

> It adapts itself automatically to changed life expectancies ...; It allows transfer mechanisms to be easily identified as in-lieu contributions: notably tax-financed credits for higher and vocational education and similar credits for educating children; ... it permits a considerable amount of flexibility for employees in choosing their retirement age; makes the inflexible and politically problematic fixation of a "normal" retirement age superfluous; and exposes the trade-off between accumulated contributions and retirement age in an internally consistent fashion; It permits easy portability of pension rights between jobs, occupations, and sectors. (Boersch-Supan 2006, pp. 44–45)

Looking backwards, it is true that "there is no such thing as 'the European Welfare State model' and that ... there is very little indication of a convergence in spite of the accelerated European integration ...". What data from the past cannot show, however, are the effects of pension reforms likely to be introduced in the near future. In particular, they give no inkling of what could be Europe's future welfare state model: a public pension system based on NDC rules, funded by a fixed contribution rate on wages,[6] and accompanied by additional benefits for the young (including pension contributions) as well as for the elderly. These would be paid for out of tax revenue and should include a minimum guaranteed pension.

The future of the welfare state depends on the ability of reformers to make workers and firms understand the economic (and ethical) value of the benefits they fund with their contributions. The NDC model provides transparent mechanisms for the transfer of property rights between generations. Broader adoption of the model could make a vital contribution to the creation and survival of a genuinely European welfare state. If this were achieved, we would have good ground to answer "no" to Boersch-Supan's first two questions.

Notes

1. It is well known that firms do not like elderly workers. In many cases in which European workers retire early, the benefits they receive should be considered as long term unemployment benefits, allowing young unemployed people to find jobs, earlier than would have been possible otherwise.
2. See Eurobarometer (2004).
3. For a microeconomic analysis of possible positive effects on well-being of a more even distribution of time, see Nisticò (2005).
4. US Social Security rules provide for three different accrual rates, corresponding to different income brackets. This mechanism does not produce the same kind of regressive redistribution observed in European schemes.
5. For the technical details on the functioning of the NDC scheme, see Gronchi and Nisticò (2006).
6. Different countries would still have different preferences for rates of contribution to compulsory pay-as-you-go public pension schemes. For a more detailed analysis of the potentialities of a European pension system, and of obstacles to implementation see Holzmann (2006).

References

Boersch-Supan, A. (2006) "What Are NDC Systems? What Do They Bring to Reform Strategies?," in R. Holzmann and E. Palmer (eds) *Pension Reform – Issues and Prospects for Non-Financial Defined Contribution (NDC) Schemes* (The World Bank).

Eurobarometer (2004) *The Future of Pension Systems*, Special Eurobarometer 161, wave 56.1, http://ec.europa.eu/public_opinion/archives/ebs/ebs_161_pensions.pdf

Gronchi, S. and Nisticò, S. (2006) "Implementing the NDC Theoretical Model: a Comparison of Italy and Sweden," in R. Holzmann and E. Palmer (eds) *Pension Reform – Issues and Prospects for Non-Financial Defined Contribution (NDC) Schemes* (The World Bank).

Holzmann, R. (2006) "Toward a Coordinated Pension System in Europe: Rationale and Potential Structure," in R. Holzmann and E.Palmer (eds) *Pension Reform – Issues and Prospects for Non-Financial Defined Contribution (NDC) Schemes* (The World Bank).

Holzmann R. and E. Palmer (2006) *Pension Reform – Issues and Prospects for Non-Financial Defined Contribution (NDC) Schemes* (The World Bank).

Nisticò, S. (2005) "Consumption and Time in Economics: Prices and Quantities in a Temporary Equilibrium Perspective," *Cambridge Journal of Economics*, 29 (6): 943–957.

3
Global Demographic Trends and Provisioning for the Future

L. Randall Wray*

3.1 Introduction

The world's population is aging, with virtually no nation immune to this demographic trend and the challenges it brings for future generations. Relative growth of the elderly population is fueling debate about reform of Social Security programs in the United States and other developed nations. In the United States, the total discounted shortfall of Social Security revenues has been estimated at about $11 trillion, of which nearly two-thirds comes after 2050. However, this chapter argues that those calling for reform have overstated the demographic challenges ahead. The reason that reformers reach the conclusion that aging poses such a serious challenge is because they focus on *financial* shortfalls. If we focus attention on demographics and on ability to produce real goods and services today and in the future, it becomes clear that the likelihood that Social Security in the United States and developed nations taken as a whole can face a *real crisis* is highly improbable, for the simple reason that demographic changes are too small relative to the growth of output that will be achieved even with low productivity increases. We will conclude with some policy recommendations that will enhance our ability to care for an aging population in a progressive manner that will not put undue burdens on future workers. Policy formation must distinguish between *financial* provisioning and *real* provisioning for the future; only the latter can prepare society as a whole for coming challenges. While individuals can, and should, save in the form of financial assets for their individual retirements, society cannot prepare for waves of future retirees by accumulating financial trust funds. Rather, society prepares for aging by investing to increase future real productivity.

3.2 The burden of aging

The data is in: we are aging – individually and collectively; nationally and globally. If you think that is a problem, consider the alternative. Aging results from the twin demographic forces of declining birth rates and rising longevity. The first is a welcome development that negated the dire "population bomb" predictions made by Club of Rome Malthusians three or four decades ago. Many developed nations are already worried about declining populations; even most emerging nations can look forward to stabilizing populations in the relatively near future. Obviously, lower fertility rates are desirable, and necessary, for achieving environmental sustainability. Rising longevity is desirable from the perspective of individuals, and also from society's vantage point. The social investment in each human is huge, and longer average life spans help society to recoup its investment. If longer life merely meant more time spent in a decrepit and dependent situation, increased longevity could be a mixed blessing. Such does not appear to be the case, although medical resources devoted to the final weeks and months of life of aged Americans is certainly rising. However, that is a largely controllable trend, if desired, through formulation of sensible health care policy – a topic beyond the scope of this chapter.

Of course, aging is considered a problem because of the burden placed on workers of supporting those aged who do not work. The most common measure of that burden is the aged dependency ratio, which is formed by taking the number of those beyond normal working age – for example, aged 65 and above – relative to the number of normal working age – say, age 18 to 64. At best, this is a very rough measure of the burden put on workers. There are a large number of factors that affect the true, real, burden. First, many people continue to work past age 65, both in formal labor markets and in informal (paid and unpaid) work. Women have traditionally provided much of the elder care, and as longevity rises, more and more women above age 65 continue to provide care for their aging relatives and others (again, in paid and unpaid work). By the same token, young people under the age of 18 work within and outside the home. Further, as we will see, it is important to note that even as the aged dependency ratio rises, the youth dependency ratio tends to fall. Thus, the total dependency burden on workers may not be rising even if the share of elderly in the population is rising.

Additionally, the labor-force participation rate, and employment rate, of people aged 18 to 64 can make a huge difference for the true burden on workers. A rising aged dependency ratio can be associated with a constant or falling burden on workers if the employment-population ratio is rising. The three most important factors that have led to changes of the employment rate across OECD (Organisation for Economic Co-operation and Development) nations in recent years have been the dramatic increase of female labor-force participation rates in some Western countries (the United States and Canada stand out), medium-term trends in unemployment rates (rising on trend in many EU nations, falling on trend in the United States), and the trend to earlier age at retirement in many developed nations (although the United States has experienced rising labor-force participation of elderly men – see below). These factors, in turn, depend on numerous variables including social norms, family structure, labor laws, economic necessity, and health. For example, falling fertility rates as well as changing views of the role of women have allowed higher female participation rates. Generous childcare systems in some nations permit even mothers with young children to work in formal labor markets. Laws protecting rights of persons with disabilities, as well as changing attitudes toward them, can increase participation rates of those formerly excluded. Improved health, perhaps due to better health care, can extend the working period for elderly persons as well as for persons with chronic and formerly debilitating health problems. Especially in Europe, very early retirement ages have been encouraged through policy, in part as a reaction to high unemployment rates. In the future, this policy could be reversed, especially if employment rates of younger adults could be increased. Higher growth of aggregate demand – as in the United States during the Clinton years – can dramatically raise employment rates, sharing the burden of supporting the aged among a larger pool of workers. By contrast, sluggish economic performance, as in many Euro nations since monetary union, raises unemployment and lowers employment rates, increasing the burden on those with jobs – a problem that should be resolved, even if the Euro nations were not aging.

Other factors that determine the burden on workers include growth of worker productivity, as well as technological improvements that allow elderly people and people with disabilities to work. Additionally, the propensity of elderly people to live alone might increase the burden on workers to the extent that this requires more resources than required to support elderly in a more traditional, extended family, arrangement. Even if independent living does not increase the total burden, it will likely shift the burden to workers in the formal sector as care that had previously been provided by family members is purchased (privately or by government). Of course, the percent of elderly persons who live independently has risen in the developed countries, but remains low in many emerging nations. (Independent living may be largely, but not entirely, determined by the nation's level of income and wealth; however, culture also matters.) Even where seniors tend to live alone, the burden on workers is complex and dynamically determined. Technological advance can reduce the burden – for example, by substituting electronic monitoring, telemedicine, and robotic service technologies for direct provision of care in the home by workers. Senior citizen communities can also reduce the resources required by achieving greater efficiency in provision of elder care.

Finally, net immigration of workers can forestall rising burdens on a nation's workers. Many developed nations are already experiencing a large shortfall of service workers needed in an aging society – including doctors, nurses, and long-term care workers. Nearly 90 percent of United States nursing homes are understaffed (AARP, 2005). At the same time, some emerging nations – especially India and the Philippines – are able to produce a large surplus of trained professionals. About 40 percent of the United States nursing workforce is foreign-born; in Italy it is estimated that 83 percent of all domestic helpers are undeclared foreign-born immigrants (AARP, 2005). The medium-term challenge is to improve training in emerging nations that currently have relatively young populations, and to relax restrictions on immigration in aged nations with excess demand. (The number of people needing long term care in Japan is expected to rise from 2.8 million in 2000 to 5.2 million in 2025, yet Japan has one of the most restrictive immigration policies among developed nations – with only 1 percent of its population being foreign-born (AARP, 2005).) It is also important to increase pay, improve working conditions, and raise the status of such jobs to attract workers and to reduce very high turnover rates. Net remittances from emigrant health care sector workers are already an important source of foreign exchange for some emerging nations. As they age, the emerging nations would begin to face their own shortages of workers to provide elder care, so they will eventually benefit directly from improved training facilities as more of their trained professionals can find jobs at home. Of course, all of this raises difficult issues regarding immigration, treatment of immigrants, and "brain drain" that can result from competition between emerging and developed nations. Still, immigration can provide needed human resources to deal with aging societies for many decades to come. Note also that net imports of goods and services is an alternative to immigration of workers in the sense that relatively "young" emerging nations with excess labor supply can export goods and services to relatively "old" developed nations with labor shortages. Again, this raises questions about "sustainability" of trade deficits and foreign indebtedness, possible impacts on employment in the importing countries, and impacts on domestic development of the exporting nations – all of which go beyond the scope of this chapter.

With these complexities in mind, let us turn to projections of global demographics and dependency ratios. This will help to provide insights into the scope of the problem, even while we recognize that demographics alone tell only a part of the story.

3.3 Demographic trends

The world's population is aging – a very unusual experience for the human population, which had previously experienced slow population growth with a fairly constant age structure (Batini et al., 2006). As briefly mentioned above, this results from the combination of falling fertility and mortality rates. The interplay of these two factors is somewhat complex. As the global population first transitioned from high fertility and high mortality rates to falling child mortality rates, the youth dependency ratio rose along with population growth rates. More female infants lived to reproduce, which actually lowered the average age of the population. Fertility rates tend to fall with a lag after mortality rates decline. This eventually produces a "demographic dividend" as youth dependency ratios fall, and the percent of the population of working age rises. Gradually, the combination of lower fertility and mortality rates causes the aged dependency ratio to rise; this population-aging process is enhanced as mortality among elderly persons falls. In addition, the population growth rate declines and turns negative for some nations – again contributing to the aging process. (See Lee 1994 for more details on the demographics of aging.)

Today the world's population is growing at about one percent per year, or 74 million people – which is the difference between 130 million births and 56 million deaths annually (CBO, 2005). It is projected that the global population will peak in 2050 and stabilize at about 9.1 billion. Developed nations taken as a whole will experience falling population, although the US population will continue to grow (ultimately expanding by about one-third); the population of emerging nations will grow just slowly enough after 2050 to replace the population lost by developed nations. Over the next 20–30 years, emerging nations will actually enjoy a demographic dividend as fertility rates fall and the percent of population of working age rises. Eventually, however, the combination of lower fertility and falling mortality will age even the emerging nations. Indeed, the aging process will be much quicker for emerging nations than it has been for the developed nations – the speed of aging is rising quickly.

There are several ways to track aging:

1. Median age: The median age of the world's population is projected to rise from 27 years in 2000 to 37 years in 2050 (Batini et al., 2006). Most industrial countries already have a median age above 31. Japan's average age recently reached 40 – the first country to achieve that feat (Bloom and Canning, 2004, p. 19); most developing countries have a median age below 25, and a few have a median below 15 years.
2. Aging index = (for example), (100)*(number aged 65+ years)/(number aged 0–17 years): This is the ratio of the aged to the young. By 2030, most developed nations will have an aging index above 100; Japan will be above 200.
3. Aged dependency ratio = (for example), (number aged 65+ years)/(number aged 18–64 years): This gives an indication of the burden placed on those of normal working age of supporting the elderly – although we must keep in mind the issues raised in the previous section. This is one of the most often cited ratios in the Social Security debate; it is closely related to the beneficiary-support ratio, which is a ratio formed by the number of Social Security beneficiaries over the population paying payroll taxes. South Korea has the fastest rising aged dependency ratio (number aged 65+/number aged 20–64): in 2000 the ratio was 10 percent, but it will rise to 69.4 percent in 2050 (AARP, 2005).

4. Youth dependency ratio = (for example), (number aged 0–17 years)/ (number aged 18–64 years): This measures the burden of supporting the young, again with the caveats noted above. As fertility rates fall, this ratio tends to fall – although that can be postponed in the case of a nation that is transitioning from very high to lower child mortality rates.
5. Total dependency ratio = aged dependency ratio + youth dependency ratio: this measures the total burden placed on those of working age.

Over the next half century, the share of the global population made up by those of normal working age will remain constant, while the youth dependency ratio will fall and the aged dependency ratio will rise. For example, if we define the working population as those aged 18 to 64 years, this remains a constant share at 59–60 percent of global population over the next 50 years (Figure 3.1).

The share of the population aged under 18 will fall from the current 34 percent to about 24 percent; the share of the population that is aged rises from 7 percent to 16 percent (CBO, 2005). Of course, the results vary across countries. In the United States, the share of the population made up by those of working age (again, defined as age 18–64) will decline by 4 percentage points; the youth dependency ratio will also fall by 4 percentage points, as the aged dependency ratio rises by 8 percentage points. Taking all the developed nations except the United States, the working age population will decline by 10 percentage points and the youth dependency ratio will fall by 2 percentage points so that the aged dependency ratio will rise by 12 percentage points. Among the emerging nations, the youth dependency

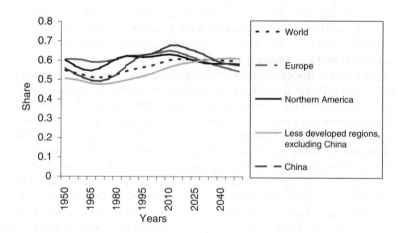

Figure 3.1 Working-age population shares

Source: Population Division, Department of Economic and Social Affairs, UN; medium variant.

ratio will fall by 15 percentage points, the aged dependency ratio will rise by 10 percentage points, and the working age population will rise by 5 percentage points (the demographic dividend). Somewhat surprisingly, China will actually be older than the United States by 2050, as its aged dependency ratio rises by 16 percentage points, its youth dependency ratio falls by 8 percentage points, and its working age population falls by 8 percentage points (all data CBO, 2005).

It is also surprising to compare these projections with historical data (Figure 3.1). The working age population was actually a lower percent of the population in the recent past than it is projected to be in the future. Most countries reached the low point some time between 1965 and 1980 – with developed nations reaching the trough earlier than emerging nations with a larger population of young. As mentioned above, the ratio is projected to remain constant for the world as a whole through 2050, but many nations will experience a falling proportion of the population of working age. Still, it is important to recognize that this ratio remains in a very tight range across the major groupings of nations, with projections of the ratio converging on 55 percent (for the more developed nations excluding the United States) to 62 percent (for less developed nations excluding China and the least developed nations) – a generally higher ratio than they had in 1950, and significantly higher than at their respective troughs. From this perspective, the globe as a whole, and even many nations individually, have already lived through the worst "demographic time bomb" in terms of the total dependency burden placed on the population of normal working age. What is new is that more of the burden is due to relative growth of the elderly population.

It is useful to examine population pyramids to get a better picture of the demographic changes involved. Figure 3.2 shows the evolution of the population pyramids for the world, while Figure 3.3 presents pyramids for the United States, each presenting a snapshot of the distribution of the population by age.

The pyramids for the world show the years 1950, 2005, and 2050, while the pyramids for the United States show the years 1951, 2004, 2050, 2075, and 2100. A "normal" pyramid would have a broad base, with each older age group having a smaller population – up to a sharp peak at the oldest age group. A sharp decline of fertility rates would reduce the size of the base; falling mortality rates among the young would tend to convert the pyramid to a column at the lower age group range. Falling death rates among middle aged and senior age groups would generate a columnar shape at the older age end of the spectrum. Finally, a baby-boom bulge would move up the age distribution through time. As these figures demonstrate, the United States is already a substantially aged society, with a distinct columnar shape (except at the oldest age groups, where the figure is sharply peaked), rather than a pyramid shape. The baby-boomer bulge is obvious as we move through time, but will have disappeared by 2050. The world population pyramid still displays a normal pyramidal shape today, except at the youngest age groups. By

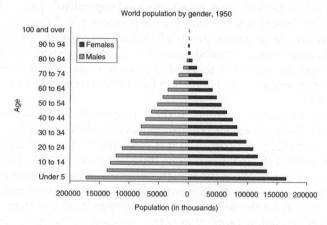
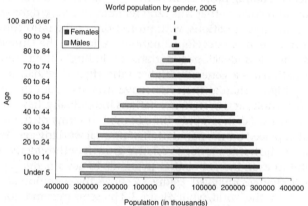
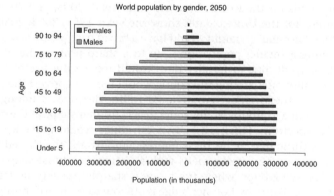

Figure 3.2 World population pyramids

Source: Population Division, Department of Economic and Social Affairs, UN; medium variant.

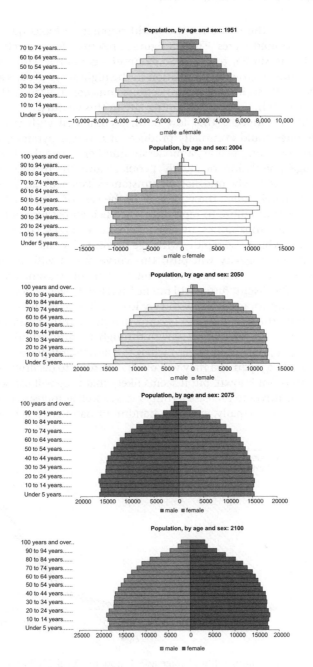

Figure 3.3 US population pyramids, selected years
Source: US Census Bureau.

2050, however, the figure for the world population looks quite similar to that of the United States. The US figures presented for projections beyond 2050 look very similar to the 2050 pyramid – columnar with a sharp peak, and with a slowly growing population in the highest age groups as longevity increases. As these long-term projections indicate, however, there are no major demographic surprises looming late in this century.

It might be supposed that low fertility combined with steadily falling mortality rates could eventually produce an inverted pyramid, with a tiny population of young people, a moderate number of people of working age, and a huge population of elderly people. However, this cannot happen except in exceedingly unusual circumstances (such as an epidemic that disproportionately killed the young; or in the case of a society that will disappear because of failure to reproduce – see below) because of the distribution of death probabilities by age. Figure 3.4 shows current US death probabilities, which rise rapidly with age beyond 70 years.

While rising longevity will push this curve out, it will not be likely to change the shape of the curve very much. For this reason, US population pyramids of the distant future will not be inverted. However, for a few nations (Japan and Italy, for example) with very low fertility rates and negative population growth, the pyramids can become inverted during a transition period. If we carry negative population growth through an infinite horizon, we eventually obtain a population of zero when the last elderly person dies. Exactly how nations like Japan and Italy will ultimately react to declining (and aging) populations is not known, but it seems likely that they will use some combination of incentives to increase fertility rates as well as increased immigration to avoid that fate. Finally, even if a handful of nations do achieve inverted

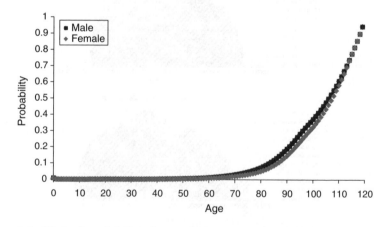

Figure 3.4 US death probabilities by age (2001, updated April 22, 2005)

Source: The 2005 Annual Report of the Board of Trustees of the Federal Old-Age and Survivors Insurance and Stability Insurance Trust Funds, US Government Printing Office Washington: 2005.

pyramids, the world as a whole will not – unless the human population is destined to shrink and finally disappear from the planet.

3.4 Implications for Social Security systems

Over the past several decades there has been rising concern about the ability of nations to provide for their aging populations. The OECD (2000) bluntly states that "[w]ithout tax increases or tax reforms, governments cannot afford to pay future retirees the benefits they are currently paying out". President Bush's Social Security reform commission even called the current program "broken" and "unsustainable" (CSSS, 2001). A number of nations have already scaled-back promises made to new and future retirees; some have moved toward privatization and others have considered various "reforms" that would put more responsibility on individuals for their own retirement. The United States, in particular, made major changes to its Social Security system in 1983 when it embraced "advanced funding" based on the notion that accumulation of a large Trust Fund surplus could reduce future burdens of supporting retiring baby-boomers. In addition, partial privatization, slower growth of benefits, and higher taxes have all been proposed. The primary driving force behind global efforts to reform Social Security systems is the perceived unsustainability of current programs in the face of rapidly aging populations. Future burdens on workers are said to be too large to permit today's systems to persist without fundamental change.

The problem, of course, is that each worker in the future will have to support more Social Security system beneficiaries. This results from low fertility and rising longevity, which means fewer people of working age and more years spent in retirement for a given normal retirement age. Even worse, working lives have been compressed in many developed countries, as working is postponed until after college and as average age at retirement falls. For example, in 1970 the average French male worker collected a pension for 11 years after retirement; today, he can expect to collect a pension for 21 years (Norris, 2005). In France, the average retirement age for both men and women is well under age 60; in Italy and Germany it is around age 60 (ibid). As the normal age of entering the workforce is postponed to 22 years, or even 28 years because of extended full-time schooling, working lives will total as little as 30 to 35 years. As a result, tax rates must rise to support "paygo" benefits systems (and individual savings must rise to support retirement).

A simplified formula for the necessary tax rate for a paygo Social Security system is:

$$T = [P(a2)]/[W(a1)]$$

where P is the average pension benefit, T is the tax rate on wages, W is the average wage, a1 is the percent of the population of working age, and a2 is the percent of the population that is aged (derived from Burtless, 2005). As a1 falls and a2 rises, the required tax rate rises for given values of wages and benefits. Hence, we can calculate the necessary increase of the tax rate to maintain a paygo system as the population ages. However, as noted above, this is far too simple because it presumes that the percent of those of working age that are working is constant, and that those who are aged do not work (or, at least, that the percent working does not change). If employment rates rise, this can offset pressures on tax rates even as the percent of the population of working age rises. As discussed above, employment rates for women in the United States have risen on a long-term trend. In addition, there has been a gradual but sustained increase of labor-force participation rates by aged men in the United States since the mid 1990s. Some European nations hope to duplicate that phenomenon, for example by making age discrimination illegal (United Kingdom, Netherlands) or by improving incentives to work longer by linking benefits to contributions (Italy, Sweden) (AARP, 2005; OECD, 2000). Falling unemployment rates also reduce the necessary tax.

Another useful measure of the rising burden of public Social Security systems is the projected rise of the ratio of publicly-provided old age benefits to GDP.

Figure 3.5 plots current and future US Social Security ((Old age and survivors and disability insurance) OASDI) expenditures as a percent of GDP, which will rise moderately from less than 4.5 percent today to over 6 percent

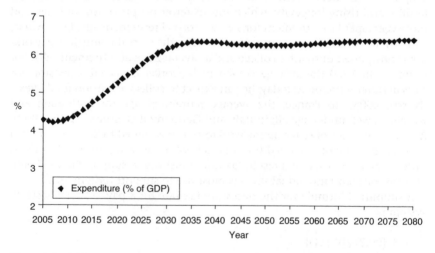

Figure 3.5 OASDI expenditures as a percent of GDP

Source: The 2005 Annual Report of the Board of Trustees of the Federal Old-Age and Survivors Insurance and Stability Insurance Trust Funds, US Government Printing Office Washington: 2005.

by 2030 as baby-boomers retire. The ratio then stabilizes at less than 6.5 percent through 2080. Burtless (2005) reports that old-age pensions as a percent of GDP also rise at a moderate pace for the G-7 nations (some actually project a falling percent); however, the relatively slow growth is in part due to recent reforms that scaled-back promises. Measured relative to GDP, the share of output that will have to be shifted to publicly-provided Social Security pensions provided to tomorrow's seniors in highly developed nations is surprisingly small, given projected demographic changes. Of course, this is only a portion of the resources that will be needed by elderly people in the future, as social security represents only one leg of the retirement stool. Still, as measured solely by the percent of GDP absorbed by Social Security, the changes are fairly moderate.

There are two separate issues regarding this future shift of resources. The first concerns the means used to achieve the redistribution. In an extended family structure, much of the shift could be achieved outside the market through redistribution of market-purchased output within the family, and through provision of elder care services (outside the market) by family members. With the growth of independent living by seniors, more of the shift of resources will be achieved through the market – with seniors using money obtained from their accumulated savings, from private pensions, and from public pensions to purchase output. Assuming that the method used to achieve the redistribution of marketed output does not impact total production, then the question comes down to designing a politically feasible policy to distribute output as desired among each age group (young, working age, elderly) and within each age group. Obviously, that is easier said than done, but will almost certainly include some combination of market and government, and will rely heavily on some sort of "tax and spend" program. There is also the possibility that output is not invariant to the redistribution method adopted. Again, that is a difficult topic. Much has been written on these issues – including a lot by me – but these matters are beyond the scope of this chapter. See Wray (1990–1991) and Papadimitriou and Wray (1999a, 1999b) for more discussion.

The second issue concerns the likelihood that future production will be adequate to meet the needs of all age groups. If not, then the method used to distribute that inadequate distribution comes down to a question of triage. Many reformers seem to presume that triage will be necessary, citing the dwindling number of workers per retiree along with projections of gargantuan financial shortfalls. However, the number of workers per Social Security beneficiary (which for the United States falls from about three today to about two in the future) provides only half the answer to the question about the ability to support future retirees. And it is probably the least important half, because growth of output will depend more heavily on growth of productivity.

Figure 3.6 shows historical data as well as projections for US labor productivity. Labor productivity has approximately doubled since 1960, and will quadruple over the next 75 year period used by the Social Security Trustees for their long range projections. The aged dependency ratio in the G-7 countries will increase by 16 percent to 38 percent (depending on the country) between 2000 and 2050. By contrast, US labor productivity is projected to increase by much more than 100 percent over the same time period. There is a lot of uncertainty associated with such long-range projections, however, the margin provided in these projections would appear to be sufficient to cover lower-than-projected productivity growth as well as higher-than-projected growth of longevity – with room to spare.

Further, there is good reason to believe that the Social Security Trustees have been overly cautious in projecting productivity growth, as their projections are influenced by the slow productivity growth from the early 1970s until the Clinton boom – arguably a historic anomaly (Papadimitriou and Wray, 1999a; see also Langer's 2000 critique of assumptions used by the Trustees). Slow growth of aggregate demand combined with rapid growth of the labor force (fueled by women and immigrants entering the labor force) led to chronically high unemployment and low wage growth. This reduced the pressure to innovate to increase labor productivity. Higher effective demand during the Clinton years, plus global competitive pressure, led to faster productivity growth in the mid-to-late 1990s (Wray and Pigeon, 2002).

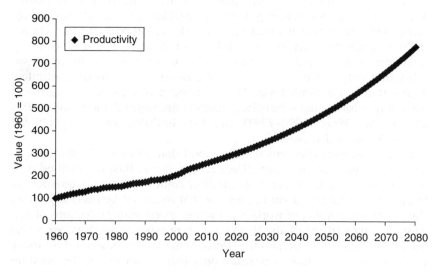

Figure 3.6 US productivity, historical and projected

Source: The 2005 Annual Report of the Board of Trustees of the Federal Old-Age and Survivors Insurance and Stability Insurance Trust Funds, US Government Printing Office Washington: 2005.

While cheap and abundant labor abroad has held down US wage growth in recent years, if labor markets of the future face shortages due to rising aged dependency ratios, this should spur better wage growth and faster productivity growth.

Indeed, it is worth noticing that between 1970 and 1995, the United States and Canada had significantly lower productivity growth (growing by only about 20 percent and 30 percent, respectively, over the 25 years) than did other OECD nations (whose productivity increased by 50 percent to 100 percent over the same period) (See Wray and Pigeon, 2002). By no coincidence, the employment/population ratio increased fastest in the United States and Canada, and slowest in those nations with the highest productivity growth (Japan and Italy actually experienced a declining employment/population ratio together with very high productivity growth). This is because the two are related through an identity: per capita GDP growth equals growth of the employment rate (workers divided by population) plus growth of productivity per worker. If demand growth is sufficient, then slow growth of the labor force can be compensated by faster growth of productivity. The evidence surveyed in Wray and Pigeon seems to indicate low productivity growth experienced in the United States (and Canada) from 1970 to 1995 was due to growth of demand that was too slow to accommodate growth of the labor force plus moderate growth of productivity. In a sense, the United States "chose" the combination of high employment growth and low productivity growth, while Europe and Japan "chose" low employment growth and high productivity growth to achieve fairly similar per capita real GDP growth.

By the mid 1990s, the Clinton boom was so strong that even robust employment growth could not accommodate all the demand. This helped to generate the famous "new economy" productivity boom (that really had little to do with the new economy – see Wray and Pigeon, 2002; as well as Gordon, 2000). Note also that fairly rapid productivity growth has continued during the "jobless" Bush recovery, as sluggish growth of aggregate demand has imposed a trade-off of productivity versus jobs, and for a variety of reasons job creation lost.

Indeed, an aging society could help to generate favorable conditions for achieving sustained high employment with high productivity growth. As the number of aged rises relatively to the number of potential workers, what is required is to put unemployed labor to work to produce output needed by seniors. Providing Social Security benefits to retirees will generate the necessary effective demand to direct labor to producing this output. Just as rapid growth of effective demand during the Clinton boom allowed sustained growth of the employment rate even as productivity growth rose nearer to US long-term historical averages, tomorrow's retirees can provide the necessary demand to allow the United States to operate near to full employment with rising labor productivity – a "virtuous combination" of the high productivity growth model followed by Europe and Japan from 1970–1995 and the high employment model followed by the United States during the 1960s as well as during the Clinton boom.

Finally, we return to the benefits of slower population growth, and to falling youth dependency ratios. As discussed, the total dependency ratios for the world as a whole, and for most countries, will not change significantly because falling youth dependency ratios will offset rising aged dependency ratios. This leads to several issues. First, it could be the case that it takes fewer real resources to take care of the young than required to care for the elderly, although that is not obvious in the case of a rich, developed nation. Note also that just as the time spent in old age is rising as longevity rises, the time spent in young age is extended by full-time study in college and graduate school. When the youth dependency ratio was higher our population was growing fast and required private and public investment in the infrastructure needed for the care of the young. Very few young people die in a rich nation – so almost all of the young grow up to be working age adults, and will become an elderly "bulge" as they retire. Much of the infrastructure we built to take care of the baby boom is still with us, and will be with us for years to come, including houses, hospitals, schools, dams, highways, and public buildings. As the baby boomers age, we may have to convert schools to senior citizen centers and hospitals to aged care facilities. However, we took care of the baby-boomers with relatively few workers in 1960, and common sense implies that we ought to be able to take care of them when they are elderly. Again, as we have discussed, once the baby-boomer bulge is gone, it appears that projected productivity growth will be more than sufficient to provide adequate output for all age groups.

The second issue generated by this demographic transition is political: workers might be more willing to support kids – especially if they have them – than the elderly. Based on current debates – which include a lot of aged bashing – that would be a safe conclusion. However, the distribution of social spending in the United States today certainly does not reflect that bias, as federal spending on the elderly is many times greater than spending on children. Even if the population truly does prefer social spending on the young – despite all evidence to the contrary – the political climate might change as the number of elderly rises relative to the number of children. The typical US worker in 1960 had 3.7 kids and perhaps one grandfather and a couple of grandmothers. In 2080, the typical worker will have fewer than two children, but might have four grandparents and some great grandparents – and maybe even a great-great grandparent to support. Further, all those elderly people will be of voting age, likely with voting rates above that of tomorrow's workers. It is hard to believe that political support for public spending on the elderly will wane as the population ages. Rather, the same sort of social effort put into preparing our nation for the wave of baby-boomer children could help us to prepare for the waves of seniors over the next couple of decades and beyond.

When formulating policy, it is necessary to distinguish between financial provisioning and real provisioning for the future. Individuals can provide for their future retirement by saving in the form of financial assets. These will then be "liquidated" to purchase the output needed during retirement. Assuming no change in the distribution of population by age, this process can work fairly smoothly as those of working age purchase the financial assets unloaded by those who are retired. Still, it is important to note that accumulation of financial assets does not guarantee that retirees will be able to obtain output – even if they can sell their financial assets – as they will be dependent upon a) those of working age to produce sufficient output, and b) a well-functioning market system in which a portion of the produced output is sold. If this is the case, the retired population bids for the marketed output, using proceeds from the sale of financial assets.

Things become more difficult if the distribution of the population by age changes significantly over time. A retiring baby boom might face a relatively small generation of those of working age willing to purchase financial assets, resulting in low sales prices on liquidation. Further, the relatively small number of workers might not produce much output. Note that in this case, it will do no good for the baby-boomers to accumulate even more financial assets in preparation for their retirement – they will still face a future in which output is relatively small and demand for their financial assets is small. Some research into equity market bull and bear runs does find that such demographic trends affect share prices. In the face of such negative demographic trends, baby-boomers could instead try to individually accumulate output (rather than financial assets) so that they could provide for their retirement in *real* terms. However, aside from housing, it is very difficult to set aside real goods and services for the distant future. Note that accumulation of equities does not guarantee access to real goods and services in the future; only accumulation of the real assets behind the equities can ensure that the retiring baby-boomer could use them to produce desired output for own use.

Can public policy prepare for a retiring baby-boom bulge through "advance funding" – that is, by accumulating a large trust fund? As I have argued in several pieces, it cannot (Wray, 1990–1991, 1998, 1999, 2005; Papadimitriou and Wray, 1999a, 1999b). Even leaving to the side the issues raised in the previous two paragraphs, a Social Security trust fund (such as that existing in the United States) provides no "financial wherewithal" to pay for a possible future revenue shortfall. To put it simply, the trust fund is simply a case of the government owing itself, an internal accounting procedure. In, say, 2050 when payroll tax revenues fall short of benefit payments, the trust fund will redeem treasury debt. To convert those securities into cash would require the Treasury to either issue new debt or generate tax revenue in excess of what will be required for other government spending in order to make the cash payment to the trust fund without increasing general budget deficits. This is exactly what would be required even if the Trust Fund had no "financial holdings" (Papadimitriou and Wray, 1999b). Government cannot financially make provision in advance for future benefit payments.

The burden of providing real goods and services to retirees in 2050, or 2075 will be borne by workers in those years regardless of the tax imposed today. If the level of goods and services to be produced in the future cannot be increased by actions taken today, then the burden that will be borne by tomorrow's workers cannot be reduced by anything we do today. This argument hinges on the assumption that accumulation of a trust fund does not directly affect the quantity of goods and services that will be produced in, say, 2050. Such an assumption might appear to be severe, but even most conventional theory concludes that the long-run growth path of the economy is not easily changed. Because accumulation of a trust fund is not likely to have a substantial impact on long-run growth, accumulation of a trust fund cannot assure the desired future aggregate production of resources, nor the desired distribution of resources (between workers and beneficiaries). If this is true, payroll taxes should be reduced now and then increased later so that Social Security program revenues and cost would be more closely aligned. Taxes on workers reduce their take-home pay, which leaves more output available for purchase by retirees. Benefit payments to retirees provide the financial wherewithal for them to buy that output. The best time to use tax-and-spend policies in this manner is the year in which it is desired to shift output to beneficiaries. The logical conclusion derived from conventional theory, then, is for the program to be run on a pay-as-you-go basis. It makes no sense to tax workers *today* to try to redistribute output to seniors *tomorrow* (Papadimitriou and Wray, 1999b). Nor does it make sense to tax workers today to try to increase the size of the pie to be distributed *tomorrow* – since even conventional theory concludes that the effects on economic growth are minimal. (Unconventional theory would conclude that higher-than-necessary taxes might even reduce growth of the economic pie by keeping effective demand low and reducing the incentive to invest in physical and human capital.)

Ultimately, what really matters is whether the economy will be able to produce a sufficient quantity of real goods and services to provide for both workers and dependents in, say, the year 2080. If it cannot, then regardless of the approach taken to finance Social Security programs (or to finance the private legs of the retirement stool), the real living standards in 2080 will have to be lower than they are today. Any reforms to Social Security systems made today should focus on increasing the economy's capacity to produce real goods and services today and in the future, rather than on ensuring positive actuarial balances through eternity. Unlike the case with individuals, social policy *can provision for the future in real terms* – by increasing productive capacity in the intervening years. For example, policies that might encourage long-lived public and private infrastructure investment could ease the future burden of providing for growing numbers of retirees by putting into place the infrastructure that will be needed in an aging society: nursing homes and other long-term care facilities, independent living communities, aged-friendly public transportation systems, and senior citizen centers.

Education and training could increase future productivity. Policies that maintain high employment and minimize unemployment (both officially measured unemployment as well as those counted as out of the labor force) are critical to maintain a higher worker-to-retiree ratio. Policy can also encourage today's and tomorrow's seniors to continue to participate in the labor force. The private sector will play a role in all of this, but there is also an important role to be played by the government.

It is ironic that reformers have put so much effort into savings promotion schemes that have never made much difference for economic growth, while ignoring labor-force policies that would have large immediate and long-lasting impacts. On balance, if we were to focus on only one policy arena today that would best enhance our ability to deal with a higher aged dependency ratio tomorrow it would be to ensure full employment with rising skill levels. Such a policy would have immediate benefits, in addition to those to be realized in the future. This is a clear "win-win" policy, unlike the ugly trade-off promoted by many reformers that pit today's workers against current seniors by proposing tax hikes and benefit cuts to increase the trust fund surplus.

Note

* The author thanks Yan Liang and Elizabeth Davidson for their research assistance in creating the tables and figures.

References

AARP (2005) "Global Report on Aging," Fall.
Batini, N., T. Callen and W. McKibbin (2006) "The Global Impact of Demographic Change," IMF Working Paper WP/06/9 (January).
Bloom, D. E. and D. Canning (2004) "Global Demographic Change: Dimensions and Economic Significance," in Gordon H. Sellon, Jr. (ed.), *Global Demographic Change: Economic Impacts and Policy Challenges*. A symposium sponsored by The Federal Reserve Bank of Kansas City, Jackson Hole, Wyoming, 26–28 August.
Burtless, G. (2005) "Can Rich Countries Afford to Grow Old?" paper prepared for a conference "An Ageing Society" Lisbon, Portugal, 19–20 May.
CBO (2005) "Global Population Aging in the 21st Century and its Economic Implications" (December).
Gordon, R. J. (2000) "Does The 'New Economy' Measure up to the Great Inventions of the Past?," *Journal of Economic Perspectives* 14(4): 49–74.
Langer, D. (2000) "Cooking Social Security's Deficit," *Christian Science Monitor*, January 4: p. 9.
Lee, R. D. (1994) "The Formal Demography of Population Aging, Transfers, and the Economic Life Cycle," in Linda G. Martin and Samuel Preston (eds),

Demography of Aging (Washington, DC: National Academies Press). Available at: http://books.nap.edu/books/0309050855/html/R1.html

Norris, F. (2005) "Live Longer, Work Longer," *International Herald Tribune*, 20–30 October, p. 18.

OECD (2000) "The Costs of an Ageing Society," No. 22, November/December (Washington, DC: OECD).

Papadimitriou, D. B. and L. R. Wray (1999a) "Does Social Security Need Saving? Providing for Retirees Throughout the Twenty-first Century," Public Policy Brief No. 55 (Annandale-on-Hudson, NY: The Levy Economics Institute of Bard College).

Papadimitriou, D. B. and L. R. Wray (1999b) "How Can We Provide for the Baby Boomers in Their Old Age?," Policy Note 1999/5 (Annandale-on-Hudson, NY: The Levy Economics Institute of Bard College).

President's Commission to Strengthen Social Security (2001) Interim Report. Available at: http://www.csss.gov/reports/Report-Interim.pdf

Social Security Administration (2005) *Annual Report of the Board of Trustees of the Federal Old-Age and Survivors Insurance and Disability Insurance Trust Funds*. Available at: http://www.ssa.gov/OACT/TR/TR05/index.html

US Census Bureau (2005) International Data Base (IDB). Available at: www.census.gov/ipc/www/idbnew.html

Wray, L. R. (1990–1991) "Can the Social Security Trust Fund Contribute to Savings?," *Journal of Post Keynesian Economics* 13(2): 155–170.

Wray, L. R. (1998) *Understanding Modern Money: The Key to Full Employment and Price Stability* (Cheltenham: Edward Elgar).

Wray, L. R. (1999) "The Emperor Has No Clothes: President Clinton's Proposed Social Security Reform," Policy Note 1999/2 (Annandale-on-Hudson, NY: The Levy Economics Institute of Bard College).

Wray, L. R. (2005) "Social Security's 70th Anniversary: Surviving 20 Years of Reform," Policy Note 2005/6 (Annandale-on-Hudson, NY: The Levy Economics Institute of Bard College).

Wray, L. R. and M. Pigeon (2002) "Demand Constraint and the New Economy," in Paul Davidson (ed.), *A Post Keynesian Perspective on Twenty-First Century Economic Problems* (Cheltenham: Edward Elgar).

Comments to Chapter 3
Richard Startz*

"Global demographic trends and provisioning for the future" reminds us to focus on fundamentals, not appearance. There are two parts to this focus: How much aging is taking place; and then how big are the consequences when compared to the real economy – emphasizing the real economy rather than the financial side. I want to build on some of the same elements in the chapter. My comments are variations on a theme presented by Wray.

Before developing that path I want to present two caveats. In talking about fundamentals we are talking economic fundamentals, not political fundamentals. Some part of what makes for a policy crisis, or not, is political response. This is particularly important in that support of the aged is a question about dividing up the pie just as much as it is a question of the size of the pie. The second issue is that provisioning for the elderly is inexorably intertwined with the question of valuation of non-market work and issues of gender. Both of these caveats are important to keep in mind but not the subject of this discussion.

Let us begin by talking about the basic problem. There are going to be a lot more elderly for each worker to support in the future. The number of old per worker is going to just about double (see Figure 3.C.1).

Suppose you thought that current production is all due to current workers and that the aged have on average the same standard of living that the young do. Both are extreme assumptions. Then right now a worker has to give over 20 percent of his production to the elderly and in 50 years will have to give over 35 to 40 percent. That is a really big change. One way to think about this chapter is that it explains why such a bold analysis leaves things out.

One thing that Wray reminds us about is that there are young dependents as well as old dependents. As the population ages, perhaps we will shift some of the money spent on schools toward seniors without having to come up with much more in total (see Figure 3.C.2).

You can see there is some truth to this. The total dependency rate has a much more modest rise, from about 0.7 to about 0.8.

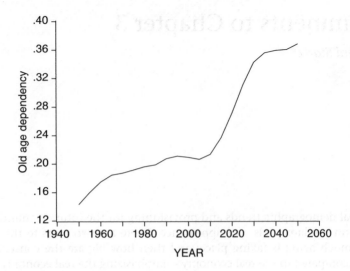

Figure 3.C.1 Old age dependency – United States
Source: David Weil.

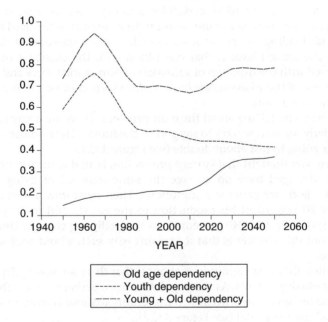

Figure 3.C.2 Dependency rates – United States
Source: David Weil.

However, to the extent we are focusing on social security and other government transfer programs, we need to weight these numbers in light of the fact that we make enormously higher transfers to the old than we do to the young. An extreme version of this is to only count transfer payments (see Figure 3.C.3).

If you take this approach, you will see the youth issue makes no difference. But doing only transfers rather than goods and services (think education) is kind of pushing it a little. The truth is probably somewhere in between looking at total dependency rates and looking only at old age dependency

Let us take a look around the world a little bit (see Figure 3.C.4).

Aging is going on around the world. But in 50 years India will look something like the United States does today. In comparison, Japan will have four times the dependency ratio of the United States.

Let us turn to another way to look at numbers. Wray says that social security expenditures will rise from under 4.5 percent of GDP to 6.5 percent. Is this a big change or a little change? One way to say this is that the share of social security is going to rise nearly 50 percent. If you say it that way, it sounds pretty big. Another way to say this is we need to find maybe two percent of GDP. Saying it that way does not sound enormous. It is about the

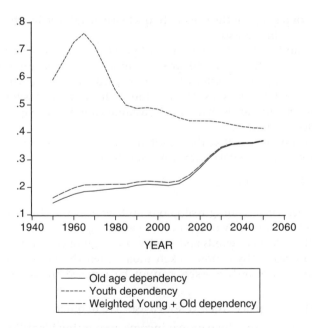

Figure 3.C.3 Weighted dependency rates – United States
Source: David Weil (for data, flakey weighting is author's).

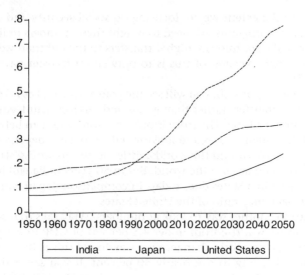

Figure 3.C.4 Old age dependency
Source: David Weil.

equivalent of paying for the wars in Iraq – twice. Bends the budget some, but not an overwhelming issue.

Keep in mind that the "size of the pie" problem is a little over two percent of GDP. If over the next 50 years, annual economic growth is four hundredths of a percent faster than is now predicted, we get the extra two percent we need. In this sense the real long run shortfall, is below measurement error. The flip side is that a small sustained lower rate of growth puts us in much deeper trouble.

I think a summary is that the shortfall is small relative to the whole pie, but large relative to how we currently allocate the pie.

Wray writes in his paper

> The burden of providing real goods and services to retirees in 2050, or 2075 will be borne by workers in those years regardless of the tax imposed today. If the level of goods and services to be produced in the future cannot be increased by actions taken today, then the burden that will be borne by tomorrow's workers cannot be reduced by anything we do today.

I think this is a place where a few caveats are in order.

First, let us consider the national income accounting identities

$C + G = Y - I + (M - X)$

Holding fixed domestic production, we can increase current consumption by importing from abroad. You cannot do this forever, but you can cover, very substantially, a long transition period by running up external credit now and then drawing it down as needed. With a net foreign asset position of around 30 percent of GDP, the United States could pay for a large part of the transition.

Well, except of course that we are 30 percent of GDP in the red and getting worse. So while in principle we might cover much of the costs of the demographic transition by saving abroad, the fact is we are developing an additional cost of roughly the same order of magnitude. As Wray has said, and as you can notice in Figures 3.C.1 through 3.C.4, the folks we owe money to are also undergoing a demographic transition. We may be getting a bill from them at just the time we need a way to provide for our own elderly.

Now let me come to my second objection in principle.

The fundamental growth accounting equation is

$$\frac{\Delta Y}{Y} \approx .75\frac{\Delta N}{N} + .25\frac{\Delta K}{K} + \frac{\Delta A}{A}$$

So if you invest now and increase the capital stock, you do increase productivity. You need something like an eight percent increase in the capital stock to get two more points of GDP. That would require a big increase in savings and investment. In principle, it is possible to provide for the future this way. I am certainly not suggesting that I think it is going to happen though.

The last objection is this business of whether in a closed economy you can increase capital now and then dissave and spend it in the future – in aggregate.

It is possible to build up capital now so that you do not need to build it in the future.

$$C + G = Y - I + (M - X)$$

By increasing the capital stock now, you can lower income (I) in the future. Wray alludes to this possibility with reference to housing. To do this effectively, you may need very durable capital. You could imagine building housing, and highways, and mass transit now, so that you can reduce capital spending in the future in favor of consumption. Since investment is about 16 percent of GDP, we are talking about a fairly drastic raising and then lowering of investment. This is again a transition issue and a fairly drastic one. To complete misquote Bob Solow, we would be talking about setting a large fraction of this generation to being construction workers so the next generation can become nurses instead.

A critical question is whether the durability of capital is indeed central. If in order to provide for 75 years in the future we need capital that lasts without substantial depreciation for 75 years, then we have a problem since few types of capital are sufficiently durable.

However, up to a point, durability is probably not an issue. Imagine a pure corn economy in which 100 bushels of corn are produced and consumed each year. Suppose corn can be costlessly preserved for one year, after which it suffers 100 percent depreciation. Now suppose that due to aging we need to change to a consumption path in which we consume 150 bushels 75 years hence and want to provision by reducing year zero consumption to 50 bushels. Can we do this?

In year zero we produce 100 bushels, consume 50, and set 50 aside. In year one, we produce 100 bushels, consume the 50 saved from year zero and 50 bushels of current production. The remaining 50 bushels of year one production are set aside. In year two we consume the corn saved from year one plus half of new production, and set aside half of year two production for year three. The pattern is repeated annually. In this way, savings from year zero can be effectively transmitted through the years even though the only available capital is very short lived.

In summary, Wray has laid out a very sensible framework for thinking about demographic change and support of the elderly in terms of fundamentals. I think we do not know enough about those fundamentals over spans of decades to be sure whether we will easily avoid a crisis or whether it might even be worse than we fear. But either way, this chapter is a good guide to how to figure out the answer.

Note

* These comments have benefited from discussion at the conference, especially from Randy Wray. Support from the Castor Professorship at the University of Washington is gratefully acknowledged. Data underlying the figures in these comments is courtesy of David Weil.

Part II

Aspects of Economic Well-being and Gender Disparities among the Elderly

4
Net Government Expenditures and the Economic Well-being of the Elderly in the United States, 1989–2001

Edward N. Wolff, Ajit Zacharias, and Hyunsub Kum

4.1 Introduction

The sustainability of, and trade-offs involved in, government expenditures for the elderly has become increasingly topical in recent years. An adequate examination of policy options has to be based on a sound assessment of the economic well-being of the elderly. The most widely used measure of economic well-being in considering the gaps between elderly and nonelderly households is money income. However, as several studies have pointed out, money income does not reflect elements that are crucial for the economic well-being of the elderly such as noncash transfers (which are completely excluded from money income) and wealth (for example, Radner, 1996; Rendall and Speare, 1993).

For instance, the economic advantage from wealth ownership reckoned in the money income measure is limited to actual property income (dividends, rent, and interest). However, a more comprehensive measure would take into account the advantage of home ownership (either in the form of imputed rental cost or annuity on home equity), and the long-run benefits from the ownership of nonhome wealth (for example, in the form of an imputed annuity) makes up the large share of economic well-being, especially, of the elderly. Government expenditure and taxes are another example. They are known to have an equalizing effect on the economic well-being between the elderly and nonelderly. The extent of the gap between the two groups, however, is sensitive to the types of expenditures and taxes that are taken into account as well as the income concept used to reckon economic well-being.

The recently developed Levy Institute Measure of Economic Well-being (LIMEW) and its associated microdatasets offer a comprehensive view of the level and distribution of economic well-being in the United States during the period 1989–2001. By means of such a comprehensive measure, it allows policymakers to gain better insights into the relative importance of different resources in sustaining or improving the economic well-being of the elderly and forces shaping inequality among the elderly.

We first describe the methodology and data sources for the LIMEW (Section 4.2). Next, we turn to estimates of the measure for both nonelderly and elderly households and for some key demographic subgroups among the elderly household population. The relative importance of different sources of income in sustaining the well-being of the elderly will be discussed. In Section 4.4, we discuss economic inequality among the elderly and the nonelderly. We also compare our findings based on the LIMEW with those based on the official measures in Sections 4.3 and 4.4. The final section contains our concluding observations.

4.2 Components of the LIMEW

The LIMEW is constructed as the sum of the following components (Table 4.1): base income; income from wealth; net government expenditures (government expenditures *minus* taxes); and household production. Our basic data is drawn from the public-use files from the Census Bureau. The calculation of base income (see below) uses values reported in the Census files for the relevant variables, without any adjustment. Additional information from Federal Reserve surveys on household wealth and surveys on time-use are incorporated into the Census files via statistical matching to estimate income from wealth and value of household production. Information from a variety of other sources, including the National Income and Product Accounts (NIPA) and several government agencies is utilized to arrive at the final set of estimates.[1]

We begin with money income and subtract the sum of property-type income and government cash transfers. We then add employer contributions to health insurance to obtain base income. Labor income (earnings plus value of employer-provided health insurance) makes up the overwhelming portion of base income and the remainder consists of pensions and other small items (for example, interpersonal transfers).

Our next step is to add imputed income from wealth. The actual, annual property income as in money income by Census Bureau is a very limited measure of the economic well-being derived from the ownership of assets. Houses last for several years and yield services to their owners, thereby freeing up resources otherwise spent on housing. Financial assets such as bank balances, stocks and bonds, can be, under normal conditions, sources of economic security in addition to property-type income.

Our approach to the valuation of income from wealth is different from the methods suggested in the literature (for example, Weisbrod and Hansen

Table 4.1 A comparison of the LIMEW and Extended Income (EI)

LIMEW	EI
Money income (MI)	Money income (MI)
Less: Property income and Government cash transfers	*Less*: Property income and Government cash transfers
Plus: Employer contributions for health insurance	*Plus*: Employer contributions for health insurance
Equals: Base income	*Equals*: Base income
Plus: Income from wealth	*Plus*: Income from wealth
Annuity from nonhome wealth	Property income and realized capital gains (losses)
Imputed rent on owner-occupied housing	Imputed return on home equity
Less: Taxes	*Less*: Taxes
Income taxes [a]	Income taxes
Payroll taxes [a]	Payroll taxes
Property taxes [a]	Property taxes
Consumption taxes	
Plus: Cash transfers [a]	*Plus*: Cash transfers
Plus: Noncash transfers [a, b]	*Plus*: Noncash transfers
Plus: Public consumption	
Plus: Household production	
Equals:	*Equals*:
LIMEW	EI

Notes

[a] The amounts estimated by the Census Bureau and used in EI are modified to make the aggregates consistent with the NIPA estimates.

[b] The government-cost approach is used: the Census Bureau uses the fungible value method for valuing Medicare and Medicaid in EI.

1968) in two significant ways. First, we distinguish between home and nonhome wealth. Housing is a universal need and home ownership frees the owner from the obligation of paying rent, leaving an equivalent amount of resources for consumption and asset accumulation. Hence, benefits from owner-occupied housing are regarded in terms of the replacement cost of the services derived from it (that is, a rental equivalent).[2] Second, we estimate the benefits from nonhome wealth using a variant of the standard lifetime annuity method.[3] We calculate an annuity based on a given amount of wealth, an interest rate, and life expectancy. The annuity is the same for the remaining life of the wealth holder and the terminal wealth is zero. (For households with multiple adults, we use the maximum of the life expectancy of the head of household and spouse in the annuity formula.) We modify the standard procedure by accounting for differences in portfolio composition across households. Instead of using a single interest rate for all assets, we use a weighted average of asset-specific and historic real rates of return,[4] where the weights are the proportions of the different assets in a household's total wealth.

In the next step we add net government expenditures – the difference between government expenditures incurred on behalf of households and taxes paid by households (Wolff and Zacharias, 2006). Our approach to determine expenditures and taxes may be called the social accounting approach (Hicks, 1946; Lakin, 2002, pp. 43–46). Government expenditures included in the LIMEW consist of cash transfers, noncash transfers, and public consumption. These expenditures, in general, are derived from NIPA (NIPA Tables 3.12 and 3.15.5). Government cash transfers are considered to be part of the money income of recipients. We value noncash transfers at the average cost incurred by the government (for example, in the case of medical benefits, the average cost for the elderly, reckoned as an insurance value, differs from that for children) rather than the fungible or cash-equivalent value (US Census Bureau, 1993: Appendix B). The other type of government expenditure that we designate as "public consumption" and include in our measure of well-being is some public expenditures on services (for example, education). When allocating these expenditures to the household sector, we attempt to follow, as much as possible, the general criterion that a particular expenditure must be incurred directly on behalf of that sector and expands its consumption possibilities. In distributing expenditures among households, we build on earlier studies that employ the government-cost approach (for example, Ruggles and Higgins, 1981).

The final step in constructing net government expenditures is concerned with taxes. Our objective is to determine the distribution of actual tax payments by households in different income and demographic groups in an accounting sense rather than incidence in a theoretical sense. We align the aggregate taxes in the Census file (imputed by the Census Bureau) with their NIPA counterparts, as for expenditures. The bulk of the taxes paid by households falls in this group – federal and state personal income taxes, property taxes on owner-occupied housing, and payroll taxes (employee portion). Our estimated total tax burden on households also includes state consumption taxes, which were not aligned with a NIPA counterpart because an appropriate NIPA benchmark was not available. Taxes on corporate profits, on business-owned property, and on other businesses, were not allocated to the household sector because we assumed that they were paid out of business sector incomes.

Ultimately, to arrive at the LIMEW, we add the imputed value of household production. We include three broad categories of unpaid activities in the definition of household production: core production (for example, cooking), procurement, (for example, shopping for groceries), and care (for example, reading to children). These activities are considered as "production", since they can be assigned, generally, to third parties apart from the person who performs them, although third parties are *not* always a substitute of the person, especially for the third activity.

Our strategy for imputing the value of household production is to value the amount of time spent by individuals on household production using the replacement cost based on average earnings of private household employees (Kuznets et al., 1941, pp. 432–433; Landefeld and McCulla, 2000). We recognize that the efficiency and quality of household production are likely to vary across households. Therefore, we modify the replacement-cost procedure and apply to the average replacement cost a discount or premium that depends on how the individual (whose time is being valued) ranks in terms of a performance index. The index seeks to capture certain key factors (household income, educational attainment, and time availability) that affect efficiency and quality differentials.

4.3 Level and composition of well-being among the elderly and nonelderly

Our unit of analysis is the household. We define an "elderly household" as one in which the "householder" is aged 65 or over and a "nonelderly" household are those in which the householder is under the age of 65. The overwhelming majority of elderly individuals live in elderly households (90.3 percent in 2001) so that our choice of unit of analysis does not lead to a biased view of the distinctions between the elderly and the nonelderly groups.

We begin by looking at the relative well-being of elderly households according to the Census Bureau's measure of gross money income. The mean and median money income of elderly households was quite low relative to nonelderly ones (see Panel A, Table 4.2). In 2001, the ratio of mean income was 0.55 and that of median income was only 0.47. There was also a decline in the mean income of elderly households relative to nonelderly ones, from 0.59 in 1989 to 0.55 in 2001. On the other hand, the ratio of median income was relatively stable over the 1990s, remaining at about 0.47.

Elderly and nonelderly households differ substantially in terms of size and composition. Such differences are taken into account in comparisons of economic well-being usually by applying some equivalence scale.[5] The adjustment results in a smaller gap between the elderly and the nonelderly households: in 2001, the ratio of elderly mean income to nonelderly was 0.68 and that of median income was 0.62 (Panel B, Table 4.2). However, the trend in the disparity was not affected by the equivalence-scale adjustment.

There are also some notable differences in the level and growth in mean money income within the elderly group (Figure 4.1).[6] The income of the older elderly (75+ group) averaged about 80 percent of all elderly in 2001. Asians (Asian or other race) had the highest income in 2001,

Table 4.2 Household money income (2005 dollars)

Characteristic of the householder	Mean				Median			
	1989	1995	2000	2001	%Chg, 89–01	1989	1995	2000	2001	%Chg, 89–01

	A. Unadjusted									
All households	56,220	57,589	64,805	64,195	14.2	45,555	43,571	47,634	46,535	2.1
Nonelderly	61,617	63,398	71,491	70,767	14.8	51,975	50,078	55,091	54,234	4.3
Elderly	36,621	36,463	39,293	38,811	6.0	24,666	24,348	26,231	25,492	3.3
Ratio: Elderly to nonelderly	0.59	0.58	0.55	0.55		0.47	0.49	0.48	0.47	

	B. Equivalence-scale adjusted									
All households	73,894	75,754	85,877	85,348	15.5	60,299	58,046	64,215	63,294	5.0
Nonelderly	78,269	80,612	91,942	91,404	16.8	66,008	64,061	71,052	70,192	6.3
Elderly	58,006	58,090	62,736	61,955	6.8	41,844	41,769	44,174	43,181	3.2
Ratio: Elderly to nonelderly	0.74	0.72	0.68	0.68		0.63	0.65	0.62	0.62	

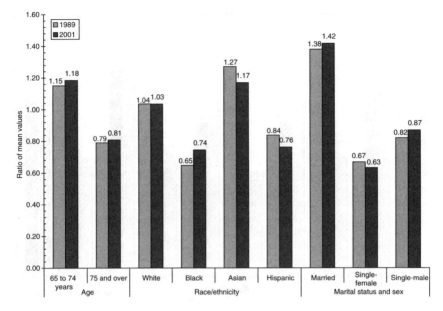

Figure 4.1 Relative well-being of elderly subgroups: money income (ratio of subgroup to overall elderly mean values)

17 percent above the overall average among elderly households, followed by non-Hispanic whites ("whites") at 3 percent above average, Hispanics at 76 percent of average, and African Americans ("blacks") at 74 percent of average. There was a notable improvement in the relative position of blacks between 1989 and 2001; in contrast, the relative position of Asians and Hispanics slipped significantly.[7] In 2001, elderly-married-couple households had the highest income among the elderly (42 percent above the overall elderly average), followed by single-male households (87 percent of average), and single females (only 63 percent of average). The relative well-being of single-male households and married couples improved, while it declined somewhat among single-female households.

The apparent advantage of Asians diminishes dramatically when an equivalence-scale adjustment is made and their equivalent income is now comparable to that of whites (Figure 4.2). It is also noteworthy that the relative disadvantage of blacks and Hispanics was larger when equivalent income is used. Disparities based on sex and marital status are lower with this adjustment, but the rank order remains the same as before. Thus, the equivalence-scale adjustment does have an effect on the measurement of the relative well-being of subgroups.

88 Economic Well-being & Gendered Disparities

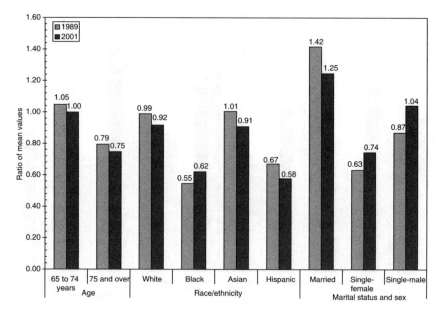

Figure 4.2 Relative well-being of elderly subgroups: equivalent money income (ratio of subgroup to overall elderly mean values)

4.3.1 Base income

We now turn to the constituent components of LIMEW. The first of these, base income, excludes both transfers and property income (Table 4.3). Not surprisingly, the ratio of base income between elderly and nonelderly households was only 0.27 in 2001, much lower than that of gross money income. There was virtually no change in this ratio between 1989 and 2001.

Among the elderly households, the relative base income of the older elderly (75+ group) was much lower than that of their relative money income (0.62 versus 0.81 in 2001, see Figure 4.3). The rank order by racial/ethnic group in base income was the same as for money income. The base income of the Asians was much greater than average money income in 2001 (a ratio of 1.39 versus 1.17), indicating that this is the main reason behind their higher money income. As with money income, positive gains in base income over the 1989–2001 period were found for blacks and losses for Asians as well as Hispanics. Married couples again ranked highest in base money income, followed by single males and then single females.

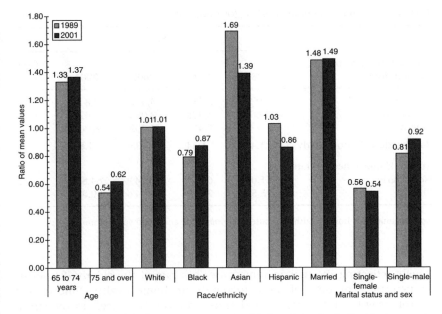

Figure 4.3 Differentials in base income among elderly subgroups (ratio of subgroup to overall elderly mean values)

Table 4.3 Household base income (2005 dollars)

	Mean				
Characteristic of the householder	1989	1995	2000	2001	%Chg, 89–01
All households	49,979	52,141	58,797	58,644	17.3
Nonelderly	59,394	61,843	69,378	69,055	16.3
Elderly	15,791	16,855	18,423	18,429	16.7
Ratio: Elderly to nonelderly	0.27	0.27	0.27	0.27	

Note: Base income equals money income *minus* all cash transfers included in it *minus* property income *plus* employer contributions for health insurance.

4.3.2 Income from home and nonhome wealth

The second component is income from home wealth, defined as the difference between imputed rent and the annuitized value of mortgage debt (Table 4.4). Differences in income from home wealth, therefore, reflect differences in the homeownership rate and home equity. In 2001, income from home wealth was much higher for the elderly than the nonelderly,

Table 4.4 Income from home wealth (2005 dollars)

Characteristic of the householder	Mean				%Chg, 89–01
	1989	1995	2000	2001	
All households	3,932	3,786	3,627	3,877	−1.4
Nonelderly	3,600	3,328	3,083	3,326	−7.6
Elderly	5,139	5,453	5,702	6,006	16.9
Ratio: Elderly to nonelderly	1.43	1.64	1.85	1.81	
Memo: Homeownership rates					
Nonelderly	61.0%	61.6%	64.4%	64.8%	
Elderly	75.5%	79.1%	80.4%	80.8%	

Note: Income from home wealth is imputed rent *minus* the annutized value of mortgage debt.

largely reflecting the higher homeownership rate of the elderly (81 versus 65 percent). The ratio of mean income from home wealth climbed very sharply over the 1989–2001 period, from 1.43 to 1.81. Indeed, income from home wealth actually declined by 7.6 percent among the nonelderly over the period.

Among the elderly, income from home wealth was 20 percent greater than average among the 65–74 age group, while among those 75 and over it was 20 percent lower (Figure 4.4), again reflecting the higher homeownership rate of the former group. Racial disparity was rather high in 2001, with nonwhites receiving only 47 percent of the average, a sharp drop from the 1989 value of 66 percent.[8] Income from home wealth was highest among married couples, and the extent of their advantage over single females and single males appeared to be roughly similar.

The disparity in income from nonhome wealth between elderly and nonelderly households is even greater than that in income from home wealth (Table 4.5). In 2001, the ratio was 3.37 between elderly and nonelderly households, about the same as in 1989. The ratio in wealth itself between elderly and nonelderly households is actually smaller – a ratio of 1.68 in 2001. The reason why the annuity ratio is higher than the ratio of actual nonhome wealth is due to the fact that elderly persons have a shorter (conditional) life expectancy than nonelderly individuals.[9] Income from nonhome wealth for the elderly climbed by an incredible 77 percent over the 1990s, a reflection largely of the surging stock market of the late 1990s.[10]

The gap between the younger and older elderly in income from nonhome wealth was somewhat smaller than that in income from home wealth (Figure 4.5). Nonwhites have only half of overall elderly average income from nonhome wealth, almost similar to their relative income from home

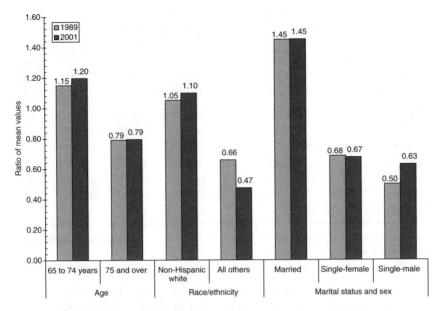

Figure 4.4 Differentials in income from home wealth among elderly subgroups (ratio of subgroup to overall elderly mean values)

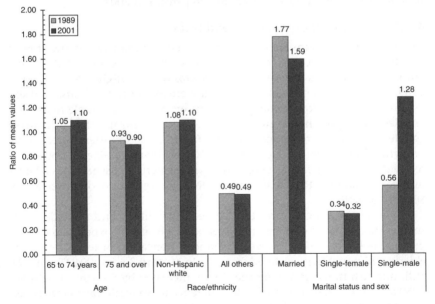

Figure 4.5 Differentials in income from nonhome wealth among elderly subgroups (ratio of subgroup to overall elderly mean values)

Table 4.5 Income from nonhome wealth (2005 dollars)

Characteristic of the householder	Mean				%Chg, 89–01
	1989	1995	2000	2001	
All households	11,943	13,503	22,951	20,628	72.7
Nonelderly	7,963	8,227	14,738	13,862	74.1
Elderly	26,395	32,691	54,292	46,768	77.2
Ratio: Elderly to nonelderly	3.31	3.97	3.68	3.37	
Memo: Mean nonhome wealth					
Nonelderly	172,572	171,541	312,711	290,789	68.5
Elderly	267,101	317,152	547,340	489,514	83.3
Ratio: Elderly to nonelderly	1.55	1.85	1.75	1.68	

Note: Income from nonhome wealth is the annutized value of nonhome wealth *minus* the annutized value of all debt other than mortgage.

wealth. Income from nonhome wealth was somewhat greater among married couples than among single males in 2001 and both were much greater than that among single females. One notable finding is that there was dramatic growth in income from nonhome wealth for single males, from 56 percent of average in 1989 to 128 percent in 2001.

4.3.3 Government expenditures and taxes

Disparities in cash transfers between the elderly and nonelderly dwarf even the differences in income from nonhome wealth (Table 4.6). In 2001, the ratio of cash transfers between the two groups was 5.6, slightly lower than in 1989. Differences among elderly subgroups are influenced by household size (Figure 4.6). The below-average cash transfers received by single males and females on the one hand, and the above-average cash transfers of married couples are largely reflections of this factor. Cash transfers received by nonwhites were about 80 percent of that the average elderly household received, even though the average, nonwhite elderly household has a larger number of adults. The racial gap is probably reflection of lower Social Security benefits.

Disparities in noncash transfers between the elderly and nonelderly are smaller than those in cash transfers (a ratio of 3.6 versus 5.6 between the former and latter in 2001). However, the ratio of noncash transfers between the elderly and nonelderly declined from 4.5 in 1989 to 3.6 in 2001 (Table 4.7). Still, noncash transfers among the elderly increased by 50 percent between 1989 and 2001. There is virtually no difference in noncash transfers between the older and younger elderly, but noticeable difference between nonwhites and whites, reflecting the higher values of means-tested benefits (primarily

Table 4.6 Government cash transfers (2005 dollars)

Characteristic of the householder	Mean				%Chg, 89–01
	1989	1995	2000	2001	
All households	5,058	5,695	5,430	5,546	9.7
Nonelderly	2,516	3,053	2,733	2,858	13.6
Elderly	14,286	15,306	15,722	15,933	11.5
Ratio: Elderly to nonelderly	5.68	5.01	5.75	5.58	

Note: Transfers received by the recipient as a cash payment (for example, Social Security).

Table 4.7 Government cash transfers (2005 dollars)

Characteristic of the householder	Mean				%Chg, 89–01
	1989	1995	2000	2001	
All households	2,781	3,969	4,037	4,551	63.6
Nonelderly	1,581	2,486	2,488	2,966	87.6
Elderly	7,140	9,362	9,951	10,674	49.5
Ratio: Elderly to nonelderly	4.52	3.77	4.00	3.60	

Note: Transfers received by the recipient as a noncash benefit (for example, Medicare).

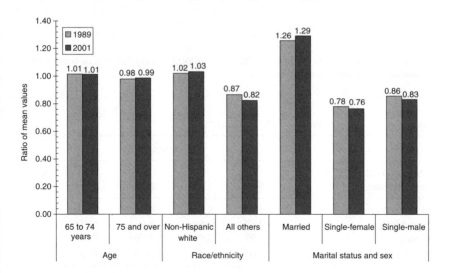

Figure 4.6 Differentials in cash transfers among elderly subgroups (ratio of subgroup to overall elderly mean values)

Medicaid and Food Stamps) for nonwhites, (Figure 4.7). Mean noncash transfers are greater for married couples than for single males or females, mainly due to the difference in the number of the elderly in the household.

Public consumption is much higher among the nonelderly than the elderly (a ratio of 2.9 in 2001), and has grown faster for the former, a 17.3 percent increase from 1989 to 2001 compared to a 7.1 percent increase (Table 4.8). These disparities largely reflect the huge role that educational expenditures play in public consumption. Public consumption was greater

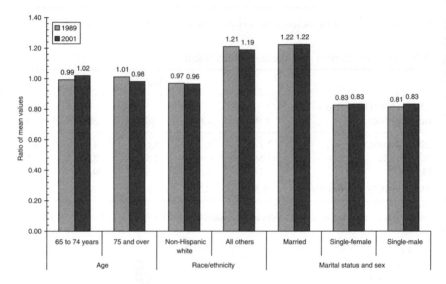

Figure 4.7 Differentials in noncash transfers among elderly subgroups (ratio of subgroup to overall elderly mean values)

Table 4.8 Public consumption (2005 dollars)

Characteristic of the householder	Mean				%Chg, 89–01
	1989	1995	2000	2001	
All households	8,178	8,504	9,347	9,591	17.3
Nonelderly	9,453	9,899	10,811	11,089	17.3
Elderly	3,550	3,430	3,764	3,803	7.1
Ratio: Elderly to nonelderly	0.38	0.35	0.35	0.34	

Note: Government consumption and gross investment expenditures allocated to households (for example, schools).

for the younger than the older elderly in 2001, and the gap widened over the 1989–2001 period (Figure 4.8). However, the most pronounced advantage in public consumption is that of nonwhites, with an average that was 40 percent more than that of the average elderly household. This is a reflection of the larger household size and the higher number of children in a typical nonwhite, elderly household. A substantial portion of public consumption (for example, public health) is distributed equally among persons and educational expenditures are distributed among school-age children. Differences in household size are also the main factor behind the below-average public consumption of single females and single males.

Taxes are much greater for the nonelderly (Table 4.9). In 2001, the ratio of mean taxes paid by the elderly to the nonelderly was only 0.38. In fact, this ratio dipped from 0.42 in 1989 to 0.38 in 2001. The average tax paid by the older elderly was only 66 percent of the overall average, while for the younger elderly, it was 133 percent (Figure 4.9). White elderly families paid, on average, 4 percent more taxes than the average elderly household and nonwhites paid 21 percent less. In 1989, the relative tax burden of the nonwhites was still lower, as they then paid 28 percent less than the average. Elderly married couples paid 50 percent more in taxes than the average elderly household, while single males and single females paid lower than average taxes. Single females had the lowest tax burden (54 percent of

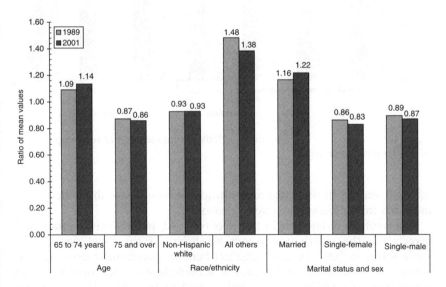

Figure 4.8 Differentials in public consumption among elderly subgroups (ratio of subgroup to overall elderly mean values)

Economic Well-being & Gendered Disparities

Table 4.9 Taxes (2005 dollars)

Characteristic of the householder	Mean				%Chg, 89–01
	1989	1995	2000	2001	
All households	14,844	15,078	19,144	18,731	26.2
Nonelderly	16,989	17,359	21,944	21,453	26.3
Elderly	7,053	6,782	8,461	8,217	16.5
Ratio: Elderly to nonelderly	0.42	0.39	0.39	0.38	

Note: Includes income taxes (federal, state, and local), property taxes, consumption taxes, and payroll taxes (employee portion only).

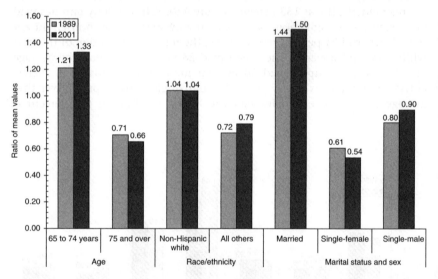

Figure 4.9 Differentials in taxes among elderly subgroups (ratio of subgroup to overall elderly mean values)

average) among all the subgroups considered here. These differences stem primarily from differences in taxable income.

As a result of differences in transfers received, public consumption, and taxes paid, the elderly was a net *beneficiary* of the fiscal system (see Table 4.10). In 2001, their average net benefit (government expenditures) amounted to $22,200. In contrast, the nonelderly was a net *payer*. Their net government expenditures averaged – $4,500 in 2001. The difference between the elderly and nonelderly was $26,600 in 2001. Average net government spending increased by 24 percent between 1989 and 2001 for the elderly, and the net government *loss* rose by 32 percent for the nonelderly. As a result, the difference between the two groups widened over the 1990s, from $21,400 to $26,600.

As shown in Figure 4.10, among the elderly, the older elderly enjoyed above-average net government expenditures (8 percent more in 2001) than the younger elderly (8 percent less). Elderly nonwhite households also enjoyed above-average net government expenditures (11 percent more in 2001), while

Table 4.10 Net government expenditures (2005 dollars)

Characteristic of the householder	Mean				%Chg, 89–01
	1989	1995	2000	2001	
All households	1,173	3,090	−329	958	−18.3
Nonelderly	−3,440	−1,922	−5,913	−4,539	32.0
Elderly	17,923	21,316	20,977	22,192	23.8
Difference: Elderly minus nonelderly	21,362	23,238	26,890	26,732	

Note: Transfers *plus* public consumption *minus* taxes.

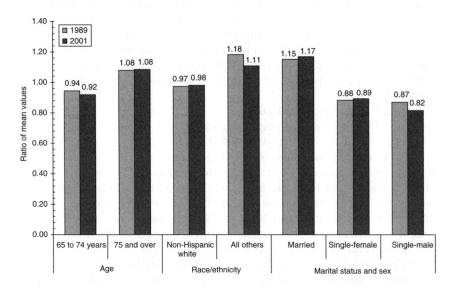

Figure 4.10 Differentials in net government expenditures among elderly subgroups (ratio of subgroup to overall elderly mean values)

elderly whites had a slightly below-average amount (2 percent less). Similarly, married couples received above-average net government expenditures (17 percent more in 2001), while single elderly received less-than-average amounts (11 percent less for females and 18 percent less for males).

Table 4.11 shows the composition of net government expenditures for both nonelderly and elderly households. We first consider all households and then discuss the differences between the elderly and nonelderly. The value of total government transfers (cash and noncash) and that of total public consumption were very close – the latter was 4 percent higher in 1989 and 5 percent lower in 2001 than the former. Social Security comprised 47 percent of total (cash and noncash) transfers in 1989 but only 41 percent in 2001. This was offset by a rise in the share of Medicare from 20 to 23 percent over this period and an even larger increase in the share of Medicaid from 10 to 17 percent. Cash transfers as a group fell from 65 to 55 percent of total transfers, while noncash transfers rose from 35 to 45 percent. Education is by far the largest component of public consumption, comprising 54 percent in 2001 – up from 51 percent in 1989. The next largest items in 2001 were public health and hospitals (10 percent), highways (9 percent) and police and fire departments (6 percent). While total public consumption rose by 17 percent between 1989 and 2001, expenditures for police and fire departments grew by a notable 40 percent and education increased by a more modest 23 percent. The remaining components of public consumption rose at below-average rates: a paltry growth of 5 percent for public health and hospitals and 15 percent for highways. If we consider both transfers and public consumption jointly, then education still ranks first in 2001, at 26 percent of government spending, followed by health spending (including Medicare, Medicaid, and public health and hospitals) at 25 percent (up from 21 percent in 1989), and then Social Security, at 21 percent (down from 23 percent in 1989).

Among the elderly, total transfers were six times as great as public consumption in 1989 and seven times as great in 2001. Cash transfers made up 67 percent of total transfers in 1989 but fell to 60 percent in 2001. Social security accounted for almost all of the cash transfers among the elderly but its share of total transfers declined from 62 to 52 percent between 1989 and 2001. Medicaid and Medicare made up almost all of the noncash transfers among the elderly. The former increased by 114 percent and the latter by 42 percent between 1989 and 2001. By 2001, Medicaid accounted for 6 percent of total transfers to the elderly, up from 4 percent in 1989, and Medicare for 33 percent, up from 29 percent. It is of interest that among the nonelderly, the biggest component of total transfers in 2001 was Medicaid (30 percent), followed by Social Security (22 percent) and Medicare (11 percent). These three programs account for the bulk of government transfers for both age groups.

Table 4.11 Government expenditures and taxes: nonelderly and elderly households (mean values, 2005 dollars)

	1989			2001			Percentage change, 89–01		
	Nonelderly	Elderly	All	Nonelderly	Elderly	All	Nonelderly	Elderly	All
Cash transfers	2,516	14,286	5,058	2,858	15,933	5,546	13.6	11.5	9.7
Social Security	1,026	13,334	3,684	1,264	15,025	4,094	23.2	12.7	11.1
Public assistance	477	67	389	194	47	164	−59.4	−28.8	−57.8
EITC	83	10	67	329	31	268	294.5	220.5	296.8
SSI	184	348	219	293	293	293	59.5	−15.8	33.7
Unemployment	275	47	226	380	69	316	38.3	45.8	40.1
Others	471	479	473	397	467	411	−15.7	−2.5	−13.0
Noncash transfers	1,581	7,140	2,781	2,966	10,674	4,551	87.6	49.5	63.6
Medicaid	825	775	814	1,738	1,661	1,722	110.7	114.2	111.5
Medicare	318	6,149	1,577	643	8,749	2,310	102.2	42.3	46.5
Food Stamps	245	71	208	186	63	161	−23.9	−10.7	−22.4
Energy assistance	21	33	24	24	30	25	13.6	−8.2	6.8
Others	193	145	183	399	201	358	106.7	38.6	96.2
Public consumption	9,453	3,550	8,178	11,089	3,803	9,591	17.3	7.1	17.3
Police and Fire	448	268	409	625	383	575	39.7	42.6	40.7
Education	5,208	511	4,194	6,321	633	5,151	21.4	23.8	22.8
Health and hospitals	985	593	900	1,026	624	943	4.2	5.3	4.8
Highways	769	626	738	882	703	845	14.7	12.2	14.5
Others	2,043	1,550	1,937	2,236	1,460	2,076	9.4	−5.8	7.2
Taxes	16,989	7,053	14,844	21,453	8,217	18,731	26.3	16.5	26.2
Federal income taxes	8,748	3,455	7,605	11,627	4,148	10,089	32.9	20.1	32.7
State income taxes	1,816	664	1,568	2,407	809	2,079	32.5	21.8	32.6
Property taxes	972	1,120	1,004	1,014	1,082	1,028	4.4	−3.4	2.4
Payroll taxes	3,923	706	3,229	4,527	842	3,769	15.4	19.1	16.7
Consumption taxes	1,530	1,107	1,439	1,877	1,336	1,766	22.7	20.7	22.7
Net government expenditures	−3,440	17,923	1,173	−4,539	22,192	958	32.0	23.8	−18.3

Public consumption was almost three times as great for nonelderly households as for elderly ones. This is due to the major role played by education in public consumption. Among the elderly, the largest component of public consumption was the residual category "other." The share of education in the public consumption of the elderly is naturally quite low as compared to the nonelderly. Other components such as highways, public health hospitals, account for a much larger share in their public consumption than in the public consumption of the nonelderly. The largest component of the taxes paid by households is federal income taxes. They comprised 54 percent of total taxes in 2001, up from 51 percent in 1989. The second largest component is payroll taxes (employee portion only), which fell from 22 percent to 20 percent in 2001. State income taxes accounted for another 11 percent in both years, state consumption taxes another 9 to 10 percent, and property taxes between 5 and 7 percent. Among the elderly, the largest tax was also the federal income tax, which accounted for about half of total taxes in 1989 and 2001, followed by consumption taxes (16 percent in both years), and property taxes (16 percent in 1989 and 13 percent in 2001).

4.3.4 Household production

The last component of LIMEW is the value of household production (Table 4.12). Disparities in household production between the elderly and nonelderly are quite small, compared to the disparities we have observed for the other components of the LIMEW. The ratio of mean household production between the elderly and nonelderly was 0.90 in 2001, down from 0.95 in 1989. However, there are some differences among the elderly subgroups in household production, especially among households differentiated by marital status and sex (Figure 4.11). The below-average values of household production of single elderly households are primarily a reflection of their smaller household size.

Table 4.12 Household production (2005 dollars)

Characteristic of the householder	Mean				%Chg, 89–01
	1989	1995	2000	2001	
All households	19,852	18,824	22,255	22,558	13.6
Nonelderly	20,053	19,223	22,614	23,036	14.9
Elderly	19,122	17,371	20,886	20,711	8.3
Ratio: Elderly to nonelderly	0.95	0.90	0.92	0.90	

Note: Value of time spent on housework (for example, cooking) and care (for example, caring for an adult).

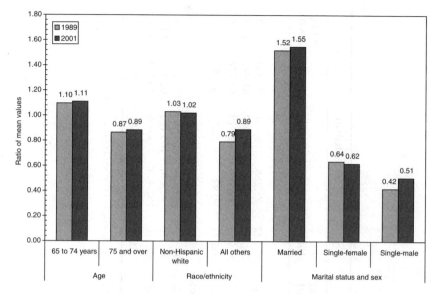

Figure 4.11 Differentials in household production among elderly subgroups (ratio of subgroup to overall elderly mean values)

4.3.5 LIMEW

We now put together all the components of LIMEW to obtain the overall measure. It is first of note that mean LIMEW for all households in 2001 was $107,000, 66 percent higher than mean money income, and median LIMEW was $79,000, 71 percent higher than median money income. The LIMEW measure thus indicates a much higher level of well-being than money income. Indeed, among the elderly, mean and median LIMEW were almost three times as great as mean and median income, respectively.

It is also apparent that the relative well-being of the elderly is much higher according to this broader measure of economic well-being. In 2001, the ratio in mean LIMEW between the elderly and nonelderly was 1.09, in comparison to a ratio of 0.55 in terms of money income. The ratio of median values in 2001 was 0.85, still much higher than the 0.47 of median money income (Panel A, Table 4.13).

When the equivalence-scale adjustment is made, the relative well-being of the elderly again seems higher (Panel B, Table 4.13). In 2001, the ratio of mean equivalent LIMEW between the elderly and nonelderly was 1.41, which is substantially higher than the corresponding ratio (0.68) of equivalent money income. The ratio of median equivalent LIMEW of the elderly to nonelderly was 1.13, compared to 0.62 for equivalent money income. However, the relative well-being of the elderly was higher in 2001 than 1989

Table 4.13 LIMEW (2005 dollars)

Characteristic of the householder	Mean					Median				
	1989	1995	2000	2001	%Chg, 89–01	1989	1995	2000	2001	%Chg, 89–01
A. Unadjusted										
All households	86,879	91,344	107,385	106,666	22.8	70,742	71,288	78,121	79,403	12.2
Nonelderly	87,570	90,700	104,000	104,740	19.6	74,226	73,899	80,087	81,741	10.1
Elderly	84,370	93,687	120,301	114,107	35.2	57,253	60,496	69,719	69,732	21.8
Ratio: Elderly to nonelderly	0.96	1.03	1.16	1.09		0.77	0.82	0.87	0.85	
B. Equivalence-scale adjusted										
All households	111,798	118,051	140,581	139,546	24.8	92,179	93,705	102,595	105,138	14.1
Nonelderly	106,202	110,003	127,678	128,760	21.2	91,320	91,496	100,132	102,778	12.5
Elderly	132,118	147,319	189,817	181,211	37.2	95,410	102,414	114,698	116,441	22.0
Ratio: Elderly to nonelderly	1.24	1.34	1.49	1.41		1.04	1.12	1.15	1.13	

Note: The LIMEW is the sum of base income, income from wealth, net government expenditure, and the value of household production.

by both adjusted and unadjusted measures, which suggests that the adjustment does not affect the trend in well-being.

The higher relative well-being of the elderly was due to a combination of higher income from wealth and higher net government expenditures for the elderly than the nonelderly. The disadvantage of the elderly in base income and, to a lesser extent, in household production was ameliorated by these two components. As shown in Table 4.14, in 2001, base income was much lower for the elderly than the nonelderly (a ratio 0.27). However, income from wealth was much higher for the elderly (a ratio of 3.1). In fact, 46.2 percent of the value of LIMEW for the elderly came from income from wealth (41 percent from nonhome wealth and 5 percent from home wealth), compared to 16.4 percent for the nonelderly. Net government expenditures were positive for the elderly ($22,100) and made up 19.4 percent of the value of LIMEW, whereas they were negative (−$4,500) for the nonelderly. The biggest difference was in taxes paid. The mean tax burden of the nonelderly was 2.6 times as great as that of the elderly. Elderly households received 5.6 times as much in the form of cash transfers and 3.6 times as much in the form of noncash transfers as the nonelderly. On the other hand, public consumption was 2.9 times as high for the nonelderly as the nonelderly. Household production was also slightly higher for the nonelderly than the elderly (a ratio of 1.11) and made up 22 percent of LIMEW for the former and only 18 percent for the latter.

LIMEW also grew much faster for the elderly than the nonelderly over the 1989–2001 period. Mean LIMEW increased by 35 percent for the elderly, compared to 20 percent for the nonelderly, while median LIMEW advanced by 22 percent for the former and 10 percent for the latter. In contrast, growth rates of money income were actually greater for the nonelderly than the elderly over this period (14.9 versus 6.0 percent for mean values and 4.3 versus 3.3 percent for median values). As a result, the ratio of mean LIMEW between elderly and nonelderly households *increased* from 0.96 in 1989 to 1.09 in 2001 and the ratio of median LIMEW from 0.77 to 0.85, while the ratio of mean money income *declined* from 0.59 to 0.55 and the ratio of median money income remained steady at 0.47. The main reason for the positive growth in the ratio of LIMEW (in comparison to the negative change in the ratio of money income) is the phenomenal increase in income from nonhome wealth of 77 percent over the period. Income from wealth also climbed as a share of total LIMEW for the elderly from 31 percent in 1989 to 41 percent in 2001. A secondary reason is the widening gap in net government expenditures between the elderly and the nonelderly, from $21,400 to $26,700.

We next turn to a comparison of the relative well-being of elderly subgroups using the LIMEW and money income (MI). The rank order of the various subgroups considered here are identical for the LIMEW and MI

Table 4.14 Composition of LIMEW and Extended Income: nonelderly and the elderly

Mean values (2005 dollars)

	LIMEW				Extended Income			
	1989		2001		1989		2001	
	Nonelderly	Elderly	Nonelderly	Elderly	Nonelderly	Elderly	Nonelderly	Elderly
Base income	59,394	15,791	69,055	18,429	59,394	15,791	69,055	18,429
Income from wealth	11,563	31,534	17,188	52,774	8,013	15,222	8,644	12,576
Home wealth	3,600	5,139	3,326	6,006	3,577	5,754	2,772	4,756
Nonhome wealth	7,963	26,395	13,862	46,768	4,436	9,469	5,872	7,820
Net government expenditures	−3,440	17,923	−4,539	22,192	−12,427	11,621	−15,539	14,506
Transfers	4,097	21,426	5,824	26,606	2,781	17,522	3,615	21,391
Public consumption	9,453	3,550	11,089	3,803				
Taxes	16,989	7,053	21,453	8,217	15,208	5,901	19,154	6,886
Household production	20,053	19,122	23,036	20,711				
Total	87,570	84,370	104,740	114,107	54,981	42,634	62,159	45,511

	Percent of total								
	LIMEW					Extended Income			
	1989		1995		1989		2001		
	Nonelderly	Elderly	Nonelderly	Elderly	Nonelderly	Elderly	Nonelderly	Elderly	
Base income	67.8	18.7	65.9	16.2	108.0	37.0	111.1	40.5	
Income from wealth	13.2	37.4	16.4	46.2	14.6	35.7	13.9	27.6	
Home wealth	4.1	6.1	3.2	5.3	6.5	13.5	4.5	10.5	
Nonhome wealth	9.1	31.3	13.2	41.0	8.1	22.2	9.4	17.2	
Net government expenditures	−3.9	21.2	−4.3	19.4	−22.6	27.3	−25.0	31.9	
Transfers	4.7	25.4	5.6	23.3	5.1	41.1	5.8	47.0	
Public consumption	10.8	4.2	10.6	3.3					
Taxes	19.4	8.4	20.5	7.2	27.7	13.8	30.8	15.1	
Household production	22.9	22.7	22.0	18.2					
Total	100.0	100.0	100.0	100.0	100.0	100.0	100.0	100.0	

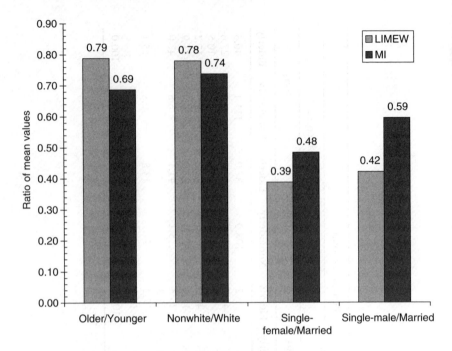

Figure 4.12a Relative well-being of elderly groups by money income and LIMEW, 1989 (ratio of subgroup to overall elderly mean values)

(Figures 4.12a and 4.12b). Differences exist, however, between the two measures regarding the relative disadvantage or advantage faced by the groups. The relative LIMEW of the older elderly was higher than their relative MI: in 2001, the ratio of mean LIMEW between the older and younger groups was 0.79 while the ratio of mean MI was 0.68. On the other hand, the opposite pattern could be observed for the relative well-being of single-female elderly: their relative LIMEW was lower than their relative MI. In 2001, the ratio of mean LIMEW between the single-female and married-couple elderly was 0.37 while the ratio of mean MI was 0.45. The smaller gap in LIMEW between the younger and older elderly is due to similar amounts of income from wealth and net government expenditures (base income was lower for the older elderly). Single females face a greater disadvantage in terms of the LIMEW because of their much lower income from wealth.

The ratio of mean LIMEW between nonwhites and whites was 0.72 in 2001, compared to a ratio of MI of 0.79, while in 1989 the ratios were, respectively, 0.78 and 0.74. Thus, the relative LIMEW of the nonwhites *fell* between 1989 and 2001, while the relative MI *rose* during the same period. The decline in the relative LIMEW of nonwhites was, in turn, due to a

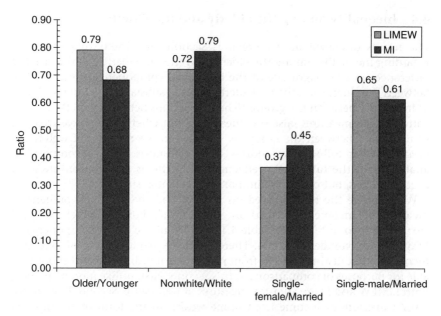

Figure 4.12b Relative well-being of elderly groups by money income and LIMEW, 2001 (ratio of subgroup to overall elderly mean values)

combination of their losing ground in income from home wealth, net government expenditures and value of household production (see Figures 4.4, 4.10 and 4.11). On the other hand, the increase in the relative MI of nonwhites appears to be not due to any improvement of their relative base income (the ratio of base income between nonwhites and whites was 0.94 in 1989 and 2001). Since the relative cash transfers of nonwhites actually dropped between 1989 and 2001 (see Figure 4.6), the explanation for the increase in their relative MI must lie with improvement in property income or pensions.

The ratio of mean LIMEW between single males and married couples was 0.87 in 2001, compared to a ratio of MI of 0.84, while in 1989 the ratios were, respectively, 0.57 and 0.81. Thus, the relative LIMEW of the single males *rose* between 1989 and 2001, while the relative MI *fell* during the same period. The increase in their relative LIMEW appears to be mainly driven by the very dramatic increase in income from wealth, especially nonhome wealth that was noted above (see Figure 4.5). On the other hand, the decline in their relative MI appears to have occurred in spite of the improvement in their relative base income (see Figure 4.3), leaving the deterioration in the property income or cash transfers as the only factors responsible.[11]

4.4 Inequality among the elderly and nonelderly

The results discussed in the previous section raise interesting questions regarding inequality among the elderly and the nonelderly. Do the striking differences in the magnitude of the individual components of the LIMEW between the elderly and the nonelderly result in substantially different levels of inequality between the groups? The distinctions between the LIMEW and conventional measures raise the question about whether the measured gap in inequality between the groups is sensitive to the measure of well-being used. In what follows, we address these questions using decomposition analysis with the full acknowledgement that this is not a substitute for a causal analysis, but only a preliminary, yet essential step.

We compare the results based on LIMEW and the most comprehensive measure of income published by the Census Bureau, which we call "extended income" (EI) (see Table 4.1 for a list of the major components of LIMEW and extended income). There are three major features of extended income EI that distinguishes it from money income and makes it more suitable for purposes of comparisons in this section. First, unlike money income, both LIMEW and EI are after-tax measures of well-being. Second, EI incorporates a measure of income from home wealth in the form of an imputed return on home equity and an expanded definition of income from non-home wealth by including, in addition to property income, the realized amount of capital gains. This makes EI particularly suitable for comparison with LIMEW as different measures of income from wealth can be compared and contrasted. Third, EI and LIMEW include the value of noncash transfers, although the method of valuation is different for medical benefits in the two measures (fungible value in EI and government cost in LIMEW).

The mean values of the two measures and their respective components for 1989 and 2001 are shown in Table 4.14. It is first of note that the relative EI of the elderly is much higher than their relative money income; the elderly to nonelderly ratio of mean values was 0.71 for EI in 2001 as against 0.55 for money income. Taking taxes and noncash transfers into account and including an expanded definition of income from wealth improves the measured relative well-being of the elderly. Of course, the extent of such improvement is still higher if LIMEW is used as the yardstick of well-being.

Comparing the EI and LIMEW shows two salient differences in terms of the disparities between the elderly and the nonelderly. First, income from nonhome wealth of the elderly relative to the nonelderly is much higher when that income is reckoned as lifetime annuity rather than as current income from assets. As discussed before, this is a reflection of the elderly's higher levels of net worth and shorter remaining years of life. The elderly to nonelderly ratio of income from nonhome wealth is 1.3 for EI in 2001 as against 3.4 for LIMEW.[12] Second, the net cost imposed by the fiscal system on the nonelderly appears to be considerably lower once public consumption is included in the equation. In both years, the net government *loss* of the nonelderly in the LIMEW is only 30 percent of its counterpart in EI. These differences in the make-up of the measures have significant impacts on the trends in inequality, as we shall now discuss.

The degree of inequality in LIMEW among the elderly is much higher than among the nonelderly (Figure 4.13). In 2001, the Gini ratio of the LIMEW for the elderly was 0.508 as against 0.402 for the nonelderly – a very high difference of 0.106 (Table 4.15). Estimates for 1989 and 1995 also show a similar gap in inequality. The gap in inequality (as well as the degree of inequality) was the highest in 2000, when the Gini ratio for the elderly was 0.130 higher than that of the nonelderly.

The amount of inequality (measured in Gini points) contributed by each component of the LIMEW for each group in 2001 is shown in Figure 4.14.[13] Base income is the major contributor to inequality among the nonelderly while income from nonhome wealth is the dominant contributor among the elderly. However, the difference in the contribution made by base income to the Gini ratios of the two groups (15.3 Gini points higher in the nonelderly) is overwhelmed by the difference in the contribution made by income from nonhome wealth (22.8 Gini points higher in the elderly). The larger contribution made by income from nonhome wealth to inequality among the elderly is *not* due to its more unequal distribution across the LIMEW distribution within this group as compared to the nonelderly.[14] Instead, it is the much bigger share of income from nonhome wealth in LIMEW among the elderly than among the nonelderly (41 versus 13.2 percent in 2001) that is responsible for the bigger amount of inequality generated by this component.

In contrast, inequality in EI is virtually identical among the elderly and nonelderly for all the years, except 1989. For example, in 2001, both had a Gini ratio of 0.399 (Table 4.15). Decomposing the Gini ratio of extended income by each major component shows that base income is the biggest contributor for both groups (Figure 4.15). However, the amount contributed by base income is about 22 Gini points higher for the nonelderly than for the elderly. But, this "excess" of Gini points is offset by taxes and transfers, and to lesser extent by income from nonhome wealth. Net government expenditures (that is, taxes and transfers taken together) reduce the inequality among the nonelderly by 15.3 Gini points while it makes no contribution to the inequality among the elderly because the contributions made by transfers and taxes cancel each other out. Income from nonhome wealth contributes almost twice as much Gini points toward the inequality among the elderly as compared to the nonelderly (12.1 versus 6.4) and the difference of 5.7 points further eliminates the "excess" of Gini points.

The results from the decomposition analysis also help to account for the fact that while inequality in LIMEW and EI is the roughly the same among

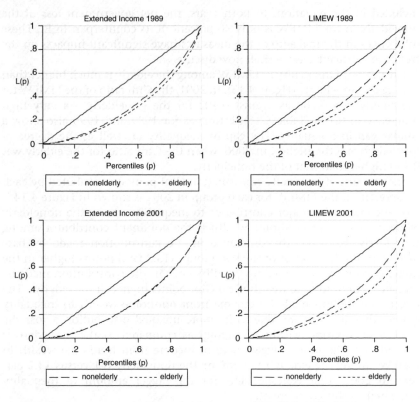

Figure 4.13 Lorenz curve for Extended Income and LIMEW: 1989, 2001

Table 4.15 Inequality among the elderly and nonelderly by measure of well-being (Gini ratios)

	1989	1995	2000	2001
		LIMEW		
Nonelderly	0.351	0.372	0.406	0.402
Elderly	0.454	0.479	0.535	0.508
		Extended income		
Nonelderly	0.356	0.387	0.403	0.399
Elderly	0.401	0.391	0.401	0.399
		Money income		
Nonelderly	0.391	0.429	0.439	0.445
Elderly	0.463	0.465	0.474	0.475

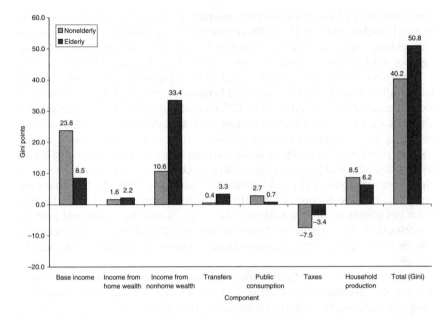

Figure 4.14 Decomposition of inequality in LIMEW, 2001

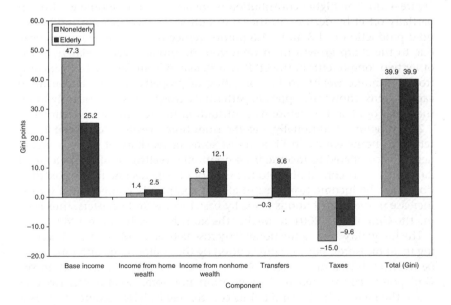

Figure 4.15 Decomposition of EI, 2001

the nonelderly (0.402 versus 0.399), inequality among the elderly in LIMEW is much higher than in EI (0.508 versus 0.399, see Table 4.15). Considering the elderly first, it can be calculated from the numbers reported in Figures 4.14 and 4.15 that the sum of Gini points contributed by base income and income from wealth in LIMEW is higher than the sum of their contributions in EI (44.1 versus 39.9) because of the much higher contribution of income from wealth in LIMEW. Household production, a component that is unique to the LIMEW, contributed an additional 6.2 points, thus resulting in a total gap of 10.9 Gini points between the two measures. Similar calculations for the nonelderly show that the sum of Gini points contributed by base income and income from wealth in LIMEW is lower than the sum of their contributions in EI (36.1 versus 55.2) because of the much higher contribution of base income in EI. However, the large negative contribution from net government expenditures in EI (−15.3) and the significant positive contribution from household production in LIMEW (8.5) help close the wedge between the two measures in the degree of inequality among the nonelderly.

Comparing time trends, we find that there is an increase of inequality among the nonelderly according to both EI and MI but little change in inequality among the elderly (Table 4.15). In contrast, according to LIMEW, inequality increased among both groups. From 1989 to 2001, the increase in the Gini points contributed by income from nonhome wealth exceeded the overall increase in the Gini of the LIMEW for the elderly (8.7 versus 5.5, see Figure 4.16). The higher contribution of income from nonhome wealth was partially offset by declines in the contributions of base income and household production (−1.3 and −1.6 points, respectively). These changes were due to the sharp growth in income from nonhome wealth relative to the other two components of the LIMEW (calculated from Table 4.14).[15] Income from nonhome wealth in EI, consisting of property income and realized capital gains, shows the opposite pattern: its growth was significantly lower than that of EI and therefore its contribution to the Gini of EI declined by 2.2 Gini points. Additionally, income from home wealth, calculated as the return to home equity in EI, also lost some of its share of EI (to a higher degree as compared to income from nonhome wealth), resulting in a fall of 2.6 points in its contribution to the Gini of EI. The decline in the contribution made by income from wealth almost completely compensated for the increase in the contributions made by base income and transfers, thus leaving the Gini of EI in 2001 at roughly the same level as it was in 1989.

The inequality among the nonelderly rose between 1989 and 2001 according to all measures, but the contribution by the components differ markedly between LIMEW and EI (Figure 4.17).[16] In the LIMEW, the increase in the Gini points contributed by income from nonhome wealth was twice as much the increase in the Gini points contributed by base income (3.5 versus 1.7 points). However, the increase in the Gini points contributed by

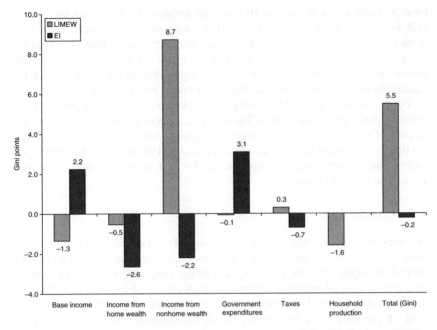

Figure 4.16 Contribution to the change in the Gini ratio of the elderly, 1989–2001

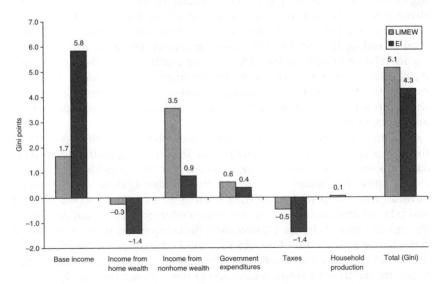

Figure 4.17 Contribution to the change in Gini ratio of the nonelderly, 1989–2001

base income alone exceeded the overall increase in the Gini ratio of EI (5.8 versus 4.3 points), and the contribution toward the increase in Gini from income from nonhome wealth was only 0.9 points. Taxes contributed toward lowering the change in the Gini of EI by 1.4 points, reflecting their growth in tandem with base income. Of equal importance in lowering the change in the Gini of EI was income from home wealth. This component of EI, consisting of return on home equity, fell by a remarkable 22 percent from 1989 to 2001 (calculated from Table 4.14). Although not shown here, the impact of this component on overall inequality was further reinforced by a decline in its concentration ratio (from 0.437 in 1989 to 0.319 in 2001) indicating that income from home wealth became more equally distributed across the EI distribution.

4.5 Conclusion

The picture of economic well-being is crucially dependent on the yardstick used to measure it. Although gross money income, the most widely used official measure, may be suitable for certain purposes, it is an incomplete measure in several important ways. The elevation of more comprehensive measures to a status that is on par with money income in the official scorecard of the economic well-being of US households (DeNavas-Walt et al., 2003) is a sure indication that academic discussion and policymaking will be increasingly informed by such measures.

The picture regarding economic well-being is substantially altered according to the LIMEW as compared to the official measures. Perhaps, our most striking result is that the elderly are much better off relative to the nonelderly in terms of our broader measure of economic well-being, LIMEW, than according to conventional income measures. The main reason for the higher relative LIMEW of the elderly is the much higher values of income from wealth and net government expenditures for the elderly than the nonelderly. The well-being measures adjusted by equivalence -scale also show the same pattern, with the relative well-being of the elderly now appearing even better.

Both mean and median LIMEW also grew much faster for the elderly than the nonelderly over the 1989–2001 period. In contrast, growth rates of standard money income were actually greater for the nonelderly than the elderly over this period. As a result, the relative LIMEW of the elderly *increased* over the period while their relative mean money income *declined* and relative median money income remained steady. The main reason for the positive growth in the LIMEW ratio (in comparison to the negative or zero change in the ratio of money income) is the phenomenal increase in income from nonhome wealth over the period. A secondary reason is the widening gap in net government expenditures between the elderly and the nonelderly.

There are pronounced differences in well-being among the population subgroups within the elderly. The older elderly are worse off relative to the younger elderly, nonwhites are worse off relative to whites, and singles are worse off relative to married couples. The disparities based on race/ethnicity, and sex and marital status, are common to the nonelderly group too, thus suggesting their salience across the elderly to nonelderly divide. These disparities are evident in both the LIMEW and money income measures. However, the extent of the disparities and their change during 1989–2001 are sensitive to the measure of well-being. In 2001, the relative LIMEW of nonwhites and single females were lower than their relative money income. The difference between the two measures can be traced primarily to the relatively lower income from wealth of these groups. From 1989 to 2001, the relative LIMEW of nonwhites fell while their relative money income actually rose. On the other hand, the gap between the older and younger elderly is smaller in the LIMEW than MI due to the fact that the two groups have similar amounts of income from wealth and net government expenditures (base income is lower for the older group).

The degree of inequality in the LIMEW is substantially higher among the elderly than among the nonelderly. In contrast, inequality in the most comprehensive measure of income published by the Census Bureau, extended income (EI), is virtually identical among the elderly and nonelderly. Thus, the measured gap in inequality among the groups is sensitive to the measure of well-being used. The main factor behind this, as the decomposition analysis reveals, is the greater size and concentration of income from nonhome wealth in the LIMEW compared to EI. Further, the change in inequality between 1989 and 2001 is also different for the alternative well-being measures. Inequality in the LIMEW grew for both the elderly and the nonelderly while the inequality in EI (as well as in standard money income) grew only for the latter group. In sharp distinction to the trends in the LIMEW for the elderly where the share of income from wealth rose significantly, the share of such income fell considerably in the overall EI for the elderly. The divergent trends in the income from nonhome wealth were the main reason behind the growing inequality in LIMEW in comparison to the stable level of inequality in EI among the elderly.

Notes

1. For details regarding the sources and methods used to estimate these components, see Wolff, Zacharias and Caner (2004).
2. This is consistent with the approach adopted in most national income accounts.
3. Our rationale for employing this method is that it is a better indicator of the resources available to the wealth holder on a sustainable basis over the expected lifetime compared to the bond-coupon method (that is, assigning a fixed rate of return such as 3 percent to all assets).

4. The rate of return that we use is real total return (the sum of the change in capital value and income from the asset, adjusted for inflation). For example, for stocks, total real return would be the inflation-adjusted sum of the change in stock prices plus dividend yields.
5. There is no agreement among economists as to which equivalence-scale is the "best", so we use the three-parameter scale employed by the Census Bureau in constructing their experimental measures of poverty (Short, 1991; Short et al., 2001). For single-parent households the scale is given by: $(A + 0.8 + 0.5 (K - 1))^{0.7}$; for all other households the scale is $(A + 0.5 K)^{0.7}$, where A is the number of adults and K is the number of children. The reference household (that is, the household for which the scale is set equal to 1) in this instance is a household with two adults and two children.
6. Due to reasons of space we discuss the differences among subgroups using only mean values, instead of using mean and median values.
7. Asians and Hispanics actually experienced declines in their mean income.
8. Because income from home wealth and the remaining components of LIMEW are imputed on the basis of a statistical matching algorithm, we show results only for the nonwhite group as a whole.
9. The annual annuity flow is distributed over the remaining lifetime of an individual so that the full value of nonhome wealth is exhausted at time of death.
10. Actually, the increase between 1989 and 2000 was even greater, followed by a 14 percent decline from 2000 to 2001, a reflection of sagging stock prices over this year.
11. We have already discussed the effects of the equivalence-scale adjustment on subgroup disparities based on money income (see Figures 4.1 and 4.2). Subgroup disparities based on the LIMEW show similar results and are hence not reported here for reasons of space. The difference in the pattern of disparities between the LIMEW and MI is not affected by adjusting the measures by the same equivalence scale.
12. Interestingly, the ratio for EI was higher at 2.1 in 1989.
13. The contribution of each component is calculated as the product of that component's concentration coefficient and its share in the LIMEW.
14. The concentration coefficient for income from nonhome wealth with respect to the LIMEW was approximately 0.81 for both groups in 2001.
15. In principle, the change in the contribution of a component is a combination of the change in its share in LIMEW and the change in its concentration coefficient. The concentration coefficients for income from nonhome wealth, base income, and household production were, however, largely unchanged over the period, thus leaving changes in income shares as the only factor behind the change in the Gini for the elderly.
16. An unknown amount of the change in official measures is due to the change in survey methods introduced from 1994 – raising the threshold for reported earnings from $300,000 to $1,000,000 and computer-assisted personal interviewing. One estimate is that these changes accounted for half of the increase in the inequality in household money income between 1992 and 1993 or about 1 Gini point (Ryscavage, 1995). The change in the Gini of the nonelderly between 1989 and 2001 for EI and MI are, respectively, 4.3 and 5.4 Gini points. It should also be noted that the growth in the inequality of LIMEW is dominated by income from nonhome wealth, a component that was unaffected by the change in survey methods.

References

DeNavas-Walt, C., R. Cleveland and B. H. Webster, Jr. (2003) US Census Bureau, Current Population Reports, P60–221, Income in the United States (Washington, DC: US Government Printing Office).

Hicks, U. K. (1946) "The Terminology of Tax Analysis." *The Economic Journal* 56(221): 38–50.

Kuznets, S. S., L. Epstein and E. Jenks (1941) *National Income and Its Composition, 1919–1938* (New York: National Bureau of Economic Research).

Lakin, C. (2002) "The Effects of Taxes and Benefits on Household Income, 2000–01," Social Analysis and Reporting Division (United Kingdom: Office for National Statistics) http://www.statistics.gov.uk/

Landefeld, J. S. and S. H. McCulla (2000) "Accounting for Nonmarket Household Production within a National Accounts Framework," *Review of Income and Wealth* 46(3): 289–307.

OECD (1995) *Household Production in OECD Countries: Data Sources and Measurement Methods* (Paris: OECD).

Radner, D. B. (1996) "Family Unit Incomes of the Elderly and Children, 1994," *Social Security Bulletin* 59(4): 12–28.

Rendall, M. S. and A. Speare, Jr. (1993) "Comparing Economic Well-Being among Elderly Americans," *Review of Income and Wealth* 39(1): 1– 21.

Ruggles, P. and M. O'Higgins (1981) "The Distribution of Public Expenditure among Households in the United States," *Review of Income and Wealth* 27(2): 137– 64.

Ryscavage, P. (1995) "A Surge in Growing Income Inequality?" *Monthly Labor Review* 118(8): 51–61.

Short, K. (2001) US Census Bureau, Current Population Reports P60–216: *Experimental Poverty Measures: 1999* (Washington, DC: US Government Printing Office).

US Bureau of the Census (1993) *Measuring the Effect of Benefits and Taxes on Income and Poverty: 1992* (Washington, DC: US Government Printing Office).

Weisbrod, B. A. and W. L. Hansen (1968) "An Income-Net Worth Approach to Measuring Economic Welfare," *The American Economic Review* 58(5): 1315–29.

Wolff, E. N., A. Zacharias and A. Caner (2004) Levy Institute Measure of Economic Well-Being, Concept, Measurement and Findings: United States, 1989 and 2000 (Annandale-on-Hudson, NY: Levy Economics Institute of Bard College) (February).

Comments to Chapter 4
Robert Haveman

In this chapter, the authors present us with a new estimate of the well-being of the elderly and assess the role of government spending and taxes in promoting well-being among this population. The estimates are based on the LIMEW model, developed by the authors at the Levy Institute. LIMEW is an ambitious effort designed to yield a more comprehensive estimate of household well-being than the measures that are commonly used by economists, namely cash money income (MI) and Census "Extended Income" (EI). I will refer to the well-being measure derived from LIMEW as full income (FI).

The chapter contains numerous comparisons of (FI) for the elderly relative to the nonelderly, and of the effects of the fisc on the elderly from 1989–2001. These include comparing the elderly with the nonelderly, and within the elderly the old-old with the young-old. In addition, comparisons are made among elderly racial groups, marital status groups, and across the MI distribution for the elderly. The contributions to these patterns of each of the modifications that LIMEW makes to the money income (MI) measure are described.

In addition, the level and trend in inequality in (FI) for both elderly and nonelderly is analyzed and compared with inequality patterns using MI and EI.

The LIMEW model

The LIMEW is designed to provide more comprehensive estimates of household well-being than those provided by MI and EI measures. Because it is an accounting exercise, it neglects any changes in behavior related to adding components of "economic well-being." The model incorporates information on values that may contribute to well-being obtained from other data sets, through statistical matching.

Conceptually, the LIMEW expands MI to reflect a variety of factors that affect well-being. These factors include employer contributions for health insurance, in-kind transfers (valued at government cost, not "recipient value"), annuitized or imputed "income" from home and nonhome assets, public consumption (the cost of public services directly received), household production, and tax liability. All of these components increase the estimated level of well-being, except the last.

Some findings from the LIMEW

An impressive set of insights result from the LIMEW estimates provided by the authors; a few of them are of particular interest. Here I present the mean values of these findings, stated in 2001 dollars.

- The full income (FI) of elderly ($114,000) is nearly three times the level of MI ($39,000) (the difference is even larger when expressed in "equivalent" terms).
- The elderly have only 55 percent of the MI of the nonelderly, but 110 percent of the FI of the nonelderly (141 percent vs. 68 percent in equivalent terms); elderly FI also grew faster than nonelderly MI.

There are several of the components of the LIMEW well-being measure that are responsible for the large increase in FI of the elderly relative to MI estimates. These include the "income" from home wealth, which adds about $6,000 to the well-being of the elderly vs. compared to only $3,000 for the nonelderly. The 600 pound elephant is the imputed "income" from non-home wealth; it adds a mean value of $47,000 to the estimated well-being of the elderly, relative to only about $14,000 for the nonelderly. Noncash transfers add about $11,000 to the well-being of the elderly, relative to only about $3,000 to the well-being of the nonelderly. Household production adds about $22,000 to the well-being of both groups.

There are other components that work the other way. For example, the value of public services adds only about $4,000 to the well-being of the elderly, but about $11,000 to that of the nonelderly. The tax component subtracts about $8,000 from the well-being of the elderly, but substantially more from the well-being of the nonelderly – $21,000 overall. The value of transfers less taxes is $18,000 for elderly and -$16,000 for the nonelderly, for an ENORMOUS difference of $34,000 in the favor of the elderly. For the entire fisc – taking account of the value of public services, the difference is $27,000 in favor of the elderly relative to the nonelderly.

In terms of the FI concept of the LIMEW model, the public sector is heavily weighted toward support of the elderly. For example, the authors find that for the elderly all of the components of the fisc are equalizing relative to base income. While the ratio of top decile of MI to bottom decile is about 74, the ratio for cash transfers is about two, noncash transfers about one, and public consumption about two. Taxes for the top decile are about 40 times that for the bottom decile. Overall, the fisc takes about $14,000 from the folks in the top MI decile, and gives about $28,000 to the folks in the bottom decile.

The authors also find that FI for the elderly is more unequally distributed than either MI or EI, and that FI inequality is growing more rapidly than inequality in the other measures. Especially relative to EI, income from non-home wealth is primarily responsible.

Thoughts on the LIMEW model

The LIMEW is heroic in its vision of a new and more comprehensive measure of economic well-being. For example, the approach extends "official efforts" to expand the well-being measure (EI) in several ways. While EI does not annuitize wealth (but does include capital gains), the model takes into account the expected life expectancy of families. Similarly, while EI does not subtract consumption taxes, adjust taxes and cash and noncash transfers to NIPA totals, or consider household production and public consumption, LIMEW and the FI concept based on it does. These are bold extensions, and in each case the authors have a rationale for their inclusion.

However, questions arise with respect to the overall robustness of the estimates that the model yields. Clearly, in assessing the model it is necessary to temper enthusiasm regarding the gains in the comprehensiveness of the estimates with an evaluation of the accuracy of the estimates themselves. In many cases, the model is required to adopt assumptions regarding unknown factors necessary to derive any kind of empirical estimate at all. Similarly, while extending the comprehensiveness of the measure of economic well-being is of value, the question of just how far to go in this process is also relevant. Several examples will make this clear.

Are we prepared to include household production in a measure of FI? Why not go all the way and add in the value of available leisure time? Because the elderly get much of their income from nonwork sources, this would benefit them greatly. However, just how should we value leisure time for people for whom market work is not a foregone option? Similarly, are we prepared to accept cost-of-provision values for noncash transfers, government services, and household production, when willingness to pay values are more relevant in assessing well-being?

The valuation and inclusion of health benefits has stumped national statisticians and policy analysts for a decade now; are we comfortable including a cost-based measure in FI? Given the large effects of Medicare and Medicaid for the elderly, should not the health needs of the elderly be accounted for in the calculation?

Should such components of MI as the value of public goods expenditures (for example, defense, statistical services) be included in the value of public consumption when these values are, by necessity, measured by the cost of producing them and the basis for allocating the benefits of public goods across individuals quite unknown? Or, again, what are the often-unstated assumptions regarding the burden of indirect taxes (for example, consumption taxes); are these generally agreed upon?

At a more detailed level, why not just annuitize net home value rather than impute rental values? Should not pension wealth be included in FI? Clearly, were it to be included the well-being gap between the elderly and the nonelderly would be even larger than that reported by the authors.

The devil is in the details

As in all cases where analysts seek to extend convention, the devil is in the details, and the LIMEW model is no exception. As indicated above, there are several aspects of their approach that need more extensive defense than that which is offered in the chapter. For example, how is the "statistical matching" done in imputing wealth information from Survey of Consumer Finances (SCF) and time use information from other surveys to the base microdata used in LIMEW? What is the basis for the adoption of the portfolio-specific interest rate used to annuitize wealth; surely, other analysts would find other options preferable? What is the justification behind the individual-performance-index weighted replacement cost value attached to household production? Again, the advantages of this option relative to others need to be defended.

Interestingly, the employer portion of payroll taxes is not included in FI. Surely, most economists would find this value relevant for assessing the economic well-being of individuals and families. Further, does LIMEW incorporate a public budget constraint? Apparently the budget does not balance, but how this is taken into account is not clear.

A bottom line

The dogged pursuit to be comprehensive embodied in the LIMEW modeling effort is to be applauded. A side effect, of course, is that one has less confidence in some of the imputed values than in others. How should the authors proceed in such a situation?

I believe that it would be helpful if the authors would distinguish their core results from those that include some of the more controversial values. Then, supplementary results including the more controversial values could be added, using a sensitivity test approach. Let the reader decide. It is, of course, a matter of judgment regarding what to include in the core and what to exclude. My candidates for the most controversial items are household production, consumption of public services, some of the indirect taxes, and the in-kind health benefits (especially Medicare and Medicaid).

With results presented in this way, the reader can proceed from estimates based on the more conventional values to those reflecting more speculative components, making the choice as to where confidence in the results gives way to skepticism. With results presented in this way, the authors can then proceed to address some more interesting policy questions with the measures developed. For example, given the money income basis of needs estimates that underlie the poverty estimates, MI and even EI can be used to measure the extent to which individuals and groups are able to meet some social standard – for example, poverty or near poverty standards. It seems impossible to use FI for this sort of exercise. Could not one fashion a reliable indicator of "minimum acceptable" family size-conditioned needs consistent with alternative LIMEW well-being estimates that could be used for assessing FI poverty and changes in it over time?

Finally, in the face of several candidates for assessing economic well-being – FI, MI, EI – is there any possibility of relating these measures to nonmonetary indicators of "well-being"? Would there be a payoff to analyzing the correspondence of FI (EI, MI) with survey indicators of "hardship", or responses regarding elements of well-being? Could not such an exercise suggest the relative merit and reliability of alternative candidates of measures of the same basic well-being value?

5
Differing Prospects for Women and Men: Young Old-Age, Old Old-Age, and Eldercare

Lois B. Shaw*

5.1 Introduction

This chapter addresses the question of government spending on the elderly from a woman's perspective. The point of view I bring is that of an *old woman*, a semi-retired feminist economist, who is a participant observer of the process of growing old. I live in a Continuing Care Retirement Community (CCRC) and so am well situated to observe the aging of my neighbors and friends as well as myself. In this chapter, I will comment on some of the policies being advocated or adopted that may affect women and men in different ways.

Although Social Security has received the most attention, expenditures for Medicare and Medicaid are projected to increase even more rapidly than Social Security spending. Some of the policies advocated for these programs may interact in unexpected ways. Regarding Social Security reform, increasing the age of eligibility to promote longer working lives has often been advocated. At the same time proposals are made to constrain Medicaid spending by shifting more of the care of the disabled elderly to unpaid caregivers, primarily women, but also some men, many at the ages when they are also being expected to do more paid work.

The elderly are conventionally defined as the population aged 65 and over, but this is a very broad age range and the capabilities of different individuals are likely to vary widely. When we consider work and retirement, we tend to be thinking about young old-age, when most people are physically active and able to care for themselves. There is considerably less research, at least by economists, on old old-age when disabilities increase, most of the elderly begin to need some assistance, and many require extensive help with the most basic activities of daily living.

Although elderly men and women encounter many of the same problems as they age, their lives are likely to follow different patterns. Men are less likely than women to live into extreme old age; women are, therefore, an increasing majority of the elderly at older ages (see Table 5.1). Men are also

Table 5.1 Percent married, probability of surviving to next age, and percent female by age

Ages	Percent married[a]		Probability of surviving to the next age[b]		Percent female[c]
	Men	Women	Men	Women	
65–74	77.6	56.1	0.747	0.828	54.2
75–84	72.8	36.6	0.485	0.606	59.2
85 and over	59.4	13.9	N/A	N/A	66.3

Source:
[a] US Census Bureau, Current Population Survey, as reported in Federal Interagency Forum on Aging-Related Statistics, 2004, Table 3.
[b] Calculated from Life Tables for Males and Life Tables for Females, National Vital Statistics Reports, 2002.
[c] Calculated from Current Population Survey, 2004; excludes population in nursing homes.

likely to have married women younger than themselves. As a result, while the majority of both men and women age 65–74 are married, by age 85 and over approximately 59 percent of men are married compared with only 14 percent of women. Then, if they become ill or disabled, men are much more likely than women to have spouses who can be caregivers whereas women are more likely to depend on adult children. These patterns will, however, certainly change with health improvements and different marital patterns as the baby boom generation ages, a topic I will return to later.

5.2 Young old-age: paid work, unpaid work, or leisure?

5.2.1 Paid work: working longer

Retirement often occurs even before age 65, most commonly at age 62 when eligibility for Social Security begins. As life expectancy increases, encouraging people to work longer seems reasonable. One proposal is to gradually increase the age of first eligibility for Social Security benefits beyond the current age of 62 years. More commonly proposed is to continue raising the age of qualification for full Social Security benefits beyond the currently scheduled changes from 65 to 67 years. Such proposals would in effect be benefit cuts for anyone who cannot work past age 62. Either proposal would cause the greatest hardship for some of the most vulnerable elderly, especially minorities and other low-income individuals who cannot continue to work because of poor health, inability to find work, or responsibilities for other family members.

Proposals for later retirement would have the greatest impact on workers in physically demanding jobs, more frequently held by men than women.

However, some occupations that are not especially demanding for younger workers become more difficult at older ages. These include many service occupations and some retail sales jobs that require standing or walking for long periods. Large proportions of these jobs are held by women. According to data from the Health and Retirement Survey (HRS), slightly more than half of workers in service occupations and about one quarter of those in sales reported that their jobs involved much physical effort all or most of the time (US Government Accountability Office, 2005b). Increasing the early or normal retirement age should be accompanied by changes that make disability benefits more readily available for people who cannot continue to work because of the physical demands of their jobs.

Working longer will only be possible to the extent that employers are willing to hire older workers. At present, companies that are downsizing often encourage their older workers to retire even before age 62. Studies show that although unemployment is generally low at older ages, older workers who do lose their jobs are unemployed for longer periods and may eventually stop trying to find work (Flippen and Tienda, 2000). Many workers believe that if they wanted to work to older ages, either their own lack of up-to-date skills or employers' discrimination against older workers would prevent them from doing so (US Government Accountability Office, 2005b).

If labor shortages develop as the baby boom generation retires, perhaps more employers will be interested in providing options such as phased retirement, allowing for part-time or part-year employment which few employers now offer (US Government Accountability Office, 2005b, p. 29). A slight trend toward more employment at older ages appears to have already begun. For example, labor force participation rates at ages 65–69 were 33.6 percent for men and 23.7 percent for women in 2005, up from 24.4 percent and 13.5 percent in 1985. These trends could reflect better job opportunities or could be due to many people feeling the need for more income as the cost of medical care increased more rapidly than inflation.

5.2.2 Unpaid work: caregiving responsibilities

Another problem of a longer working life that is seldom recognized is that many women and some men in their 50s and 60s may find it difficult to continue working for pay because they are needed as caregivers for their spouses, parents or other relatives. Research suggests that informal care by spouses or adult children delays the use of nursing home care and reduces the use of formal paid home care (Charles and Sevak, 2005; Van Houtven and Norton, 2004). Consequently, encouraging care by family members is frequently mentioned as an option for reducing pressures on public programs (Wolf, 1999). Additionally, reductions in Medicaid availability at both state and federal levels may well be forcing families to assume this responsibility.

Relatively small amounts of assistance can usually be combined with paid employment, and when family relationships are good, may be very satisfying to the caregiver. Sometimes elderly parents who are in relatively good health can reciprocate by occasionally or even regularly taking care of grandchildren. On the other hand, caring for those who require considerable help with the so-called instrumental activities of daily living (IADL) may be quite time-consuming.[1] Even more difficult to combine with paid work is the more intensive care required for those who need assistance with the such activities of daily living (ADL) as dressing, bathing, eating, moving around indoors, and using the toilet.

This country appears to be following the path taken by some European countries: encouraging more paid work *and* increased unpaid eldercare (OECD, 2005; Stark, 2005). Women are more likely than men to be involved in these conflicting demands. In the United States spouses and daughters are the most common caregivers; wives are approximately 60 percent of spouse caregivers, although husbands play a significant role as well, in part because they are so much more likely than women to be married. Among adult children, daughters (or daughters-in law) are much more likely to provide extensive care than are sons, sons-in-law, or other relatives or friends (Johnson and Wiener, 2006; Wolf, 2004).[2]

Nearly all spouse caregivers are over age 55, approximately one third of them in the 55–69 age range, the ages when more paid employment is being advocated (Johnson and Wiener, Table 5.6). Nearly one-quarter of daughter caregivers are age 60 and over, approximately one-third are in their 50s, and another third are in their 40s; many of them are employed (Johnson and Wiener, Table 5.5). Thus the conflict between paid work and care-giving may arise for women and some men, not only when they are raising children but also at older ages when they must provide care for spouses or elderly parents (Gross, 2006). Some of the younger caregivers may be caring for both parents and children.

When increased family care is recommended as a way to reduce dependence on expensive nursing home care, the most intensive kind of care is implied, and coresidency is often required. Wolf (1999) argues that care by family members, specifically adult children, can be more efficient than paid care. Coresident care can indeed offer economies of scale. In some cases, a parent's retirement income can also make a substantial contribution to the family's welfare.

On the other hand, the potential stress for both the recipient and the caregiver should not be ignored. Bringing a parent into the home of an adult child can require difficult adjustments for both parent and child. A Canadian study finds that providing care for a parent living in the household is far more stressful than the same amount of child care (MacDonald, Phipps, and Lethbridge, 2005). Intensive care, especially for an elderly person with dementia can put enormous strains on the caregiver. Those who have to give up their jobs or reduce their hours of paid work may also be jeopardizing their own retirement incomes.

The value of caregiving to society may well exceed its net value to the caregiver who pays much of the personal and financial cost. Therefore, public support to encourage caregiving by family members is warranted (Wolf, 1999; Folbre, 2004). For example, the use of adult day care can allow the caregiver some respite to do necessary tasks such as shopping. In some cases, such an arrangement can even allow caregivers to continue with their regular jobs. However, adult day-care facilities are not available in many communities and are rather expensive, even though costing considerably less than nursing home care. Some states permit Medicaid to pay for adult day care.

Countries such as Australia, Canada, Sweden, and the United Kingdom have tried to ameliorate the eldercare problem by providing allowances to support caregivers (OECD, 2005). Some of these countries have also provided social insurance benefits for caregivers. Proposals for caregiver tax credits or added years of Social Security coverage have been made in the US Congress, but have not been enacted (Wolf, 2004).

5.2.3 Leisure?

If we make adequate provisions for those who are not able to work because of disability, care responsibilities, or inability to find a suitable job, it should be possible to encourage longer working lives for those in young old-age who are able and willing to work for pay. The question arises, however, whether we should not also allow a place for leisure at some point before old old-age? Policies to encourage more paid work even past age 70 sometimes take on a rather puritanical tone that is reminiscent of the old hymn, "Work for the night is coming when man's work is done." This hymn enjoins us in successive verses to work through the morning hours, through the sunny noon, and while the night is darkening; the work ethic indeed.[3]

Perhaps we are a bit influenced by the media view of the wealthy young-old people who go on cruises and other exotic vacations and live in retirement communities with golf courses. This picture may apply to some members of the upper-middle class and many of the upper class, but for most other people, the reality is very different. Many are caring for aging spouses or even still working, at least at part-time paid jobs. For most, leisure is more likely to consist of simpler pleasures like gardening, visiting with neighbors, napping, and playing with grandchildren. Even this last activity, for women especially, sometimes becomes part or even full-time caregiving to help their daughters or daughters-in-law hold paid jobs. In African-American and other low-income communities, grandmothers are sometimes raising their grandchildren alone (Joslin and Brouard, 1995).

5.3 Old old-age and the need for care

At the same time that life expectancy has been increasing, disability among the elderly has decreased (Cutler, 2001). Many women and men who live into old old-age remain in relatively good health, but as they reach their late 70s and into their 80s, more of them develop problems that may interfere with their ability to live independently (see Table 5.2).[4] Low vision becomes an increasing problem, and many old people lose some of their independence because they can no longer drive a car.

Although women are more likely to live to older ages, they are also more likely than men to have mobility problems at each age. Women are more likely than men to be disabled because of arthritis, osteoporosis or after a fall, conditions that are usually not fatal, but can lead to long periods of disability. Men, on the other hand, are more often disabled because of heart disease or strokes and do not live as long with these conditions (Guralnik et al., 1997). Dementia, probably the most disabling and most feared disability, rises rapidly with age to affect approximately 17 percent of women and 21 percent of men by age 80 and 30 percent of both men and women aged 85 years or over (Federal Interagency Forum, 2004, p. 90).[5]

Among married couples, caring for an ailing spouse is common. Approximately 45 percent of spouse caregivers are in their 70s and some are in their 80s, when their own health may be a constraining factor (Johnson and Weiner, 2006). Although most eldercare is provided by spouses or other

Table 5.2 Disabilities and nursing home residence by age and gender

Ages	Trouble seeing[a]	Impaired mobility[b]	Nursing hme residence[c]
(Percentages)			
MEN			
65–74	13.3	13.0	1.0
75–84	16.2	21.3	3.1
85 and over	29.2	35.1	11.7
WOMEN			
65–74	15.5	26.0	1.1
75–84	19.1	32.9	5.1
85 and over	34.7	59.5	21.1

Source:
[a] Federal Interagency Forum on Aging Related Statistics. Older Americans 2004: Key Indicators of Well-Being. Table 16a, Non-institutionalized civilian populations, 2002.
[b] Table 19c, Medicare enrollees, 2002.
[c] Table 35a, Percent of age group, 1999.

unpaid caregivers in the community, many of those needing care, women especially, live alone and have no relative who can assist them. After age 75, the majority of women are not married (Table 5.1) and nearly half live alone (Shaw and Lee, 2005).

Among the elderly residing in the community[6], about 20 percent of those who need assistance with either activities of daily living (ADL) or instrumental activities of daily living (IADL) rely on paid caregivers (Wolf, 2004). More women than men rely on paid care, even though they have less income and fewer assets than men. The majority of paid caregivers are also women, predominately African-Americans or Hispanics (Wiener and Tilly, 2002). The work is usually low-paid and seldom provides benefits. Turnover is high, leading to a high level of insecurity for those relying on this kind of care.

Formal long-term care is most commonly provided in nursing homes, although some small room and board facilities also offer complete care. Residence in nursing homes increases rapidly with age. In 1999, approximately 3 percent of men and 5 percent of women lived in nursing homes at ages 75–84, and the percentages increased to 11 percent of men and 20 percent of women of age 85 and over (see Table 5.2). Approximately three-quarters of nursing home residents are women. About 72 percent of nursing homes are operated for profit, and the quality of care is often poor (Eaton, 2005).

The average cost of a year in a nursing home is $70,000 (Metlife Mature Market Institute, 2004). While the median net worth of elderly married couples was $170,000 in 2000, median net worth of female householders aged 65 years and over was $75,275, barely enough to cover one year in a nursing home (US Census, 2000). Hence many nursing home residents exhaust their savings within a year or two of entry, and then become dependent on Medicaid. Nursing homes may be reluctant to take people who are on Medicaid, making it more difficult for lower-income people to find accommodations. (Harrington Meyer, 2001).

5.3.1 Paying for long-term care

For elderly women, especially, paying for the care they need is often a major problem whether they remain in their homes or go into nursing homes. Over half of long-term care for the elderly is paid for by federal and state governments: Medicaid paid for 35 percent and Medicare 25 percent in 2004. Only 4 percent was paid for by insurance; the rest (36 percent) was paid for out of pocket by the recipients, their families, or other sources such as charitable funds (Johnson and Uccello, 2005; CBO, 2004).[7]

Nursing home care, however, involves much higher Medicaid expenditures than home-based care. In 2004, Medicaid covered approximately 40 percent of nursing home expenses compared with 25 percent of home-based care expenses. Medicaid is not an entitlement and is administered by the states, which can determine eligibility within limits set by federal law. Medicaid has been described as insurance in which the deductible is your life savings and the co-payment is your annual income (Quoted in Clark et al., 2004, p. 326). More stringent rules for Medicaid eligibility is a favorite recommendation for curbing government expenditures on the elderly (CBO, 2004, Chapter 3). Women are not only the primary recipients of Medicaid, but also the primary caregivers who will be under pressure to provide more unpaid care.

Medicare plays a larger role in home-based long-term care because it pays for skilled nursing care that is provided at home on a daily basis. It also pays for short-term care in nursing homes that provide skilled nursing care after hospitalization, but does not pay for custodial care on a long-term basis (Johnson and Uccello, 2005).

Private spending by the care recipient or her/his family also represents a major source of payment for long-term care. Out-of-pocket medical expenditures of all kinds are usually largest in the last years of life, reaching approximately one quarter of annual income for the median couple and over one-half of annual income for 20 percent of elderly couples (McGarry and Schoeni, 2005). If assets are drawn down to pay for medical expenses, the surviving spouse, most commonly the wife, will be less likely to be able to pay for her own expenses in her last years.

One possible remedy is long-term care insurance, which is relatively new but is likely to become a more important way of paying for long-term care in the future. Premiums at age 65 average approximately $2,000 per year for a guarantee of an inflation-adjusted payment of a stated amount for 3–6 years (CBO, 2004, Table 1–3). Purchase of life-time coverage is even more expensive. Premiums increase rapidly with age, and are considerably lower if purchased before age 65. However, Consumer Reports does not recommend earlier purchase because of the risk of having to drop the insurance if income should decrease or premiums should be increased enough to make them unaffordable (Consumer Reports, 2003).[8] Furthermore, an estimated 15 percent of those applying for policies are turned down for health reasons, and some purchasers have also found it difficult to get companies to pay when long-term care is needed. Therefore, long-term care insurance can by no means solve everyone's problems.

5.4 Eldercare in the future

In 20 years, members of the large baby boom generation (born in 1946–1964) will all be in what is now the usual retirement ages, and the oldest will have reached age 80. The situation I will discuss here is based on current trends, but disasters such as abrupt climate change, wars over energy sources, or epidemics could completely change this picture.

Although the baby boom generation will probably be healthier than today's elderly, total medical expenditures are not likely to decline because of their large numbers (Wiener and Tilly, 2002). The decrease in disabilities that has occurred in recent years has been greatest for the well-educated and relatively wealthy (Schoeni et al., 2005). Therefore, increasing income inequality as well as increasing disability at younger ages owing to such factors as increasing obesity (CBO, 2004, Box 1–2), portend smaller decreases in old-age disability than in the past. In any event both Medicare and Medicaid are likely to be under great pressure because of the size of the baby boom generation (US Government Accountability Office, 2005a). A likely outcome is that eligibility or payments are likely to be further reduced, putting more of the burden on families for unpaid care.

At the same time, family care is likely to be less available than it has been. It is uncertain whether as much spouse care will be available for either women or men. On the one hand, fewer of those in their 40s and 50s are married than was the case for the current elderly population. On the other hand, increasing life expectancy may reduce the likelihood of becoming widowed. In any case a larger percentage of the younger generation is predicted to be divorced or never married (Butrica, Iams, and Smith, 2003).

Another important difference between today's elderly and baby boomers is that the latter have had far fewer children than their parents. Nearly 60 percent of women who are now in their 70s had had three or more children by ages 40–44, compared with only about 30 percent of women born in 1956–1960. Similarly only 10 percent of the older women had no children by their early 40s, compared with 19 percent of the younger group (US Census, 2005). Therefore, care by children, mainly daughters, such an important source of care for elderly women today, will also become much less common.

For all these reasons, additional sources of eldercare may be necessary in the future. Sons and sons-in-law may need to provide more care than at present. Siblings, friends, and perhaps nieces and nephews may also become more important sources of care. In any event, it is probable that an increased reliance on paid care will be necessary. Until now, nurses and other health care workers have often been recruited from the developing world to alleviate shortages (Callahan, 2001). Immigration, especially large flows of migrants from Latin America, has now become the subject of much controversy. Rather than depending so heavily on poorly paid immigrants, a better policy would surely be to provide higher wages and better working conditions for care workers in order to attract and retain high-quality workers, whether native-born or immigrants.

Higher rates of saving could potentially reduce the need for higher government spending on eldercare when the large baby boom generation retires. Members of this generation are expected to have higher incomes than the current elderly generation and would clearly benefit from saving more. Nevertheless, the increasingly unequal distribution of income means that many of them, including families with below-average incomes and the majority of unmarried women, will not be able to save enough to pay for long-term care if they need it (Van Derhie and Copeland, 2003).

In addition, fewer workers in the future will have income from defined benefit pension plans, and the defined contribution plans that are replacing them are usually taken as lump-sum benefits rather than annuities (Shaw and Hill, 2002). This exposes retirement income to investment risk, especially since many people do not have the skills required for successful long-term management of assets (Copeland, 2005). Hence, the risk of outliving assets may very well increase for this generation.

Long-term care insurance will probably become a more important part of paying for long-term care. Federal employees, for example, already have the option of including long-term care insurance as a fringe benefit. Long-term care premiums are at present deductible as medical expenses once total medical expenses exceed the required percentage of income, but this is most useful for the wealthy in higher tax brackets. Use of home equity to buy long-term care insurance through reverse mortgages has been suggested, but is not yet widely practiced. Reverse mortgages could also be used to pay for long-term care directly (Rich and Porter, 2006), but this again is most useful for those who own expensive homes.

In the past ten years Germany, Japan, Austria, and Luxembourg have instituted state-provided long-term care insurance systems (OECD, 2005). These systems might provide useful models and should be studied carefully as they mature. Adding long-term care insurance to Medicare might be a good option for the United States as well. This might be done by increasing the payroll tax, but could be accomplished in a less regressive way by reinstituting the estate tax at higher levels and dedicating the proceeds to universal long-term care insurance.

An important strategy to reduce long-term care expenditures is to delay the need for full-time care by helping the individual to remain active longer. Assistive devices such as walkers and motorized scooters allow old people to move about more easily and have been found to reduce the number of hours of personal assistance needed (Hoenig, Taylor, and Sloan, 2003). Also, medical advances such as cataract surgery, hip and knee replacement, and various treatments for heart conditions have allowed people to live longer active lives. Here as in other aspects of government spending, increased (decreased) spending of one type (Medicare) may lead to reduced (increased) need for other spending (Medicaid).

Retirement communities with services are a growing source of support for the elderly with mild disabilities or those who anticipate that they may need services in the future. Because providing care at home or in communities with services is less expensive than nursing home care, some states are attempting to shift funds for seniors in this direction. About 7 percent of the population age 85 and over at present live in such senior communities (Federal Interagency Forum, 2004, p. 54). Some communities offer senior low rent housing and services such as transportation to stores. Congregate housing facilities usually offer individual apartments with common dining facilities and other common areas. Assisted living facilities usually provide all meals and services such as laundry, housecleaning, and assistance with medications for those who need such help, but are still able to do many things for themselves. This kind of assisted living usually costs considerably less than nursing home care.

Continuing care retirement communities offer a range of services including independent living, assisted living, and full nursing home care. Communities of this kind provide settings in which it is easy for elderly people to help each other in various ways that can delay the time when more expensive formal care is needed and thus reduce government expenditures on Medicaid. It is my hope that the baby boom generation will be able to think of still other ways to help themselves and each other in old age.

Appendix

An Example of a Continuing Care Retirement Community (CCRC)

The CCRC I live in has features that allow the elderly, especially those living alone, to delay the time when they will need the full care of a nursing home. We are a not-for-profit community with over 1,000 residents, the majority living in independent living apartments. One meal a day is covered by the monthly fee, but breakfast and lunch are available if desired. A small grocery store, beauty salons, doctor's offices, and a pharmacy are on the premises. About three-quarters of the residents are women, the majority of whom are widowed, divorced, or never married. According to a recent survey, only 2 percent are in their 60s, about 35 percent are in their 70s, over half are in their 80s, and 10 percent are 90 years old or over. (These figures may under-represent those in their late 80s and beyond as they are probably less likely to respond to written surveys.)

Although the population is definitely middle or upper middle class, it is not limited to such a high-income population as some have supposed. Our friends are retired teachers, librarians, and housewives. Most of the men were civil servants, but one we particularly enjoy talking to was a train conductor. We continually meet people who have lived here for more than 10 years, some more than 20 years. Those who need daily help usually move into assisted living, but a few hire their own helpers. A nursing home provides after-hospital care and physical therapy for those recovering from hip or knee surgery. Full long-term care is also available, including a special wing for care of Alzheimer patients. There is also an adult day-care unit used as respite care by spouses of residents as well as by people in the surrounding community with early-stage Alzheimer's.

Residents offer each other help of various kinds. Those who still drive may take others shopping or to doctor's appointments. Many who are becoming forgetful have friends to remind them to come to meals. People in the nursing home unit after surgery usually have well-wishers who send cards or flowers and visit them when they are well enough. This kind of friendly environment is particularly important for those who have no family or friends living nearby.

Although the nursing home unit does depend partly on Medicare and Medicaid funding, there is also a benevolent fund to help those whose income and assets fail to cover all their costs. Many residents contribute to this fund as do people in the surrounding community. No one has ever been asked to leave because of insufficient funds. In an area with lower housing costs than the one in which we are located, this kind of nonprofit community, organized by religious or other voluntary groups, could offer a retirement alternative to a broader range of older people living alone.

Notes

* Acknowledgments: I thank my daughter Sarah Shaw Tatoun as well as Brittany Stalsburg and Erica Williams of the Institute for Women's Policy Research for their expert assistance in preparing references and tables, my daughter Rachel Shaw for her careful reading and encouragement, and my colleagues Marianne Ferber, Nancy Folbre, and Barbara Gault for their thoughtful comments.

1. IADLs include being able to manage money and medications, use the telephone, shop, cook and do light housework.
2. Estimates of the characteristics of caregivers of the elderly vary across years, source of the data, and the kind and amount of care being provided. The estimates shown are for those helping with ADLs.
3. For the complete hymn see www.cgmusic.com/cghymnalothers/workforthenight.htm.
4. Some part of these age differences could, of course, be due to cohort effects.
5. These figures are underestimates because they include only the noninstitutional population.
6. Most community-based care is provided in private homes, but as discussed later, assisted living and other arrangements are becoming increasingly popular. Residents of assisted living facilities, in particular, are considered part of the noninstitutional population, but may not be adequately represented in surveys (Schoeni et al., 2005).The Federal Interagency Forum on Aging-Related Statistics recommends more attention to these newer kinds of living arrangements for the elderly to be sure that their residents are accurately counted (Federal Interagency Forum, p. 60).
7. These figures do not take into account the value of unpaid care. According to the CBO (2004, Figure 1), the value of unpaid care could account for as much as 36 percent of long-term care expenses, bringing the total amount from private sources both paid and unpaid to over 60 percent of total costs. Wolf (2004) explains some of the different ways of valuing unpaid care, and some of the sources of both over and underestimation.
8. While premiums are supposed to be fixed at the age of purchase, insurance companies have sometimes been successful in getting grants from state regulators

for large increases in premiums if they find their premiums are not covering costs (Johnson and Uccello, 2005). Over a long period of years, there is also greater risk of company bankruptcy as well.

References

Butrica, B. A., H. M. Iams and K. E. Smith (2003) "It's All Relative: Understanding the Retirement Prospects of Baby Boomers," (Washington, DC: The Urban Institute).
Callahan, J. J., Jr. (2001) "Policy Perspectives on Workforce Issues and Care of Older People," *Generations* XXV(2).
Charles, K. K. and P. Sevak (2005) "Can Family Caregiving Substitute for Nursing Home Care?" *Journal of Health Economics* 24 (November): 1174–1190.
Clark, R. L., R. V. Burkhauser, M. Moon, J. F. Quinn and T. M. Smeeding (2004) *The Economics of an Aging Society* (Malden, MA: Oxford and Melbourne: Blackwell).
CBO (2004) *Financing Long-Term Care for the Elderly* (Washington DC: Congressional Budget Office).
Consumer Reports (2003) "Do You Need Long-term-care Insurance?" 68(3) (November): 20–24.
Copeland, C. (2005) "Changes in Wealth for Americans Reaching or Just Past Normal Retirement Age," Employee Benefit Research Institute, No. 277 (Washington, DC: EBRI).
Cutler, D. M. (2001) "The Reduction in Disability among the Elderly," *Proceedings of the National Academy of Sciences* 98(12): 6546–6547.
Eaton, S. C. (2005) "Eldercare in the United States: Inadequate, Inequitable, but Not a Lost Cause," *Feminist Economics* 11 (July): 37–52.
Federal Interagency Forum on Aging-Related Statistics (2004) *Older Americans 2004: Key Indicators of Well-Being*, Federal Interagency Forum on Aging-Related Statistics (Washington, DC: US Government Printing Office).
Flippen, C. and M. Tienda (2000) "Pathways to Retirement: Patters of Labor Force Participation and Labor Market Exit among the Pre-retirement Population by Race, Hispanic Origin, and Sex," *Journals of Gerontology: Series B: Psychological Sciences and Social Sciences* 55B (January): S14–S27.
Folbre, N. (2004) "A Theory of the Misallocation of Time" in Nancy Folbre and Michael Bittman (eds) *Family Time: the Social Organization of Care* (London and New York: Routledge) pp. 7–24.
Gross, J. (2006) "As Parents Age, Baby Boomers and Business Struggle to Cope," *New York Times*, March 25.
Guralnik, J. M., S. G. Leveille, R. Hirsch, L. Ferrucci and L. P. Fried (1997) "The Impact of Disability in Older Women," *Journal of the American Medical Women's Association* 52 (Summer): 113–120.
Harrington Meyer, M. (2001) "Medicaid Reimbursement Rates and Access to Nursing Homes: Implications for Gender, Race, and Marital Status," *Research on Aging* 23 (September): 532–551.
Hoenig, H., D. H. Taylor, Jr. and F. A. Sloan (2003) "Does Assistive Technology Substitute for Personal Assistance among the Disabled Elderly?" *American Journal of Public Health* 93(2) February: 330–337.
Johnson, R. W. and C. E. Uccello (2005) *Is Private Long-Term Care Insurance the Answer?* Center for Retirement Research at Boston College. Issue Brief.

Johnson, R. W. and J. M. Wiener (2006) "A Profile of Frail Older Americans and Their Caregivers," Urban Institute, The Retirement Project, Occasional Paper No. 8 (Washington, DC: Urban Institute).

Joslin, D. and A. Brouard (1995) "The Prevalence of Grandmothers as Primary Caregivers in a Poor Pediatric Population," *Journal of Community Health* 20(5): 383–401.

MacDonald, M., S. Phipps and L. Lethbridge (2005) "Taking Its Toll: The Influence of Paid and Unpaid Work on Women's Well-Being," *Feminist Economics* 17 (March): 63–94.

McGarry, K. and R. F. Schoeni (2005) "Medicare Gaps and Widow Poverty," *Social Security Bulletin* 66(1): 58–74.

MetLife Mature Market Institute (2004) *The MetLife Market Survey of Nursing Home and Home Care Costs: September 2004* (Westport, CT: MetLife Mature Market Institute).

OECD (2005) *Long-Term Care for Older People* (Paris: OECD).

Rich, M. and E. Porter (2006) "Increasingly, the Home is Paying for Retirement," *International Herald Tribune*, February 26.

Schoeni, R. F., L. G. Martin, P. M. Andreski and V. A. Freedman (2005) "Persistent and Growing Socioeconomic Disparities in Disability Among the Elderly: 1982–2002," *American Journal of Public Health* 95 (November): 2065–2070.

Shaw, L. B. and S. Lee (2005) "Growing Old in the US: Gender and Income Adequacy," *Feminist Economics* 11 (July): 163–198.

Shaw, L. B. and C. Hill (2002) *The Gender Gap in Pension Coverage: What Does the Future Hold?* (Washington, DC: Institute for Women's Policy Research).

Stark, A. (2005) "On the Need of a New World Order of Care," (2005) *Feminist Economics* 11 (July): 7–36.

US Bureau of the Census (2000) *Wealth and Asset Ownership*. http://www.census.gov/hhes/www/wealth/1998_2000/wlth00-1.htm (accessed April 2006).

US Bureau of the Census (2005) "Fertility of American Women, June 2004," *Current Population Reports*, December 2005.

US Government Accountability Office (2005a) *Long-Term-Care Financing: growing Demand and Cost Are Straining Federal and State Governments.* GAO-05–546T.

US Government Accountability Office (2005b) *Labor Can Help Employers and Employees Plan Better for Their Future.* GAO-06–80.

VanDerhei, J. and C. Copeland (2003) *Can America Afford Tomorrow's Retirees: Results from the EBRI-ERF Retirement Security Projection Model*, EBRI Issue Brief No. 263 (Washington, DC: Employee Benefits Research Institute).

Van Houtven, H. and E. C. Norton (2004) "Informal Care and Health Care Use of Older Adults," *Journal of Health Economics* 23 (November): 1159–1180.

Wiener, J. M. and J. Tilly (2002) "Population Aging in the United States of America: Implications for Public Programs," *International Journal of Epidemiology* 31: 776–781.

Wolf, D. A. (1999) "The Family as Provider of Long-Term Care: Efficiency, Equity, and Externalities," *Journal of Aging and Health* 11 (August): 360–382.

Wolf, D. A. (2004) "Valuing Informal Eldercare," in Nancy Folbre and Michael Bittman (eds) *Family Time: The Social Organization of Care* (London and New York: Routledge) pp. 110–129.

Comments to Chapter 5
Rania Antonopoulos

"Differing Prospects for Women and Men: Young Old-Age, Old Old-Age, and Eldercare" identifies a very important issue that is easy to miss, especially if demographic trends are treated as mere averages. Care for the elderly is gendered and therefore differences must be recognized and asymmetries taken into account for sound policy design. To begin at the beginning, the economic resources available to the elderly follow gendered distinctions and this contributes to the kind and amount of care received. Equally important is the amount of care-work men and women contribute that differs and is based on lifecycle patterns of division of labor of those who are the providers of daily care to the elderly. This is the main message of Lois Shaw's chapter. Men and women have, on the average, significantly different life expectancies, an empirically shown fact, but seldom recognized sufficiently when entitlements to the elderly are considered for reform.

There is little, if anything, to disagree with Shaw's poignant and fitting representations of the plight of elderly women. The chapter concentrates almost exclusively on Medicaid (a long-term care means-tested program) although some issues have important implications for Medicare and Social Security. She provides, in the chapter, ample justification of the stark differences of the division of labor between what women and men do during the years of their young old-age and old old-age respectively. For this division of labor is predicated within and outside the labor market along gendered lines. During the early years the questions center on "who takes care of the kids and old parents?" and later in life "who takes care of the male spouse?" and even much later "who takes care of the old women"? Shaw answers the latter questions admirably, marshalling a lot of empirical evidence. Women are the primary caregivers to their spouses, she writes, who for the most part are older than them, and since women's life expectancies are longer, ultimately, they are not able to care for themselves and become dependent on either the state or their children for the provisioning of long-term care. Ample evidence documents that caregiving has been provided mostly by women – wives, daughters, and daughters-in-law – than men – husbands or sons – and Shaw draws on the available official statistics to reach her conclusions.

The chapter contains demographic transition comparisons of elderly men and women, gendered probabilities of surviving to the old old-age, and incidences of disability and needs for long-term care. All these point to the special needs that public policy must address when attempting to reform spending toward the elderly. Reducing Medicaid spending, for instance, predictably reinforcing asymmetry as more unpaid care would be provided to the disabled aged by the majority of women. Unlike other Organisation for Economic Co-operation and Development (OECD) countries providing allowances to support caregivers or including long-term care insurance coverage, the United States exemplifies the model of an inadequate and gender biased eldercare system (Eaton, 2005); and this policy is continued despite projections that a majority of the aged – 65 and over – will find themselves needing long-term care at some point in the remaining years of their lives (Cadette, 2003).

Shaw suggests a number of changes to the existing policy in the United States with which I am in complete agreement. I would recommend, however, that we seriously consider supplementing these with those advocated by the late Susan Eaton (2005) that included both far more generous public provisioning of eldercare and also, a regulatory reform that addresses the problems of the nursing home industry. The model of the state of Massachusetts Nursing Home Quality Care Initiative, instituted in 2000, coupled with the Extended Care Career Ladder Initiative (ECCLI) which is designed to train, retain and promote caregivers are examples of much needed organizational reform and implementation; these types of structures promote organizational change of culture that leads to more individualized and higher quality care as well as to a gender equitable society.

References

Cadette, W. M. (2003) "Caring for a Large Geriatric Generation: The Coming Crisis in US Health Care," Policy Note 2003/3 (Annandale-on-Hudson, NY: The Levy Economics Institute of Bard College).

Eaton, S. C. (2005) "Eldercare in the United States: Inadequate, Inequitable, but Not Lost Cause," *Feminist Economics* 11 (July): 37–52.

Part III

Changing Patterns of Retirement Behavior

ns
6
Working for a Good Retirement

Barbara A. Butrica, Karen E. Smith, and C. Eugene Steuerle*

6.1 Introduction

One way of relieving the economic pressures created by an aging population is to encourage workers to delay retirement. When people leave the workforce, they forgo earnings. To replace these earnings, many retirees begin collecting pensions and/or drawing down their assets. Most retirees also begin collecting Social Security benefits. At the same time, retirees pay fewer taxes – not just payroll taxes that support Social Security, but also federal, state, and local income taxes that support other government programs. Thus, the retirement of the boomer generation, some 76 million people, is expected to have a large impact on individuals, the retirement system, and the economy.

The oldest boomers will turn age 62 – the age of first eligibility for Social Security benefits and the age at which the majority of retired workers elect to receive benefits – beginning in 2008. Because people are living much longer than before, even substantial increases in work duration would leave future generations with more years of retirement on average than almost all generations living in the past. When Social Security benefits first became payable in 1940, the average worker retired at 68. To retire for an equivalent number of years in 2005 would mean retiring at 74; by 2050, that equivalent age would increase to 78. However, in 2005, workers on average retired at about age 63 (Steuerle, 2005).

When people work longer, they earn more income, usually save some of that income, allow existing assets to grow, increase their lifetime Social Security benefits, and increase their annual Social Security benefit even more when their lifetime benefits are withdrawn over a shorter period of time. Butrica et al. (2004) estimate that people could increase their annual consumption at older ages by more than 25 percent by simply retiring at age 67 instead of age 62.

An aging population and the approaching retirement of the largest birth cohort in US history could mean an insufficient income stream to pay promised Social Security benefits in 2017. Delaying retirement could ease this logjam. In 2004, the Social Security Old-Age and Survivors Insurance and Disability Insurance (OASDI) Trust Funds paid about $493 billion in Social Security benefits and received about $658 billion in revenue. About 84 percent of this revenue came from payroll taxes paid by employees, employers, and the self-employed. Another 2 percent came from income taxes paid on Social Security benefits, and 14 percent came from interest income on OASDI Trust Funds (Board of Trustees, 2005).

The Office of the Chief Actuary (OCACT) projects that OASDI revenues (payroll taxes, interest on the OASDI trust funds, and income taxes on Social Security benefits) will be more than enough to pay promised benefits through 2016. After that, boomers retiring in hoards would require trustees to begin redeeming the bonds held by the OASDI Trust Funds. According to current projections, all assets in the Trust Funds will be depleted by 2041. Without reform, benefits received after 2041 will have to be paid solely out of payroll tax and the proceeds from income tax on benefits, which will fall short of benefits promised under the current law (Board of Trustees, 2005). So working longer would inject the Trust Funds with much-needed cash, especially from the additional payroll taxes.

What's more, workers who delay retirement produce additional goods and services for the economy and pay additional income taxes that increase general revenues used to support other government programs (or, for that matter, used to cover some of Social Security reforms). At the same time, these additional revenues from a larger national income reduce tax pressures on younger workers or, alternatively, allow government to spend more on programs other than for the elderly.

This chapter is the first comprehensive look at how changes in retirement behavior and reforms that encourage workers to delay retirement could impact individual retiree benefits, the solvency of the Social Security Trust Funds, and general revenues. The specific ripple effect of delayed retirement is gauged using projections of retirement age, Social Security take-up age, pensions, Social Security benefits, taxes, and other important sources of income in retirement from the Urban Institute's Dynamic Simulation of Income Model (DYNASIM3).[1] We increase the retirement and Social Security take-up age of nondisabled workers and estimate their Social Security benefits, payroll taxes, and federal and state income taxes. While the report shows the extraordinary possibilities additional work generates, it is not a behavioral study of exactly how people respond to existing incentives. Instead, it measures the economic consequences of delaying retirement under a range of specified behavioral responses. Additional work requires individuals to give up leisure time, but for many individuals, work also comes with improved physical and mental well-being (Calvo, 2006).

Findings show that the Social Security earnings generated from just one additional year of work are almost equal to the entire 2045 Social Security shortfall (of benefits from taxes) projected under the baseline scenario. A share of those earnings is paid to the government in the form of taxes, including Social Security taxes. The additional Social Security taxes generated by five years of work alone offset more than half of the Social Security shortfall in 2045. Further, if one takes into account the additional income tax revenues, the government's gain to its unified account is far greater than the size of the Social Security deficit. While it is harder to depend upon additional work only to close the gap between projected Social Security income and outlays, various combinations of benefit cuts and additional work can still leave the average retiree with significantly higher average retirement income than he or she otherwise might have. The increase in personal wealth from added work more than offsets any decrease in personal wealth due to simulated Social Security benefit cuts. Under all of the simulated reform options, added work leads to a more solvent and more financially secure retirement.

6.2 Literature review

Although numerous studies have examined how our tax and benefit systems affect work incentives, previous research has not measured the combined impact of Social Security, taxes, and employee benefits on the returns to work at older ages. Gokhale, Kotlikoff, and Sluchynsky (2002), for example, compare lifetime earnings for a representative two-earner couple to lifetime taxes and the lifetime value of transfer payments they lose because of work, and conclude that workers give up nearly 50 cents in tax payments and foregone transfers for every dollar they earn. The authors do not, however, examine returns to work at older ages or how returns vary with age. A number of studies have investigated the impact of financial incentives on retirement behavior, especially the role of Social Security and employer-sponsored pension and health plans (Coile and Gruber, 2004; Johnson, Davidoff and Perese, 2003; Lumsdaine, Stock and Wise, 1992, 1994; Samwick, 1998; Stock and Wise, 1990), but they have not focused on how total returns to work change as adults age. Finally, Diamond and Gruber (1999) compute implicit tax rates and replacement rates for prototypical workers, but they ignore the role of federal income taxes and employer-sponsored pension and health insurance plans, which have important effects on work incentives.

Research by Butrica et al. (2004) attempts to fill the gap in this literature by describing the combined impact of Social Security, typical employee benefits, and the tax system on the tax rates, replacement rates, and retirement wealth of representative workers. The authors find that the implicit tax rate on work increases rapidly at older ages, and by age 65, people can typically receive nearly as much in retirement as they can by working (see Figure 6.1). However, the authors also find that older individuals could substantially increase their financial resources in retirement by working longer.[2]

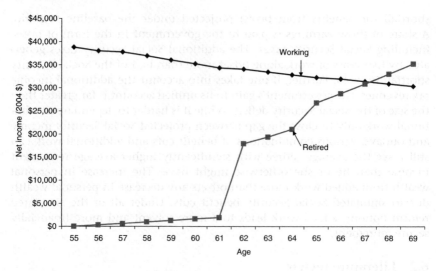

Figure 6.1 Net income of a hypothetical worker by age and employment status
Source: Urban Institute tabulations of DYNASIM3.

For example, the representative worker could nearly double his real annual income at age 75, net of health insurance premiums and federal taxes, by stopping work at age 65 instead of age 55. By waiting until age 68 to retire, he would accumulate enough wealth (from pensions, Social Security, and saved earnings) to finance an annual consumption stream at older ages of $60,000 per year, nearly three times as much as he could finance if he retired at age 55.

This chapter builds on the research of Butrica et al. (2004) in two primary ways. First, the results are based on a nationally representative sample of the US population, rather than on prototypical individuals. Second, it examines the consequences of delaying retirement both at the macro and individual level, rather than just the individual level. Specifically, this chapter considers how additional work influences the Social Security deficit and the taxes that would go to support all government programs within a unified budget, in addition to the lifetime and annual benefit payments in Social Security.

6.3 Interaction of Social Security, pensions, earnings, and taxes

This chapter accounts for the complex interaction between Social Security benefits, pensions, earnings, and taxes to assess how working longer influences individual retiree benefits, the solvency of the Social Security Trust Funds, and general revenues. This section briefly describes how working longer might influence each income source, as well as taxes. Butrica et al. (2004) provide more detail about the provisions of Social Security, tax law, and employer benefit policies as they pertain to the decision to work at older ages.

Working an additional year will generally increase future Social Security benefits, for example, but the relationship between work history and Social Security is complex. Social Security reduces payments for those who collect benefits before the normal retirement age (NRA) and increases benefits for those who delay collecting until after the NRA.[3] But delaying take-up also reduces the number of payments they receive. The optimal age of take-up depends in part on mortality expectations: those who survive until very advanced ages will gain more from claiming later than those who do not live as long. In addition, beneficiaries who continue to work are subject to the retirement earnings test. For those below the NRA, Social Security withholds $1 in benefits for every $2 of earnings in excess of the exempt amount − $12,480 in 2006. The reduction in benefits is partly offset by higher future benefits.

Traditional defined benefit plans often introduce strong disincentives to work at older ages. Workers with defined contribution pension plans can build up the assets in these accounts through their own, and possibly their employers', contributions. With defined benefit pension plans, however, additional work does not necessarily translate into higher benefits. For instance, many traditional defined benefit plans penalize those who continue on the job after they qualify for full retirement benefits, reducing the lifetime benefits they receive from the plan. Some plans also cap the number of service years that workers can credit toward their pensions, and others cap the share of pre-retirement earnings that the plan will replace in retirement. In addition, for every year that workers remain on the job past the plan's retirement age, they forgo a year of retirement benefits. Pension wealth declines when the increase in annual benefits from an additional year of work is insufficient to offset the loss due to a reduction in the number of pension installments.

Delaying retirement increases lifetime earnings and the ability to support, and possibly increase, current and future consumption. Yet, the individual returns to work are somewhat reduced because workers must pay both payroll and income taxes on most of their earnings. For society as a whole, however, those additional taxes now become available for other purposes, such as covering the cost of Social Security and Medicare.

6.4 Methodology

The Urban Institute's DYNASIM3 is used to determine the individual and budgetary consequences of working longer. In DYNASIM, retirement is defined as substantial, but not necessarily complete, withdrawal from the labor force. Specifically, DYNASIM's retirement age represents the age at which a worker experiences at least a 50 percent drop in earnings compared with average earnings earned between age 45 and 50. (The drop in earnings must last for at least two years.) Defining the retirement age this way allows DYNASIM to simulate more gradual transitions to full retirement. A separate DYNASIM module projects Social Security take-up age using discrete-time hazard models based on age, expected benefit amount, spousal characteristics, and Social Security policy parameters. (See Favreault and Smith [2004] for more detailed information.)

The DYNASIM retirement and Social Security take-up age is increased by one or five years to simulate delayed retirement. We do this for those who (1) are not disabled, (2) did not die before the model predicted their retirement or Social Security take-up, (3) retired or took up Social Security benefits before age 70 or the end of the projection period, and (4) are still in the labor force and are not collecting Social Security benefits in 1993, the first year of DYNASIM projections. For example, in the "work one more year" scenario, if DYNASIM projects a worker to retire at age 60 and to begin receiving Social Security benefits at age 62, we force the worker to retire at age 61 and to take up Social Security benefits at age 63. In the "work five more years" scenario, we force the worker to retire at age 65 and to take up Social Security benefits at age 67. We then insert the worker's pre-retirement earnings, indexed by wage growth, in each simulated extra year of work. We also shift the worker's original post-retirement earnings to reflect his or her additional work effort. After adjusting the earnings and benefit take-up age, we let the model re-estimate pensions, Social Security benefits, and federal and state income taxes.

Working longer by itself may not close the gap between projected Social Security income and outlays, and Social Security benefit changes may induce additional work. Experimenting with alternative Social Security benefit structures, we conduct five policy simulations that differ from Social Security current law (summarized in Table 6.1):

Table 6.1 Summary of policy simulations

Option	Work adjustment	Change in EEA	Change in NRA
Baseline	–	–	–
Pure work effect	Work+N	–	–
Pure benefit cut	–	–	↑
Partial work no benefit cut	Work+N before EEA	↑	–
Partial work with benefit cut	Work+N before EEA	↑	↑
Full work with benefit cut	Work+N	↑	↑

Notes: N equals one for the one-year scenarios and five for the five-year scenarios. Dash indicates no change compared to the baseline scenario. Arrow indicates an increase compared to the baseline scenario.

- *Pure Work Effect*: All nondisabled individuals delay retirement and benefit take-up and work one (or five) additional year(s). In this simulation, retirees receive Social Security benefits, which may stay constant or increase because of a delayed retirement credit or adjustment in the retirement earnings test, over a shorter period of time.
- *Pure Benefit Cut*: An across-the-board benefit cut that is unaccompanied by any change in work effort. This is represented by an increase in the Social Security NRA, which forces an actuarial reduction in the benefit at every age of retirement.[4] While this simulation does not generate income for the Social Security Trust Funds, it does decrease costs substantially.
- *Partial Work, No Benefit Cut*: An increase in the Social Security early entitlement age (EEA) accompanied by an increase in the work effort of individuals who originally retired before the new EEA.[5] If the EEA increases by five years, then workers who used to retire at or before age 62 would retire five years later, those who used to retire between ages 63 and 66 would retire at age 67, and those who used to retire at age 67 or later would not change their retirement age. This simulation raises income slightly because workers who delay retirement continue to pay taxes. But it also raises costs slightly because no one receives a benefit cut, they just delay their Social Security take-up and benefits are reduced less for early retirement.
- *Partial Work with Benefit Cut*: An increase in the EEA and the NRA, accompanied by an increase in the work effort of individuals who originally retired before the EEA. This is similar to the previous simulation except that it decreases costs because the increase in the NRA is essentially a benefit cut.
- *Full Work with Benefit Cut*: Finally, an increase in the EEA and NRA, accompanied by an increase of similar magnitude in the work effort of all individuals. For example, if the EEA and NRA increase by one year, the work effort of all individuals, excluding the disabled, increases by one year. This simulation is identical to the previous one, but with a much larger impact since everyone increases work effort in addition to the EEA and NRA changes.

For each of these simulations, we examine how individual retirement annuity income and wealth, Social Security income and costs, and general revenues change compared to the baseline (no reform).[6]

Because we are interested in highlighting how an individual's work decision can impact his or her retirement income, each of these sources of wealth reflects only the wealth created by the individual. That is, we only include retired-worker benefits in the Social Security wealth calculation (we exclude Social Security auxiliary benefits), and pension wealth excludes survivors' benefits, inheritances, and benefits obtained through divorce. Each component of total retirement wealth is measured as the present discounted value (PDV) of the expected future stream of benefits or payments from age 50 until death, and then put into constant 2006 dollars. The computations assume a real interest rate of 2 percent. The measure shows net resources (from earnings, pensions, and Social Security) available to finance consumption after age 49, evaluated in the year 2006.

We also annuitize the value of retirement wealth to show how real annual consumption changes with additional work. We take the level of retirement wealth that accumulates over the individual's lifetime and divide it by the real annuity factor at age 50. The resulting value of the annuity shows how much could be consumed every year from age 50 until death, if the retiree chose to equalize real annual consumption after age 49.[7] If retirees saved their additional wealth from working longer and annuitized *the additional amount* at retirement, their annual annuity payments would be much higher. To show this, we compute a second annuity, which is the sum of two different annuities – a baseline annuity purchased at age 50 and another purchased at the later of retirement age or Social Security take-up age. To compute the second annuity, we calculate the change in total net wealth between the baseline and alternative scenario, grow it from age 50 until the later of retirement or Social Security take-up age by a real interest rate of 2 percent, divide it by the real annuity factor that corresponds to that age, and add it to the baseline annuity.

At the macro level, we calculate the change in the Social Security deficit and in general revenue due to additional work. To do this we aggregate Social Security benefits and revenues over all individuals in the population and compare the projected total number of OASDI beneficiaries, the total benefits that will be paid to them, the total number of covered workers, and the total general revenue (payroll and income taxes) generated by their work under the baseline and alternative scenarios. For these analyses, we include both the individual's Social Security retired-worker and auxiliary benefits to represent more accurately the total costs to the system. We calculate the change in Medicare Hospital Insurance (HI) tax from additional work, but we exclude these funds in our Social Security deficit reduction calculations.

6.4.1 Description of DYNASIM

DYNASIM is a useful tool for gaining insights into the future retiree population and their retirement incomes.[8] The model starts with a self-weighting sample of about 100,000 individuals from the 1990 to 1993 Survey of Income and Program Participation. DYNASIM ages this starting sample in yearly increments to 2050, using parameters estimated from longitudinal data sources. The model integrates many important trends and differentials in life course processes, including birth, death, schooling, leaving home, first marriage, remarriage, divorce, disability, work, and earnings. Important for this study, DYNASIM projects retirement age and Social Security take-up age. DYNASIM also simulates the major sources of retirement income – specifically

Social Security benefits, pension income, income from assets, earnings, Supplemental Security Income (SSI), imputed rental income, and income from nonspouse co-resident family members. Finally, the most recent version of DYNASIM also includes federal and state income taxes, which are calculated using the income tax calculator developed by Jon Bakija (2005). This calculator accurately models current law taxes including the Economic Growth and Tax Relief Reconciliation Act (EGTRRA), the Jobs and Growth Tax Relief Reconciliation Act (JGTRRA), the AMT, and the taxation of Social Security benefits and pension income. (See the appendix for more details on DYNASIM.)

6.5 Increase in income and wealth for individuals

Table 6.2 shows net retirement wealth and its components in our DYNASIM baseline. It also describes the change in wealth due to working both one and five years longer. In our baseline scenario, retirees who survive to 2049 and are receiving Social Security benefits accumulate an average net retirement

Table 6.2 Mean baseline respondent wealth and change from additional work (2006 $)

	Baseline	Change from baseline	
		Work one more year	Work five more years
Social Security	$199,378	$5,937	$28,864
DB pensions	39,576	−421	−2,517
DC pensions	54,633	2,028	10,859
Earnings	477,862	35,579	180,658
Federal/State income taxes	110,982	8,736	44,157
Payroll taxes	34,491	2,489	12,715
Total net wealth	625,976	31,897	160,992
Annual annuity at age 50	26,570	1,317	6,688
Annual annuity at retirement		2,402	14,888
%Change total net wealth		5%	26%
%Change annual annuity at age 50		5%	25%
%Change annual annuity at retirement		9%	56%

Notes: Based on 17,547 unweighted observations of persons who are alive in 2049 and retired and receiving Social Security benefits. See Appendix Table 6.A.2 for more detail.
1. Annuity at age 50 is total net wealth divided by the real annuity factor at age 50.
2. Annuity at retirement is the change in total net wealth between the baseline and alternative scenario, grown from age 50 until the later of retirement or Social Security take-up age by a real interest rate of 2 percent, divided it by the real annuity factor that corresponds to that age, and added to the baseline annuity.

Source: The Urban Institute tabulations of DYNASIM3.

wealth of $625,976 (2006 dollars). This is the sum of $199,378 in Social Security wealth, $39,576 in defined benefit pension wealth, $54,633 in retirement account balances (defined contribution pensions), and $477,862 in earnings wealth, less $110,982 in lifetime federal and state income taxes and $34,491 in OASDI and HI payroll taxes. This retirement wealth could support an annual consumption stream of $26,570 per year from age 50 onward.[9]

If everyone delayed their retirement by just one year (Pure Work Effect), the average net retirement wealth would increase by $31,897 and the average annuity at age 50 would increase by $1,317 per year (5 percent). If retirees saved their additional wealth from working another year and annuitized it at retirement (for example, 401[k] balances were left untouched until retirement), their annual annuity would increase by $2,402 per year (9 percent) compared to the baseline. When workers work an additional five years, average net wealth increases $160,992 (26 percent) compared to the baseline. Annuitized at retirement, this extra wealth would increase annual retirement income by $14,888 per year – a 56 percent increase in retirement income compared to the baseline. While average Social Security wealth and retirement account balances increase with extra work, the big gains in net wealth for the individual come from his or her additional earnings. This additional wealth also generates additional taxes that can then be used to support more government spending for the retired population or for the population as a whole. The pure addition of extra work has a large positive impact on retirement income, at least as measured by potential consumption.

Table 6.3 shows the change in net wealth and the annual annuity under our five reform scenarios working an additional one year and five years compared to the baseline.[10] The baseline and "Pure Work Effect" columns show the same results as in Table 6.2.

Increasing the NRA without changing work behavior (Pure Benefit Cut) has a large negative impact on retirement wealth because it is essentially a benefit cut. With a one-year increase in the NRA and no work response, average net wealth would decline by $12,169. The average annual annuity at age 50 would fall by $515 (2 percent), and the average annual annuity at retirement would fall by $936 (4 percent) compared to the baseline. With a five-year increase in the NRA, average net wealth would decrease by over $60,000 and the average annuity at retirement would fall by 17 percent.

Next, consider a delay in retirement but only by workers who originally retired before the new EEA. If the EEA were increased one year in this "Partial Work No Benefit Cut" scenario, average net wealth would increase by $21,685 and pay out an annual annuity that is $882 higher or even $1,497 higher (if the additional annuity did not begin until retirement) than the baseline. If the EEA were increased five years and early retirees worked five more years, average net wealth would increase by $132,716 and the annual annuity at retirement would increase by $11,264 (42 percent). Note that

Table 6.3 Mean respondent wealth and annuity income in 2049 under current law and estimated change under alternate reform scenarios (2006 $)

	Baseline	Change due to the reform compared to baseline				
		Pure work effect	Pure benefit cut	Partial work no benefit cut	Partial work and benefit cut	Full work and benefit cut
Work one more year						
Net wealth	$625,976	$31,897	−$12,169	$21,685	$9,661	$20,016
Annuity at age 50	26,570	1,317	−515	882	374	816
Annuity at retirement		2,402	−936	1,497	554	1,449
% Change annuity at age 50		5%	−2%	3%	1%	3%
% Change annuity at retirement		9%	−4%	6%	2%	5%
Work five more years						
Net wealth	625,976	160,992	−60,256	132,716	73,331	100,344
Annuity at age 50	26,570	6,688	−2,549	5,482	2,968	4,127
Annuity at retirement		14,888	−4,617	11,264	5,948	8,993
% Change annuity at age 50		25%	−10%	21%	11%	16%
% Change annuity at retirement		56%	−17%	42%	22%	34%

Notes: Based on 17,547 unweighted observations of persons who are alive in 2049 and retired and receiving Social Security benefits. See Appendix Table 6.A.2 for more detail.
1. Annuity at age 50 is total net wealth divided by the real annuity factor at age 50.
2. Annuity at retirement is the change in total net wealth between the baseline and alternative scenario, grown from age 50 until the later of retirement or Social Security take-up age by a real interest rate of 2 percent, divided it by the real annuity factor that corresponds to that age, and added to the baseline annuity.

Source: The Urban Institute tabulations of DYNASIM3.

what goes on here is that lifetime Social Security benefits go up (the actuarial adjustment is more than fair) slightly, some workers labor for an additional year and get more earnings, there are additional savings in defined contribution plans, and there are more taxes paid on the work.

In contrast to pure benefit cuts that decrease average net wealth, benefit cuts that are accompanied by additional work actually increase average net wealth. If only early retirees worked one more year but we increased the NRA one year (Partial Work and Benefit Cut), net wealth would increase $9,661. This would increase the average annuity at retirement by 2 percent. If every eligible worker changed his work behavior on top of a benefit cut (Full Work and Benefit Cut), net wealth would increase $20,016 and the annuity at retirement would increase 5 percent. Under these scenarios, workers get the wealth benefit from the extra work, but the gain is partly offset by a reduction in Social Security benefits due to the benefit cut. The more workers who work longer, the larger the net gain.

If we focus just on the change in annuity income at retirement under our alternate reform scenarios, bigger increases in work effort yield bigger gains in retirement income. Reductions in Social Security benefits reduce retirement income, but benefit cuts in conjunction with additional work will ultimately lessen the size of any benefit cut needed to achieve solvency.

Lower-income workers get larger gains from additional work than do higher-income workers (see Figure 6.2). Partly because of the progressive Social Security and income tax systems, lower-income workers keep a greater share of additional earnings because of lower tax rates compared with higher-income workers. Of course, since lower-income workers also tend to have somewhat higher mortality rates than higher-income workers, their additional earnings are spread over fewer years of remaining life. This mortality differential is captured in our calculated annuity income through education. While DYNASIM projects that the average annuity at retirement from one year of work, given no changes in Social Security policy, would increase 9 percent, workers in the bottom fifth of lifetime earnings distribution would get an average increase of 16 percent in their annuity at retirement from one year more work and a 98 percent increase from five more years of work. Benefits from work are still large for the top lifetime earners, but only about half as large as for the lowest earners.

Not all low-income workers can achieve this gain, of course. This chapter does not examine all the policy options that one may also want to enact in conjunction with efforts to increase working years. But note that the relative gains increase well up the income scale, so that even the second richest quintile has a larger percentage increase in annual income than does the richest. Still, the gains are sizable in every quintile.

Most individuals are healthy and able to work at older ages. Only about 20 percent of recent early Social Security claimants report having a health condition that limits the amount or type of work they can do (Panis et al., 2002).[11] Most of these individuals would be eligible for Social Security

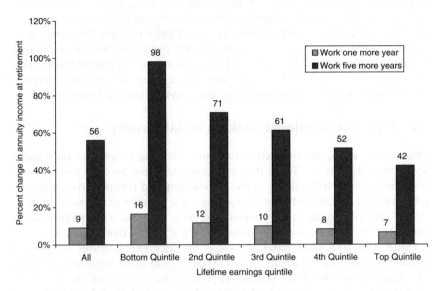

Figure 6.2 Percent change from baseline in average annuity income at retirement by lifetime earnings quintile and additional work effort
Source: Urban Institute tabulations of DYNASIM3.

disability insurance and are not included in our simulations. Panis et al. (2002) find that only about 5 percent of early claimants would be disadvantaged by an increase in the EEA due to poor health, lack of pension, and physically demanding jobs. This leaves a large share of healthy workers who are potentially able to increase their work effort.

Substantial increases in work at older ages may be dependent on some amount of policy reform. Changing the symbolism of defining 62 as old age may itself have long-term effects if people begin to realize that at that age they often have one-third of their adult lives on average remaining before them. Policy reform – whether it changes symbols or incentives or both – is likely to change work behavior (although we do not examine how much in this chapter). As a bottom line, however, neither the "Pure Work Effect" nor the "Pure Benefit Cut" scenarios is realistic. Rather, reforms that include both work increases and benefit cuts are a more likely outcome.

Our examination of the potential change in retirement age brings to mind two very important problems that should be addressed. First, an increase in the retirement age for some individuals means an actual loss in defined benefits under current private plan practices. These net losses for individuals in some cases are offset by an equal and opposite net gain to employers. If one believes that employees could capture these gains, then the table understates the net gains to employees; either way it understates the net gains to the economy. Second, the actuarial adjustments in Social Security are quite generous as one moves into the future – in fact, they are more than actuarially fair from a benefit standpoint.[12] Adjustments in retirement age need to be done in a way that avoids large unintended losses by relying on old formulas for what makes actuarial sense. For example, the "Pure Work Effect" scenario not only increases taxes paid by workers, it also bumps up their average lifetime benefits.

6.6 Effects of additional work on Social Security

This section examines the extent to which working longer can help make Social Security solvent. To do this, we aggregate Social Security benefits and revenues over all individuals in the population and compare the projected total number of OASDI beneficiaries, the total benefits that will be paid to them, the total number of covered workers, and the total payroll taxes generated by their work under the baseline and alternative scenarios.

Under the DYNASIM baseline, Social Security expenditures on benefit payments will exceed income from OASDI payroll taxes beginning in 2023 (see Figure 6.3).[13] By 2045, DYNASIM projects Social Security income to be $3,791 billion and costs to be $4,430 billion – a deficit of $638 billion. If everyone worked one more year (Pure Work Effect), this would reduce the deficit by 2 percent (see Table 6.4). However, working five more years (Pure

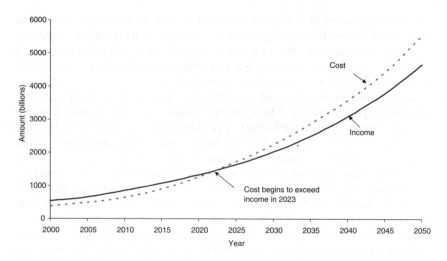

Figure 6.3 Aggregate income and costs to the Social Security system, under the baseline, 2000–2050

Source: Urban Institute tabulations of DYNASIM3.

Table 6.4 Total Social Security income, cost, Social Security deficit in 2045 by reform scenario (dollars in billions)

	Baseline	Pure work effect	Pure benefit cut	Partial work no benefit cut	Partial work and benefit cut	Full work and benefit cut
Work one more year						
Social Security earnings	$30,575	$31,161	$30,575	$30,944	$30,944	$31,161
Social Security income	3,791	3,864	3,791	3,837	3,837	3,864
Social Security cost	4,430	4,492	4,250	4,511	4,309	4,317
Social Security deficit (OASDI)	638	628	459	674	472	453
Percent change in deficit		−2%	−28%	6%	−26%	−29%
Work five more years						
Social Security earnings	$30,575	$33,481	$30,575	$32,873	$32,873	$33,481
Social Security income	3,791	4,152	3,791	4,076	4,076	4,152
Social Security cost	4,430	4,602	3,548	4,652	3,777	3,775
Social Security deficit	638	450	−243	576	−299	−377
Percent change in deficit		−29%	−138%	−10%	−147%	−159%

Notes: Includes all surviving US residents in 2045 (146,555 unweighted observations). See Appendix Table 6.A.3 for more detail.
1. Social Security earnings includes only covered earnings below the taxable maximum. Social Security income includes OASI and DI taxes. Social Security cost includes OASI and DI adult benefits.
2. The numbers in the table may not add due to rounding.

Source: The Urban Institute tabulations of DYNASIM3.

Work Effect) would reduce the deficit by 29 percent, still leaving a Social Security deficit of $450 billion. Unfortunately, working longer by itself does not close the gap between projected Social Security income and outlays.[14]

Combining additional work with changes in Social Security policy has a much larger impact on the Social Security deficit than just working longer by itself. For example, if everyone delayed retirement by five years and, at the same time, both the EEA and NRA were increased by five years (Full Work and Benefit Cut), Social Security could remain solvent beyond 2049 (the last year in the projection period). The deficit in 2045 would be reduced by 159 percent to become a surplus of $377 billion. Even under the "Partial Work and Benefit Cut" scenario, where not everyone delays retirement, the deficit in 2045 would be reduced by 147 percent to become a surplus of $299 billion. Increasing the NRA five years alone (Pure Benefit Cut) would achieve solvency, reducing the deficit by 138 percent to become a surplus of $243 billion in 2045.

Even though delaying retirement by itself (Pure Work Effect) does not close the deficit, it does reduce it by 2 percent for one more year of work and by 29 percent for five more years of work. Thus, more work allows a much higher benefit level to be sustained (at any tax rate). The Social Security earnings from one additional year of work ($586 billion) in 2045 are almost equal to the entire 2045 Social Security deficit projected under

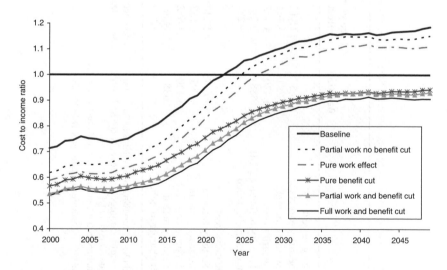

Figure 6.4 Social Security cost to income ratio under various working five more years reform scenarios, 2000–2049

Source: Urban Institute tabulations of DYNASIM3.

the baseline scenario (see Appendix Table 6.A.3). Also, the additional Social Security taxes generated by five years of work ($361 billion) is more than half of the Social Security shortfall in 2045 (see Appendix Table 6.A.3).

Figure 6.4 shows aggregate income and costs to the Social Security system under the baseline and alternate scenarios assuming workers delay retirement by 5 years. As the cost to income ratio illustrates, under the baseline, the year of insolvency is 2023. It moves to 2027 under the "Pure Work Effect" scenario, to 2025 under "Partial Work Effect No Benefit Cut" scenario, and beyond 2049 under all other scenarios.

6.7 Effects of additional work on general revenues

Additional work also increases general revenues through federal and state income taxes. While this extra revenue is not earmarked for Social Security, it does represent additional resources available to cover other government spending or to help avoid higher taxes. We add this additional revenue to our measure of deficit reduction to calculate the change in the unified deficit. If all eligible workers worked one more year (Pure Work Effect), general revenues would increase $170 billion (see Table 6.5).[15] The extra general tax revenue combined with the $10 billion Social Security deficit reduction (from Table 6.4) would generate $180 billion additional revenue – that is a 28 percent reduction in the baseline Social Security deficit, compared with only a 2 percent reduction when the extra general tax revenue is excluded. A benefit cut without any additional work (Pure Benefit Cut) also lowers the Social Security deficit, but because it produces less income tax revenue, it reduces the total reform savings.

The impact of increased general revenues would be substantially greater if everyone delayed retirement by five years. For example, under the "Pure Work Effect" scenario, the Social Security deficit would decline by 29 percent, but the unified deficit would decline by 159 percent – more than enough to pay promised Social Security benefits in 2045. In fact, accounting for the increase in general revenues, all of the five-year scenarios modeled would be solvent throughout the projection period (see Figure 6.5).

While none of our one-year scenarios generate enough additional revenue to close the long-term Social Security deficit, all of the five-year scenarios are more than sufficient. The more we can encourage workers to delay retirement, the less we will have to reduce promised benefits to achieve solvency. (The net fiscal cost will depend on the net cost of the reform option used to induce the retirement change.) More work also increases retirement income through increased personal savings and a shorter spend-down period. The less we need to cut benefits to close the spending gap, the more we can promise in Social Security. Since Social Security is still the most important asset for most retired households,

Table 6.5 Total change in income tax, Social Security deficit, and unified deficit in 2045 by reform scenario (dollars in billions)

	Pure work effect	Pure benefit cut	Partial work no benefit cut	Partial work and benefit cut	Full work and benefit cut
Work one more year					
Increase in income tax	170	−23	97	69	139
Reduction in Social Security deficit	10	180	−36	167	185
Reduction in unified deficit	180	157	62	236	324
Percent change in Social Security deficit	−2%	−28%	6%	−26%	−29%
Change in unified deficit as a percent of the Social Security deficit	−28%	−25%	−10%	−37%	−51%
Work five more years					
Increase in income tax	824	−110	610	473	684
Reduction in Social Security deficit	188	882	63	938	1,015
Reduction in unified deficit	1,012	772	672	1,411	1,700
Percent change in Social Security deficit	−29%	−138%	−10%	−147%	−159%
Change in unified deficit as a percent of the Social Security deficit	−159%	−121%	−105%	−221%	−266%

Notes: Includes all surviving US residents in 2045 (146,555 unweighted observations). See Appendix Table 6.A.3 for more detail.
1. Percent change based on projected baseline Social Security deficit of $638 billion in 2045.
2. Income tax includes both federal and state income tax.
3. The numbers in the table may not add due to rounding.

Source: The Urban Institute tabulations of DYNASIM3.

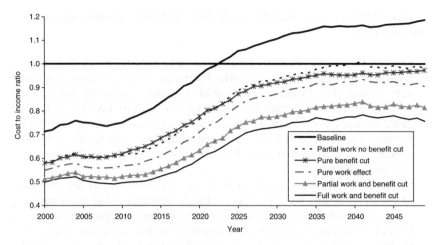

Figure 6.5 Social Security cost to income ratio under various working five more years reform scenarios including additional income tax, 2000–2049
Source: Urban Institute tabulations of DYNASIM3.

additional work goes a long way toward ensuring retirees a comfortable retirement in the decades to come.

Looking narrowly at the Social Security system and ignoring the individual's additional earnings, at any given tax rate, additional work allows Social Security on average to pay a higher level of lifetime benefits (because there are more taxes to be shared). If people also stop increasing their number of years of benefits as their lifespans increase, their annual benefits in retirement can be maintained at a higher rate. As a corollary, for any Social Security system with any (reformed or unreformed) tax rate, a higher average retirement age (however induced) means higher lifetime benefits and much higher annual benefits than in a system with a lower retirement age.

6.8 Discussion

A number of policy changes have already occurred that encourage more work at older ages. These include the increase in the Social Security NRA, the shift from defined benefit to defined contribution pensions, and the scaling back of retiree health insurance. However, these changes alone will probably not be enough. The revenue impact of additional work can significantly lessen the amount of benefit cuts necessary to make Social Security solvent. Any reform that increases work effort allows substantially higher levels of consumption for the population and higher Social Security benefits for retirees.[16]

Some options to consider that would encourage work at older ages include the following:

- Change the Social Security actuarial adjustments to boost the rewards for working longer and the penalties for retiring younger – even if actuarially neutral. For instance, one could consider decreasing early Social Security benefits and increasing delayed Social Security benefits. Note that distributional issues can be met several ways, such as providing a minimum benefit, or applying this type of actuarial adjustment only for marginal benefits above some minimum (so that only retirees with higher lifetime earnings were affected).
- Increases in the benefit entitlement age for both Social Security and Medicare. Indexing the NRA and the EEA to changes in life expectancy by itself would help reverse past trends where, because people were receiving benefits earlier and earlier relative to expected death, smaller and smaller shares of total benefits were being paid to the truly old (for example, those in the last ten years of their lives).
- Many incentives for early retirement are outside of the Social Security system. Regulatory barriers (for example, from the tax code, the Employee Retirement Income Security Act of 1974 [ERISA], and the Age Discrimination in Employment Act [ADEA]) discourage the offering of phased retirement. For instance, some regulations prevent workers from collecting their defined benefit pensions while continuing to work for the plan sponsor, forcing workers to either retire or lose substantial pension wealth (Penner, Perun and Steuerle, 2002). The Pension Protection Act of 2006 has relaxed these regulations by allowing pension plans to make distributions to participants who are 62 and still working.
- The elimination of the requirement that Medicare serve as the secondary payer for workers with employer-sponsored coverage. The high cost of medical insurance for older workers discourages employers from retaining or hiring workers over age 65. Allowing Medicare (whatever the initial age of eligibility) to be the primary payer would lower employment costs and reduce the implicit tax rate faced by older workers, increasing work incentives at older ages.

6.9 Conclusion

Previous work has shown that the economic pressures of an aging population can be relieved considerably for particular hypothetical workers if they can be encouraged to delay retirement. The choice of retirement age is the most important portfolio choice most workers will make – far exceeding in importance such issues as whether to invest their 401(k)s in stocks or bonds. Working longer increases the net output and productivity of the economy, generates additional payroll and income tax revenue, and reduces the average number of years in which people receive retirement benefits. This chapter extends that previous research by demonstrating for the population as a whole just how much of a difference additional years of work can make for retirement income, for closing the gap in the Social Security deficit, and for producing other taxes that can be used to support the government as a whole.

We find that people could increase their annual consumption at older ages by 5 percent if they worked one more year and by 25 percent if they worked five more years – assuming an annuity purchased at age 50. The gains from working longer would be even greater if retirees saved their additional wealth and annuitized it at retirement – a 9 percent increase in consumption from one more year of work and a 56 percent increase from five more years of work. Lower-income workers gain more from additional work than higher-income workers, but all workers gain.

The Social Security earnings generated from one additional year of work are almost equal to the entire 2045 Social Security shortfall (of benefits from taxes) projected under the baseline scenario. Also, the additional Social Security taxes generated by five years of work offset more than half of the Social Security shortfall in 2045. While working an additional five years reduces the Social Security deficit, it is not enough to completely erase it. However, combining additional work with a corresponding change in the NRA means that Social Security could remain solvent beyond 2049 (the last year in the projection period). Accounting for the federal and state income taxes generated from additional work, no other changes in Social Security policy would be needed for the system to remain solvent throughout the projection period. Interpolating between the one-year and five-year projections suggests that if workers would increase their work over the next 45 years roughly in proportion to their increase in life expectancy, they would likely increase payroll and income taxes by enough to wipe out almost any deficit in old age insurance payments between benefit payments and Social Security taxes currently collected.[17] In this last case, we are not arguing that all those tax dollars should be devoted to Social Security, but only how powerful the effect of additional work can be.

Appendix

Appendix Table 6.A.1 summarizes the basic processes modeled in DYNASIM, along with the data on which the module's parameters are estimated. Favreault and Smith (2004) provide a fuller description of each of the modules used in DYNASIM. More details on the modules directly related to this report are provided below.

Table 6.A.1 Summary of core processes modeled in DYNASIM

Process	Data	Form and predictors
Birth	*Estimation*: NLSY (1979–94); VS; *Target*: OCACT	7-equation parity progression model; varies on the basis of marital status; predictors include age, marriage duration, time since last birth; uses vital rates after age 39; sex of newborn assigned by race; probability of multiple birth assigned by age and race
Death	*Estimation*: NLMS (1979–81); VS (1982–97); *Target*: OCACT	3 equations; time trend from Vital Statistics 1982–1997; includes socioeconomic differentials; separate process for the disabled based on age, sex, age of disability onset, and disability duration derived from Zayatz (1999)
Schooling	NLSY (1979–94), CPS (Oct. 1995)	10 cross-tabulations based on age, race, sex, and parent's education
Leaving home	NLSY (1979–94)	3 equations; family size, parental resources, and school and work status are important predictors
First marriage	NLSY (1979–93)	8 equations; depends on age, education, race, earnings, presence of children (for females); uses vital rates at older ages
Spouse selection		Closed marriage market (spouse must be selected from among unmarried, opposite-sex persons in the population); match likelihood depends on age, race, education
Remarriage	VS (1990)	Table lookups, separate by sex for widowed and divorced
Divorce	PSID (1985–93)	Couple-level outcome; depends on marriage duration, age and presence of children, earnings of both spouses
Labor supply and earnings	*Estimation*: PSID (1980–93); NLSY (1979–89); *Target*: OCACT (LFP, wage/price growth)	Separate participation, hours decisions, wage rates for 16 age-race-sex groups; all equations have permanent and transitory error components; some wage equations correct for selection bias; key predictors include age splines, marital status, number and ages of children, job tenure, education level, region of residence, disability status, schooling status, unemployment level, and age spline – education-level interactions

Continued

Table 6.A.1 Continued

Process	Data	Form and predictors
Disability	SIPP (1990)	Separate entry (by sex)/exit (pooled) equations; include socio-economic differences (education, marital status, earnings history)
DI take-up	SIPP (1990–93)	2 separate equations (by sex) predict take-up of those eligible for disabled worker benefits (ages 19 though the normal retirement age); key predictors include age, disability status, education, marital status, recent earnings
Pensions (DB, DC, IRAs, Keoghs)	BLS (1999–2000); EBRI/ICI; SIPP (1990–93); PENSIM (PSG) and PIMS models (PBGC)	Uses SIPP self-reports on past and current pension coverage with job changes and future coverage simulated using PENSIM; uses PIMS for DB formulas (with separate procedure for DBs from government jobs); DC balances projected using SIPP self-reports of account balances and contribution rates and EBRI/ICI data asset allocations and contribution rates for new participants
Wealth	PSID (1984–94); SIPP (1990–93)	4 random-effects models for ownership/value given ownership separately for housing and non-housing wealth; additional models for spend-down after first OASDI receipt; key predictors include age, race, marital status, family size, birth cohort, dual-earner status, pension coverage, recent earnings
OASI take-up	SIPP (1990–93)	Eligibility is deterministic; 3 separate equations (separate for workers by lagged earnings, and auxiliary beneficiaries) predict take-up of those eligible for retired worker benefits (ages 62 and older); key predictors include age, disability status, education, marital status, recent earnings, pensions, lifetime earnings, and spouse characteristics; take-up of survivor benefits at 60 and 61 is deterministic (i.e., mandatory if earnings are below the exempt amount)
OASDI benefits	Rule-based	Sophisticated calculator incorporates entire work and marriage histories, auxiliary benefits for spouses/survivors and former spouses, and the retirement earnings test.

Continued

Table 6.A.1 Continued

Process	Data	Form and predictors
SSI benefits	SIPP (1990–93)	Eligibility is deterministic; 2 equations predict take-up of the aged; key predictors include demographics, state supplement, resources
Living arrangements	SIPP (1990–93)	Logistic regression that considers health, resources, and kin availability (number of children ever born); resources of co-residing family members are imputed using donor families sampled from current co-residing aged individuals in SIPP.
Immigration	PUMS 1980, 1990, 2000. INS yearbook 2001	Add target number of immigrants based on Dowhan and Duleep (2002), which are based on sex, country of origin, and age at immigration

Abbreviations: BLS = Bureau of Labor Statistics; CPS = Current Population Survey; EBRI = Employee Benefits Research Institute; DB = defined benefit; DC = defined contribution; DI = Disability Insurance; ICI = Investment Company Institute; INS = US Immigration and Naturalization Service; LFP = labor force participation; NLMS = National Longitudinal Mortality Study; NLSY = National Longitudinal Survey of Youth; OASDI = Old-Age, Survivors, and Disability Insurance; OCACT = Office of the Chief Actuary intermediate assumptions; PBGC = Pension Benefit Guarantee Corporation; PIMS = Pension Insurance.

Sample

DYNASIM begins with a self-weighting sample of 103,072 individuals from the 1990–1993 Survey of Income and Program Participation (SIPP) data. The SIPP data provide starting values for age, sex, race, education, marital status, immigrant status, earnings, pension characteristics, financial asset, home equity, earnings, Social Security, and SSI.

Earnings

Projections of pension and Social Security wealth depend on earnings. DYNASIM has historic individual earnings from 1951 to 1992 and projected earnings from 1993 to 2050. These historical data are based on earnings records that are statistically matched from longitudinal earnings histories taken from the 1968–1994 PSID and the 1973 March Current Population Survey (CPS) matched to the Social Security Administration Summary Earnings Record.[18] Projected labor supply and earnings are based on a complex set of regressions from the PSID and the National Longitudinal Survey of Youth (NLSY) and calibrated to 2005 Social Security Office of the Chief Actuary (OCACT) assumptions about future labor force participation and wage growth.

Taxes

DYNASIM has the capacity to estimate payroll taxes, as well as state and federal income taxes. The DYNASIM tax calculator accurately models current law taxes including EGTRRA, JGTRRA, the AMT, and the taxation of Social Security benefits and pension income. The tax calculator also simulates future tax law. For short-term projections (through about 2010), it holds constant the current law tax rates and adjusts the brackets as appropriate for expected inflation. It holds the Social Security taxation thresholds at their current law values, since these are not indexed for inflation. The calculator also price indexes the provisions of the alternative minimum tax (AMT) beyond the current period, even though these provisions are not currently indexed. Without this adjustment, many middle-class taxpayers would end up paying the AMT (Burman, Gale and Rohaly, 2003). Since wages are expected to increase faster than prices, the tax calculator indexes the brackets and provisions of the AMT to wages instead of prices for the long-term projections. Doing this will avoid real-bracket creep and prevent the ratio of taxes to gross domestic product (GDP) from rising steadily over time. It also continues to hold the Social Security taxation thresholds at their current law values.

Pensions

DYNASIM projects pension amounts in defined benefit (DB) plans and defined contribution (DC) plans, as well as from IRA and Keogh plans. Pensions are based on an individual's entire work history (real and simulated) up to the projected retirement date. Baseline information regarding pension coverage on current and past jobs is based on SIPP self-reports. To impute future job changes and pension coverage on future jobs, DYNASIM incorporates data on synthetic work histories from the Policy Simulation Group's PENSIM model, developed for the Department of Labor, Pension, and Welfare Benefits Administration.[19]

DYNASIM next projects pension benefits from past, current, and future jobs. In general, DB plan benefits are projected using pension plan formulas from the Pension Benefit Guarantee Corporation (PBGC)'s Pension Insurance Modeling System (PIMS). DC account balances are projected using self-reported information on the SIPP regarding account balances and contribution rates, as well as asset allocations and future contribution rates that vary by age according to EBRI/ICI data on 401(k) asset allocations (VanDerhei et al., 1999). The proportion of initial contributions and balances allocated to equities varies by age category. Then, every five years, the model rebalances the portfolios according to the allocation strategy for the individual's attained age category. Subsequent contributions are allocated to match the allocation strategy of the attained age, if different.

DYNASIM accumulates DC account balances assuming a Consumer Price Index (CPI) growth rate of 2.8 percent (the growth rate assumed by OCACT), a real rate of return for stocks of 6.50 percent, and a real rate of return for bonds of 3.30 percent. One percent is subtracted from each of the stock and bond real rates of return to reflect administrative costs. Investment experience varies by individual and by year, by setting the rates stochastically (assuming a standard deviation of 17.28 percent for stocks and 2.14 percent for bonds).

The SIPP also includes information regarding IRA/Keogh account balances and contributions. Similar to DC plans, IRA/Keogh account balances are accumulated to the retirement date, along with any new contributions and interest earnings. IRA/Keogh contribution rates are allowed to vary over time by age and earnings, using the same method used for DC plans. IRA/Keogh contributions are capped according to the legal limits that vary by year. IRA/Keogh assets are allocated the same way as DC assets and rates of return are set stochastically using the same method as that used for DC plans. Only those with IRA/Keogh coverage at the time of the SIPP interview have IRAs/Keoghs. No new IRA/Keogh participation is simulated in DYNASIM.

Social Security benefits

DYNASIM also includes a detailed Social Security benefit calculator that uses earnings and marital histories to estimate Social Security benefits – either retired-worker, spouse, or survivor benefits. The current benefit calculator is based on the 2005 OCACT assumptions about future price and wage growth. In each year, from the projected year of first benefit receipt until the projected year of death, DYNASIM computes a respondent's Social Security benefit that reflects his or her earnings and marital history at that point in time. The calculator first establishes benefit eligibility based on personal characteristics such as age, number of covered quarters, disability status, marital status, and length of marriage. For those who qualify, the model computes Social Security benefits – either retired worker, spouse, divorced spouse, or survivor benefits. The calculator then checks an individual's take-up age against his or her NRA, reducing benefits for those who retire before their NRA and increasing benefits for those who retire later. Social Security estimates are based on the assumption that current-law benefits will be payable throughout the projection period. However, the Social Security OASDI Trust Funds are projected to be exhausted by 2041 and OCACT estimates that benefits would need to be reduced by 12.8 percent starting in 2005 in order for the trust funds to remain solvent (Board of Trustees, 2005). If the benefit cuts are delayed, the average percentage reduction would need to be larger. Our Social Security wealth estimates are based on the assumption that future retirees will receive the current law benefits they were promised, not the benefits that current trust fund receipts will finance in the long run. But the model is capable of simulating the effects of alternative benefit levels.

Table 6.A.2 Mean respondent wealth and annuity income in 2049 under current law and estimated change under alternate reform scenarios (2006 $)

	Baseline	Pure work effect	Pure benefit cut	Partial work no benefit cut	Partial work and benefit cut	Full work and benefit cut
Work one more year						
Social Security	199,378	205,315	185,796	203,055	189,563	191,804
DB pensions	39,576	39,155	39,576	39,550	39,550	39,155
DC pensions	54,633	56,661	54,633	55,760	55,760	56,661
Earnings	477,862	513,441	477,862	501,860	501,860	513,441
Federal/State income taxes	110,982	119,718	109,569	116,438	114,970	118,089
Payroll taxes	34,491	36,981	34,491	36,126	36,126	36,981
Total net wealth	625,976	657,873	613,807	647,661	635,637	645,991
Annual annuity at age 50	26,570	27,887	26,056	27,452	26,944	27,386
Annual annuity at retirement		28,972	25,635	28,067	27,124	28,020
Percent change in net wealth		5.1%	−1.9%	3.5%	1.5%	3.2%
Change total net wealth		31,897	−12,169	21,685	9,661	20,016
Change annual annuity at age 50		1,317	−515	882	374	816
Change annual annuity at retirement		2,402	−936	1,497	554	1,449

Continued

Table 6.A.2 Continued

	Baseline	Pure work effect	Pure benefit cut	Partial work no benefit cut	Partial work and benefit cut	Full work and benefit cut
Work five more years						
Social Security	199,378	228,242	132,816	222,480	154,651	158,694
DB pensions	39,576	37,060	39,576	40,610	40,610	37,060
DC pensions	54,633	65,492	54,633	62,095	62,095	65,492
Earnings	477,862	658,520	477,862	623,259	623,259	658,520
Federal/State income taxes	110,982	155,139	104,676	145,156	136,712	146,239
Payroll taxes	34,491	47,207	34,491	44,596	44,596	47,207
Total net wealth	625,976	786,968	565,720	758,692	699,307	726,320
Annual annuity at age 50	26,570	33,258	24,021	32,052	29,538	30,698
Annual annuity at retirement		41,458	21,953	37,834	32,518	35,563
Percent change in net wealth		26%	−10%	21%	12%	16%
Change total net wealth		160,992	−60,256	132,716	73,331	100,344
Change annual annuity at age 50		6,688	−2,549	5,482	2,968	4,127
Change annual annuity at retirement		14,888	−4,617	11,264	5,948	8,993

Notes: Based on 17,547 unweighted observations of persons who are alive in 2049 and retired and receiving Social Security benefits.
1. Annuity at age 50 is total net wealth divided by the real annuity factor at age 50.
2. Annuity at retirement is the change in total net wealth between the baseline and alternative scenario, grown from age 50 until the later of retirement or Social Security take-up age by a real interest rate of 2 percent, divided it by the real annuity factor that corresponds to that age, and added to the baseline annuity.

Source: The Urban Institute tabulations of DYNASIM3.

Table 6.A.3 Aggregate impact of working one and five years longer on Social Security and general revenues (population in millions and amounts in billions)

	Baseline	Pure work effect	Pure benefit cut	Partial work no benefit cut	Partial work and benefit cut	Full work and benefit cut
Work one more year						
Total population	369	369	369	369	369	369
Covered worker population	188	191	188	190	190	191
Retiree population	85	82	85	84	83	82
Total earnings	32,284	32,929	32,284	32,706	32,706	32,929
Taxable earnings	30,575	31,161	30,575	30,944	30,944	31,161
OASI tax	3,241	3,303	3,241	3,280	3,280	3,303
DI tax	550	561	550	557	557	561
Total OASDI tax	3,791	3,864	3,791	3,837	3,837	3,864
Total HI tax	887	904	887	897	897	904
Total income tax	8,438	8,608	8,414	8,535	8,507	8,577
Total revenue (OASDI+Δincome tax)	3,791	4,034	3,768	3,935	3,906	4,003
Total benefits	4,430	4,492	4,250	4,511	4,309	4,317
Social Security deficit (OASDI tax)	638	628	459	674	472	453
Social Security deficit (total revenue)	638	458	482	577	403	314

Continued

Table 6.A.3 Continued

	Baseline	Pure work effect	Pure benefit cut	Partial work no benefit cut	Partial work and benefit cut	Full work and benefit cut
Work five more years						
Total population	369	369	369	369	369	369
Covered worker population	188	203	188	199	199	203
Retiree population	85	71	84	74	73	70
Total earnings	32,284	35,454	32,284	34,823	34,823	35,454
Taxable earnings	30,575	33,481	30,575	32,873	32,873	33,481
OASI tax	3,241	3,549	3,241	3,485	3,485	3,549
DI tax	550	603	550	592	592	603
Total OASDI tax	3,791	4,152	3,791	4,076	4,076	4,152
Total HI tax	887	971	887	953	953	971
Total income tax	8,438	9,262	8,328	9,047	8,911	9,122
Total revenue (OASDI + Δincome tax)	3,791	4,976	3,681	4,686	4,549	4,836
Total benefits	4,430	4,602	3,548	4,652	3,777	3,775
Social Security deficit (OASDI tax)	638	450	−243	576	−299	−377
Social Security deficit (total revenue)	638	−374	−133	−34	−773	−1,061

Notes: Includes all surviving US residents in 2045 (146,555 unweighted observations). Total Revenue includes OASI, DI, and the change in federal and state income tax. HI tax is not included.

Source: The Urban Institute tabulations of DYNASIM3.

Notes

* The research reported herein was performed pursuant to a grant from the US Social Security Administration (SSA) to the Center for Retirement Research at Boston College (CRR). The opinions and conclusions are solely those of the authors and should not be construed as representing the opinions or policy of SSA or any agency of the Federal Government or of the CRR, or the Urban Institute, its board, or its sponsors. The authors thank Richard Johnson for his advice on this and related projects.

1. DYNASIM uses OCACT 2005 economic and demographic assumptions including labor force participation rates, average earnings, and mortality.
2. Some of the implicit taxes are returned to workers in the form of higher Social Security benefits and pension income in retirement. Saved earnings from additional employment will increase consumption without increasing taxable income.
3. Social Security reduces benefits by 5/9 of 1 percent for each month that benefits are received before the NRA, up to 36 months. The benefit is further reduced by 5/12 of 1 percent for every month before the NRA in excess of 36. Benefits are increased by 3/4 of 1 percent for each month that initial take-up exceeds the NRA, up to age 70. No credit is given for delaying initial take-up beyond age 70.
4. Increasing the NRA as a way of cutting benefits is not unprecedented. The 1983 Social Security Amendments raised the NRA from age 65 to 67 over a 22-year period beginning in 2000. This provision was designed to increase the benefit reduction at age 62 from 20 percent in 1999 to 30 percent in 2022, and to institute a reduction in benefits at age 65 by as much as 13.4 percent in 2022. In our simulation, 62-year-old claimants in 2022 would face a 35 percent benefit reduction if the NRA were increased by one additional year, and a 45 percent benefit reduction if it were increased by five additional years.
5. The early entitlement age, currently age 62, is the earliest age that individuals may take up Social Security benefits. However, annual benefits are then reduced to adjust for the fact that early retirees receive benefits over a longer period.
6. In order to analyze the change in net wealth and annual future consumption made possible by additional work, we first define total retirement wealth (TW) as the sum of Social Security wealth (SW), defined benefit pension wealth (DBPW), defined contribution account balances (DCPW), and earnings wealth (EW), less federal and state income taxes (IT) and payroll taxes (PT): TW = SW + DBPW + DCPW + EW − IT − PT.
7. The annuity is price-indexed (inflation protected) and is based on the average mortality by age, cohort, sex, race, and education. The real rate of return is 2 percent.
8. DYNASIM has been used to simulate how potential changes to Social Security will affect the future retirement benefits of at-risk populations (Favreault and Sammartino, 2002; Favreault, Sammartino and Steuerle, 2002), how annuitization affects outcomes under a Social Security system with personal accounts (Uccello et al., 2003), the potential retirement consequences of rapid work effort growth among low-wage, single mothers in the late 1990s (Johnson, Favreault and Goldwyn, 2003), the implications of recent earnings inequality patterns for future retirement income (Smith, 2002), and patterns of wealth accumulation and retirement preparedness (Butrica and Uccello, 2004).
9. Reported numbers include Social Security beneficiaries in 2049 age 60 and older. We also ran these analyses for the cohorts born between 1964 and 1966 and found very similar results. For this reason, we present only the results of the larger sample.

10. Appendix Table 6.A.2 provides more details on how the sources of net wealth change with both one year and five years of additional work.
11. Panis et al. (2002) is based on the first five waves (1992, 1994, 1996, 1998 and 2000) of the Health and Retirement Study among individuals born between 1931 and 1941.
12. Given expected increases in life expectancy of future retirees, the actuary reduction for early benefits does not reduce benefits enough to compensate for the additional years of expected benefits. The reduction factors are based on life expectancy of earlier cohorts.
13. OCACT projects that Social Security outlays will first exceed revenues in 2017 (Board of Trustees, 2005). The Congressional Budget Office projects this year to be 2020 (Congressional Budget Office, 2005). Our estimates will differ from either of these sources because (1) DYNASIM does not project children's Social Security benefits, (2) our measure of Social Security revenue includes only payroll taxes and excludes interest and taxes on benefits, and (3) there are small differences in lifetime earnings of workers and their spouses.
14. Of course, increasing work beyond five years may be enough to close the gap. But this policy seems unrealistic.
15. Additional work also increases HI taxes. We do not include the additional HI revenue in our measure of revenue gains from work. The HI values are reported in appendix Table 6.A.3.
16. Although some reform options would require additional government spending, they would improve work incentives at older ages.
17. According to OCACT, the life expectancy in 2004 was 74.6 years for men and 79.6 years for women (Board of Trustees, 2005). Under their intermediate assumptions, life expectancies in 2050 will increase by 4.8 years for men and 3.6 years for women.
18. Smith, Scheuren, and Berk (2001) show that these earnings histories match up quite well with actual earnings histories that are available on a confidential basis at the Social Security Administration.
19. See Holmer, Janney, and Cohen (2006) for more detail on the PENSIM model.

References

Bakija, J. (2005) "Documentation for *IncTaxCalc*: A Federal-State Personal Income Tax Calculator Covering the Years 1900–2002," unpublished manuscript.

Board of Trustees (2005) "The 2005 Annual Report of the Board of Trustees of the Federal Old-Age and Survivors Insurance and Disability Insurance Trust Funds," (Washington, DC: Social Security Administration). http://www.ssa.gov/OACT/ TR/TR05/tr05.pdf

Burman, L. E., W. G. Gale and J. Rohaly (2003) "The Expanding Reach of the Individual Alternative Minimum Tax," *Journal of Economic Perspectives* 17(2): 173–186.

Butrica, B. A., R. W. Johnson, K. E. Smith and C. E. Steuerle (2004) "Does Work Pay at Older Ages?" (Washington, DC: The Urban Institute). http://www.urban.org/url.cfm?ID=411121

Butrica, B. A. and C. E. Uccello (2004) "How Will Boomers Fare at Retirement?" Final Report to the AARP Public Policy Institute (Washington, DC: AARP).

Calvo, E. (2006) "Does Working Longer Make People Healthier and Happier?" Work Opportunities for Older Americans, Series 2. Chestnut Hill, MA: Center for Retirement Research at Boston College. http://www.bc.edu/centers/crr/ wob_2.shtml.

Coile, C. and J. Gruber (2004) "The Effects of Social Security on Retirement in the United States," in David A. Wise (ed.) *Social Security Programs and Retirement Around the World: Micro Estimation* (Chicago: University of Chicago Press), pp. 691–730.

CBO (2005) "Updated Long-Term Projections for Social Security," (Washington, DC: The Congress of the United States, Congressional Budget Office). http://www.cbo.gov/ftpdocs/60xx/doc6064/03-03-LongTermProjections.pdf

Diamond, P. and J. Gruber (1999) "Social Security and Retirement in the US" in Jonathan Gruber and David A. Wise (eds.) *Social Security and Retirement Around the World* (Chicago: University of Chicago Press), pp. 437–474.

Dowhan, D. and H. Duleep (2002) "Projecting Immigrants for MINT," (Washington, DC: Social Security Administration).

Favreault, M. M. and F. J. Sammartino (2002) "Impact of Social Security Reform on Low-Income and Older Women," Final Report to the AARP Public Policy Institute (Washington, DC: AARP).

Favreault, M. M., F. J. Sammartino and C. E. Steuerle (2002) *Social Security and the Family Addressing Unmet Needs in an Underfunded System* (Washington, DC: Urban Institute Press).

Favreault, M. M. and K. E. Smith (2004) "A Primer on the Dynamic Simulation of Income Model (DYNASIM3)," Discussion Paper, The Retirement Project (Washington, DC: The Urban Institute).

Gokhale, J., L. J. Kotlikoff and A. Sluchynsky (2002) "Does It Pay to Work?" NBER Working Paper No. 9096 (Cambridge, MA: National Bureau of Economic Research).

Holmer, M. R., A. Janney and B. Cohen (2006) "Overview of PENSIM," Report for the US Department of Labor, Employee Benefits Security Administration. http://www.polsim.com/overview.pdf.

Johnson, R. W., A. J. Davidoff and K. Perese (2003) "Health Insurance Costs and Early Retirement Decisions," *Industrial and Labor Relations Review* 56(4): 716–729.

Johnson, R. W., M. M. Favreault and J. H. Goldwyn (2003) "Employment, Social Security, and Future Retirement Outcomes for Single Mothers," CRR Working Paper No. 2003–14 (Chestnut Hill, MA: Center for Retirement Research at Boston College). http://www.bc.edu/centers/crr/wp_2003-14.shtml

Lumsdaine, R., J. H. Stock and D. A. Wise (1992) "Three Models of Retirement: Computational Complexity Versus Predictive Validity," in David A. Wise (ed.) *Topics in the Economics of Aging* (Chicago, IL: University of Chicago Press), pp. 19–57.

Lumsdaine, R., J. H. Stock and D. A. Wise (1994) "Pension Plan Provisions and Retirement: Men and Women, Medicare and Models," in David A. Wise (ed.) *Studies in the Economics of Aging* (Chicago, IL: University of Chicago Press), pp. 183–212.

Panis, C., M. Hurd, D. Loughran, J. Zissimopoulos, S. Haider, P. St. Clair (2002) "The Effects of Changing Social Security Administration's Early Entitlement Age and the Normal Retirement Age," Report for the Social Security Administration (Santa Monica, CA: RAND).

Penner, R. G., P. Perun and E. C. Steuerle (2002) "Legal and Institutional Impediments to Partial Retirement and Part-Time Work by Older Workers," (Washington, DC: The Urban Institute). http://www.urban.org/url.cfm?ID=410587

Samwick, A. A. (1998) "New Evidence on Pensions, Social Security, and the Timing of Retirement," *Journal of Public Economics* 70(2): 207–236.

Smith, K. E. (2002) "How Will Recent Patterns of Earnings Inequality Affect Future Retirement Incomes?" Final Report for AARP (Washington, DC: The Urban Institute).

Smith, K. E., F. Scheuren and J. Berk (2001) "Adding Historical Earnings to the Survey of Income and Program Participation (SIPP)," in *2001 Proceedings, Statistical Computing Section*. [CD-ROM]. American Statistical Association.

Steuerle, C. E. (2005) "Alternatives to Strengthen Social Security," Testimony before the US Committee on Ways and Means of the US House of Representatives, May 12.

Stock, J. H. and D. A. Wise (1990) "Pensions, the Option Value of Work, and Retirement," *Econometrica* 58(5): 1151–1180.

Uccello, C. E., M. M. Favreault, K. E. Smith and L. H. Thompson (2003) "Simulating the Distributional Consequences of Personal Accounts: Sensitivity to Annuitization Options," (Washington, DC: The Urban Institute). http://www.urban.org/url.cfm?ID=410960

VanDerhei, J., R. Galer, C. Quick and J. Rea (1999) "401(k) Plan Asset Allocation, Account Balances, and Loan Activity," EBRI Issue Brief No. 205 (Washington, DC: Employee Benefit Research Institute).

Comments to Chapter 6
Lucie G. Schmidt

This chapter is one in a series of papers by researchers at the Urban Institute who are using a microsimulation model to look at a variety of interesting policy issues. For many of these questions – those that require complex forecasting of behavior and the modeling of interactions between demographic and labor market outcomes – these microsimulation models can be extremely useful. In this chapter, the authors examine how an additional one or five years of work, under a number of different policy scenarios, affect both individual-level outcomes, such as total net wealth, its components, and its annuitized value, as well as macro-level outcomes such as the Social Security deficit.

The microsimulation model provides a useful and informative comparison of outcomes under 5 scenarios: (1) full additional work with no benefit cut; (2) benefit cut but no additional work; (3) partial additional work with no benefit cut; (4) partial additional work with benefit cut; and (5) full additional work with benefit cut. Each of these scenarios is a different combination of varying two policy levers: first, the amount of additional work; and second, whether or not there is a benefit cut. In the "full additional work" scenario, all individuals are projected to increase both their retirement age and their Social Security take-up age by one or five years. In the "partial additional work" scenario, the authors project an increase in work effort only for those who originally were predicted to retire before the new early eligibility age (EEA). Finally, in the "benefit cut" simulations, the authors examine the effects of an across-the-board cut in benefits, represented by an increase in the normal retirement age (NRA), which forces an actuarial reduction in the benefit at every age of retirement.

The authors find that the choice of retirement age is important for individuals' financial well-being, but that a pure work change will not eliminate the Social Security deficit. However, they find that combining a work increase with a benefit cut could increase the solvency of the Social Security system.

Comments

The chapter would benefit from clarification of the scenarios examined. For example, how should we think about the additional work scenarios? Should we think of these as a voluntary increase in work, or as a policy-induced increase in work through changes in the EEA/NRA? Second, the authors simulate "delayed retirement" by increasing both the predicted retirement age and the predicted Social Security take-up age by either one or five years. The example given by the authors is that an individual who is projected to retire at age 60 and take up benefits at 62 is now projected to retire at 61 and take up benefits at 63. But if the individual who was projected to retire at age 60 was only taking up Social Security at age 62 because this is the EEA, and would actually prefer to take up earlier, it seems equally plausible that the "delayed retirement" scenario would mean retirement at age 61 and benefit take up at age 62. So the authors report this as the result of increasing work by a year, but it is really the result of increasing both work and take-up age by a year. This needs to be clarified in the text.

In addition, the authors model an across-the-board benefit cut as an increase in the NRA. This approach seems to entangle the two dimensions under consideration – increasing work and decreasing benefits. I would have preferred to see this modeled as a decrease in benefits holding the NRA constant. I am sure there is a good modeling reason for doing this the way it was done, but it would be useful for that to be laid out for the reader. The current approach leads to things like Scenario #3, in which the EEA is increased by either one or five years, with no change in the NRA. What does it mean to increase the EEA 5 years but not change the NRA?

More general comments

1. Does a delay in retirement in the context of the microsimulation model affect decisions made before the retirement date?

If I choose to delay retirement for a year, but I know that I will be delaying retirement (and therefore having fewer years of retirement to finance), I might change my preretirement behavior on a number of dimensions. It was not clear from the chapter exactly what assumptions were made when conducting this thought experiment.

2. General equilibrium effects of the increase in labor supply?

Simulations that involve all individuals working an additional year or 5 years increase labor supply by a *large* number of person-years. The authors should take into account the potential general equilibrium effects that this increase in labor supply may have on wages. These effects could be added in – some estimate could be made of the decrease in wages and who it would likely affect (depending on the substitutability of older workers for younger workers). If older workers' wages fall, then the positive effects on consumption and well-being for older workers are overstated. If instead the wages of younger individuals fall, this will also have tax and transfer implications.

3. Automatic responses versus behavioral responses

The model suggests that an increase in work leads to an increase in wealth. However, it would be useful to clarify which responses in the model are automatic and which are behavioral choices. The effect of an extra year of work on Social Security wealth is automatic, conditional on the rules of the system. But the effect of an extra year of work on DC pension contributions would depend upon the choices of the individual. The model assumes that workers with DC pension plans, if they work for an additional year, will continue to build up the assets in these accounts through their own and possibly their employers' contributions.

If individuals work an additional year, they could consume all the additional wealth and not save any. Furthermore, related to my earlier comment, if they planned on working an additional year, they could actually reduce savings in previous years, knowing that they would have one additional year to work (and one fewer year of retirement to finance). Explicitly laying out the mechanisms through which each of these measures of wealth increases would be useful.

4. Consumption ≠ well-being

The chapter is viewed as "... demonstrating for the population as a whole just how much of a difference additional years of work can make for individual well-being." However, consumption and "individual well-being" are not necessarily the same thing. Increased consumption does not necessarily equal increased well-being if we appropriately value leisure and nonmarket production. Nonmarket production could be particularly important if we consider caregiving, either of a spouse, or the increasing tendency in some demographic groups for individuals to care for grandchildren. A related point is that we might expect the disutility associated with work to increase with age, as the health of an individual or their spouse deteriorates.

5. Differential impacts by group

The introduction of the chapter asks "How would delaying retirement influence individual Social Security benefits in particular and retirement income and adequacy more generally? What is the differential impact by age, marital status, race, education, and income level?"

The chapter addresses the differential effects by income quintile, but does not look at these other dimensions yet. We can guess at the direction of some of these effects on the basis of what we know about the distribution of replacement rates and life expectancies, but it will be interesting to be able to actually compare magnitudes. These dimensions could be particularly important given demographic differences in health status and the propensities to engage in nonmarket production.

7
Net Intergenerational Transfers from an Increase in Social Security Benefits

Li Gan, Guan Gong, and Michael Hurd

7.1 Introduction

When the age of death is uncertain, individuals will leave bequests even if they have no desired bequests, simply because they will hold wealth against the possibility of living longer. Bequests are accidental. Starting from a baseline level of Social Security benefits, an increase in benefits will cause consumption to increase. However, consumption may not increase by as much as the increase in Social Security, which would cause wealth to be greater than under the baseline scenario. The higher wealth levels would translate into greater bequests, even when there is no bequest motive and all bequests are accidental. Therefore, an increase in Social Security benefits may not be a complete transfer from the younger generation to the older generation: some of the increase in benefits may be bequeathed back to the younger generation. Whether this happens depends on the form of the utility function, the amount of bequeathable wealth, and whether there is a bequest motive. The objective of this chapter is to quantify how much of an increase in Social Security benefits would be bequeathed back to the younger generation. We will use an estimated life-cycle model for consumption by singles.[1]

7.2 Life-cycle model

A broad characterization of the situation at retirement is the following. People reach retirement with an array of economic resources: a claim on Social Security; a claim on Medicare; pension rights; and bequeathable wealth. An appropriate theoretical framework to analyze this situation is the life cycle model of consumption that goes back to Modigliani and Brumberg (1954), with extensions to account for a bequest motive (Hurd, 1989). In life-cycle models of consumption under uncertainty, individuals make choices in the current period on the basis of current information and beliefs so as to maximize the expected discounted present value of utility. The expected discounted present value of utility is the sum of utility in the current period based on current choices and the current state of the world, and the expected discounted present value of future utility, which depends on the probability of survival to each future period, the return to saving, budget constraints, and optimal consumption choices at each period in the future, and the value of financial bequests at the death.

We base the analysis on a somewhat restricted version of the life-cycle model. Life-time utility is based on time-separable utility from consumption and from bequests (Yaari, 1965); the only uncertainty is date of death; resources are initial bequeathable wealth, rights to pensions, and a stream of annuities such as Social Security; bequeathable wealth cannot become negative, and, therefore, borrowing against future annuities is not allowed. Because it does not have a provision for the choice to work, it is applicable only to respondents after they enter retirement or disability.

7.3 Model of consumption by singles

These assumptions lead to the following behavioral model for a single person: maximize expected lifetime utility Ω over the consumption path $\{c_t\}$

$$\Omega = \int_0^N u(c_t)e^{-\rho t}a_t dt + \int_0^N V(w_t)e^{-\rho t}m_t dt. \qquad [1]$$

The first term is expected discounted utility from consumption, where

$u(\cdot)$ = the utility flow from consumption;
ρ = the subjective time rate of discount;
a_t = the probability of being alive at t; and
N = the maximum remaining years of life ($a_N = 0$).

The second term is the expected discounted utility of bequests, where

$V(\cdot)$ = utility from bequests that may depend on the personal characteristics of potential inheritors such as the economic status of any children in an altruistic or strategic bequest model;
w_t = bequeathable wealth at t;
m_t = probability density of dying at t.

The constraints on the maximization are as follows: initial bequeathable wealth w_0 is given; the nonnegativity constraint $w_t \geq 0$ $\forall t$; and the rate at which bequeathable wealth changes is given by

$$\frac{dw_t}{dt} = rw_t - c_t + A_t, \qquad [2]$$

in which r = real interest rate (constant and known) and A_t = flow of annuities at time t.

The nonnegativity constraint on bequeathable wealth can be justified by a legal ban on borrowing against Social Security benefits. In addition, in the data very few are observed with negative wealth, and those few tend to have negative wealth as the result of negative business wealth. This is likely to be the result of unanticipated losses rather than borrowing for consumption purposes. The importance of taking account of the corner solution ($w_t = 0$) is seen from the fraction of single elderly with approximately zero nonhousing wealth. In 1993, about 19 percent of those aged 70–79 and about 40 percent of those aged 90–100 had wealth of less than $1,000.

The model places considerable emphasis on annuity income, which is based on the empirical observation of its importance: in 1994, 94 percent of the elderly (65 or over) had some annuity or pension income (including Social Security); 79 percent had more than half of their income from annuities or pensions.

The solution to the single's problem is (Hurd, 1989)

$$\begin{cases} \dfrac{du_t}{dt} = u_t(h_t + \rho - r) - h_t V_t & \text{for } w_t > 0; \\ c_t = A_t & \text{for } w_t = 0, \end{cases} \qquad [3]$$

where w_0 is given and

$u_t = du(c_t)/dc_t$ = marginal utility of consumption at time t;
$h_t = m_t/a_t$ = mortality risk (mortality hazard) at time t; and
$V_t = dV(w_t)/dw_t$ = marginal utility of bequests at time t.

The model does not admit an analytical solution because of the boundary condition and because of the bequest motive. The optimal consumption path must be found numerically: conditional on the specification of the utility function, the equation of motion of consumption is given implicitly by [3], and the level is found from the lifetime budget constraint.

A typical solution as found in prior estimation based on the Retirement History Survey (Hurd, 1989) is shown in Figure 7.1. This is the consumption path for a man aged 75 with initial bequeathable wealth of $100,000 and Social Security income of $10,000. By age 92 all bequeathable wealth has been consumed and the consumption path will follow the path of Social Security.

Once the optimal consumption path has been found, predicted wealth $\{\hat{w}\}$ is calculated from the equation of motion of wealth [2]. Therefore, for each

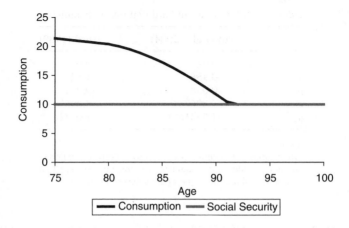

Figure 7.1 Consumption path
Source: Retirement History Survey (Hurd, 1989).

individual the model can be used to forecast consumption and wealth. Income can be forecast from observed annuity income and from capital income as rw_t.

7.4 Estimation of the model

In previous work we have estimated the model of consumption by singles (Gan, Gong et al., 2004). We specified that the utility function is the constant relative risk aversion utility function

$$u(c) = \frac{1}{1-\gamma} c^{1-\gamma}$$

and that the bequest function is

$$V(w) = (\alpha_0 + \alpha_1 n)w$$

if n, the number of children, is positive; otherwise $V(w) = 0$. We estimated this model over two waves of data from the Asset and Health Dynamics study (AHEAD).[2]

An important determinant of the consumption path is mortality risk h_t in [3]. While prior work simply used life tables to construct h_t for each individual, we use individual reports on subjective survival probabilities

Table 7.1 Interest rate and utility function parameters

	Gan et al., (2004)	Hurd (1989)
r	0.04	0.03
γ	0.986	1.12
ρ	0.058	−0.011
α_0	$3.8067e^{-7}$	$3.8067e^{-7a}$
a_1	$1.0431e^{-6}$	$1.0431e^{-6a}$

Notes
[a] Hurd estimated a bequest parameter to indicate any children, but not an additional parameter for the number. For that reason we will use the bequest parameters from Gan.

(Hurd and McGarry, 1995, 2002). A subjective survival probability as measured in AHEAD is a respondent's estimate of the probability of surviving to a "target" age. For example, a 71-year-old would be asked about his or her subjective probability of surviving to age 85, while a 77-year-old would be asked about survival to age 90. Following Gan et al., (2005) we estimated individualized survivor curves that depend on both the life table and on subjective survival. Briefly, we used a statistical method to combine them such that someone who reported subjective survival chances greater than the life table survival chances at the target age would be given an individualized survival curve that is greater than the life table curve at all ages. In our estimation at each age h_t depended on the individualized survival curve.

Our preferred estimation results produced the parameter values conditional on an assumed real interest rate of 0.04 as shown in Table 7.1. These differ from those in Hurd (1989), which are also shown in the Table. In our simulations we will use both sets of parameters.

7.5 Expected bequests

Our model solves for the optimal consumption path conditional on initial bequeathable wealth, Social Security benefits (Social Security wealth), age, sex, and the number of children. Then, using the equation of motion of wealth we find the optimal path of bequeathable wealth. From these paths we can calculate the expected present value of consumption and of Social Security benefits (Social Security wealth). A bequest happens when someone holding wealth dies. The expected bequest at some future time τ conditional on surviving to time t is just $w_\tau m_\tau$, that is wealth held at τ times the probability of dying at τ. The expected present value of bequests is just the discounted sum of the $w_\tau m_\tau$. From these calculations we form a lifetime balance sheet. On the receipt side there is initial bequeathable wealth plus Social

Security wealth; on the expenditure side there is the expected present value of consumption and the expected present value of bequests.

Figure 7.2 shows the consumption and wealth paths for a single woman initially aged 65. Her initial bequeathable wealth is $100,000 and Social Security income is $10,000. The consumption path in this figure differs from the consumption path in Figure 7.1 because it pertains to a woman aged 65 and because it is based on the parameters in Table 1 of Gan et al., (2004).

Our method of finding the effect of changes of Social Security on bequests is to first conduct a simulation such as that which produced the wealth and consumption paths in Figure 7.2. Then resimulate the model but increase Social Security benefits by some given amount. On comparison of the change in the expected present value of bequests, the expected present value of consumption and Social Security wealth will show how much of the increase has been used for bequests and for consumption.

Figure 7.3 shows an example of these simulations. The baseline or initial simulation is for a woman aged 65 with three children. The parameters are from Table 1 (Hurd, 1989). The baseline wealth, consumption, and Social Security benefits paths are shown in the thicker lines. Baseline Social Security is $10,000 per year; baseline initial wealth is $100,000. Baseline initial consumption is about $12,900 per year and increases to $17,100 at age 81 and then declines until age 94 when wealth is exhausted. After this age she would consume $10,000 per year. Wealth declines continuously until age 94 when it reaches zero. Under this scenario expected bequests are $30,200.

The simulation results with Social Security benefits of $20,000 are shown in the thin lines. Initial consumption is $21,000 under this scenario. It increases until age 82 after which it declines until age 93 when wealth is exhausted. Should this woman survive until 93 she would consume Social

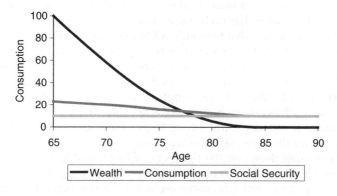

Figure 7.2 Consumption and wealth paths
Source: Table 1 (Hurd, 1989).

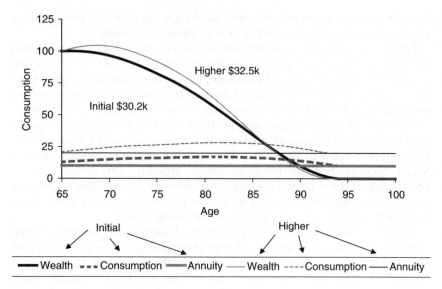

Figure 7.3 Response to increase in Social Security
Source: Table 1 of Gan et al. (2004).

Security benefits of $20,000 until the end of her life. Wealth increases until age 69 after which it declines continuously reaching zero at age 93. Under this scenario the expected present value of bequests is $32,500 thousand. Even though wealth is exhausted sooner under this scenario, bequests are greater because more wealth is held at ages 75–85 when the probability of death is large.

Table 7.2 shows a summary of these kinds of simulations. The table pertains to a 65-year-old man. In the two left-side panels are results under the assumption that he has no bequest motive (no children). In the left-most panel his initial bequeathable wealth is $100,000 and annual Social Security benefits are $10,000. The expected present value (discounted at a 4 percent real interest rate) of Social Security benefits (Social Security wealth) is $107,600. According to the estimated optimal consumption path the expected present value of consumption is $193,200 and the expected present value of bequests is just $12,800. Thus the model predicts that 12.8 percent of initial wealth will be bequeathed, and because there is no bequest motive these bequests are accidental.

The next panel shows similar figures but when Social Security benefits are $20,000 each year. Social Security wealth is twice as large, but the expected present value of consumption increases by $109,000 which is more than the increase in Social Security wealth. Because the lifetime budget constraint must be satisfied, the expected present value of bequests must decline, and,

Table 7.2 Bequeathable wealth, Social Security benefits, expected present value of consumption and bequests (thousands) 65-year-old male

	No children		Three children	
	Initial Social Security	Increased Social Security	Initial Social Security	Increased Social Security
Initial bequeathable wealth	100.0	100.0	100.0	100.0
Initial Social Security benefits	10.0	20.0	10.0	20.0
Social Security wealth	107.6	215.3	107.6	215.3
Expected PV consumption	193.2	302.2	193.0	302.1
Expected PV bequests	12.8	10.1	13.0	10.4

Source: Parameters from Table 1 (Gan et al., 2004).

indeed, a direct calculation shows that it does. Therefore, for this example, an increase in Social Security benefits is entirely consumed by the receiving cohorts, and they even consume a little more out of their own bequeathable wealth. The net effect is a decrease in bequests.

The right two columns have similar results but now the man is assumed to have three children. A comparison of columns one and three, which holds Social Security benefits constant but changes the bequest motive, shows that the bequest motive is weak: the expected present value of bequests increases by just $200 or 2.6 percent. We should not expect, therefore, that increases in Social Security benefits will cause a change in the expected present value of bequests that is much different from the comparisons of columns one and two. And that is the case: As the last two column show, the expected present value of bequests falls by $2,600 rather than by $2,700 as in columns one and two. Thus the bequest motive causes an additional $100 in bequests out of an increase in the present value of Social Security benefits of $107,700.

Table 7.3 has similar results but they are for a 65-year-old woman. The difference in inputs that causes the difference in results is that women face substantially lower mortality risk and have greater life expectancy. Thus Social Security wealth is about $15,000 higher. This lower risk causes the optimal consumption level initially to be lower but consumption is achieved over a longer lifespan so that total consumption is higher than for a 65-year-old man. Because consumption is initially lower, wealth is held for a longer time. Even though more wealth is held, it is held earlier in life when mortality risk is fairly low. Thus, compared with a man the bequests are lower.

As with the 65-year-old man, the woman's expected bequests decline when Social Security benefits are increased from $10,000 to $20,000 per year.

Table 7.3 Bequeathable wealth, Social Security benefits, expected present value of consumption and bequests (thousands) 65-year-old female

	No children		Three children	
	Initial Social Security	Increased Social Security	Initial Social Security	Increased Social Security
Initial bequeathable wealth	100.0	100.0	100.0	100.0
Initial Social Security benefits	10.0	20.0	10.0	20.0
Social Security wealth	122.6	245.2	122.6	245.2
Expected PV consumption	212.1	335.8	211.9	335.2
Expected PV bequests	9.8	7.5	10.1	7.7

Source: Parameters from Table 1 (Gan et al., 2004).

Table 7.4 Bequeathable wealth, Social Security benefits, expected present value of consumption and bequests (thousands) 65-year-old male

	No children		Three children	
	Initial Social Security	Increased Social Security	Initial Social Security	Increased Social Security
Initial bequeathable wealth	100.0	100.0	100.0	100.0
Initial Social Security benefits	10.0	20.0	10.0	20.0
Social Security wealth	115.7	231.5	115.7	231.5
Expected PV consumption	189.5	307.7	188.2	304.1
Expected PV bequests	27.6	25.4	29.0	29.2

Source: Parameters from Table 1 (Hurd, 1989).

Table 7.5 Bequeathable wealth, Social Security benefits, expected present value of consumption and bequests (thousands) 65-year-old female

	No children		Three children	
	Initial Social Security	Increased Social Security	Initial Social Security	Increased Social Security
Initial bequeathable wealth	100.0	100.0	100.0	100.0
Initial Social Security benefits	10.0	20.0	10.0	20.0
Social Security wealth	132.9	265.8	132.9	265.8
Expected PV consumption	206.2	340.3	204.6	336.3
Expected PV bequests	29.2	28.8	30.9	33.0

Source: Parameters from Table 1 (Hurd, 1989).

As shown in the right-hand columns, bequests decrease even when there is a bequest motive.

Tables 7.4 and 7.5 have results similar to those in Tables 7.2 and 7.3 except that different parameters are used for the model, those shown in Table 7.1, column "Hurd (1989)". The time rate of discount, is much lower so that the start of the consumption path is lower, causing more wealth to be held. A consequence is that bequests are substantially higher even without a bequest motive (left columns): thus 28 percent – 29 percent of bequeathable wealth is accidentally bequeathed. Even so, increasing Social Security causes bequests to decrease by $2,200 for the 65-year-old man and $400 for the 65-year-old woman.

When there is a bequest motive, an increase in Social Security benefits does cause an increase in bequests. In the case of the 65-year-old woman, the increase is by $2,100 which is an increase of 6.8 percent. However, Social Security wealth increased $132,900 so all but a trivial fraction of the increase in Social Security benefits was used for consumption.

7.6 Conclusion

Although in principle an increase in Social Security benefits could result in substantial increases in bequests whether they are accidental or not, the empirical finding is that they do not or at least not substantially. In fact, under a model of life-cycle consumption by singles, which was estimated over two different data sets, bequests actually decrease in the absence of a bequest motive. Only in one of the estimated models that allowed for a bequest motive did bequests increase, and even then the increase was trivial. We explored many more cases such as variation in the level of Social Security benefits, the number of children and the age of the single person (not shown). In no simulation did we observe any significant increase in bequests in response to an increase in Social Security benefits. We conclude that, at least for singles, increases in Social Security benefits are unlikely to be offset by bequests.

Results for couples are unlikely to be substantially different simply because at the death of a spouse about 75 percent of the wealth goes to the surviving spouse (Hurd and Smith, 2001). At that point the surviving spouse follows the consumption path generated by the singles' model. As we have seen the singles' model does not produce any important bequest offset to an increase in Social Security benefits.

An unanswered question, however, is the role of *intervivos* transfers. They are fairly large, and perhaps they would be increased in response to an increase in Social Security benefits. To answer that question would require the specification and estimation of a considerably more complex model than the one used here.

Notes

1. A similar model for couples is much more complex and will be an objective of future work.
2. See Soldo, et al. (1997) for a description of AHEAD.

References

Gan, L., G. Gong, M. Hurd and D. McFadden (2004) "Subjective Mortality Risk and Bequests," NBER Working Paper 10789 (Cambridge, MA: National Bureau of Economic Research).

Gan, L., M. D. Hurd and D. McFadden (2005) "Individual Subjective Survival Curves," in David A.Wise (ed.), *Analyses in the Economics of Aging* (Chicago, IL: University of Chicago Press) pp. 377–402.

Hurd, M. D. (1989) "Mortality Risks and Bequests," *Econometrica* 57(4): 779–813.

Hurd, M. D. and K. McGarry (1995) "Evaluation of the Subjective Probabilities of Survival in the HRS," *Journal of Human Resources*, 30: S268–292.

Hurd, M. D. and K. McGarry (2002) "The Predictive Validity of Subjective Probabilities of Survival," *The Economic Journal* 112(482): 966–985.

Hurd, M. D. and J. P. Smith (2001) "Anticipated and Actual Bequests," in David A. Wise (ed.) *Themes in the Economics of Agingr* (Chicago, IL: University of Chicago Press) pp. 357–389.

Modigliani, F. and R. Brumberg (1954) "Utility Analysis and the Consumption Function: An Interpretation of Cross-sectional Data," in K. Kurihara (ed.) *Post Keynesian Economics* (New Jersey, NJ: Rutgers University Press).

Soldo, B., M. D. Hurd, W. Rodgers and R. Wallace (1997) "Asset and Health Dynamics Among the Oldest-Old: An Overview of the Survey," *Journal of Gerontology* 52B (May): 1–20.

Yaari, M. (1965) "Uncertain Lifetime, Life Insurance, and the Theory of the Consumer," *Review of Economic Studies* 32(2): 137–150.

Comments to Chapter 7
Daniel L. Thornton

Gan, Gong, and Hurd (2006) have written a very nice chapter and it is a pleasure to discuss it. The chapter asks the question: Is an increase in Social Security benefits a complete transfer from the younger to the older generation, or does some of the increased benefit gets transferred back to the younger generations via bequests? To answer this question, following Hurd (1989) they write down a simple model of utility maximization for a single person with a bequest motive, that is, utility from leaving money to the person's heirs. They assume a constant rate of relative risk aversion utility function and a bequest function that is multiplicatively linear in wealth and the number of children. If there are no children, the bequest function is zero. They estimate the parameters of the model over two waves of data form the AHEAD – the Asset and Health Dynamics study. They simulate the consumption and bequest paths associated with two paths for Social Security benefits, $10,000 and $20,000 for a person with $100,000 of initial wealth. The simulations suggest that little or none of the increase in Social Security benefit gets transferred back to the younger generations via bequests. Indeed, for some simulations, bequests actually decline. They conclude that "at least for singles, increases in Social Security benefits are unlikely to be offset by bequests."

I have no substantive comments on the work because it is very carefully and competently done. I have a few questions and concerns, however. Several places in the chapter the authors hint at public policy implications of such analyses. Since their work suggests that Social Security benefits should not be increased to raise the welfare of succeeding generations, I am comfortable with the implied public policy recommendation – Social Security benefits not be raised. Would I have been as comfortable had their evidence suggested that a large part of an increase in Social Security benefit would have been passed on to the next generation? I think not for a variety of reasons. First, and perhaps foremost, there is simply not enough heterogeneity in the model. Their model does not consider aspects of the social safety net other than Social Security. It does not incorporate working after retirement (indeed, there is no labor income). They do not consider reasons for bequests other than children. Furthermore, their analysis does not consider that there are ways to leave bequests before death.

Second, their simulations are for an individual with relatively little wealth and no other sources of income other than Social Security and pensions. The Employee Benefit Research Institute's estimates suggest that, at best, this model applies to about half of the elderly's income during the period 1974–2003.

Third, some important aspects of the model and simulations were chosen on the basis of 1993 and 1994 data, before the significant rise in the stock market beginning in the mid-1990s. It seems likely that some things that were true prior to mid-1990s, may be less relevant today. More generally, I believe that Social Security is one area where simulations based on the past are likely to be misleading guide for the future for the simple reason that the future is likely to be very different from the past. People will live and work longer. Individuals will have more (and perhaps better) opportunities for part-time work and semi-retirement. Moreover, but extremely important is the likelihood that saving habits will change with the continued reduction in Social Security benefits and the like. For these reasons and others, it seems that any policy recommendations made on simulations of such models are likely to be misleading.

Finally, I would note that the results of the chapter are not surprising in light of recent research by one of the authors. Specifically, in a very careful paper, Hurd (2003) investigates whether there is a bequest motive and finds that "for all practical purposes the bequest motive is not operative." If bequests occur by accident rather than design, it is hardly surprising to find that essentially none of an increase in Social Security benefits is returned to the younger generation in the form of bequests.

References

Hurd, M. D. (2003) "Bequests: By Accident or by Design?" in Alicia H. Munnell and Annika Sundén (eds) *Death and Dollars: The Role of Gifts and Bequests in America* (Washington, DC: Brookings Institution Press) pp. 93–118.

Hurd, M. D. (1989) "Mortality Risks and Bequests," *Econometrica* 57(4): 779–813.

Part IV
Interaction between Private and Public Provisioning

Part IV

8
The Changing Role of Employer Pensions: Tax Expenditures, Costs, and Implications for Middle-class Elderly

Teresa Ghilarducci

8.1 Introduction

What puzzles the nation is why pensions can be so expensive and deliver so little. All workers are feeling the pension pinch: those without pensions, those with pensions, and those who have lost pensions. The stagnation in pension coverage coupled with employer adoption of 401(k) plans means the hopes of those without pensions are smaller; those with pensions have experienced more risks and responsibilities for saving and investing; and those who have lost pensions feel robbed and forced to work longer.

Here are some key findings of this chapter.

- Tax favoritism, and consequently tax expenditures, are key pieces of federal retirement income security policy. The tax expenditures for employer-pensions are the largest of any category and the composition is changing from subsidizing defined benefit (DB) plans to 401(k) plans. See Section 8.2.
- Employer pensions are institutionalized savings and the key component of American household savings to a middle-class retiree standard of living. See Section 8.3.
- Paradoxically, pension participation is stagnating despite the rapid increase in: defined contribution (DC) coverage, tax expenditures, and pension spending, which increased faster than cash compensation and medical insurance (MI). See Section 8.4.
- The participation/spending paradox may be explained by the distribution of pension coverage shifting to higher income workers and away from middle-class workers and the motives of employers to make the shift. See Section 8.5.

- Younger workers could be worse off with the typical 401(k) plan than the typical DB plan, because job tenure is not diminishing and 401(k) plans are used mostly as severance plans, rather than pension plans. See Section 8.6.
- There are good reasons why employer-based pension plans may and should survive (retirement financing is inextricably tied to work; occupational plans help raise productivity and retain older workers – a major future human resource challenge). Social Security expansion can help most workers, which can be funded from rearranging tax expenditures for 401(k) plans and Individual Retirement Accounts (IRAs). See Section 8.7.
- The proposed "so-called" winning solution to strained pension budgets of people working until age 70 may not be possible, as jobs held by the elderly become more difficult. In addition, though some elderly may find work attractive as retirement income fails older people lose the ability to seek the work on their terms, and the terms of the employer prevail; see Appendix.

8.2 Government spending on the elderly and tax expenditures

Every year the federal government spends a little over one third of its budget on programs and transfer payments for people 65 -years- old and over. Most of the spending is on entitlement programs – programs whose expenditures are based on the costs of the services or transfers to those eligible and collecting. Of these, Social Security and Medicare take up the lion's share. In 2010, projected spending on the elderly is $471 billion for Social Security, $10 billion for Supplemental Security, and $377 billion for Medicare. Currently, total federal spending for the elderly is $ 1,026 billion, $441 billion is in Social Security (CBO, 2000).[1]

These direct costs understate the true spending on programs directed at retiree well-being. American legislators have long used tax policy, through "tax expenditures," to direct private spending in socially approving ways. Tax expenditures are the value of the tax code's exemption of income that is generated for certain activities.

Tax expenditures for private retirement plans – including revenue not collected because earnings and contributions in traditional employer pensions DB plans, in 401(k) plans, in IRAs,; and in similar savings vehicles dedicated for disbursement at older ages totaled one-fourth of total annual Social Security contributions were – $114 billion in 2004. Even more amazing, total household saving, at $102 billion, was lower than the federal pension tax expenditure (Bell, Carasso, and Steuerle, 2005). Federal spending in the form of tax expenditures for 401(k) plans is expected to grow 28 percent by 2009, while that for traditional plans is falling by 2.1 percent (see Table 8.1). Since tax expenditures aim to meet a social purpose, this

Table 8.1 Selected tax expenditures for the US budget

	2005	2009	Growth rate
	(billions of dollars)		
Net exclusion of pension contributions and earnings: 401(k) plans	58.9	75.4	28.0%
Net exclusion of pension contributions and earnings: Employer plans	61.7	60.4	−2.1%
Exclusion of employer contributions for medical insurance premiums and medical care (the largest)	112.9	150.3	33.1%
Deductibility of mortgage interest on owner-occupied homes	69.7	87.9	26.1%

Source: US budget 2004. Analytical Perspectives, Table 18–3.

study focuses on how this shift affects workers and retirees and assesses whether the $114 billion could be spent in better ways.

Tax expenditures have distributional effects, and since higher income individuals with higher marginal tax rates have the greatest financial incentive to take advantage of this source of federal spending, tax policy can be partially blamed for the relatively small rates of pension coverage among lower-income workers. The distribution of tax expenditures can be inferred by who is covered by the various forms of tax-favored plans.

8.3 Middle-class retirement income and household saving

Social Security benefits replace about 41 percent of income for retirees who were average career earners.[2] But financial planners recommend a minimum 70 percent replacement rate so middle-class workers reach that target mainly through employer-linked pension plans. In 2002, elderly households in the middle of the income distribution (the middle 20 percent) received 9.2 percent of their total retirement income from private employer pensions, which is lower than the 13.8 percent the top quintile receives.[3] Yet, the gap in personal assets is much larger. Middle-class households obtained 7.4 percent of their retirement income from personal assets, including 401(k) plans, whereas the top 20 percent of households receive a much larger share, 18.9 percent, from personal assets. It seems the top-heavy distribution of personal assets is caused partly by 401(k) plans being more unevenly distributed than private pension plans. Wolff (2007) reports that inequality is much higher among households with pension wealth and is much higher for those with DC accounts than with those with DB accounts. It is clear, combined with Social Security, traditional employer pensions are the key to middle-class status in old age and 401(k) plans help higher income workers more.

It also seems these institutionalized forms of savings are the only reason that the overall savings rates are not smaller (Bosworth and Bell, 2005; Munnell, Golub-Sass, and Varani, 2005). In 2005, Americans spent more than their income, yet 20 years ago savings rates were 10 percent (Munnell, Golub-Sass, and Varani, 2005). This is mysterious. Savings should be increasing. Middle-aged workers save more, and more workers are middle aged. Educated people save more, and more workers are educated. Most savings comes from the households at the top of the income distribution, and these have had the most income gains (Bosworth and Bell, 2005). Although Americans practically stopped saving out of take-home pay in the 1980s, the deep decline in contractual savings, especially by traditional DB pension plans, explains a large part of the current savings rate decline. Therefore, the savings drop is directly caused by diminishing DB pension. Yet, tax expenditures for retirement plans are going up by almost 26 percent! Part of the paradox is explained by stagnating coverage among lower income and middle class workers and increasing coverage and tax deductible limits increasingly utilized by upper income workers. First we discuss workers and their pensions.

8.4 Employer pension coverage is shrinking among middle-class workers

Despite considerable federal tax incentives to employer provided pensions, workers surveyed in the Current Population Survey (CPS) report that their participation in an employer pension plan has been falling for years: the pension participation of workers who work full time and for an entire year fell from 54.1 to 53.4 percent between 2003 and 2004 (Purcell, 2005a).

The Department of Labor's survey of private employers, the 2005 National Compensation Survey (NCS), also reports stagnation, although employers report pension coverage and participation rates recently rose slightly. In 2005, employers reported a 2 percentage point increase in private sector participation to 50 percent from 48 percent in 1999. (The comparable participation figure – for all private sector workers in the 2005 CPS – is a lower 46 percent participation rate.)[4] There is a great deal of variation of participation rates among workers and whether the pension is a DB or DC-type plans, like 401(k) plans. 401(k) type plans are growing and DBs are not. For some, union workers and workers in small firms, coverage rates increased 7.6 percent and 8.8 percent respectively. Manufacturing workers and nonunion workers had the least growth in pension participation (see Table 8.2).

DCs are increasingly dominating DB plans: DB participation rates have been flat since 2004 while DC rates are up 19.4 percent. Remarkably, the growth in DC plans has not raised pension participation rates. In 2005,

Table 8.2 Pension participation and growth rates of all private sector workers by selected category and ranked by participation rates in 2005

	Participation rates in all pension plans		Participation rates in DB pension plans		Participation rates in DC pension plans		Changes from 1999–2005		
	1999	2005	1999	2005	1999	2005	Changes in overall pension participation	Changes DB participation	Changes DC participation
Union	79	85	70	72	39	43	7.6%	2.9%	10.3%
Firms over 100	64	67	37	36	46	53	4.7%	−2.7%	15.2%
Goods-producing	61	64	36	32	44	50	4.9%	−11.1%	13.6%
Full time	56	60	25	25	42	50	7.1%	0.0%	19.0%
Service industries	44	47	17	18	34	39	6.8%	5.9%	14.7%
Non union	44	46	16	15	35	41	4.5%	−6.3%	17.1%
Small firms 0–99	34	37	8	9	27	32	8.8%	12.5%	18.5%
All workers	48%	50%	21%	21%	36%	43%	4.2%	0.0%	19.4%

Note: All participation rates are in percent.
Source: The source of the data is the National Compensation Survey: employee benefits in private industry, author's computations from the data available on the website: www.nbls.gov/ncs/ebs

employers reported that 43 percent of workers participated in DC plans and 21 percent participated in DB plans. If these shares were added, 64 percent of the workforce would be in retirement plans, but only 50 percent are. If DC coverage and participation growth expanded access to pension plans rather than replacing or supplementing an already existing DB plan, then growing DC rates should have pulled up total pension coverage and participation rates.[5] The correlation between the overall expansion of pension participation and DB participation rates is a strongly positive 79 percent. However, the correlation between all pension and DC growth is a negative 10 percent. This means that groups with the highest growth rates in DC plans are less likely to experience a significant increase in pension access. The highest growth rate in DB coverage was 12.5 percent for workers in small firms, and this group also happened to have the largest increase in overall growth rates – a boost of 8.8 percent.

More troubling is that the gap between the participation rates and coverage rates has grown larger. In 1983, some 54 percent of workers were covered by a pension plan whereas only 43 percent of those workers participated in the plan their employer sponsored. This means, the fraction of workers participating in a pension plan among those who were covered by a plan was 82 percent. That fraction fell to 75 percent by 2004.[6] The coverage rates exceed participation rates because workers can choose not to be covered only in a 401(k) and they can be disqualified from a plan if they have less than one year of service or work fewer than 1,000 hours per week. Yet, as DC plans become more important the voluntary participation feature of 401(k) plans becomes more significant for whether lower-income workers are covered (Purcell, 2005b). Since 1983 (which is about the time 401(k) plans were being adopted widely) participation rates have fallen behind coverage rates.

The bottom line is that regardless of the database used, pension coverage is stagnating as a percentage of the labor force. Furthermore, the evidence suggests that increases in DC plan coverage have not been correlated with increases in total pension coverage, perhaps because DCs relentlessly exclude many lower-income workers.[7] This conclusion begs the question whether pension tax expenditures meet social goals.

8.5 The disconnect between employer pension spending and pension security

It makes sense that tax expenditures are increasing because pension spending has risen dramatically, though it might not make much sense that many workers are not benefiting. According to the Chamber of Commerce's survey of private sector employers, from 1989 to 2005, the nominal increase in total compensation for all employees in manufacturing was 56.5 percent; but, the increase for DB spending was 450 percent.[8] DC costs increased by 90.9 percent.

In 2005, the average DB pension cost for all employees in private manufacturing was $4.40 per hour; DC costs were $2.10 per hour. In the nonmanufacturing sector, the growth in spending for all types of compensation was more balanced. Between 1989 and 2005, DB pension spending rose by 60 percent, DC by 120 percent, and total compensation increased by 66 percent (see Table 8.3).

Companies, especially in manufacturing, had to increase pension spending dramatically in 2004 and 2005 when the sudden declines in the stock market placed company DB plans in a severely underfunded position. It may be difficult to feel sympathy for companies that were required to sharply increase DB contributions because many had taken pension holidays in the 1990s when the stock market returns and interest rates were such that assets grew at the very same time liabilities fell (the high interest rates deeply discounted them). To their credit these companies did not ask for pity, instead they boosted DB contributions and many planned their exit out of DBs. Some used bankruptcy courts and exited in a nonorderly and brutal way (some airline pilots lost 80 percent of their expected pensions), and many other employees will never get what they expected from their DB plan (VanDerhei, 2006): other companies emphasized their 401(k) supplement and eased out of the DB plan. Some companies officially froze their healthy DB plan.[9]

Table 8.3 DB pension spending has increased faster than cash compensation and medical insurance for all workers (production and salary expressed in dollars per hour)

	Manufacturing			Growth	
	1989	1998	2005	1998–2005	1989–2005
DB[a]	$0.80	$1.20	$4.40	266.7%	450.0%
DC	$1.10	$1.40	$2.10	50.0%	90.9%
Retiree health	$1.00	$1.00	$1.20	20.0%	20.0%
Medical insurance	$8.30	$6.90	$9.40	36.2%	13.3%
Total compensation	$14.48	$20.58	$22.67	10.1%	56.5%

	Nonmanufacturing			Growth	
	1989	1998	2005	1998–2005	1989–2005
DB	$2.50	$3.90	$4.00	2.6%	60.0%
DC	$1.00	$2.10	$2.20	4.8%	120.0%
Retiree health	$0.80	$0.90	$0.50	−44.4%	−37.5%
Medical insurance	$7.90	$6.40	$10.90	70.3%	38.0%
Total compensation	$14.67	$18.82	$24.35	29.4%	66.0%

Note: [a] DB includes cash balance and hybrid plans.
Source: Employee Benefits Report, US Chamber of Commerce various years, Table 1.

Tax and accounting rules have been blamed for causing employers to move away from DB pensions.[10] But I argue here that the primary reason is more straightforward. Many employers switch to DC plans to lower costs. IBM, Hewlett Packard, Motorola, and other major corporations announced that this was the rationale for changing their pension policies. IBM's savings are projected in the billions of dollars (Walsh, 2006). (A full accounting of healthy companies freezes are available from Munnell, Golub-Sass, and Francis, 2006.)

8.5.1 How firms save money with DC plans

VanDerhei (2006) argued that though firms cited cost volatility as the DB feature firms wanted to avoid, the Aon company found that 45 and 35 percent of the companies they surveyed froze their DB plans for reasons identified as "the amount of contribution" required or "the impact on corporate expense." The human resource consulting firm, Mercer, found that 25 percent of their surveyed firms froze their DB plan for "long-term cost savings." VanDerhei found that there is tremendous variability regarding what types of workers were fully compensated by employer 401(k) plan contributions when they lost DB benefits. He concludes, in general, older, longer-tenured workers are less likely than younger workers to be compensated. And, if workers do not earn over 4 percent return on the 401(k) plan contributions and remain with the firm between 10 and 14 years, they will more likely lose from a DB to 401(k) switch.

The 2005 costs for DBs are much larger than DC plans which makes the simplest and most obvious reason employers may prefer DC plans to DB plans the chief explanation for the shift – shifting to DCs lowers worker pay without workers retaliating. In other words, the fact that 401(k) plans can reduce pension costs powerfully motivates some employers to choose 401(k) plans despite DBs positive effects in retaining and attracting older workers – an especially important feature as the workforce ages. The motivation is apparent when the vexing problem that eligible employees irrationally "leave money on the table" by not participating in 401(k) plans is viewed from the vantage of the employers' delight, not the policy-economist's dismay.

In addition to the public announcements made by firms cutting DBs is the evidence that despite the convenience of payroll deduction and the proliferation of expensive investor education programs the average participation rate for 401(k)-eligible workers has stagnated at about 80 percent. Twenty percent of employees do not take advantage of an employer's match or tax break. Pension experts and academics invariably write this off to "quirky" human nature (Turner, 2006). This view ignores the obvious reality that when workers leave money "on the table" they leave it on the employers' table and that the outcome could be anticipated and factored into the employers' compensation strategy.[11] In fact, if all eligible workers participated in their employers' 401(k) plans between 2002 and 2004, employers would have had to contribute 26 percent more – for an annual total of $3.18 billion. Employers not wanting 100 percent participation solve some of the mystery why, although automatic enrollment is a documented, effective way to increase participation in 401(k) plans, 82 percent of 401(k) sponsors do not offer it. As mentioned above, one-fifth of employers are credited with providing a pension even though they contribute nothing to their employees' 401(k)s.[12] Ghilarducci, Sun, and Nyce (2004) and Ghilarducci and Sun (2006) found that merely adopting a 401(k) can reduce pension costs by as much as 25 percent. Crucially, the cost savings from switching from a DB to a DC is not distributed equally; it is likely for numerous reasons that the biggest losers are lower-paid workers.

Indirect evidence that profit maximization motivates firms to discourage 401(k) participation can be found in the fact that those employers with the highest participation rates are primarily not-for-profit firms and government agencies. In 2003, *Plan Sponsor magazine* celebrated these employers for above average participation rates in 401(k) type plans. Those achieving 99 to 100 percent participation used a simple, surefire method: they mandated participation. Therefore, what is not so obvious is made clear. The long-standing stagnation in pension coverage is partially explained by firm's ability to reduce employee compensation by replacing DB plans with 401(k) plans. Evidence above showed that increasing DC coverage is correlated with slow growth in pension coverage, whereas growth in DB coverage is associated with an increase in coverage. Cost savings in DC plans may explain the reason.

Employers move from DB plans to DC plans, in part, because such a move saves money without an appreciable loss in productivity. Employers are able to adopt inferior pension plans, in part, because the workers are not resisting the loss. As noted earlier, one of the most important sources of climate change threatening pensions is the decline in unions. Collectively bargained compensation packages traditionally contain more employee benefits and other forms of non-wage compensation than non-union compensation packages. There are various mechanisms that explain the union effect on employee benefits. Unions may facilitate benefits by informing and educating members about the importance of insurance and pensions. Unions also may promote employee benefits relative to cash wages because unions represent the older worker rather than the marginal, younger worker who likely prefers cash relative to insurance. Union workers have almost twice the coverage rates for lower-income workers and over 10 percent more for higher paid workers.

8.6 Are DCs better for workers and retirees in a changing world?

A main argument against DBs is that they are, supposedly, a bad fit with today's workers. An extreme form of the argument is that DBs reward workers who stay with the same employer for their entire career and if workers are more mobile this pension form makes little sense – young workers hardly vest or only accumulate miniscule DB credits. Yet, the mobility argument is fragile, built on exaggerated claims about worker mobility.

In fact, younger workers have always engaged in "job hopping" but formerly they were more likely to end up in a beneficial DB plan. In this way mobile workers benefit from the existence of a DB plan even if they do not settle into a job or jobs until age 40. After 10 years at an advanced age, a worker can lock in a significant DB pension benefit. DBs allow middle-aged workers to accumulate a reasonable retirement income in their 40s and 50s even if they've changed jobs a lot in their 20s and 30s. Furthermore, the fact that most workers use their 401(k) account balances as severance payments, spending them when they quit, are laid off or fired means that job-hopping has even worse consequences for retirement savings in a 401(k) world.

However, before we allow that mobility determines the most effective pensions, we need to know the facts. Mobility trends differ depending on the point of view – what time period, what industries, what aged workers, for men or for women. In many ways, workers have become more stable. One measure is that the share of employees with more than 10 years of service has increased since 1996, up for men from 30.5 to 30.6 percent and women up from 27.9 to 28.6 percent (Wiatrowski, 2005). It is true that compared to the 1970s and early 1980s men are staying less times in their jobs (the share of male employees with 10 or more years of tenure was 37.7 percent in 1983). In addition, older men, who experience more job displacement and have lost their employer pensions have had "to screw their courage to the sticking-place" in order to save for retirement on their own. In 1983, over 57 percent of men aged 45–50 years would have been with their current employers for over 10 years; that probability fell to 48.1 percent in 2004. Nevertheless, women have become more stable: the probability that a woman in this age group would have been with her employer for over 10 years increased from 33 percent to 36.2 percent from 1983 to 2004.

Another reason mobility increases are exaggerated is that mobility actually is *decreasing* in industries where the most new jobs are appearing. Industries adding the most jobs are retail trade, employment services and computer design, state and local governments, food services, and in healthcare: offices of health practitioners, ambulatory healthcare services and hospitals. In all but one of these large job growth areas mobility is decreasing and tenure is increasing. Over all, the average growth in job tenure for most of the fastest growing industries is 16.3 percent, compared to the average of 14.3 percent

Table 8.4 Changes in job tenure for industries with the largest job growth

Industries expected to grow the fastest (2002–2012)	Average years of tenure with current employer January 2000	Increase in job tenure to January 2004 (in percentage)
Retail trade	2.5	12.0
Employment services and computer design[a]	2.6	38.5
State and local government[b]	5.5	16.4
Food services	1.4	14.3
Offices of health practitioners, ambulatory services	3.2	3.1
Construction	2.7	11.1
Educational services	3.2	18.8
Hospitals	5.1	−7.8
Average for all industries		13.3
Average for all industries without hospitals	3.5	14.3

Notes:
[a] The job tenure figures often include categories that do not correspond with the employment growth categories. The tenure figures are for professional and technical services, which is a larger category than 'employment services and computer design.'
[b] The job tenure figures only include state employment because the employment growth categories are reported in larger categories than for job tenure. (Average tenure in local employment decreased slightly from 6.7 to 6.4.)
Source: US Census, Statistical Abstract of the United States: 2004–2005.

(see Table 8.4). Furthermore, the average tenure for all workers over age 16 increased from 3.5 years to 4 years from January 2000 to January 2004, which means more workers will have reached the 5-year mark when they must be vested (Bureau of Labor Statistics, 2004). Bottom line: job security has improved slightly rather than the workforce becoming more mobile. This means the environment is favorable to DB plans.

8.6.1 Head on comparisons: DB versus 401(K) simulations

A simulation of a worker working in three scenarios shows that even in a mobile society a worker would likely accumulate a pension worth much more when DB plans exist rather than when all plans are 401(k) plans. The simulation assumes a worker has three jobs after age 30 and four jobs before age 30. The simulation also assumes that the worker with a 401(k) saves 25 percent of his/her 401(k) balance when he/she changed jobs before age 30 and then 100 percent after age 30. Participation in 401(k) plans is voluntary and there are many exclusions so most workers do not participate (Munnell and Sunden, 2004, p. 56), but participation rates do increase with a person's age. Munnell and Sunden (2004, p. 56) calculate that participation rates are about 28 percent until age 30 and then grow gradually to 44.2 percent by age 45, and then drop down to 38.8 percent. Assuming that workers and employers together contribute 9 percent to a 401(k) (Munnell and Sunden, 2004, p. 58) and it earns 3 percent per year (after adjusting for risk and fees), then under real life circumstances this worker will accumulate $33,335. This amount is not far-fetched since the median account balance for a 60–64 year old is $59,000 (Munnell and Sunden, 2004). The annuity value is only about $2,700 per year.[13] On the other hand, the DB annuity accumulated under a common formula of 2 percent of salary per year of service credit adds up to $35,000 per year. Workers are automatically in a DB plan and the amounts are guaranteed by the government agency, the Pension Benefit Guarantee Corporation (PBGC). The 401(k) is worth more only under ideal circumstances, which are that the worker never skips a contribution, always participates, and never withdraws. Under these ideal circumstances, the lump sum is over $647,000 and the annuity value is over $51,000 per year.

However, the ideal 401(k) world in which young workers always have a job, steadily save 12 percent of their income, always get low fees, and never touch the accrual or principal is in the big rock candy mountain in the sky, not on this planet, even with investor education.

Employers are causing the move away from DB plans. Employers, not workers, determine pension design. However, not all employers are alike and not all are adopting individual-based employee benefits. As argued above, many employers who do adopt the individual model choose 401(k)-style plans in order to lower short-term pension costs and help manage cash flow problems. A firm offering 401(k)s does not have to commit to contributions at all. In fact, over 20 percent of employers stopped contributing to their 401(k) plans in 2001 (Munnell and Sunden, 2004). While DBs are superior in retaining workers in their late 40s and early 50s (Johnson and Uccello, 2004), and employers face impending shortages of skilled labor, worker loyalty seems less highly valued today by some large firms. It has always been the case that some business models stress low pay labor and a tolerance for high turnover. A memo from Wal-Mart's human resource director leaked to the press (Greenhouse and Barbaro, 2005) advised supervisors to include vigorous physical tasks in all jobs so that senior workers, who are paid higher wages, are subtlety encouraged to quit.

These trends away from offering pay to longer tenure employees may come back to haunt firms. Industries enjoying rapid growth may face high turnover costs, especially if they must recruit from other companies making hiring more expensive than retaining older workers. As the baby-boomers retire over the next 20 years, and more companies – especially those that depend on skilled and semi-skilled labor – find it difficult to hire without raising wages, they likely will regret not having DBs. Certainly, many successful employers maintain DBs or DB hybrids in order to attract and retain older workers. Federal policy should not make DBs extinct for lack of action or imagination or because fads are moving in another direction in the short term.

Table 8.5 Pension benefit simulations: of a 401(k) and typical DB plan under ideal and probable conditions

Age	Salary	Years on the Job	Contribution rate 9%	Real life 401(k) plan			Ideal behavior in a 401(k) plan				Average DB
				Withdrawal rates	Participation rates	Net at age 65	Job	Withdrawal	Participation	Lump and annuity	Formula 2% for each service year
20	$35,000	2	0.09	75%	0.28	$1,482	1	0%	1	$21,177	0
22	36,050	3	0.09	75%	0.28	$2,224	2	0%	1	$32,718	0
25	37,132	1	0.09	75%	0.28	$678	3	0%	1	$11,233	0
26	38,245	1	0.09	75%	0.28	$699	4	0%	1	$11,570	0
27	39,393	3	0.09	75%	0.28	$1,862	5	0%	1	$35,752	0
30	49,241	15	0.09	0%	0.416	$14,916	6	0%	1	$223,452	$14,772
45	50,718	10	0.09	0%	0.442	$6,025	7	0%	1	$153,437	$10,144
55	52,240	10	0.09	0%	0.388	$5,448	8	0%	1	$158,040	$10,448
65	Same	0	0	Lump sum		$33,335 or $2,628 per year for life	Retire	Annuity		$647,379 or $51,072 per year for life	$35,364 per year for life

Source: Author's calculations.

8.6.2 Under real life conditions DBs are better than 401(k)s

This is a simulation of a worker's pension accrual. This simulation assumes that the worker and the employer contribute the average to their 401(k) and participate at the average rates if they are covered by a DB or DC plan. The resulting pensions under both types of plans are compared with a career where the worker has the ideal rates of contribution, withdrawal, and participation.

This simulated worker has eight jobs, retires at age 65 with an ending salary of $52,240. Ideally, he/she would have $647,379 in his/her account and take it out in an annuity of $51,072 per year. The ideal 401(k) is better than the average DB plan, which yields $35,364 for life. However, under real-life conditions, the real-life 401(k) is worth $33,335 or $2,628 per year for life for a woman aged 65 (see Table 8.5).

8.7 Policy implications

Conventional wisdom explaining the DC dominance over DBs takes on an evolutionary view that DB plans are dinosaurs that could not evolve to meet the demands of the new economic environment. The "dinosaur" interpretation argues that employees have come to prefer the 401k-type DC plan to the traditional DB plan because workers are mobile and the DC accounts are transparent, that is, workers can better understand their benefits. I argue that DB plans are more like pandas, a worthwhile species endangered by shortsighted policies and decisions. This "DB pensions are pandas" interpretation holds that DB coverage rates have stagnated because many companies have adopted 401(k) plans to take advantage of temporary changes in accounting standards and to lower pension costs, not to respond to worker preferences for DC plans or to changes in labor processes and technology.

Appropriate government policy should look like a retirement policy designed on purpose. In basic public finance economics, social security systems have clear goals: adequacy, efficiency, horizontal and vertical equity, and contribution to economic growth. Giving tax favoritism to qualified private sector plans reasonably extends these goals to voluntary employer plans. Since the plans are voluntary, employers' needs are key: employers want to provide personnel tools and limit risk and volatility. Also for employer pension plans to have a social purpose and justify their tax expenditures, they must make sense in people's lives. Given the recent wave of DB and DC pension plan, all three groups of workers – the more than 50 percent without a pension at any one point in time; workers who have lost or spent their DB and DC plans; and those with pensions – are worried about retirement security.

There is great opportunity for policy makers to reverse this deterioration of retirement income. In particular, policies should be designed to encourage efficient pension plans and voluntary working. Although not a focus of this chapter, the contours of pension reform include the following platforms:

First, policy goals should ensure more coverage in defined benefit (DB) type plans. This can be accomplished in two ways: (1) by expanding the traditional multiemployer portable DB plans that have existed in dynamic industries with mobile workforces for 40 years; and, (2) by bringing more DB features into defined contribution (DC) plans; for instance by instituting a "DB(k)," which is an Academy of Actuaries proposal which allows workers to supplement their DB plan with their own contributions (Gebhardtsbauer, 2004).

New Jersey hospital nurses offer an example of the first option. In the late 1990s, these nurses finally obtained a longstanding demand in collective bargaining to join the multiemployer pension plan that the hospital's operating engineers belonged to. Why operating engineers? The hospital had changed ownership so many times that each single employer plan ended when another firm bought the hospital. The employees did not move – it was the employers who were mobile. Joining the multiemployer plan let the nurses build up credits in one DB plan (Ghilarducci, 2003). There should be more single employer plans merged with multi-employer plans. Through collective bargaining, the union representing mechanics and other workers brought in employees from United, US Airways, and Aloha airlines after their other plans terminated and were taken over by the PBGC. This means that when the single employer DB plan in the airline industry failed, the International Association of Machinists multiemployer plans stepped up to replace them, offering better benefits than the airlines' proposed DC plans for the same contribution. The plan is more stable for the workers because it is a DB plan that includes the other airlines. These workers could lose their jobs at US Airways or any other airline, but not necessarily active membership in their pension plans.

Promoting the transfer of single employer DB plans to multiemployer DB plans cannot be done easily without enabling legislation and regulatory changes. The law is not helpful, nor is the PBGC, in preventing single employer terminations. The PBGC should encourage multiemployer plans to take on distressed single-employer plans by offering financial assistance. This may be much cheaper than taking over an entire plan. The law already allows the PBGC to financially assist a distressed multiemployer plan by letting it merge into another multiemployer plan. Why not help a distressed single employer plan merge into a multiemployer plan? A demonstration project in the airline or auto parts industries could greatly expand the multi-employer universe.

Policies that bring DB designs into DC plans include DB hybrid pension designs that could help calm those now in existing DB plans as long as current expected benefits are protected. Good policy would devise incentives to keep firms from exiting the DB system (GAO, 2005b; Weller, 2005). Also, sensible protections that already govern the investment behavior of DB plan fiduciaries could be a good place to start, as, for example, in the percent of a portfolio allowed to be in the employee's company's stock. Other considerations include mandatory minimum contributions, incentives for at least partial annuitization, and limits on fees.

The latter can be accomplished by allowing individuals to use efficient not-for-profit individual account vendors such as Michigan Governor Jennifer Granholm's proposal to let Michigan small businesses use the Michigan state pension fund to administer their 401(k) plans (Plan Sponsor, 2006) and the proposed legislation in Washington State that would give state residents access to the professionals managing the state employee pension funds (Watkins, 2002).

Economist Zvi Bodie (2001) has suggested that workers should be able to top off their Social Security benefits with an investment in government inflation indexed bonds. Others have also argued that expanding Social Security is the only way to secure middle and lower income workers retirement. Options to expand Social Security are beyond this study, but there could be ample money to do so if the tax expenditures for 401(k) plans were restricted to 90 percent of workers not in the top 10 percent of the earnings distribution.

Last, as explained in the appendix, there are several pieces of evidence that suggest that older workers may be working under duress. Labor market policies should protect older workers and ensure that work after an advanced age is under workers' terms. Perhaps, extending the American with Disabilities Act protections could help protect older workers and help employers resist the temptation to solve perceived labor supply shortages by cutting pensions.

8.8 Conclusion

DB plans seem more suitable to a rapidly aging workforce and the projected labor skill shortage because older workers respond well to DB plans. Four environmental changes create a hostile environment for DB plans: (1) the national decline in union contracts help employers adopt 401(k) plans without an apparent loss in productivity; (2) the regulatory environment is inhospitable for DB plans relative to its friendliness toward DC plans (Gebhardtsbauer, 2004; Eickelberg, 2005, Mercer, 2004) as is the dramatic shift in Presidential and Congressional attitudes that reduce employer and government responsibility for social insurance; (3) uncertainty over DB pension costs has made DC plans more attractive (Weller, 2006); and (4) commercial vendor interests in marketing 401(k)-type accounts has increased relative to their interest in selling traditional defined benefit pensions (McCaw, 2004), (this is an important topic for another paper).

In sum, the shift to DCs corresponds with paradoxical trends: federal costs for pensions are increasing through tax expenditures while pension participation rates are stagnating. It seems companies are switching to save money. This adds up to a conclusion that pensions are become more skewed toward upper income workers (Wolff and Weller's 2005 study of household wealth comes to the same conclusions). The American system of retirement security is in transition. Private sector DB plans, which never covered more than 40 percent of the work force, are declining. Meanwhile, 401(k) plans have grown by leaps and bounds. Yet none of this growth is likely to increase the number of workers covered by pensions or reduce their risk of losing them. Ultimately, it matters less which pension systems we use to achieve a secure national retirement system: what really matters is that we ensure a secure retirement for all American workers and their families.

Appendix

Impact of changing pensions on workers: more savings or more work

The changes in employer spending on pensions means that large, trend-setting employers are eroding retirement income security for most workers who will never efficiently accumulate enough assets nor effectively choose payout options to provide a steady adequate amount of income for life after retirement. It is doubtful that employees will save vigorously in voluntary retirement savings vehicles given that the 20-year old experience with 401(k) plans reveals that employees have been either unwilling or unable to save enough (Munnell and Sunden, 2004; Vanguard Group, 2005). Only one-third of workers are on track to achieve the 70 percent target retirement income replacement rate (Vanguard Group, 2005). Although a full 90 percent of workers have thought about how much income they would need in retirement, only 41 percent of workers have specific plans about how to obtain the necessary assets. Some 40 percent of households are at risk of not having enough income in retirement; to avoid this problem they would need to double their savings rates or defer retirement until age 70. When it comes to planning for an adequate retirement income, there is a large disconnect between thinking and doing. Financial education (FE) does not help much: only 40 percent of those who receive counseling or attend a FE class change their saving behavior. In fact, planning itself may be on the decline! The percentage of workers who thought about calculating savings needs ranged from 31 to 53 percent in 2000; then it to fell to 42 percent in 2004 (EBRI, 2004). If pensions are not enough the elderly will have to work – indeed Butrica et al. (2003) predict that earnings from work will be a greater source of retirement income for baby-boomers. The fact that earnings will become more important than investment income for future American retirees makes sense. Thus, to emphasize, the elderly will seek work as pensions fall short but on whose terms? There is no reason to believe that the employer attitudes and work conditions will welcome the older worker.

More seek work at older ages

Since 1949, men and women over age 65 have left the labor market in recessions. Men withdrew from the labor force at the average yearly rate of 2.4 percent and women by 1.5 percent. Yet, in the most recent recession, men over age 65 left at a rate of 3.9 percent, but women entered the work force by increasing work effort by 5.3 percent. The labor force participation rate for slightly younger men and women, aged 55 to 64, was higher over the most recent business cycle. However, labor force participation and working are not the same thing. Despite the rapid increase in labor force participation, many of the elderly found unfavorable working conditions. If the elderly were laid off, they had half as much chance of being reemployed than younger people. The average duration of unemployment is higher for older workers and rose in 2002; the average search for job seekers over age 55 was 16 weeks, up from 12.7 in 2001. Significantly, older men's job security has gotten much worse; their median years of tenure – the number of years a person has been employed by their current employer – has fallen dramatically, by almost 50 percent from 15.3 years for men aged 55–64 to just 10.2 years. (The decline is much smaller for women, from 9.8 years in 1983 to 9.6 years in 2002.)

Jobs for older workers are not getting easier for old people to do

A recent Urban Institute study (Chapter 6 this book) makes a clear hard-hitting case for the most sought after policy solution: a win-win opportunity. They argue that everyone wins if workers are persuaded to work more years. Social Security, Medicare, and workers all win if workers would work until age 70. Their simulations reveal that workers especially win. If they work several years longer they could enjoy a 25 percent increase in their standard of living. This finding is suspicious. A neoclassical economist would reject this conclusion faster than saying Economics 101. Since a standard of living consists of money and leisure, and if workers could have enjoyed more money by working longer and they wanted to they would have. We would have to assume workers have revealed their preferences for leisure over a 25 percent increase in income by retiring, unless Butrica and colleagues argue that something like ignorance, custom, discrimination, and heuristic problems (all of which I am disposed to accept) bar, cajole, and inhibit workers from working more. Nevertheless, the paper makes no such claims. The puzzle why workers retire despite the huge gains from working longer might be understood by recognizing the disutility of working for older people. An obvious reason people retire instead of working to gain 25 percent more income is that the value of time increases as time becomes scarce, as one approaches death.

A fundamental question for policy makers and for our scrutiny of federal spending on the elderly is whether federal policy is creating more older workers because they want jobs or because they have lost pensions. Currently, it seems employers are offering jobs to older people that employers have reserved for other marginal workers. Instead of 60 being the new 30, it has become the new 17 as older people fill the job segment with the predicted largest growth in new job – retail clerks. This is the direction we appear to be headed.

There is little evidence that older people have an increased ability to work longer. In fact, since 1981, the share of older workers reporting limitations in their ability to work has stayed steady at about 15–18 percent. While jobs demanding heavy lifting, stooping, and kneeling, and overall physical effort are declining, especially for men, older workers report an increase over 17 percent in job stress and the need for intense concentration. Older women report an increase over 17 percent in jobs requiring good eyesight. See Table 8.A.1. Only magical thinking can conclude that the computer has made jobs easier for older workers. (Johnson, 2004).

Table 8.A.1 Selected characteristics of job as reported by people working age 55–60 in 2002

	Percentage change since 1992	
	men	women
Good for older people		
Hardly any lifting heavy loads required	8.60%	17.10%
Hardly any stooping or kneeling required	6.90%	0%
Hardly any physical effort	26%	2.90%
Difficult for older people		
Always or almost always requires good eyesight	8%	17.70%
Always or almost always requires intense concentration	17.80%	15.10%
Strongly agree that job involves a lot of stress	18.10%	17.80%

Source: Johnson 2004.

The fact that older people find jobs harder to get, more difficult to perform, and unemployment duration much longer suggests that older people are forced into the market because of eroding pensions. In the last recession, the unemployment rate went up faster for older women than any other group, while in the subsequent economic recovery the unemployment rate declined for older men and women more slowly than for younger workers.

Since older people are working more today, we need policies that speak to their special needs. The elderly will likely be attracted to the fastest-growing jobs, which happen to be dominated by women and ironically are those serving the elderly. The two occupations experiencing the fastest growth are registered nurses and nursing for home health care and personal health care aids. These jobs are better for the client and worker, no matter how old, when collective bargaining determines wages, hours, and working conditions. Older people in these jobs need the protections that the Americans with Disabilities Act provides such as the right for reasonable accommodations in scheduling and equipment. In the end, the only way to ensure that older workers have jobs on their terms depends on them having secure retirement income.

Impact on employers of workers working longer

What Butrica, Smith, and Steuerle (Chapter 6 this book) do not address is whether extending work life will help employers out. Clearly, some workers will want to work longer, at least part time. It is not clear, however, that employers will provide the jobs older workers want. All older workers want to work on their own terms, but if pension and retiree health care is less secure that may not be possible. Robert Hutchens (Hutchens and Grace-Martin, 2004; Hutchens and Papps, 2005) shows that the overwhelming number of employers and workers tell researchers that they would be open to phasing in retirement but, in fact, such arrangements hardly ever exist. One reason may be that what older workers want from employers is not what employers want from workers.

Notes

1. Other federal spending for the elderly includes pensions for federal and military personnel, the portions of the food stamp and Medicaid (the federal share) programs spent on the elderly, elder housing assistance, veterans' compensation and pensions, and Home Energy Assistance Program spending for the elderly.
2. The average Social Security replacement rate will fall in the two decades to 30.5 percent as the average benefit decreases due to the NRA rising to age 67 and increases income taxes and Medicare premiums (Munnell, 2003, Table 4, p. 3).
3. Employer pensions are important for middle class retirees

	First	Second	Third	Fourth	Fifth
Social Security	82.6	84.0	67.0	47.0	19.8
Private pensions or annuities	2.5	4.1	9.2	13.8	10.0
Income from assets	2.4	3.6	7.4	9.8	18.9
Earnings	1.1	2.3	7.0	14.7	38.4
Government employee pensions and railroad	1.0	2.7	5.8	11.7	10.5
Other	1.5	1.7	2.7	2.9	2.4
Public assistance	8.9	1.6	1.0	0.2	0.1

Notes: Total income to each quintile by source of income of household units with member over Age 55. Quintile upper limits are: $9,721, $15,181, $23,880, $40,982.
Source: Table 7.5 percentage distribution, by marital status and quintiles of total money income www.ssa.gov/policy/docs/statcomps/income_pop55/2002 released March 2005.

4. The actual number is probably closer to the National Compensation Survey (NCS) results because employers have a better idea of who is covered than workers do. Also, many CPS respondents are not the actual worker but his or her spouse or other relative and may not be knowledgeable about the employee's pension plans.
5. Union workers experienced one of the largest increases in pension coverage rates – from 79 percent in 1999 to 85 percent in 2005 – and this group had already started from a high base remarkably this group also had one of the largest increases in DB coverage – 70 percent to 72 percent – and a large increase in DC coverage – from 39 to 43 percent. Because unions usually bargain DC plans to complement DB plans, we can be certain that in this case, the increase in the DB rate likely boosted pension access. This relationship holds up in an evaluation of the correlation between general pension and DB participation rates.
6. Private sector nonagricultural wage and salary workers, aged 21[a] and over

	Coverage rates (%)	Participation rates (%)	Sponsored-participation rate[a] (%)
1979	54	43	80
1983	49	40	82
1988	51	37	73
1993	55	39	71
2004	55	41	75

Private sector nonagricultural wage and salary workers, aged 21 and over
[a] for 2004 the age range is only 21–64.
Source: for years 1979–1993 the data comes from the Employee Benefits Research Institute, 1995, EBRI Data book on Employee Benefits. EBRI, Washington DC, and the data for 2004 comes from EBRI, 2005, "Employment–Based Retirement Plan Participation: Geographic Differences and Trends, 2004." Issue Brief. No. 286. October page 7.

7. There are significant differences in pension coverage and the share of workers who actually participate in a plan. DB plan coverage, with some exceptions for part-time or newly hired employees, is largely universal. In contrast, while DC plans may be offered to a large majority of a sponsoring employer's workforce, employee nonparticipation rates can average over 20 percent (Purcell, 2005a).
8. Manufacturing firms do not have more DB plans, nor are the benefit levels higher, but the pension holidays may have been more prevalent. In 2005, 23 percent of non-manufacturing firms and 18 percent of manufacturing firms offered DB plans in the Chamber of Commerce's sample (p. 40) and the average employer costs were $1,985 for non-manufacturing firms and $1,410 for manufacturing firms (Chamber of Commerce, 2005, p. 10).
9. The Employee Benefit Research Institute (VanDerhei, 2006) surveyed DB plan changes and found that the PBGC concluded most frozen plans were small and, if they were large, the companies were in some financial distress. If the firms surveyed by Aon consulting firm that say they are considering a plan freeze actually do, then in a few years, 23 percent of their 1000 clients surveyed with DB plans will have frozen their plans. Watson and Wyatt surveyed Fortune 1000 firms revealed 11 t of firms that froze their plans were below invest grade ratings, meaning they were in poor financial health (VanDerhei, 2005).
10. The funding rules affect pension plan contributions in a variety of ways. For example, some rules allow plan sponsors to choose interest rates that can reduce plan liabilities; other rules limit the maximum amount of contributions that a sponsor can make, while others permit the use of "credits" earned from passed asset gains as a substitute for cash contributions. See GAO 2005a.
11. Ippolito (1997) and Burham (2003) argue that the voluntary participation feature of 401(k)s help employers screen for the most productive employees. The idea is that workers who save are more productive. The forms can passively and easily tie compensation to productivity by matching the voluntary savings of what turns out to be their best workers.
12. I used information from Munnell and Sunden (2004) on participation rates, average contribution levels by earnings, the distribution of employees by earnings (Calculated from the CPS, 2003) to make the three billion dollar estimate. The average saving per worker is $156, Madrian, Choi, and Laibson (2005) calculated for their sample of over 800 employees in one firm that the employer saved over $250 per older worker who did not participate in the 401(k) even when they were eligible.
13. Calculated from immediateannuity.com 7 May 2006.

References

Bell, E., A. Carasso, and C. E. Steuerle (2005) "Strengthening Private Sources of Retirement Savings for Low-Income Families," Opportunity and Ownership Project Brief #5. (Washington, DC: Urban Institute). <http:// www.urban.org/ url.cfm? ID= 311229>

Bodie, Z. (2001) "Financial Engineering and Social Security Reform," in J. Y. Campbell and M. Feldstein (eds) *Risk Aspects of Investment-Based Social Security Reform* (The University of Chicago Press) pp. 292–305.

Bosworth, B. and L. Bell (2005) "The Decline in Saving: What Can We Learn from Survey Data?," unpublished draft written for the 7th Annual Joint Conference of the Retirement Research Consortium, "Creating a Secure Retirement" (Washington,

DC, August 11–12). <http://www.bc.edu/centers/crr/dummy/seventh_annual.shtml>
Bureau of Labor Statistics (2004) "Employee Tenure in 2004," September 21 http://www.bls.gov/news.release/tenure.t05.htm Table 5. (Median Years of tenure with current employer).
Burham, K. (2003) 401(k)s "As Strategic Compensation: Align Pay With Productivity And Enable Optimal Separation," Ph.D. Dissertation (Notre Dame, IN: University of Notre Dame).
Butrica, B. A., H. M. Iams, and K. E. Smith (2003) "It's All Relative: Understanding the Retirement Prospects of Baby-Boomers," Working Paper #2003-21 (Boston, MA: Center for Retirement Research).<http://www.bc.edu/centers/crr/dummy/wp_2003-21.shtml>
Chamber of Commerce (2005) *Employee Benefits* (Washington, DC: US Chamber of Commerce) p. 10.
CBO (2000) "Federal Spending on Elderly and Children," (Washington, DC: Congressional Budget Office).
Current Population Survey (CPS), maintained by the Department of Labor and the US Census Department available at www.census.gov/cps
Eickelberg, H. (2005) Testimony before the House Ways and Means Subcommittee on Select Revenue Measures on the Administration's proposal for Single-employer Pension Funding Reform, March 8. On behalf of the American Benefits Council of Life Insurers: Business Roundtable Committee On Investment Of Employee Benefits.
Employee Benefit Research Institute (2004) "Will Americans Ever Become Savers?" The 14th Retirement Confidence Survey, 2004, Issue Brief #268 (Washington, DC: Employee Benefit Research Institute). <http:// www.ebri.org/ publications/ib/index.cfm?fa=ibDisp&content_id=496>
Gebhardtsbauer, R. (2004) "A Balancing Act: Achieving Adequacy and Sustainability in Retirement Income Reform: What Are the Tradeoffs?," see Appendix A paper presented by Ron Gebhardtsbauer at the AARP/CEPS Forum, Hotel Astoria, Brussels, Belgium, 4 March. http://www.actuary.org/pdf/pension/tradeoffs_030404.pdf
Ghilarducci, T. (2003) "Delinking Employee Benefits from a Single Employer: Alternative Multiemployer Models," in D. S. Blitzstein, O. S. Mitchell, M. Gordon, and J. F. Mazo (eds) *Benefits for the Workplace of the Future* (Philadelphia, PA: University of Pennsylvania Press) pp. 260–284.
Ghilarducci, T. and W. Sun (2006) "How Defined Contribution Plans and 401(k)s Affect Employer Pension Costs," *Journal of Pension Economics and Finance* (Cambridge University Press) pp. 175–196.
Ghilarducci, T., W. Sun, and S. Nyce (2004) "Employer Pension Contributions and 401(k) Plans: A Note," *Industrial Relations* 43(2): 473–479.
Government Accountability Office (2004) Private Pensions: Multiemployer Plans Face Short and Long-Term Challenges, GAO-04-423 (Washington, DC: GAO).
Government Accountability Office (2005a) Private Pensions: Recent Experiences of Large Defined Benefit Plans Illustrate Weaknesses in Funding Rules, GAO-05-294 (Washington, DC: GAO).
Government Accountability Office (2005b) Private Pensions: Information on Cash Balance Pension Plans, GAO-06-42 (Washington, DC: GAO).
Greenhouse, S. and M. Barbaro (2005) "Wal-Mart Memo Suggests Ways to Cut Employee Benefit Costs," *The New York Times*, October 26, p. C1.

Hutchens, R. M. and Grace-Martin, K. (2005) "Who among White Collar Workers Has an Opportunity for Phased Retirement? Establishment Characteristics," (May 2004) IZA Discussion Paper No. 1155. Available at SSRN: http://ssrn.com/abstract=554023

Hutchens, R. M. and K. L. Papps (2004) "Developments in Phased Retirement,". Pension Research Council Working Paper, PRC WP 2004–14 (Philadelphia, PA: Pension Research Council). http://rider.wharton.upenn.edu/~prc/PRC/WP/WP2004-14.pdf

Ippolito, R. A. (1997) *Pension Plans and Employee Performance: Evidence, Analysis, and Policy* (Chicago, IL: University of Chicago Press).

Johnson, R. W. (2004) "Job Demand Among Older Workers," *Monthly Labor Review* (July) 48–56.

Johnson, R. W. and C. E. Uccello (2004) "Cash Balance Plans: What Do They Mean for Retirement Security?," *National-Tax-Journal*, Part 1 (June) 57(2): 315–328.

Madrian, B., J. Choi, and D. Laibson (2005) "$100 Bills on the Sidewalk," prepared for the 7th Annual Joint Conference of the Retirement Research Consortium, "Creating a Secure Retirement" (Washington, DC, August 11–12). http://www.bc.edu/centers/crr/papers/Seventh_Paper/Choi2.pdf

McCaw, D. (2004) "Strengthening Pension Security for All Americans: Are Workers Prepared for a Safe and Secure Retirement?," testimony for the House Committee on Education and the Workforce, 25 February.

Mercer (2004) Analysis Presented at the ERISA Industry Committee on January 14 (members only access to forum in ERIC.org website) quoted in "Our Non-Level Playing Field Will Eliminate Defined Benefit Plans (Or How to Hurt Retirement Security in American for Decades to Come)," 2005 (Washington, DC: Center for American Progress).

Munnell, A. H., F. Golub-Sass, M. Soto, and V. Francis (2006) "Why are Healthy Firms Freezing Their Defined Benefit Pension Plans?," Issue in Brief 44 (Chestnut Hill, MA: Center for Retirement Research).

Munnell, A. H., F. Golub-Sass and A. Varani (2005) "How Much are Workers Saving?," Issue in Brief 34 (Chestnut Hill, MA: Center for Retirement Research). <http://www.bc.edu/centers/crr/ib_34.shtml>

Munnell, A. H. and A. Sunden (2004) *Coming Up Short: The Challenge of 401(k) Plans* (Washington, DC: Brookings Institution Press).

Munnell, A. H. and A. Sunden (2003) "Suspending the Employer 401(k) Match," Issue in Brief 12 (Chestnut Hill, MA: Center for Retirement Research). http://www.bc.edu/centers/crr/dummy/pr_2003-06-30.shtml

Plan Sponsor (2006) "Michigan's Granholm Announces New 401(k) Plan Proposal," January 26 (PLANSPONSOR.com).

Purcell, P. (2005a) "Pension Sponsorship and Participation: Summary of Recent Trends," (Findings from the Domestic Social Policy Division), CRS Report #RL30122 (Washington, DC: Congressional Research Service).

Purcell, P. (2005b) "Retirement Plan Participation and Contributions: Trends from 1998 to 2003," (Findings from Domestic Social Policy Division), CRS Report #RL33116 (Washington, DC: Congressional Research Service).

Turner, J. A. (2006) "Designing 401(k) Plans That Encourage Retirement Savings: Lessons From Behavioral Finance Research Report," AARP Public Policy Institute (March). http://www.aarp.org/research/financial/pensions/

VanDerhei, J. (2006) "Defined Benefit Plan Freezes: Who's Affected, How Much, and Replacing Lost Accruals," Issue Brief 291 (Washington, DC: Employee Benefit Research Institute) Available at SSRN: http://ssrn.com/abstract=891170.

Vanguard Group (2005) Vanguard Annuity Options, "Create Your Own Personal Pension Plan With an Income Annuity," accessed at vanguard.com, 15 October.
Walsh, M. W. (2006) "IBM to Freeze Pension Plans to Trim Costs," *The New York Times* (6 January), Section A, Column 5, p. 1.
Watkins, M. (2002) "Washington Voluntary Accounts: A Proposal Key Elements," Economic Opportunity Institute (January) available Dec. 2004 at http://www.econop.org/Policy-WVA.htm
Watson Wyatt Worldwide (2005) "Recent Funding and Sponsorship Trends among the FORTUNE 1000," Insider (Washington DC: Watson Wyatt Worldwide) On the web at http://www.watsonwyatt.com/us/pubs/insider/showarticle.asp?ArticleID=14750
Weller, C. (2005) "Ensuring Retirement Income Security with Cash Balance Plans," September (Washington, DC: Center for American Progress).
Weller, C. (2006) Presentation on "The Immediate Future of Pension Security," March (Washington, DC: Center for American Progress).
Wiatrowski, W. J. (2005) "Retirement Plan Design and the Mobile Workforce," (Washington, DC: Bureau of Labor Statistics). Originally posted: 28 September. http://www.bls.gov/opub/cwc/cm20050926ar01p1.htm
Wolff, E. N. (2007) "The Adequacy of Retirement Resources among the Soon-to-Retire, 1983–2001," in D. B. Papadimitriou (ed.) *Government Spending on the Elderly* (United Kingdom: Palgrave Macmillan).
Wolff, E. N. and C. Weller (2005) *Retirement Insecurity* (Washington, DC: Economic Policy Institute).

Comments to Chapter 8
Zvi Bodie

In my comments I will first briefly summarize Teresa Ghilarducci's main points and then offer some additional thoughts. Here is my quick summary of the key points in her chapter:

1. The current US occupational pension system is heavily "subsidized" through favorable tax treatment.
2. Yet coverage is only 50 percent of the labor force.
3. Coverage is skewed toward those who have the best jobs.
4. The shift from DB to DC has not improved coverage, but it has made people far more insecure by subjecting them to risks they are not qualified to manage.

Teresa's main conclusion is that government pension policy ought to be changed. It should seek to expand pension coverage to those in lower paid jobs, and it should seek to enhance retirement income security. I find myself in complete agreement with Teresa's analysis and conclusions. Therefore, I will focus on some additional points that I think need to be emphasized in the current discussion about occupational pensions.

Some additional thoughts

Self-directed 401(k) plans were originally created as a tax-advantaged way to encourage employees to *supplement* Social Security and DB pension plans. The natural investment vehicle for that purpose was the mutual fund. But now that 401(k) plans have become a *substitute* rather than a complement for DB pension plans, there ought to be a safe, inexpensive, and simple way for aging employees to replace their income from work – a contract similar to Social Security or a DB pension. Teachers Insurance and Annuity Association (TIAA), a DC plan created in 1921 in lieu of a traditional DB plan for college teachers, originally was set up as an insurance company and sold only deferred fixed annuity contracts. Decades later, in the 1950s, it created College Retirement Equities Fund (CREF) to offer equity exposure.

The pioneers in the 401(k) market, however, have been investment management companies like Fidelity and Vanguard. Their main products are mutual funds. The investor "education" materials they provide are heavily biased toward equities, the asset class on which the funds charge the highest fees. They encourage people to stay heavily invested in equities even after retirement. When customers choose to take a lifetime annuity at retirement, mutual funds call it "annuicide."

I believe that in the next five to ten years, as large numbers of "Boomers" start to retire and roll over their 401(k) accumulations into IRAs, there will be a shift to insurance contracts. Plan participants will demand simple and safe products that generate secure lifetime income. Competition among providers will drive innovation and bring lower prices. The new financial technology that has revolutionized corporate risk management will be applied to efficiently create mass-produced retirement income contracts tailored to the needs of different classes of people.

What should the role of government be?

There are several things that the US government can do to help the transition to a new and more efficient pension system:

- Promote truthful advertising.
- Issue new "building block" securities to complete the markets for risk sharing.
  - Treasury inflation-protected securities (TIPS) and Inflation-indexed Bonds (IBonds).
  - A potential example: sell inflation-protected life annuities.
- Let the free market price and allocate these securities.
- Eliminate barriers to development of more robust financial institutions that employ the most efficient financial technology.

9
Retiree Health Benefit Coverage and Retirement

*James Marton and Stephen A. Woodbury**

Labor markets and health insurance are closely linked in the United States because many employers provide health insurance to both current and retired workers. Economists and policy analysts have paid much attention to the reasons for and consequences of employer provision of health insurance (HI) to current employees – see, for example, Rosen (2000) for a review and discussion – but retiree health benefits (RHB) have received far less attention, at least in part because data on them have been scarce.

Nevertheless, RHBs raise important issues for public policy. Offers of employer-provided retiree benefits – especially offers to early retirees – have become less common in recent years (see Section 9.1).[1] By definition, early retirees are not yet eligible for Medicare and may not be able to afford private coverage. Moreover, their expected health care expenses are larger than those of younger workers. If society values the consumption of health care coverage by early retirees, employer-provided retiree coverage is likely to be a public policy concern.

Any number of public policies could increase the HI coverage of early retirees. For example, Medicare could be extended to early retirees, or new incentives could be created (or mandates adopted) for employers to offer additional retiree health coverage. However, given the link between health markets and the labor market, such policies could have the unintended consequence of increasing the incentive to retire early in order to take advantage of the expanded health coverage. The extent to which this is a problem depends on the strength of the relationship between the availability of RHBs and labor supply (in this case, retirement).

Our main goal in this chapter is to add to the evidence on the effects of RHBs on retirement. We do this by examining data from the Health and Retirement Study (HRS), a major longitudinal survey sponsored by the National Institute of Aging and conducted by the University of Michigan. Unlike early work using the HRS, we use information on the availability of

RHBs and pensions in more than one year; in particular, we estimate a pair of two-year retirement transitions, 1992 to 1994 and 1994 to 1996, for a sample of men who were employed full-time in 1992, allowing for changes in RHBs and pensions between 1992 and 1994. Also, because labor force participation of a spouse may well be important to a man's decision to retire, we add variables to the model capturing the employment of each man's wife. Finally, we include in the models a control for self-reported health status in order to obtain additional evidence on the correlation between health and retirement decisions.

The next section describes the extent to which workers are covered by RHBs, examines trends in that coverage over time, and discusses reasons for the trends. We also follow a panel of men from the HRS over time, illustrating their retirement behavior and changes in their health benefit coverage using probability trees. We then describe the existing literature on health benefit coverage and retirement and discuss how our analysis contributes to this literature. The following sections describe the HRS data we use, the retirement models we estimate, and the results of estimation. We conclude with a summary of our findings, a discussion of policy implications, and some suggestions for extending the analysis.

9.1 Trends and changes in retiree health coverage

How widespread are RHBs, and how has retiree health coverage changed over time? Figures 9.1 through 9.4 show, for various types of employers, trends in the percentage who offer RHBs to their workers. The data underlying the figures come from the Insurance Component of the Medical Expenditure Panel Survey (MEPS-IC), a survey of employers conducted by the Agency for Health Care Research and Quality of the US Department of Health and Human Services. Figure 9.1 shows that about 20 percent of private employers offered RHBs in 1997, but this had fallen to about 13 percent by 2003. Figure 9.2 shows that large employers are far more likely than private employers taken as a whole to offer RHBs.

A comparison of Figures 9.1 and 9.3 shows that government employers are more likely to offer RHBs than are private employers. Despite this difference, offers of RHBs among public employers are also becoming less common (Figure 9.3). The trend appears to be confined to local government employers, however, as the percentage of state government employers that offer RHBs has increased since 1997 (Figure 9.4). In 2003, 88 percent or more of state government employers offered RHBs to their employees.

The above figures pertain to the percentage of employers offering RHBs. But what percentage of workers is covered by RHBs? Fronstin (2005) has generated estimates from the Survey of Income and Program Participation (SIPP) showing that in 1997 about 50 percent of workers aged 45 to 64 expected to receive RHBs upon retirement. This percentage had dropped

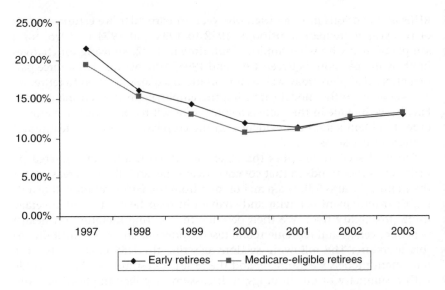

Figure 9.1 Percentage of private-sector establishments offering health insurance to retirees, 1997–2003

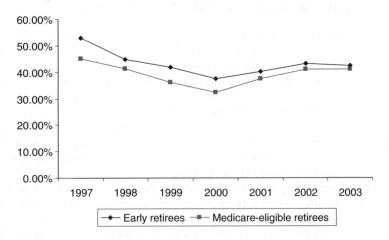

Figure 9.2 Percentage of private-sector establishments with > 1,000 employees offering health insurance to retirees, 1997–2003

to roughly 47 percent by 2002. For males, the percentages are slightly higher – 57 percent in 1997, and 51 percent in 2002. These latter percentages are comparable to those for the HRS sample we examine in this chapter. What is especially interesting about Fronstin's estimates, though, is that they far exceed the percentage of retired individuals who report

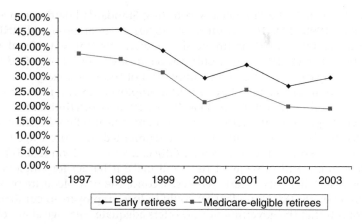

Figure 9.3 Percentage of public-sector establishments offering health insurance to retirees, 1997–2003

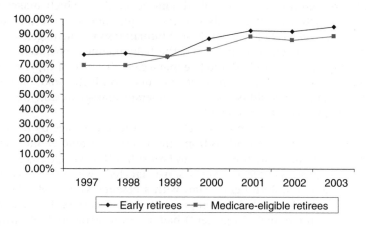

Figure 9.4 Percentage of state government establishments offering health insurance to retirees, 1997–2003

actually receiving RHBs (Fronstin, 2005, pp. 12–15). In 1997, 39 percent of early retirees and 28 percent of Medicare-eligible retirees reported that they were receiving RHBs, and these figures had fallen to 28 percent and 26 percent by 2002. It is reasonable to infer that many workers who expect RHBs do not receive them.

Fronstin (2001, 2005) and Schieber (2004) attribute the decline in retiree health coverage largely to Financial Accounting Statement No. 106 (FAS 106) – "Employers' Accounting for Postretirement Benefits Other Than

Pension" – which the Financial Accounting Standards Board approved in December 1990. FAS 106 requires employers to treat promised RHBs as financial liabilities in their financial statement starting with fiscal years after December 15, 1992. The result was reconsideration of promised RHBs and, in many cases, reduction or elimination of those promises.

Two more recent factors may also lead employers to curtail early RHBs. First, a federal court ruling in 2000 held that it is discriminatory for an employer to provide early retirees more generous health benefits than those provided by the employer and Medicare (combined) to retirees age 65 and older (US Government Accountability Office, 2005). As Moon (2005) points out, this ruling and subsequent rules will make it harder for employers to provide health benefits to early retirees. Second, the new Medicare prescription drug benefit (Medicare Part D) could induce employers to cut RHBs on the grounds that the government now offers adequate coverage at age 65. As Moon (2005) again points out, for employers who are planning to reduce or eliminate RHBs, the Medicare drug benefit offers an excuse for opting out.

On the other hand, it is also possible that employers have reduced RHBs out of a recognition that the baby-boom generation, which makes up a disproportionate part of the labor force, is aging and may be difficult to replace. *The Economist* (2006) has quoted human resource managers who say that they are concerned that "When the baby-boomer generation retires, many companies will find out too late that a career's worth of experience has walked out the door, leaving insufficient talent to fill the void." It follows that reducing RHBs could be part of a deliberate strategy to slow the loss of older skilled workers to retirement.

We can gain further insight into changes in RHB coverage by tabulating the longitudinal data on workers from the HRS that we analyze more extensively below. To illustrate how access to retiree health coverage changes over time for a given sample of workers, we created two probability trees, Figures 9.5 and 9.6. Both figures start with a baseline sample of 3,172 men who were 51 to 61 years old and employed full-time in 1992. The tree shows that 1,775 of these men (56 percent) had access to RHBs in 1992, whereas 1,397 (44 percent) did not. Branches of the tree to the right of the dashed line show how many of these workers remained in the sample, had retired, remained employed full-time, or had moved to some other labor force state (employed part-time, unemployed, partly retired, disabled, or not in the labor force) by 1994 (Figure 9.5) or 1996 (Figure 9.6). Continuing to the right, further branches subdivide retired workers by their health insurance status (employer-provided health insurance (EPHI), other health insurance (HI), or uninsured), employed full-time workers by whether they continued to have access to retiree health benefits (RHB or no RHB), and men in other labor force states by their HI status (insured or uninsured), in 1994 or 1996.

Four main findings emerge from Figures 9.5 and 9.6. First, some workers who had RHBs in 1992 no longer had them in 1994 or 1996. Figure 9.5

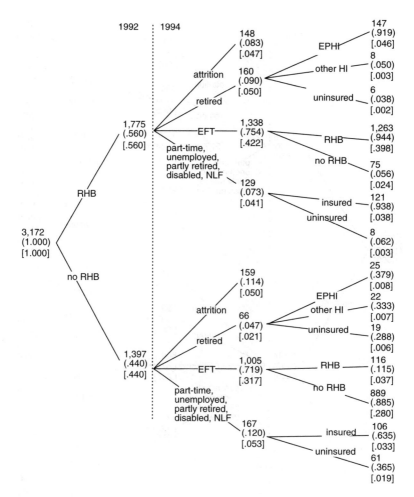

Figure 9.5 Transitions of employed full-time workers ages 51–61 with and without retiree health benefits, 1992–1994

Note: Each cell shows the individual raw count, the probability of being in a branch conditional on being in the previous branch (in parentheses), and the unconditional probability of being in that branch [in square brackets].

Key:
RHB – covered by retiree health benefits
EFT – employed full-time
NLF – not in the labor force
EPHI – covered by employer-provided health insurance
other HI – covered by health insurance other than EPHI

Source: Authors' tabulations of Health and Retirement Study data. See text for discussion.

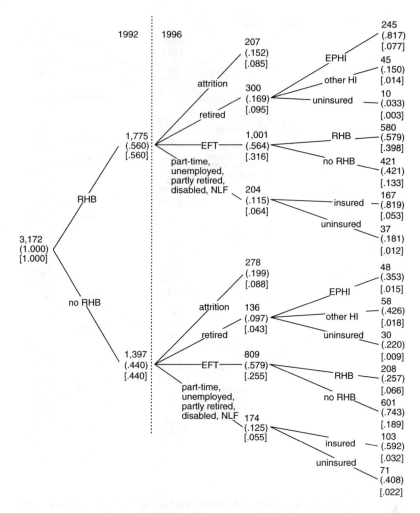

Figure 9.6 Transitions of employed full-time workers ages 51–61 with and without retiree health benefits, 1992–1996

Note: Each cell shows the individual raw count, the probability of being in a branch conditional on being in the previous branch (in parentheses), and the unconditional probability of being in that branch [in square brackets].

Key:
RHB – covered by retiree health benefits
EFT – employed full-time
NLF – not in the labor force
EPHI – covered by employer-provided health insurance
other HI – covered by health insurance other than EPHI

Source: Authors' tabulations of Health and Retirement Study data. See text for discussion.

shows that, of the full-time employed men who were covered by RHBs in 1992, 75 percent (1,338/1,775) were still employed full-time in 1994, and 94 percent of the latter (1,263/1,338) were still covered by RHBs; however, 6 percent (75/1,338) of those who remained employed full-time had lost their RHBs. It follows that 4 percent (75/1,775) of the employed full-time men who were covered by RHBs in 1992 had lost that coverage by 1994. Figure 9.6 shows that by 1996, only 56 percent of full-time covered men (1,001/1,775) remained employed full-time, and only 58 percent of the latter (580/1,001) were still covered by RHBs. That is, of the 1,775 employed full-time men who were covered by RHBs in 1992, 24 percent (421/1,775) had lost retiree health benefit coverage by 1996.

Why did so many workers lose RHBs between 1992 and 1996, compared with 1992 to 1994? A significant part of the explanation may be that the HRS question on RHBs differed between 1994 and 1996. The 1994 questionnaire asked HRS respondents whether their EPHI was "available to people who retire" (question R8 of the 1994 survey). This question is ambiguous in at least two ways. First, a respondent could interpret it to pertain to either early retiree benefits or Medicare-eligible retiree benefits. Second, a respondent could interpret it to apply either to himself or to any other worker. The 1996 questionnaire asked respondents a more specific question – whether the respondent's EPHI could be continued up to the age of 65 if he or she left the employer at the time of the interview (questions R34 and R35 of the 1996 survey). This question is restricted to the availability of early retiree benefits (rather than all retiree benefits) to the respondent (rather than any worker), so by definition it will elicit fewer positive responses than the 1994 question. It could well be that RHB offers dropped between 1994 and 1996, but the drop is likely to be exaggerated by comparing Figures 9.5 and 9.6.

A second finding from Figures 9.5 and 9.6 is that some workers who lacked retiree benefits in 1992 had gained them by 1994 or 1996. Figure 9.5 shows that of the full-time employed men who lacked RHBs in 1992, 72 percent (1,005/1,397) were still employed full-time in 1994. Although 89 percent of the latter (889/1,005) still lacked RHBs, 12 percent (116/1,005) had gained them. So 8 percent (116/1,397) of the employed full-time men who lacked RHBs in 1992 had gained coverage by 1994. Figure 9.6 shows that by 1996, 58 percent of full-time men without RHBs (809/1,397) remained employed full-time, and 74 percent of the latter (601/809) still lacked RHBs; however, 26 percent (208/809) had gained coverage. That is, 15 percent (208/1,397) of the employed full-time men who lacked RHBs in 1992 had gained coverage by 1996. The finding suggests that as older workers increase their job tenure, they thereby become eligible for RHBs.

Taken together, these first two findings indicate that retiree health coverage of a given worker does change over time, which suggests in turn the importance of allowing retiree health coverage to be a time-varying covariate in empirical models of retirement.

Third, some workers who reported having RHBs in 1992, and who had retired by 1994 or 1996, did not have employer-provided health benefits in retirement. For example, Figure 9.6 shows that of the full-time employed men who were covered by RHBs in 1992, 17 percent (300/1,775) had retired by 1996, and 82 percent of the latter (245/300) were receiving employer-provided RHBs; however, 15 percent (45/300) were receiving other HI, and 3 percent (10/300) were uninsured. Although the percentage uninsured is quite small, the data displayed in Figures 9.5 and 9.6 give some longitudinal support to Fronstin's (2005) inference that "workers are more likely to expect RHBs than retirees are actually likely to have those benefits."

Fourth, workers with RHBs are more likely to retire than those without. Consider first changes between 1992 and 1994. Whereas 9 percent of workers with RHBs had retired by 1994 (and more than 90 percent of these were covered by employer-provided health benefits), less than 5 percent of workers who lacked RHBs in 1992 had retired by 1994 (and only 38 percent of these had EPHI). Changes between 1992 and 1994 tell a similar story: 17 percent of workers with RHBs had retired by 1996, but only 10 percent of workers who lacked RHBs in 1992 had retired by 1996. These figures give a first hint that RHBs are related to earlier retirement.

9.2 Retiree health benefits and retirement: existing research

Reductions in RHB coverage could lead government to respond by expanding Medicare or by regulating retiree benefits. In the absence of a government response, reductions in the availability of retiree health coverage could lead workers to change their labor supply behavior and work more or longer, because if they do not, they or their dependents will not be covered by HI.

Much public discussion in recent decades has suggested that a government response to declining RHBs would be appropriate. Efforts to create universal health insurance coverage – through a single payer or some other means – would obviously eliminate the problem implied by declining employer-provided retiree coverage. Government provision of HI would in turn have other consequences – workers who might otherwise continue working would retire because they would not need to work in order to maintain HI coverage. It follows that estimates of workers' labor supply response to RHBs constitute an important part of the debate over government provision of RHBs.

Much empirical research has investigated the effects of pensions, social security, and assets on the decision to retire, but relatively little research has examined the impact of HI coverage on retirement.[2] Previous research has used data from the Retirement History Survey, conducted mainly during the 1970s (Rust and Phelan, 1997), the SIPP (Karoly and Rogowski, 1994; Madrian, 1994), the Current Population Survey (Gruber and Madrian, 1995), and the National Medical Expenditure Survey (Madrian, 1994). These studies uniformly conclude that availability of RHBs (or continuation coverage in the case of Gruber and Madrian) significantly increases the probability that an older worker will retire.

Hurd and McGarry (1993), Rogowski and Karoly (2000), and Blau and Gilleskie (2001) examine the relationship between retirement (or retirement expectations in the case of Hurd and McGarry) and RHBs using the HRS. The HRS has the unique advantage of being longitudinal and including questions on both retirement and the availability of RHBs. As a result, studies based on these data are among the most convincing in this literature. Hurd and McGarry (1993) examine Wave 1 (1992) of the HRS and find that workers eligible to receive RHBs that are partly or fully paid by the employer are significantly less likely than other workers to report that they expect to work past age 62. Rogowski and Karoly (2000) and Blau and Gilleskie (2001) each take advantage of two waves of the HRS and find that workers with an offer of RHBs are significantly more likely to retire than workers without. Rogowski and Karoly find that workers with RHBs in 1992 were about 11 percentage points more likely to be retired in 1996 than those without. Blau and Gilleskie examine the transition to retirement between 1992 and 1994 and find that RHBs increased the probability of retirement by 2 to 6 percentage points, depending on the extent to which retirees share in the cost of those benefits.

9.3 Empirical model and data

Both Rogowski and Karoly (2000) and Blau and Gilleskie (2001) leave open three issues that we explore here. First, they use observations on RHB coverage, pension coverage, and other variables in 1992 (Wave 1 of the HRS) to predict labor force participation in 1994 (Wave 2) or 1996 (Wave 3). However, as seen in Figures 9.5 and 9.6, retiree health coverage is not constant for each worker but varies over time. Accordingly, in the estimates below, we allow the availability of RHBs and pensions to vary from year to year. Second, a small literature has examined the effect of one spouse's labor supply behavior on the other's labor supply (for example, Buchmueller and Valletta, 1999; Wellington and Cobb-Clark, 2000; Olson, 2000), so we add to the model variables capturing the employment of each man's wife. Third, because health is such an important factor in people's retirement decisions, we add to the list of health indicators each individual's self-reported health status. Our aim in making these changes is to check whether estimates of the impact of RHBs on retirement are sensitive to changes in model specification.

We estimate the correlation between retiree health coverage and retirement over three time periods (1992–1994, 1994–1996, and 1992–1996) for a sample of men in the HRS born between 1931 and 1941 working full-time (at least 35 hours per week) as of 1992.[3] The retirement decision between 1992 and 1994 is conditioned on health benefit and pension coverage in 1992, whereas the retirement decision between 1994 and 1996 is conditioned on health benefit and pension coverage in 1994. For comparison, we also estimate a four-year retirement transition, between 1992 and 1996, in which we condition only on health benefit and pension coverage in 1992.

Specifically, we estimate three probit models of the conditional probability that individual i (working in 1992 or 1994) will be retired in a subsequent year (1994 or 1996):

$$\Pr(retired_{i,1994} = 1|\bullet) = F[\beta_0 + \beta_1(rhb_{i,1992}) + \beta_2(pension_{i,1992}) + \beta_3(health_{i,1992}) + \beta_4(spouse_{i,1992}) + \beta_5(X_{i,1992})] \quad (1)$$

$$\Pr(retired_{i,1996} = 1|\bullet) = F[\beta_0 + \beta_1(rhb_{i,1994}) + \beta_2(pension_{i,1994}) + \beta_3(health_{i,1994}) + \beta_4(spouse_{i,1994}) + \beta_5(X_{i,1994})] \quad (2)$$

$$\Pr(retired_{i,1996} = 1|\bullet) = F[\beta_0 + \beta_1(rhb_{i,1992}) + \beta_2(pension_{i,1992}) + \beta_3(health_{i,1992}) + \beta_4(spouse_{i,1992}) + \beta_5(X_{i,1992})] \quad (3)$$

In these probits, rhb_{it} denotes a set of dummies indicating whether worker i was offered RHBs in year t (either 1992 or 1994), $pension_{it}$ is a set of indicators of whether worker i was included in a pension plan (or plans) in year t, $health_{it}$ is a set of variables modeling the health of the worker in year t, $spouse_{it}$ is a set of variables indicating whether the worker was married and whether his spouse was working in year t, and X_{it} is set of demographic variables. We specify these retirement equations as probits (F denotes the standard normal cumulative density), but linear probability models would serve just as well.

The sample starts with the 3,172 men ages 51–61 and employed full-time in 1992 (Wave 1) from the HRS. Over the subsequent four years, some men left the study (due to death or for other reasons), some retired, others continued to work full time, and still others moved to part-time work, unemployment, partial retirement, disability, or left the labor force (the "other" category). Figure 9.7 illustrates these transitions. In 1994, 307 men left the study, so 2,865 men remained for estimating equation 1. Of these, 226 (8 percent) had retired by 1994. Between 1994 and 1996 another 183 left the sample, so 2,146 men remained to estimate equation 2. Of these, 228 (11 percent) had retired by 1996. The four-year retirement transition modeled by equation 3 is not shown in Figure 9.7, but between 1992 and 1996, a net total of 446 men left the study, so 2,726 remained to contribute to the estimation of equation 3. Of these, 449 (16 percent) had retired by 1996.

Table 9.1 displays sample means of the independent variables included in the models. The first column gives means of the "starting sample" – that is, the 3,172 men in the HRS who were employed full-time 51–61 years old in 1992. The second and third columns show sample means of the "transition

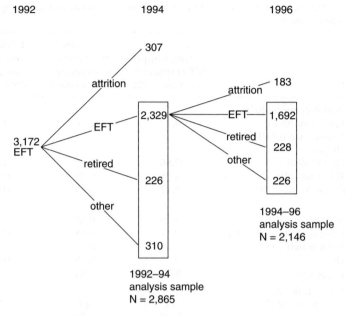

Figure 9.7 HRS analysis samples illustrated
Notes:
EFT refers to employed full-time workers.
"Attrition" includes those who were not interviewed or died.
"Other" includes part-time, unemployed, disabled, and not in the labor force.
Source: Authors' tabulations of Health and Retirement Study data. See text for discussion.

samples" – that is, the samples used to estimate equations 1 and 2. Comparison of the columns suggests that attrition results in samples of men who are more likely to have HI, more likely to be covered by a pension, and more likely to be married. Although the attrition does appear to be nonrandom, it does not appear severe enough to make attrition bias a serious concern.

We model coverage by RHBs (rhb_{it}) in year t using a set of four mutually exclusive dummy variables:

- a dummy equal to 1 if the worker had EPHI but *no offer of RHBs*[4] (this is the reference category).
- a dummy equal to 1 if the worker had EPHI and *would receive health benefits if he retired*.
- a dummy equal to 1 if the worker had no EPHI but was *covered by some other type of health insurance*.
- a dummy equal to 1 if the worker had *no HI* coverage.

Table 9.1 Summary statistics of samples used in estimation (sample proportions except where noted)

Variable	Starting sample: (FT employed males in 1992)	1992–1994 transition sub-sample (1992 values)	1994–1996 transition sub-sample (1994 values)
Retiree health benefits (RHB)			
has employer-provided health insurance (EPHI) but no RHB (ref)	0.24	0.24	0.25
has EPHI and RHB	0.56	0.57	0.60
no EPHI but has other coverage	0.08	0.08	0.07
no health insurance (HI)	0.12	0.11	0.08
Pension			
none or unknown (ref)	0.39	0.38	0.34
has defined contribution (DC)	0.18	0.18	0.20
has defined benefit (DB)	0.25	0.25	0.33
has both	0.17	0.18	0.12
has but type unknown	0.01	0.01	0.01
Health status indicators			
body mass index (BMI)	27	27	27
multiple chronic conditions	0.20	0.20	0.23
reports fair or poor health	0.12	0.12	0.12
Spousal labor supply			
not married (ref)	0.16	0.15	0.13
married, spouse works full time (FT)	0.38	0.39	0.38
married, spouse works part time (PT)	0.15	0.15	0.16
married, spouse not working	0.31	0.31	0.33
Age at time of 1992 interview	55.7	55.7	55.4
Nonwhite	0.16	0.15	0.14
Years of schooling	13	13	13
Months between interviews	N/A	22	24
Sample size	3,172	2,865	2,146

Notes: The starting sample includes employed full-time men ages 51–61 in 1992. The transition subsamples drop workers who had left the survey by 1994 or 1996. See Figure 9.7.

Source: Authors' tabulations of HRS data. See text for discussion.

As mentioned earlier, Fronstin (2005) found that roughly 57 percent of men ages 45–64 reported being covered by RHBs in the 1997 SIPP, so the percentages of workers covered by RHBs in the HRS samples we are using (between 56 and 60 percent) seem reasonable. Note that the percentages are somewhat higher for the 1992–1994 and 1994–1996 subsamples than for the starting sample.

A second set of dummies (*pension$_{it}$*, again mutually exclusive) models whether the worker was included in a pension plan or tax-deferred savings plan through his work in year *t*:

- a dummy equal to 1 if the worker was *not included in any pension plan* or did not know whether he was included (the reference category).
- a dummy equal to 1 if the worker was included in one or more *defined contribution (DC)* pension plans (but not included in any defined benefit plans).
- a dummy equal to 1 if the worker was included in one or more *defined benefit (DB)* pension plans (but no defined contribution plans).
- a dummy equal to 1 if the worker was included in *both a DC and a DB* pension plan.
- a dummy equal to 1 if the worker said he was included in a pension plan but *did not know the type*.

Nearly two-fifths of this sample was not covered by any employer-sponsored pension plan in 1992, typical of the population of working men in 1992.

Rogowski and Karoly (2000) included two variables to capture each worker's health status (*health$_{it}$*) in year *t*. The first is body mass index (BMI) in year *t* – weight in kilograms divided by height in meters squared – which has come to be widely used in the development literature as a measure of maximum physical capacity. The second is a dummy equal to 1 for workers who report having two or more chronic health conditions in year *t*, such as high blood pressure, diabetes, cancer, chronic lung disease, heart disease, stroke, or arthritis. The latter is only a rough indicator of a respondent's health, in part because it does not distinguish more serious from less serious conditions; however, limitations of the HRS make it difficult to construct a more telling health indicator based on a respondent's report of specific illnesses. Accordingly, we add to the model a dummy variable equal to 1 for respondents who report being in fair or poor health in year *t*.

Because the labor force status of a spouse is likely to be important to a man's decision to retire, we add to the model a set of dummies capturing the employment status of each man's wife in year *t*:

- a dummy equal to 1 if the worker was *not married* (the reference category).
- a dummy equal to 1 if the worker was *married to a woman working full time*.
- a dummy equal to 1 if the worker was *married to a woman working part time*.
- a dummy equal to 1 if the worker was *married to a woman who does not work* (is unemployed, partly retired, retired, disabled, or not in the labor force).

Because labor supply decisions by couples are likely to be joint, we are concerned that this set of indicators is endogenous. This is a difficult issue, and the literature on HI and labor supply (cited above) has not addressed it. We include these variables to see whether estimates of the impact of RHBs are sensitive to their inclusion or exclusion, and leave the endogeneity of spousal labor supply to future work.

The demographic controls included in the model (X_{it}) are age in 1992, an indicator equal to 1 for nonwhites, and years of schooling. Like Rogowski and Karoly (2000), we also include a variable indicating the length of time between wave interviews because that time varies across respondents.

9.4 Empirical findings

Table 9.2 displays estimates of the probit models described above, with one panel for each model. Each panel gives probit βs, P-values, marginal effects, and marginal effects relative to the base probability of retirement. (Each marginal effect is the expected percentage point change in retirement probability from a one-unit change in the independent variable at the sample mean.)

The key variable in each model is the indicator of EPHI with RHB coverage ("has EPHI and RHB"). The relationship between RHBs and retirement is strong and statistically significant in each model. A worker with RHBs in 1992 was 4 percentage points more likely to be retired in 1994 than was a comparable worker who had employer-provided health benefits but no RHBs (1992–1994 model). This is a 55 percent increase in the baseline probability of retirement between 1992 and 1994 of 8 percent. Also, a worker with RHBs in 1994 was 3 percentage points more likely to be retired in 1996 than a comparable worker who had no RHBs (1994–1996 model) – a 29 percent increase in the baseline retirement probability between 1994 and 1996.

It follows that the relationship between RHBs and retirement was stronger between 1992 and 1994 than between 1994 and 1996. This is a key finding. During 1992–1994, the cohort we are analyzing was younger than during 1994–1996. The stronger relationship between RHB offers and retirement during 1992–1994 than during 1994–1996 suggests that workers with RHBs tend to take advantage of those benefits when they are relatively young. This makes sense because RHBs are more valuable to a worker at age 55 than at age 65 – the younger worker receives the benefit over more years. To a worker eligible for RHBs, each year of delayed retirement represents a year of lost benefits. As a result, we would expect the impact of RHBs on retirement to fall as workers approach age 65. An important implication is that RHBs are likely to be expensive precisely because they are more likely to be accepted by workers who are younger and further from Medicare eligibility. It is hardly surprising, then, that employers have been trimming their offers of RHBs.

The 1994–1996 model differs from earlier RHB models estimated with the HRS because it updates the observations of RHBs and other independent variables. For comparison, the 1992–1996 model estimates the probability of

Table 9.2 Probit estimates of retirement probability between 1992–1994, 1994–1996, and 1992–1996, full-time older male workers in the HRS (probit betas, with P-values and marginal effects)

Independent Variable	1992–1994				1994–1996				1992–1996			
	Probit β	P-value	Marginal effect (%)	M.E./base (%)	Probit β	P-value	Marginal effect (%)	M.E./base (%)	Probit β	P-value	Marginal effect (%)	M.E./base (%)
Retiree health benefits(RHB) [ref: has employer-provided health insurance (EPHI) but no RHB]												
has EPHI and RHB	0.39	0.00	4	55	0.24	0.01	3	29	0.33	0.00	7	41
no EPHI but has other coverage	0.38	0.02	6	70	0.16	0.40	2	22	0.23	0.12	5	32
no health insurance	0.19	0.24	2	31	−0.18	0.39	−2	−20	0.11	0.43	2	14
Pension (ref: none or unknown)												
has defined contribution (DC)	0.02	0.86	0	3	0.06	0.64	1	8	0.16	0.12	3	21
has defined benefit (DB)	0.35	0.00	5	58	0.68	0.00	11	101	0.48	0.00	11	68
has both	0.28	0.02	4	47	0.47	0.00	8	76	0.52	0.00	13	78
has but type unknown	−0.15	0.75	−2	−19	0.70	0.10	15	139	0.71	0.02	20	124
Health status indicators												
body mass index (BMI)	0.01	0.11	0	2	0.01	0.25	0	1	0.01	0.17	0	1
multiple chronic conditions	0.19	0.03	2	30	−0.02	0.85	0	−2	0.11	0.16	2	14
reports fair or poor health	0.20	0.07	3	33	0.39	0.00	7	61	0.31	0.00	7	45

Continued

Table 9.2 Continued

Independent Variable	1992–1994				1994–1996				1992–1996			
	Probit β	P-value	Marginal effect (%)	M.E./base (%)	Probit β	P-value	Marginal effect (%)	M.E./base (%)	Probit β	P-value	Marginal effect (%)	M.E./base (%)
Spousal labor supply (ref: not married)												
married, spouse works full time (FT)	−0.44	0.00	−5	−60	−0.29	0.03	−4	−34	−0.23	0.02	−5	−28
married, spouse works part time (PT)	−0.56	0.00	−5	−60	−0.17	0.26	−2	−19	−0.19	0.09	−4	−23
married, spouse not working	−0.32	0.00	−3	−42	−0.08	0.54	−1	−9	−0.18	0.06	−4	−22
Age in 1992	0.12	0.00	1	17	0.16	0.00	2	20	0.16	0.00	3	20
Nonwhite	−0.07	0.54	−1	−9	−0.07	0.54	−1	−8	−0.05	0.58	−1	−6
Years of schooling	0.00	0.82	0	0	−0.04	0.00	−1	−5	−0.04	0.00	−1	−5
Months between interviews	0.01	0.44	0	2	0.01	0.75	0	1	0.00	0.80	0	0
Intercept	−9.08	0.00			−10.81	0.00			−9.93	0.00		
Log likelihood	−698				−600				−1032			
Sample size	2,865				2,146				2,726			
Number retired	226				228				449			
Percent retired	8%				11%				16%			
Left survey (all reasons)	307				183				446			

Notes: Probit estimates from samples of employed full-time men ages 51–61 in 1992. See Figure 9.7 and Table 9.1 for more on the samples.

Source: Authors' calculations from HRS data. See text for discussion.

retirement in 1996 using only explanatory variables from 1992. That model suggests that a worker with RHBs in 1992 was 7 percentage points more likely to be retired in 1996 than a comparable worker without RHBs (1992–1996 model) – a 41 percent increase in the baseline retirement probability between 1992 and 1996 (16 percent). Although the finding is consistent with the findings from the separate 1992–1994 and 1994–1996 models, it masks the main finding from the separate models – that the relationship between RHBs and retirement was stronger in the 1992–1994 transition – when the workers in the sample were younger – than in the 1994–1996 transition.

Rogowski and Karoly (2000) estimate a model similar to Table 9.2's 1992–1996 model and find a marginal effect of RHB coverage of 11 percentage points – representing a 68 percent increase in their baseline probability of retirement – substantially larger than our estimate. Why the difference? We believe the main factor is that Rogowski and Karoly used the alpha release of the HRS Wave 3 data, whereas we use the final release of the Wave 3 data as further cleaned by the RAND Corporation. We end up with a larger sample than theirs (2,726 vs. 2,638), more retirees (449 vs. 422), and a slightly higher baseline retirement probability (16.5 percent vs. 16.0 percent) over the four years. A related point is that Rogowski and Karoly's coding of the RHB and pension indicators may differ from ours (which is based on RAND's coding in the RAND HRS data). Because Rogowski and Karoly do not report sample descriptive statistics, it is difficult to know how our sorting of workers into different RHB and pension categories differs from theirs.[5]

Table 9.2 also suggests that workers covered by a DB pension in 1992 were 5 percentage points more likely to be retired in 1994 than those with no pension. Workers with both DB and DC pensions in 1992 were 4 percentage points more likely to be retired in 1994 than those without. These represent increases of 58 percent and 47 percent in the baseline probability of retirement between 1992 and 1994. The effects of pension coverage in 1994 on the probability of being retired in 1996 are even stronger, which suggests that this cohort of workers became more likely to accept a DB pension as it aged. In striking contrast, workers covered by DC pensions were no more likely to retire than were those with no pension. These findings make sense because DB pensions tend to be structured so as to induce workers to retire between ages 62 and 65, whereas DC pensions do not create strong retirement incentives (Lazear, 1998, chapter 15). Because the cohort of men we are analyzing was 51 to 61 in 1992, it makes sense that the impact of a DB pension on retirement would increase in later years (that is, as the cohort aged and the bulk of the cohort drew closer to age 62).

The models also include a measure of self-reported fair or poor health ("reports fair or poor health"), in addition to the BMI and chronic conditions health indicators included by Rogowski and Karoly (2000). Fair or poor health is statistically significant in all three models – men who report fair or poor health are between 3 and 7 percentage points more likely to be retired two to four years in the future than men who do not report fair or poor health. BMI is not significant in any of the models, and the indicator of multiple chronic conditions is significant only in the 1992–1994 model. (The latter suggests that having two or more chronic conditions in 1992 leads to a 30 percent increase in the baseline probability of retirement in 1994.)

The relationship between spousal labor supply and retirement is quite strong and suggests the importance of including spousal labor supply variables in retirement models. Men who had a full-time or part-time working wife in 1992 were 5 percentage points less likely to be retired in 1994 than were men who were not married. This represents a 60 percent drop in the baseline probability of retirement. The relationship between marriage to a full-time working spouse and retirement is smaller but still statistically significant for the 1994–1996 retirement transition. (The relationship between marriage to a part-time working spouse and retirement is insignificant for 1994–1996.) The findings are consistent with the idea that couples make decisions about retirement jointly – men and women with working spouses try to time retirement so as to retire at the same time as their spouse (Hamermesh, 2002).

An important caveat applies to all the above estimates – they should not be interpreted causally. Although the findings do suggest that RHBs cause earlier retirement, as we would expect, it is likely that workers who would like to retire before age 65 choose (or self-select into) jobs that offer RHBs. If so, this self-selection would lead to upward-biased estimates of the causal effect of RHBs on retirement – workers who are covered by RHBs would have retired somewhat earlier even if they were not eligible for those benefits. Without further efforts to identify the true relationship between RHBs and retirement, we cannot say anything about the size of this bias, but the issue is ripe for future research.

9.5 Summary, implications, and extensions

Paul Fronstin (2001, 2005) has shown clearly that during the past decade, fewer employers have offered RHBs, and fewer workers have been covered by such benefits. Because early RHBs provide a bridge to Medicare for dislocated workers in their 50s and early 60s, the decline of RHBs leaves an increasing number of older workers vulnerable to loss of health insurance if they lose their job. However, past evidence, which we reconfirm here, suggests that RHBs also induce workers to retire earlier than they would otherwise. Intentionally or not, RHBs draw experienced and productive workers out of the labor force.

In this chapter, we have used data from the Health and Retirement Study to extend past work on RHBs in three main ways. First, we develop a descriptive analysis of RHB coverage that compares the coverage of workers in 1992 with their coverage two and four years later. The analysis, summarized in two probability trees (Figures 9.5 and 9.6) shows the following:

- Of the full-time employed workers who had RHBs in 1992, about 4 percent were still full-time employed in 1994 but had lost their RHBs.
- Of the full-time employed workers who lacked RHBs in 1992, about 8 percent were still employed full-time in 1994 and had gained RHBs.
- It follows that retiree health coverage of a given worker changes over time, so it may be important to account for such changes in formulating empirical models of retirement.
- Some full-time employed workers who thought they had RHBs in 1992, and who had retired by 1994 or 1996, did not have employer-provided health benefits in retirement. Of the full-time employed men who were covered by RHBs in 1992 and had retired by 1994, 4 percent were uninsured, and 5 percent were covered by HI other than EPHI.

The analysis is limited by changes in key survey questions between the 1994 and 1996 waves of the HRS, and we believe that further work with post-1996 HRS waves would be useful.

Second, in modeling the relationship between RHBs and retirement, we have analyzed two separate two-year transitions in which the explanatory variables are updated for the second transition. The approach is a simplified survival analysis or event history analysis with time-varying covariates, and it allows us to observe different impacts of RHBs on retirement as the cohort of workers ages. It contrasts with the approach taken in earlier work, where a single two- or four-year transition is analyzed. The main findings can be summarized simply:

- For the 1992–1994 transition, workers with RHBs were 4 percentage points more likely to retire than those without – a 55 percent increase in the retirement probability.
- For the 1994–1996 transition, workers with RHBs were 3 percentage points more likely to retire than those without – a 29 percent increase in the retirement probability.

We infer that this cohort of workers was most likely to accept RHBs when they were relatively young, then grew less likely to do so as they aged. The implications are twofold. From a modeling perspective, the findings suggest the importance of examining repeated transitions and accounting for changes over time in the explanatory variables. From a policy perspective, the findings are important because they suggest that workers who are eligible for RHBs tend to take advantage of them when they are young. This makes sense because RHBs accepted when a worker is younger yield a benefit for longer and hence are more valuable. The implication, though, is that RHBs represent an expensive benefit that tends to induce experienced workers with several remaining productive years to retire. Policies that create additional retiree health coverage need to account for the reduction in labor supply that may be an unintended consequence of such policies.

Third, we have attempted to improve on the previous literature by including the employment status of each worker's spouse in the retirement models. The findings suggest strongly that men with a full-time working spouse are less likely to retire than men who are not married. This suggests that husbands and wives view each others' leisure time as complementary; hence, couples time their retirements to coincide. Including spouse's employment status does not seem to appreciably change the estimated relationship between RHBs and retirement (see Note 5).

At least three extensions of the work presented here would be useful. First, it would clearly be interesting to examine additional two-year retirement transitions by adding more recent HRS waves to the analysis. Second, it may well be possible to do a better job of controlling for the health of the workers in the sample by including different health indicators from the HRS that we have not exploited. Third, in recent years the HRS has added cohorts of "War Babies" (born between 1942 and 1947), and of "Early Baby Boomers" (born between 1948 and 1953). Examining the behavior of these younger cohorts and comparing it with the behavior of the original HRS sample could have important implications for public policy. We hope to pursue these extensions in future work.

Notes

* For helpful advice and comments, we thank participants at The Levy Economics Institute's Conference on Government Spending on the Elderly, Steven Haider, Susann Rohwedder, and, particularly, Barbara L. Wolfe.

1. Because most retirees are eligible for Medicare at age 65, employer-provided RHBs are of two kinds – first, coverage for early retirees (those younger than 65), which often continues the HI a worker had while employed until age 65; second, coverage for the Medicare eligible (those 65 or older), which supplements Medicare so that retirees have comprehensive HI. Alternatives to employer-provided RHBs do exist, but they are usually more expensive or less generous than EPHI. For example, early retirees may buy private health insurance, and retirees age 65 and older may buy Medigap insurance or enroll in Medicare Advantage (Medicare, Part C, a private plan administered through Medicare).
2. See Gruber and Madrian (2004) and Madrian (2006) for more complete reviews of the literature and additional background.
3. For the empirical analysis, we started with the RAND HRS Data file, Version F, which is a simplified longitudinal data set based on the HRS data. See St. Clair et al. (2006).
4. As discussed earlier, the 1992 and 1994 question reads, "Is the health insurance plan [that currently covers you] available to people who retire?" The 1996 and later

waves of the HRS ask explicitly whether the respondent's health benefit plan would cover him if he retired before age 65.
5. Two obvious differences between Rogowski and Karoly's specification and ours do not seem to underlie the difference in estimated impact of RHBs. First, Rogowski and Karoly included a dummy variable indicating whether a worker was married, whereas we include a set of indicators of the employment status of each worker's spouse. However, we have estimated the model with a dummy variable for married replacing the spouse employment status indicators, and the results (not reported) are essentially similar. Second, Rogowski and Karoly controlled for the cost sharing associated with RHBs, whereas we have not. We omit cost sharing because HRS data on cost sharing are omitted from the RAND HRS Data file we are using. However, in a draft of this chapter, we used the original HRS data, included cost sharing indicators, and like Rogowski and Karoly, found them to have little impact on retirement probabilities. The finding is surprising in light of other findings on the relationship between health insurance costs and decisions to retire (Johnson, Davidoff, and Perese, 2003).

References

Blau, D. M. and D. B. Gilleskie (2001) "Retiree Health Insurance and Labor Force Behavior of Older Men in the 1990s," *Review of Economics and Statistics* 83: 64–80.

Buchmueller, T. C. and R. G. Valletta (1999) "The Effect of Health Insurance on Married Female Labor Supply," *Journal of Human Resources* 34: 42–71.

The Economist (2006) "Special Report: The Aging Workforce," 18 February, 65–67.

Fronstin, P. (2001) "Retiree Health Benefits: Trends and Outlook," Issue Brief No. 236 (Washington, DC: Employee Benefit Research Institute).

Fronstin, P. (2005) "The Impact of the Erosion of Retiree Health Benefits on Workers and Retirees," Issue Brief No. 279 (Washington, DC: Employee Benefit Research Institute).

Gruber, J. and B. C. Madrian (1995) "Health Insurance Availability and the Retirement Decision," *American Economic Review* 85: 938–948.

Gruber, J. and B. C. Madrian (2004) "Health Insurance, Labor Supply and Job Mobility: A Critical Review of the Literature," in Catherine G. McLaughlin (ed.) *Health Policy and the Uninsured* (Washington, DC: Urban Institute Press) pp. 97–178.

Hamermesh, D. S. (2002) "Timing, Togetherness, and Time Windfalls," *Journal of Population Economics* 15: 601–623.

Hurd, M. and K. McGarry (1993) "The Relationship between Job Characteristics and Retirement Behavior," Working Paper No. 4558 (Cambridge, MA: National Bureau of Economic Research).

Institute for Social Research, University of Michigan. The Health and Retirement Study. Full documentation and data available at <http://hrsonline.isr.umich.edu>

Johnson, R. W., A. J. Davidoff, and K. Perese (2003) "Health Insurance Costs and Early Retirement Decisions," *Industrial and Labor Relations Review* 56: 716–729.

Karoly, L. A. and J. A. Rogowski (1994) "The Effect of Access to Post-Retirement Health Insurance on the Decision to Retire Early," *Industrial and Labor Relations Review* 48: 103–123.

Lazear, E. P. (1998) *Personnel Economics for Managers* (New York: Wiley).

Madrian, B. C. (1994) "The Effect of Health Insurance on Retirement," *Brookings Papers on Economic Activity* No. 1 (Washington, DC: The Brookings Institution) pp. 181–232.

Madrian, B. C. (2006) "The US Health Care System and Labor Markets," Working Paper No. 11980 (Cambridge, MA: National Bureau of Economic Research).
Moon, M. (2005) "Retiree Health Coverage: Individuals Picking Up Bigger Tab," *TIAA-CREF Trends and Issues*, July (New York: TIAA-CREF).
Olson, C. A. (2000) "Part-time Work, Health Insurance Coverage, and the Wages of Married Women," in W. T. Alpert and S. A. Woodbury (eds) *Employee Benefits and Labor Markets in Canada and the United States* (Kalamazoo, MI: W.E. Upjohn Institute for Employment Research) pp. 295–324.
Rogowski, J. and L. Karoly (2000) "Health Insurance and Retirement Behavior: Evidence from the Health and Retirement Survey," *Journal of Health Economics* 19: 529–539.
Rosen, S. (2000) "Does the Composition of Pay Matter?," in W. T. Alpert and S. A. Woodbury (eds) *Employee Benefits and Labor Markets in Canada and the United States* (Kalamazoo, MI: W.E. Upjohn Institute for Employment Research) pp. 13–30.
Rust, J. and C. Phelan (1997) "How Social Security and Medicare Affect Retirement Behavior in a World of Incomplete Markets," *Econometrica* 65: 781–831.
St. Clair, P. et al. (2006) *RAND HRS Data Documentation, Version F.*, May (Santa Monica, CA: Labor and Population Program, RAND Center for the Study of Aging).
Schieber, S. J. (2004) "The Outlook of RHBs," TIAA-CREF Institute Research Dialogue, Issue No. 81, September (New York: TIAA-CREF).
United States Government Accountability Office (2005) "RHBs: Options for Employment-Based Prescription Drug Benefits under the Medicare Modernization Act," GAO Report to Congressional Committees, GAO-05-205, February (Washington, DC: GAO).
Wellington, A. J. and D. A. Cobb-Clark (2000) "The Labor Supply Effects of Universal Coverage: What Can We Learn from Individuals with Spousal Coverage?" *Research in Labor Economics* 19: 315–344.

Comments to Chapter 9
Barbara Wolfe

The goals of this very interesting chapter are to (1) describe the provision of retiree health benefit (RHB) coverage over time and (2) analyze the implications for retirement behavior paying particular attention to the influence on employees in their 50s. This chapter thus addresses an increasingly important topic as fewer employers now offer RHBs than in the past. The shift in employer-sponsored retiree health insurance benefits started in the early 1990s and it continues today.

The major reason for the initial decline in coverage was a major change in the accounting standards for post-retirement benefits other than pensions (FAS 106). These new standards required companies to include the expense of such benefits in their profit and loss calculations. These requirements created a liability for companies that negatively influence their bottom line. In response many firms were eager to reduce this obligation. The future outlook suggests further reductions as the increasing cost of providing such benefits (due to increasing health care costs and longer life expectancies) combined with the new accounting standards is likely to lead many more firms to decrease their RHBs.

This shift means a loss to those employees who would have had employer-provided coverage. Some firms have retained coverage but shifted a portion of the expense of RHBs to the retiree. For retirees this shift is not attractive and the consequences are more severe than a similar shift for active employees. While individuals are active employees, the employer share of health care benefits is not counted as income and in some cases, neither is the employee contribution. And, active employees can pay out-of-pocket medical expenses out of flexible spending accounts (if their employers offer such a plan), which also is on a pretax basis. However, for retired employees, premium contributions and out-of-pocket health care expenses must meet a 7.5 percent adjusted gross income test before these expenses are deductible from taxable income. Only the portion spent above the 7.5 percent level is tax deductible. Thus, the costs of coverage, which are shifted to the retired employee, have to be paid with post-tax dollars.

All of this means that we should expect more and more firms to decrease RHBs and more and more retirees to go without the private coverage. But will this lead to later ages at retirement? The figures in the chapter provide a descriptive view of changes in coverage through the early 2000s. My only question on these is related to Figure 9.2 on the provision of benefits by large employers. Below I show a graph with a longer time trend. The levels and trend over the period 1997–2003, included in the chapter, differ from Figure 9.C.1 and I do not understand why. The trends in coverage shown in the chapter are clearly considerably less than those in the figure below raising some question of the representativeness of the sample, the accuracy of the responses of those in the Health and Retirement Survey or possibly the weighting of the sample. All figures do show the expected decline in RHBs over time.

Turning to the regression based analysis, the authors estimate a model that is an extension of the Rogowski and Karoly model. Unfortunately they do not substantially improve upon the health measures used in that analysis, which included Body Mass Index (BMI) measured continuously and the presence of two or more chronic illnesses. Turning to BMI, I am concerned with the use of BMI as a continuous variable. BMI has an optimal or normal range and a range of too low weight in addition to one of too high (overweight and obese). The continuous measure used is not very satisfactory as a measure of health. Not surprisingly the results are consistent with this critique – no tie is found

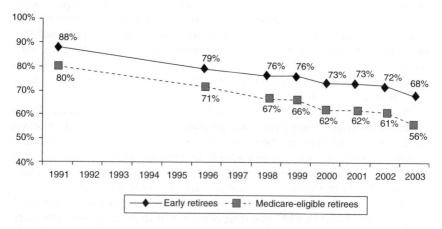

Figure 9.C.1 Provision of Retiree Health Benefits by Employers with 1,000+ Employees, 1991–2003

Source: Frank McArdle et al., *Retiree Health Coverage: Recent Trends and Employer Perspectives and Future Benefits* (Menlo Park, CA: The Henry J. Kaiser Family Foundation, October, 1999); Steve Coppock and Andrew Zebrak, "Finding the Right Fit: Medicare Prescription Dugs and Current Coverage Options," testimony before the U.S. Senate, Committee on Finance, and Hewitt Associates, personal communication.

between continuously measured BMI and retirement. The continuous measure may hide any real tie between BMI and work, especially in an older population where being underweight may be a risk factor or indicator of significant health problems. In terms of the use of multiple chronic illnesses, those included appear to be very different illnesses: for example, treated high blood pressure is quite different from chronic lung disease; skin cancer is generally very different from lung cancer or stomach cancer. Thus a simple count is not a revealing measure of health. A tie to functional limitations may well be a better indicator of health (that is, using an indicator that combines conditions with limitations). The authors do add self reported health in the form of a variable indicating poor or fair health and that is clearly an improvement to the previously estimated Rogowski-Karoly model, as seen in the empirical results.

The findings of the importance of RHBs are the core results and they are strong. The authors' findings suggest that on average for workers 51–61 in 1992, there was a 55 percent increase in the probability of retiring in the subsequent two years if they had both employee health benefits and RHBs than if they had only employee health benefits. In the next two years, there was a smaller though still large 29 percent increase in the probability of retiring for a comparison of the same two benefit groups. The authors reasonably suggest this is because RHBs are worth more prior to eligibility for Medicare, which occurs at age 65 (except for those with significant disabilities). In order to test this I would suggest estimating the same model on smaller age cohorts, say those 55–58 and those 59–61. If the authors are correct, for the earliest two-year time period, the results should be stronger for the younger group than the older group. And a test over those 59–61 from 1992–1994 and then another similarly age group from 1994 to 1996 will allow the authors to test if it is the age of the cohort or the change in the economy and other changes in the health care coverage market that lie behind the differing results.

Of course, as the authors note, spouse coverage is very relevant here. If an employee has a spouse that has health care coverage that could cover the employee, retiree coverage should be far less important in any retirement decision. The authors attempt to incorporate this by including a set of indicator variables that indicate the presence of a spouse and if present, the spouse's work status. This is not entirely satisfactory. The authors note the limitation in terms of joint decision-making. There is also a possibility that they have a retired spouse whose employer offers retiree health insurance coverage. This would not be included through the current set of indicator variables. For all of these reasons, I think they may wish to separately estimate their model for singles, who obviously do not have spousal coverage, and see if these estimates are greater than those of the full cohort.

Finally, there are some additional issues of measurement worth keeping in mind when viewing these results. First, there may be a correlation between information on pensions and retiree coverage and plans to retire. That is, those who plan to retire sooner should be better informed. The reported elasticity then would not be correct. Let us consider for example the following possibility. Consistent with the discrepancy between the reported proportion with RHBs in the figure above, and the lower proportion in the sample used in this chapter (as shown in Figure 9.2 of the chapter), those who plan to retiree know they have coverage (or do not have coverage) while those who do not plan to retire soon are uncertain if they have coverage but answer no to whether or not they have coverage. Then, the estimates presented here would be overestimates. (If the response of those who are not informed were instead to incorrectly answer yes to benefits, then the reported estimates are likely to be underestimates of the true elasticity.)

Second, there is a question as to whether workers' behavior is tied to expectations or to reality. It seems important to know in order to model the tie between benefits and employment correctly. The authors note the discrepancy between expectations and reality; they do not model or test the question. Third, there is a question of the correct definition of retirement. Individuals may "retire" from one employer and begin work with another. This would appear to be a different decision than retiring without subsequent work. And it is a different decision in terms of public finance of Medicare (and Social Security) and for the employer who offers RHBs.

To conclude, this chapter is on a topic that is increasingly important given the reduction in employer-based retiree coverage, the reduction in employer based coverage for active workers, the increasing cost of health care, increasing longevity, and the increasing costs of Medicare and payroll tax that finance Medicare. I compliment the authors for research on this increasingly important issue and encourage them to continue to conduct research on this topic. This is a very good start.

Reference

Karoly, L. A. and J. A. Rogowski (1994) "The Effect of Access to Post-Retirement Health Insurance on the Decisions to Retire Early," *Industrial and Labor Relations Review* 48: 103–123.

Part V
Budgetary and Macroeconomic Implications of Aging

Part V

10
Population Forecasts, Fiscal Policy, and Risk

Shripad Tuljapurkar

10.1 Introduction

This chapter describes stochastic population forecasts as they relate to the development of policies related to government spending on the elderly, mainly in the context of the industrialized nations. I begin by discussing methods for projecting demographic rates, mortality, fertility, and immigration, using probabilistic forecasts. I show how these are combined to make stochastic forecasts of population number and composition, illustrating with forecasts of the US population. Next I discuss how demographic models and economic models can be combined into an integrated projection model of transfer systems such as Social Security. I show how these integrated models describe various dimensions of policy-relevant risk and discuss the nature and implications of risk in evaluating policy alternatives. Finally, I consider briefly the distinct issues in the projection of health care spending.

The background to this chapter will be familiar to many readers. US demography in the early 21st century will be shaped first by the aging of the baby-boom and then by the sustained increase in human life span that began over a century ago. These factors will result in an unprecedented increase in the proportion of people who are over 65 years old, starting about 2010. Since existing public programs for pensions and health care are largely paid for by transfers from taxpayers (in the prime working ages of 20–65) to people over 65, the fiscal cost of these transfers will likely have to go up unless there are changes in the benefits paid by these public programs. Much the same phenomenon is taking place contemporaneously across the industrialized world and will also occur after some decades in most other countries of the world, including notably India and China. Research on this topic addresses the possible individual and policy responses to these forthcoming demographic changes. At the aggregate level, the central quantities of interest are the taxes collected to pay transfers and the size of the total transfer paid to the older population. These have two components, per-capita tax, and transfer rates, and the numbers of taxpayers and recipients. If we focus on the rates, as Richard Disney said in his 1996 book, projected fiscal changes have nothing to do with demography. If we focus on the second, demography matters. Of course in the real world both matter, as does the interaction between them. In this chapter my primary focus is on demography but the integrated models discussed here provide a tool for the exploration of interactions, as I will illustrate.

The next section of this chapter discusses the determinants of population change and the nature of stochastic forecasting models, then considers in turn mortality, fertility, and migration. Section 10.3 discusses stochastic population projections for the United States and some of their features. Section 10.4 considers integrated projection models that combine economic, policy and demographic variables, and presents in outline such a model for the US Social Security system. Results from this model are used to illustrate and discuss policy analysis in the context of the substantial uncertainty in our projections of the future. In particular, I discuss ways in which one constructs and analyzes measures of risk. In Section 10.5 I indicate how the integrated model of Section 10.4 can be adapted to address health care costs, and conclude with some reflections on the value of these methods.

Much of the work underlying this chapter has been done in collaboration with Ronald Lee over the past 15 years. Significant contributions to parts of this effort have also been made by Mike Anderson, Carl Boe, and Ryan Edwards. My goal here is to present the current state of this work, so the citations here are not exhaustive.

10.2 Demographic forecasts: vital rates

Demographers study and forecast the numbers and composition of populations. It is possible to subdivide populations quite finely, for instance by age, sex, ethnicity, education, marital status, and household status. But our ability to accurately model the dynamics involved decreases as disaggregation increases, so most forecasts only project population composition by age and sex. To do this we require forecasts of age-specific and sex-specific vital rates, fertility, mortality, and immigration. Given a launch year, say 2005, and the population composition in that year, plus projections of all of rates for every year in the forecast horizon, the population forecast is simply a bookkeeping exercise called the cohort-component method. The key to the stochastic forecasting approach is that it incorporates the temporal volatility of vital rates and projects these into the future to produce a range of forecasts with associated probabilities. The hard part of this is to project the rates.

10.2.1 Mortality

Mortality rates for large national populations have a characteristic age pattern for ages through 85 and the age pattern of mortality at ages between 85 and 110 is now also fairly well understood (Thatcher, Kannisto, and Vaupel,

1998). To make projections we want to know how the level of mortality falls at all ages, and reliable forecasts are made possible by Lee and Carter's (1992) discovery that mortality rates in the United States have fallen at roughly the same age-specific exponential rate over many decades. Lee and Carter's conclusion has been found to apply to virtually every industrial country, starting with the G-7 countries (Tuljapurkar, Li, and Boe, 2000), and represents the most striking discovery about mortality change in the industrial age. Letting M(x,t) be the central death rate for age x in year t, the Lee-Carter model can be written in the form,

$$\log M(x,t) = \log M(x,t-1) - z\, b(x) + E(t). \tag{1}$$

Here z is a rate of decline common to every age and b(x) is an age-specific response factor that tells us the relative rate of decline specific to age x, and E(t) is a residual that is typically small in magnitude. The constancy of the rate of decline z means that mortality falls at a roughly constant exponential rate over time.

For a forecaster the Lee-Carter model has the equally important feature that deviations around the long-run trend can be effectively modeled using stochastic processes. Fitting the model (1) yields residuals E(t) that have no trend but can be described by a relatively simple stochastic process. Lee and Carter (1992) and many subsequent studies find that E(t) is well described by a random walk; some variants of this model use low-order autoregressive processes (UK Government Actuary, 2001). The model in equation (1) and a stochastic model for E(t) are fitted to some span of historical data. Starting with known mortality rates in a launch year one can then generate an infinity of forecasts for subsequent years: first project a sample path w of the residual process, say E(t,w) for each forecast year t, and then use (1) to compute a corresponding forecast M(x,t,w). The probability distribution of the sample paths E(t,w) can be derived from the fitted model (analytically or by simulation), and this yields the probability distribution of M(x,t,w). Finally, these forecasts of central death rates are converted to age-specific probabilities of death using standard demographic methods.

Several recent studies have tested and extended the Lee-Carter method. The original method has been simplified slightly (Tuljapurkar, Li, and Boe, 2000), tested using historical data and found accurate (Lee and Miller, 2001), modified slightly for particular countries (Booth, Maindonald, and Smith, 2002), better algorithms have been developed to guarantee smoothness and to generate optimal forecast models for the E(t) process (Hyndman and Booth, 2006), and alternative models for E(t) have been estimated and tested (UK Government Actuary, 2001). The largest systematic application of the Lee-Carter method has been done by the European DEMWEL project, covering 19 countries in and neighboring the EU; these results are soon to be published. A recently proposed new method to forecast mortality applies the extrapolative insight of the Lee-Carter method to the age distribution of deaths (Bongaarts, 2005); the latter has not been tested against the Lee-Carter method. The power of the Lee-Carter result is that the linearity of the mortality trend in equation 1 is revealed by an analysis of the variance in the data, and is not imposed. Most alternatives, including the Bongaarts approach, assert a model and fit its parameters; there has not been much systematic comparison of competing models.

Figure 10.1 shows forecasts of life expectancy at birth derived by the Lee-Carter method for the United States for both sexes combined with a launch date in 2001. These are 100-year forecasts – it is a brave assumption that the model will hold for a century, but the model does accurately describe the past seven decades of mortality experience. The forecast is displayed as a set of 3 lines – the lowest indicates the 2.5 percentile level of the forecast in each year, meaning that the probability that the life expectancy falls below that lowest line in any year is 2.5 percent. The middle and upper lines are the median (50th percentile) and the 97.5 percentile. Thus this forecast provides a range of outcomes that are predicted to contain the future life expectancy with high probability. In addition, this method provides any desired number of sample paths of forecast mortality rates, and in a simulation these sample paths will have a probability distribution that is reflected in the prediction

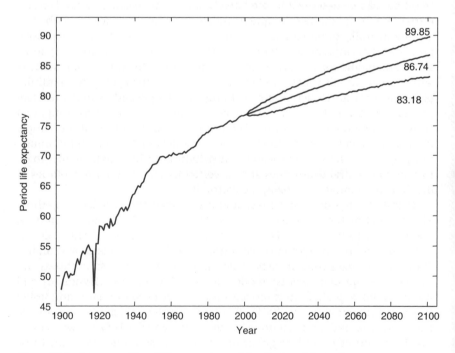

Figure 10.1 Sexes-combined life expectancy, historical and forecast

intervals shown in Figure 10.1. Note the 95 percent prediction interval for life expectancy is 2.5 years wide after 25 years and 5 years wide after 50 years. The median life expectancy forecast one hundred years out is about 87 years; by way of comparison, the life expectancies in both Japan and Sweden today are over 85 years.

10.2.2 Fertility

Fertility is described by age-specific birth rates per person year for women between (usually) ages 15 and 50. The sum of the age-specific fertility rates over the reproductive ages is the total fertility rate (TFR). The most noticeable empirical fact about fertility in the past half-century or so is that it has varied enormously over the years. From the 1950s to the 1970s many industrialized countries experienced first a boom and then a bust in TFR, leading to large baby booms. Fertility change in recent decades in many industrial countries has put a dent in a long-held belief that TFR should stabilize at or close to the population replacement value of 2.05. Among the rich industrialized countries, the United States now stands out with a relatively high (though below replacement) fertility that has held stable for over a decade; France is not far different. Virtually all other rich industrialized countries have experienced declines in fertility to TFR levels well below replacement. Although demographers have argued that this decline is a temporary consequence of much-delayed childbearing, TFR levels have stayed low for several years, and there seem to be no reasons to expect a sizeable rebound (Lesthaege and Willems, 1999). Economists have advanced endogenous theories of fertility that predict swings in fertility in response to changing population composition, most famously Easterlin's (1976) cohort size story for the United States, but these have found little empirical support and do not seem useful in a serious forecasting model.

The volatility of fertility over time means that we do not have a strong trend to exploit in making forecasts, in contrast to what we know about mortality. However, the age pattern of fertility (that is, the relative as opposed to absolute fertility of different ages) changes relatively slowly over time, even though the levels of TFR can change relatively rapidly over time. In making a forecast it seems sensible to expect that past volatility in fertility is likely to continue in the coming decades. Given this state of understanding, Lee and Tuljapurkar (1994) proposed a stochastic model of fertility that is conceptually similar to the Lee-Carter mortality model but has very different dynamics. The model involves two equations,

$$F(x,t) = A(x) + B(x) F(t), \qquad (2)$$
$$F(t) = F^* + c(F(t-1) - F^*) + u(t) + d\, u(t-1) \qquad (3)$$

Equation 3 is a stochastic model for fertility $F(x,t)$ of age x in year t, $A(x)$ and $B(x)$ are constant age-specific schedules; the level of fertility is governed by the time-factor F(t) and the constant F*, and the u(t) are stochastic innovations. Equation 2 takes the output from equation 3 and translates it into fertility change. A key assumption in this model is that the expected value of the TFR will converge over time to a specified value F*. This is a subjective assumption made in all long-run fertility forecasts that I am aware of; Tuljapurkar and Boe (1999) examine the consequences of assuming that the long-run mean F* is drawn from a prior distribution that reflects our uncertainty about long-run trends. We estimate the fertility model starting with an a priori specification of the long-run constraint F* and historical data. Just as with mortality, this estimation process yields a forecast engine that generates sample paths F(x,t,w) of age-specific fertility over time. An alternative approach to forecasting fertility (Alho and Spencer, 1997) uses a more flexible parameterization of the stochastic process that generates uncertainty over time, but yields similar qualitative predictions.

Figure 10.2 displays probabilistic forecasts of TFR for the United States with a launch date of 2003. As with the life expectancy forecasts in Figure 10.1, the plot displays several forecast lines: shown here are five annual percentile bounds ranging from a 2.5 percent low to a 97.5 percent high. In contrast with Figure 10.1, in which mortality forecasts display a modest rate of increase in uncertainty with forecast horizon, the uncertainty range for TFR in Figure 10.2 rises extremely rapidly with forecast horizon. It

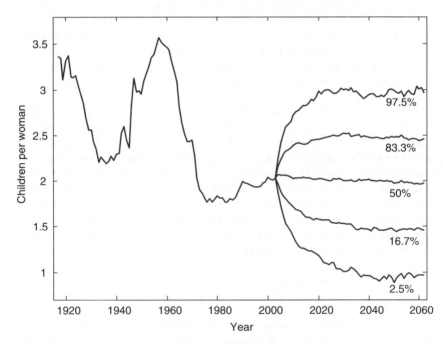

Figure 10.2 Total fertility rate, historical and forecast

is important to note that any actual forecast will not follow the percentile lines but will fluctuate over time between the highest and lowest percentiles. It is also worth pointing out that the 2.5 percentile of projected TFR approaches about 1.0, a value close to that currently observed in South Korea, Italy, and several other countries, whereas the 97.5 percentile of projected TFR approaches about 3, a value substantially below US TFR at the peak of the baby-boom. Thus the uncertainty shown in Figure 10.3 may be high but is certainly consistent with historical experience.

10.2.3 Migration

This is the final component of vital rates and is driven largely by policy so that it does not make much sense to model the historical dynamics. For US forecasts we adopt a scenario method and use (with equal probability) high–medium–low immigration alternatives in line with either the US Census Bureau or the Social Security Administration. The medium scenario is simply a continuation of recent past patterns and includes both legal and illegal migrants.

10.3 Population projections

Given stochastic models for mortality and fertility as well as migration scenarios, we start with the population in a launch year and generate a large

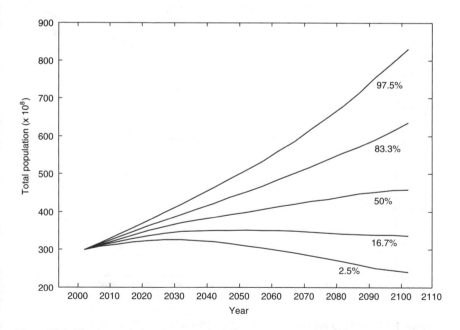

Figure 10.3 Total population forecasts ($\times 10^8$)

number of sample paths of the vital rates and then corresponding sample paths of population forecasted by age and sex over time. Using a large number of sample paths (several thousand) allows us to estimate prediction intervals that contain any desired probability for population numbers and ratios. It is worth noting that in general the forecast uncertainty obtained using stochastic methods is much wider than the uncertainty indicated by typical scenario forecasts.

The effects of combining stochastic projections of mortality, fertility, and immigration into a population forecast for the United States are illustrated by considering several aspects of the projected population. A much broader set of forecasts for the G-7 countries is presented and discussed in Anderson, Tuljapurkar, and Li (2001). Figure 10.3 displays percentile prediction intervals for US total population starting in 2003. Note that the uncertainty in the forecast increases with the forecast horizon as indicated by the growing width of the 95 percent prediction interval relative to the median forecast – for total population the 95 percent prediction interval is about 20 percent of the median forecast after 25 years and increases to 40 percent after 50 years.

Figure 10.4 displays probability percentiles for projections of the old age dependency ratio (population over 65 divided by population 20–64). The size of this old age dependency ratio is a key determinant of the balance of

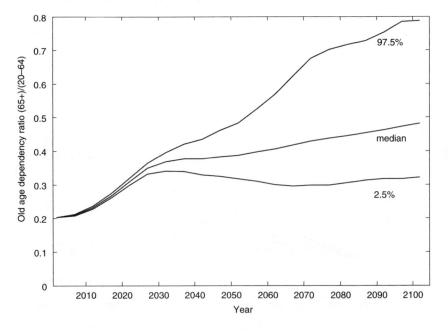

Figure 10.4 Old age dependency ratio (65+)/(20–64)

flows in any transfer system for old age populations, whether for pensions or health care. As is well known, the net balance of payments in any such transfer system depends on a product of two ratios: the dependency ratio, and the ratio of per-capita transfer payments to per-capita receipts. The projected dependency ratio has small uncertainty until 2030 because most of the change in this ratio until then is due to the aging of the baby-boom. Note that the aging of the baby-boom will with near-certainty increase the dependency ratio from its 2003 value of about 0.2 to a value of 0.35 by 2030. The prediction intervals for the dependency ratio are not as wide as for total population; the 95 percent prediction interval in Figure 10.3 is about 0.1 of the median projection after 25 years and just over 0.2 after 50 years. It is striking that even after the baby-boom has largely passed, from 2050 onwards, the probability that the dependency ratio will fall below 0.35 is only about 1/6 – a striking result given the large uncertainty about the predictions.

Figures 10.5, 10.6, and 10.7 display the uncertainty differently, in terms of population pyramids shown at 5-, 25-, and 50-year forecast horizons. Each figure shows a standard population pyramid with age groups arranged vertically for ages up to 105 years – for simplicity I show the total population at

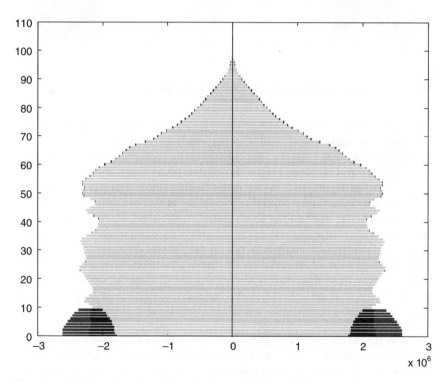

Figure 10.5 Projected US population 2010; uncertainty is 95 percentile range

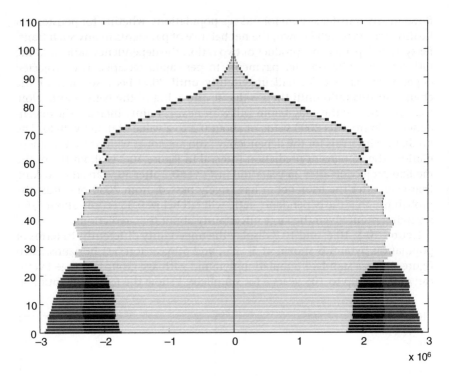

Figure 10.6 Projected US population 2025; uncertainty is 95 percentile range

each age and do not distinguish the two sexes. In each figure the 2.5 percent (yellow), 50 percent (blue), and 97.5 percent (red) of the population forecast in each age interval. Observe that the largest numerical uncertainty is at the younger ages and is driven by the substantial uncertainty about fertility that is illustrated in Figure 10.2. As we move further out in time, from 5 to 25 to 50 years, the uncertainty band due to fertility at the younger ages moves up the pyramid. The uncertainty in mortality projections, shown by the multi-colored bands at the highest ages, is modest by comparison to the uncertainty in fertility, although it is not in fact trivial in absolute terms. The pattern of growth of uncertainty in these pyramids corresponds directly with the growth of uncertainty shown for the old age dependency ratio in Figure 10.4 – that ratio becomes increasingly uncertain as the number of working age people becomes uncertain, that is, at a time horizon greater than 20 years.

These stochastic forecasts give us a complete set of probabilistic projections of population number and composition over time. Since the method generates a probability distribution over sample paths (that is, possible futures), there is complete consistency of the prediction probabilities for

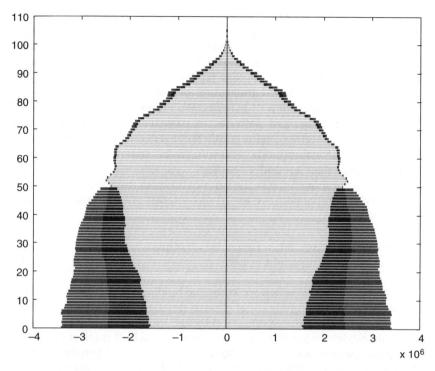

Figure 10.7 Projected US population 2050; uncertainty is 95 percentile range

numbers in various age segments (for example, children or retirees) with prediction probabilities for ratios such as the old age dependency ratio.

10.4 Pension systems and risk

The approach we take to model pension systems and other fiscal expenditures (Lee and Tuljapurkar, 2000; Tuljapurkar, Anderson, and Lee, 2003) builds on the work of the Social Security Administration (SSA) actuaries in the United States, but is simpler in that we do not disaggregate as much as they are required to do. We follow SSA in modeling both disability and old age support to produce a model of the US old age and survivors and disability insurance (OASDI) system. The analytical structure is straightforward – we project labor force participation rates, productivity growth, real interest rates, and returns on the stock market (the S&P 500) using multivariate autoregressive models that test for correlations between the series. The economic models are estimated using historical data in conjunction with expert opinion where necessary – for example we constrain the long-run behavior of real interest rate and labor force participation rates. These models are used to generate stochastic sample paths for the economic variables by Monte Carlo simulation. To complete the model we need tax schedules that determine payments into the system, and benefit schedules that determine payments out of the system. We take tax and benefit schedules to be given by existing law, including the indexation of wages for the computation of benefits, and the indexation of benefits. We follow SSA in using historical data to estimate retirement patterns, in particular the fractions of each cohort that opt to receive benefits at different ages in the retirement window. We also follow SSA assumptions concerning behavioral responses to planned changes in retirement age and incentives.

The core of our models tracks the balance B(t,w) in the Social Security trust fund on every sample path we use in our forecast of economic and demographic variables,

$$B(t,w) = (1 + r(t,w))*B(t - 1,w) + \{\text{Tax receipts } t - 1,w\} - \{\text{Benefits paid } t - 1,w\} \qquad (4)$$

Given a launch year in which we know the holdings of the fund, and some forecast horizon, we employ the stochastic population projections to generate a sample path of future population by age and sex in each year, and the economic models to generate a sample path for each of interest rate, labor force participation, wages, taxes, beneficiary status, and benefit payment schedules by age in each year. The latter schedules are applied to the projected population to generate the flows on the right side of equation (4). Thus the final output is a sample path of the flows into and out of the Trust fund as well as the level of the fund itself. The resulting set of forecast sample paths can be used to assess the state of the system. To explore the effects of privatization we use our joint stochastic model of interest rates and the rate of return on the S&P 500 index of equities. For any particular privatization scheme, we modify equation (4) appropriately to incorporate both risky and risk-free components of the fund.

The way in which we use these projections is to ask: given some fiscal quantity, what is its predicted probability distribution over time? An illustration is given in Figure 10.8 that describes the probability distribution of the projected actuarial balance under current law. This is a summary measure that can be interpreted as the additional tax, as a percentage of income that would balance the flows in equation (4) over a specified time horizon. The histogram shown in Figure 10.8 indicates the distribution of projected actuarial balances for the US OASDI over a 75-year horizon. The vertical lines indicate the SSA low, medium, and high actuarial balances. What is striking is that even with the substantial uncertainty in economic and demographic variables, there is a projected probability of over 50 percent that the additional tax will lie between 1 percent and 3 percent. In addition, the probability that

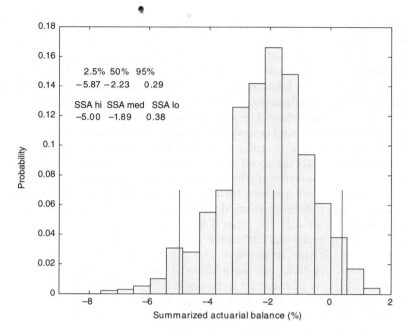

Figure 10.8 75-year summarized actuarial balance

fortuitous combinations of future conditions (for example, higher than expected wage growth, high interest rates, high fertility) will keep the actuarial balance at or above zero is only about 0.05. The probabilistic approach gives us a nuanced understanding of how economic and demographic changes affect the system over time, and also gives us the odds are that they will generate particular outcomes.

Another, and possibly more important, application of this model is to explore the impact of policy changes on particular outcomes of interest. To model a policy change, say an increase in the normal retirement age (NRA), requires that we must incorporate not simply a shift in benefit schedules but also any resulting shift in behavior. Thus an increase in the NRA may change the probabilities with which people opt to claim benefits at different ages, their labor force participation rates, and also payouts from the disability program. We proceed by incorporating the responses or mechanisms predicted by other models (behavioral, endogenous economic, empirical) to provide information on such shifts. Our modeling approach would also allow us to incorporate uncertainty about these responses, although we have not done so.

I provide two illustrations of the analysis of policy options based on Anderson, Tuljapurkar, and Lee (2003). In these examples, I focus on the

262 Budgetary and Macroeconomic Implications

solvency of the trust fund as a criterion of interest; this is not the most important criterion but is simply convenient for illustrative purposes. Solvency simply tells us whether in any given year t the balance in equation (4) is positive. The probability of solvency in any future year t is found directly by counting the fraction of sample paths w for which $\{B(t,w) > 0\}$, and the answer will clearly depend on the time horizon, here indicated by t. In the illustration that follows I use a time horizon of 50 years and examine the probability that the fund is solvent in each of those 50 years. Under current law it is well known that the fund will almost certainly be insolvent before these 50 years are up, so we will use the models to ask what happens to the probability of solvency if we change policy in specified ways.

As a first example, we ask how solvency is affected by a combination of two policy changes to be implemented immediately – one is to raise the taxes collected for Social Security, the other is to invest some fraction of the trust fund (collectively) in the S&P 500 index. Figure 10.9 shows how the probability of solvency changes in response. The current situation is indicated by the origin where we have neither additional taxes nor investment, and shows the probability of solvency to be essentially zero. If we move along either of the horizontal axes we are tracking either an increase in tax by the specified percentage, or the immediate investment of a specified proportion of the Trust Fund surplus into equities. As we move into the interior we are tracking the joint effect of both kinds of change. A really interesting

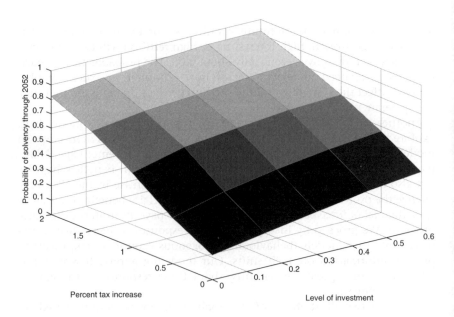

Figure 10.9 Chance of solvency until 2052: tax increase and investment

feature of the plot is the synergy between the two policy variables. A tax increase of 1 percent by itself raises solvency probability from near zero to about 40 percent. If we also invested 20 percent of the trust fund in the stock market, we get up to solvency probability of about 60 percent.

As a second illustration, we again consider the probability of solvency over 75 years but examine the effect of a different pair of policies. One policy, as before, is to raise the taxes going into Social Security, the other is to increase the NRA to 67, 68, or 69 on a more accelerated schedule. The final NRA values and the target dates for their achievement are shown in the figure. In the baseline case at the origin we have current law taking us to an NRA of 67 in 2022. Other possibilities shown are achieved by a steady increase over the periods indicated starting immediately. The results of these changes on solvency over 50 years are shown in Figure 10.10. Here again, we observe synergies between the two policy options and they are even bigger than those in Figure 10.9. A tax increase of 1 percent by itself raises solvency probability from near zero to about 40 percent. If we also increase the NRA steadily up to age 69 by 2024, we get up to a solvency probability of about 80 percent.

The analyses illustrated in Figures 10.8 and 10.9 can be conducted for other objective functions under other policy scenarios. These analyses reveal unexpected synergies between policy options and also the importance of the

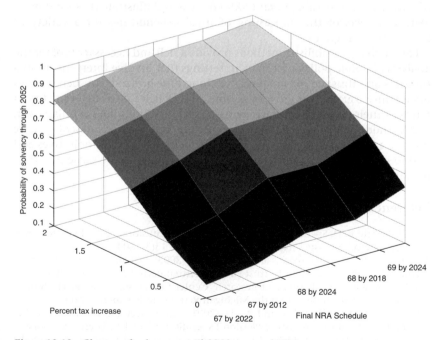

Figure 10.10 Chance of solvency until 2052, tax and NRA

timing of policy change. The analyses also highlight the fact that many policy options can improve the fiscal situation of the OASDI program but still leave us with a substantial probability that some target, such as solvency, will not be achieved. Thus we can rank alternative policies in terms of the probabilities that they will achieve some set of targets.

10.5 Modeling health expenditure and modeling policy

Public health care spending can be modeled in much the same way as we model the OASDI system. The key step is to determine age-schedules of expenditure by sex and to describe how these schedules will evolve over time. As the population ages, we expect a long-run shift in the age profiles themselves – the large expenditures that characterize the last two years of life will progressively occur at later ages. In addition, and this is critical, we must project changes in the absolute level of expenditure at all ages over time. The latter is well known to be driven by cost inflation in the short run, but may also change over time in response to trends in health. It is easy to see that if costs increase faster than wages then the transfers needed to pay for these costs must also increase, and eventually any such system will be unsustainable. Forecasts usually analyze alternative long run scenarios of change while incorporating historical volatility as we did with our models of fertility. Lee and Tuljapurkar (2000) discuss and illustrate these and more general aspects of the forecasting of fiscal expenditures for a variety of government programs.

I argue that probabilistic methods provide a rich and necessary tool for the analysis of public policy especially in settings that involve intergenerational transfers and thus require analyses over long time horizons. In such settings uncertainty usually will grow over time, and policies must be evaluated in terms of their probability of achieving targets of various kinds (Tuljapurkar, 1997; Anderson, Tuljapurkar, and Lee, 2003). The methods described here provide a natural setting in which to evaluate multiple policy objectives and also to identify policy combinations that are optimal in the sense that they maximize the probability of achieving particular goals.

References

Alho, J. M. and B. D. Spencer (1997) "The Practical Specification of the Expected Error of Population Forecasts," *Journal of Official Statistics* 13(3): 203–225.

Anderson, M., S. Tuljapurkar, and R. D. Lee (2003) "Chances are ... Stochastic Forecasts of the Social Security Trust Fund and Attempts to Save It". Presented at the 1999 Conference on Retirement Research, Center for Retirement Research, Boston College. Available online from the Michigan Retirement Research Center.

Anderson, M., S. Tuljapurkar and N. Li (2001) "How Accurate are Demographic Projections Used in Forecasting Pension Expenditure?," in Tito Boeri, Axel Borsch-Supan, Agar Brugiavini, Richard Disney, Arie Kapteyn, and Franco Peracchi (eds)

Pensions: More Information, Less Ideology (Norwell, MA: Kluwer Academic Publishers) pp. 9–27.

Bongaarts, J. (2005) "Long-Range Trends in Adult Mortality: Models and Projection Methods," *Demography* 42(1): 23–49.

Booth, H., J. Maindonald, and L. Smith (2002) "Applying Lee-Carter under Conditions of Variable Mortality Decline," *Population Studies* 56: 325–336.

Disney, R. (1996) *Can We Afford to Grow Older? A Perspective on the Economics of Ageing* (Cambridge, MA: MIT Press).

Easterlin, R. A. (1976) "The Conflict between Aspirations and Resources," *Population and Development Review* 2: 417–425.

Hyndman, R. J. and H. Booth (2006) "Stochastic Population Forecasts Using Functional Data Models for Mortality, Fertility and Migration," Working Papers in Demography, 99, Australian National University. Available on the web at demography.anu.edu.au/Publications/WorkingPapers/99.pdf

Lee, R. D. and L. Carter (1992) "Modeling and Forecasting US Mortality," *Journal of the American Statistical Association* 87(419): 659–671.

Lee, R. D. and T. Miller (2001) "Evaluating the Performance of the Lee-Carter Method for Forecasting Mortality," *Demography* 38: 537–549.

Lee, R. D. and S. Tuljapurkar (2000) "Population Forecasting for Fiscal Planning: Issues and Innovations," in Alan Auerbach and Ronald Lee (eds) *Demography and Fiscal Policy* (New York, NY: Cambridge University Press) pp. 7–57.

Lee, R. D. and S. Tuljapurkar (1994) "Stochastic Population Forecasts of the US: Beyond High, Medium, Low," *Journal American Statistical Association* 89: 1175–1189.

Lesthaege, R. and P. Willems (1999) "Is Low Fertility a Temporary Phenomenon in the European Union?" *Population and Development Review* 25: 211–228.

Thatcher, A. R., V. Kannisto, and J. W. Vaupel (1998) *The Force of Mortality at Ages 80 to 120* (Odense: Odense University Press).

Tuljapurkar, S., N. Li, and C. Boe (2000) "A Universal Pattern of Mortality change in the G7 Countries," *Nature* 405: 789–792.

Tuljapurkar, S. (1997) "Uncertainty in Demographic Forecasts: Methods and Meanings." Proceedings of the 1996 Conference on Applied Demography, Bowling Green State University, Ohio.

Tuljapurkar, S. and C. Boe (1999) "Validation, Information and Probabilistic Priors in Stochastic Forecasts," *International Journal of Forecasting* 15: 259–271.

Tuljapurkar, S., M. Anderson, and R. D. Lee (2003) "Effects of Changing the Social Security Retirement Age on the Dynamics of the OASDI Program." Presented at the October 1998 meeting of the Social Security Advisory Board, Capitol Hill, Washington DC. Available online from the Michigan Retirement Research Center.

UK Government Actuary (2001) National Population Projections: Review of Methodology for Projecting Mortality, by the Government Actuary's Department, National Statistics Quality Review Series Report No. 8.

Comments to Chapter 10
Clark Burdick

I was very pleased to be asked to discuss the chapter, "Population Forecasts, Fiscal Policy, and Risk," by Shripad Tuljapurkar. This chapter advocates a "stochastic modeling" approach to the analysis of Social Security. This stochastic modeling approach to policy analysis, pioneered by Tuljapurkar and a collection of co-authors, has been my primary research interest with the Social Security Administration's Office of Policy. For much of the past seven years at SSA, I have been employing, adapting, interpreting, and extending the types of approaches and methods advocated in this chapter. Needless to say, I liked the chapter a great deal, and I believe that the stochastic modeling approach it describes represents an important tool for long-range policy analysis.

Stochastic modeling is an approach that attempts to quantify the uncertainty surrounding long-range forecasts of policy outcomes, typically outcomes that depend on both demographic and economic factors. Stochastic modeling was first developed by demographers and economists (primarily Tuljapurkar and a collection of co-authors that I just mentioned) to study the fiscal impact of an aging population. These researchers recognized that fiscal policy is influenced by both the size and age distribution of the population. Entitlement spending on the elderly and education spending on the young are the two most obvious examples.

Long-range forecasts are required to study the impact of population changes on the economy because demographic change generally occurs slowly over long periods of time. Despite the gradual nature of these demographic shifts, however, the fiscal impact of an aging population is large. According to the 2005 Annual Report of the OASDI Trustees, the Social Security system faces unfunded obligations totaling $11.1 trillion in present value over the infinite future. Of these obligations, $7.1 trillion accrue in the years 2079 and beyond.[1] While some may question how meaningful these infinite horizon projections are, I do not think it is controversial to claim that the years 2079 and beyond represent the long run or that $11.1 trillion is a big number.

Unfortunately, even short-range forecasting is hard, and long-range forecasting is very hard. But short- and long-range forecasting typically correspond to time horizons of something like two quarters ahead and eight quarters ahead, respectively. Social Security, by contrast, is required to forecast 75 years ahead. If forecasting eight quarters ahead is very hard, forecasting 300 quarters ahead is darn near impossible!

Forecasting over very long time horizons is particularly difficult for a number of reasons. In addition to all of the difficulties faced by shorter run forecasts, there are additional complications that arise over longer time horizons. Over long periods of time, some variables seem to undergo regime switches that alter their behavior in ways that are difficult to capture with standard models. Take average labor productivity (ALP) for example. In the early 1970s, the mean growth rate of ALP dropped unexpectedly. This new lower mean growth rate persisted through the early 1990s when, just as unexpectedly, the mean growth rate of ALP rose back up even higher than its pre-decline level. Economists have been unable to identify any plausible explanation for the 20-year period of low average growth in ALP, and we have insufficient data to reliably estimate the relative likelihood or duration of future spells of low ALP growth.

Other variables change behavior for reasons that are well understood but can be similarly difficult to forecast. The level of legal immigration, for example, is determined almost exclusively by legislative action. Congress periodically raises or lowers the limits set on the number of legal immigrants allowed annually, and immigration data rise and fall accordingly. In the absence of a model of future Congressional decisions, the level of legal immigration can be very difficult to forecast reliably.

A very long forecasting horizon also leaves open the possibility of unprecedented events. The past 90 years included two World Wars and the global Spanish flu pandemic. How many World War scale conflicts and global pandemics might we experience in the next 75 years? It seems prudent to include some possibility of these or similar events in very long-range forecasts, but there is a paucity of data available to reliably estimate the frequency or likelihood of such events in the future.

Perhaps the biggest challenge of very long-range forecasting is accounting for possible interactions between demographic and economic factors. It is well known that income and wealth are negatively correlated with mortality (wealthier individuals tend to live longer on average), but the economic and demographic professions have not yet developed well-established models that are capable of capturing even this well-understood feedback effect between demographic and economic factors. Similarly, few economists or demographers would dispute the possibility, or even likelihood, of the interaction of wealth and fertility decisions over the long run, but once again we lack well-established models that capture these feedback effects. In the case of fertility, we are not even sure which sign the possible correlation might take. If children are modeled as a consumption good that provides utility directly to the parents, then higher wealth should be associated with higher fertility. But if, on the other hand, children are modeled as an investment good, to provide care for the parents in their old age, then higher wealth may be associated with lower fertility levels.[2]

I hope I have argued convincingly to this point that long-range forecasting is both very difficult and necessary for analyzing the fiscal impact of an aging population in general and for analyzing a public pension system like Social Security in particular. Given the extreme difficulties in forecasting important variables and their interactions reliably over such a long time horizon, it becomes increasingly important to quantify the degree of uncertainty surrounding the projections. Quantifying this uncertainty is the goal of stochastic modeling.

Traditionally, a scenario approach has been used to attempt to quantify the uncertainty surrounding long-range policy projections. Unfortunately, the scenario approach suffers from several rather serious limitations. The scenario approach is based on analyzing future policy outcomes under three alternative scenarios, sometimes referred to as pessimistic, intermediate, and optimistic. The policy outcomes are derived by assuming that each variable assumes a single constant value over most of the forecasting period. The intermediate projection is considered to be the "most likely" or "best guess" or "long-run expected value" outcome. The policy outcomes for the alternative scenarios are derived by assuming that the input variables are consistently above or below their intermediate values.

One major problem with the scenario approach is that the grouping of input variables into the alternative (non-intermediate) scenarios is arbitrary and inconsistent across applications. The Census Bureau, for example, groups higher-than-expected mortality together with higher-than-expected fertility in one scenario, while the Trustees' Report groups higher-than-expected mortality together with lower-than-expected fertility. Thus, fertility and mortality are perfectly positively correlated in the Census scenarios, while they are perfectly negatively correlated in the Trustees Report scenarios. As a result, the Census scenarios indicate much greater uncertainty surrounding the intermediate projections of the total dependency ratio with very little uncertainty surrounding the old age dependency ratio, while the opposite is true of the Trustees' Report projections.

Furthermore, the assignment of variables to alternative scenarios is often theoretically and empirically suspect. The pessimistic scenario used in the Trustees' Report for its long-range projections assumes both above-average inflation and above-average unemployment. While high inflation and high unemployment can, and have, occurred jointly in the past, a 75-year period of continuous stagflation is highly implausible on the grounds of both theory and evidence.

The scenario approach also provides very little empirical content. The alternative scenarios are intended to indicate the range of possible policy outcomes that might be experienced in the future, but they provide no indication of the relative likelihood that the upper and lower bounds might be exceeded or, if so, by how much and/or how often. This type of information about the relative likelihood of alternative outcomes can be invaluable for the design and evaluation of alternative policies.

The stochastic modeling approach advocated in Tuljapurkar's chapter provides an alternative method to quantify the uncertainty surrounding long-range policy forecasts. This stochastic modeling approach provides valuable information about the relative likelihood of alternative outcomes and avoids many of the pitfalls inherent in the previously described scenario approach. The stochastic modeling approach pioneered by Shripad Tuljapurkar and various co-authors applies Monte Carlo simulation methods to subjectively calibrated time series models to approximate the entire probability distribution of future policy outcomes.

The stochastic modeling approach is based on the assumption that the variability of each variable around its mean or expected value and the covariation between variables will be the same in the future as it has been in the past. Standard time series models are used to capture this variability and covariation between variables, but these series models are generally calibrated to match subjective expert opinion about the long-run mean or expected value of the variables in question. This subjective calibration is needed because, while stochastic modeling is predicated on the assumption that the variability of the variables will be the same in the future as it has been in the past, there are often good reasons to believe that the mean or expected value of these variables may be different in the future than in the past.

One major reason that such subjective calibration is necessary is the inability of currently available models to capture important interactions between economic and demographic factors. The growth rate of GDP, for example, is approximately equal to the growth rate of average labor productivity plus the growth rate of the labor force. A time series model of economic variables will miss this demographic dependency and will tend to predict a future mean value of GDP growth equal to its historical mean. If demographic changes are expected to slow the rate of growth of the labor supply, however, then future GDP growth may in fact be lower than its historical average, and the mean rate of GDP growth should be subjectively lowered in our economic model. At least until the economic and demographic professions develop more comprehensive models that are able to capture all demographic and economic interactions, such judgmental adjustments, though unappealing, will continue to be necessary.

Of course the need to subjectively calibrate a time series model raises the obvious question of what values the model should be calibrated to. Typically the intermediate values used in the previously discussed scenario approach are used. Recall that the major problems with the scenario approach were with the quantitative measurement of uncertainty, not with the measure of central tendency. And furthermore, the goal of stochastic modeling is not to produce more accurate forecasts locationally but to quantify the uncertainty surrounding policy outcomes in the far distant future.

Monte Carlo simulation methods are used to simulate multiple time paths for the future values of each variable that influences the policy outcomes of interest. From these synthetic paths, synthetic policy outcomes are constructed. When tabulated across the multiple Monte Carlo simulations, the collection of policy outcomes generated represents an approximation of the entire probability distribution of possible policy outcomes. By construction, the mean or median of this approximate probability distribution will be determined by the subjective intermediate values that the time series models were calibrated to. But such an approximate probability distribution also provides very detailed information about how future policy outcomes may vary around the mean or median. That is, the stochastic modeling approach provides a complete quantitative characterization of the uncertainty surrounding the policy forecasts.

While stochastic modeling provides a powerful new tool for policy analysis, the approach is not without its own difficulties. Most stochastic modeling exercises are very complex, involving multiple component models each used to simulate different collections of variables. Economic variables and demographic models are typically modeled separately. Furthermore, each of the component models is typically calibrated, or adjusted, to equate the models' long-run mean with some subjective long-range projection. These factors make it very challenging to vet the results against those of other alternative models.

Typically, time series models are estimated on the basis of some notion of statistical optimality such as least squares or maximum likelihood. Unfortunately, the act of calibrating a time series model, as is done in stochastic modeling, alters the inferential structure of the model and generally invalidates the use of these usual metrics. It can be extremely difficult to establish the statistical optimality of even the component models in a stochastic modeling exercise, let alone the overall results. Instead, researchers must argue that the model being employed is "subjectively best" in some sense. Many models can produce a probability distribution of future policy outcomes that seems reasonable, but meaningful results require that the resulting probability distribution accurately reflect the demographic and economic processes at work. Settling for results that are "subjectively adequate" can come perilously close to accepting results that are "not obviously wrong."

Choosing the "subjectively best" model is not always easy. Joyce Manchester and I wrote a survey article[3] that showed that several different stochastic models, each taking a different approach with different assumptions, all produced broadly consistent estimates of OASDI trust fund outcomes. While measures of statistical optimality are generally not available, there are other tools available that can help stochastic modeling practitioners decide between competing models in cases like this. Ex-post validation and Bayesian posterior predictive assessment are techniques that can be used to evaluate the predictive performance of alternative models. Although not yet widely used, tools such as these should help researchers select appropriate models and establish the validity of their stochastic modeling results as the field matures.

The main reason tools like ex-post validation are not yet widely used is that stochastic modeling is still a relatively young field. The models surveyed in the article mentioned above are among the first comprehensive stochastic models of OASDI trust fund outcomes. In the future I expect to see larger stochastic models that incorporate additional variables being developed. Javier Meseguer and I are currently exploring Bayesian techniques that will permit the estimation of much larger and more complicated models than are currently being used. Bayesian techniques can also be used to add parameter estimation uncertainty to stochastic modeling results. Bayesian techniques can even incorporate alternative model uncertainty, by averaging results across competing models.

Many classes of models remain relatively unexplored by stochastic modelers. Markov regime switching models and the use of the Kalman filter to estimate models with unobserved components are but two examples of potentially fruitful models that have not yet been explored. Clearly, much research remains to be done before the promise of stochastic modeling is fully realized, but stochastic modeling already represents a powerful new tool for policy analysis – an approach that is able to shed light on the complete range and distribution of policy outcomes that might occur in the future.

Notes

1. The 2005 Annual Report of the Board of Trustees of the Federal Old Age and Survivors Insurance and Disability Insurance Trust Funds, Table IV.B6, p. 59.
2. Consideration of children as an investment good is probably more relevant to developing economies but may still influence the total fertility level even in developed nations.
3. "Stochastic Models of the Social Security Trust Funds," Clark Burdick and Joyce Manchester, Research and Statistics Note, Social Security Administration Office of Policy, March 2003.

11
Wage Growth and the Measurement of Social Security's Financial Condition

*Andrew G. Biggs and Jagadeesh Gokhale**

11.1 Introduction

It is often argued in both policy circles and the popular media that faster economic growth could significantly reduce Social Security's long-term funding imbalance.[1] If, as many argue, Social Security Trustees' projections for economic growth are unduly pessimistic, policy makers may ignore calls for policies to reform the system in the belief that faster economic growth will "bail us out." However, Social Security's financial status is normally analyzed under a truncated horizon of 75 years. Does the positive association of faster economic growth with improvement in the system's actuarial balance survive under longer horizons? If not – that is, if faster economic growth fails to improve or even worsens Social Security's actuarial balance over very long horizons – failure to enact reforms to make the system sustainable would be a more serious lapse than many policy makers and budget analysts realize.

The current Social Security benefit formula indexes workers' earnings through age 60 for wage growth when calculating their average indexed monthly wage (AIME), which is the basis for computing Social Security benefits.[2] Benefits are calculated at retirement by applying a progressive formula to the AIME, so that a larger fraction of pre-retirement earnings are replaced by Social Security benefits for low-wage workers compared to higher earners. Post-retirement, benefits are increased annually with the Consumer Price Index (CPI) to maintain their purchasing power. Each worker cohort's retirement benefits – as calculated when its members retire – reflect that cohort's higher labor productivity and wages during its lifetime compared to that of the immediately preceding cohort. Thus, average benefits for succeeding cohorts of retirees will tend to rise at the rate of average wages. And for each cohort, once the benefit level is established, its purchasing power is maintained by allowing the dollar amount to grow at the rate of general price inflation.

Actuarial balance is the most prominent of a number of measures that the Social Security Trustees use to assess the program's long-term finances. It equals the present value of the system's annual net income expressed as a percentage of payrolls over the measurement period.[3] As described by the Trustees,

> actuarial balance is a measure of the program's financial status for the 75-year valuation period as a whole. It is essentially the difference between income and cost of the program expressed as a percentage of taxable payrolls over the valuation period. This single number summarizes the adequacy of program financing for the period.

While the Trustees have traditionally measured actuarial balance over 25, 50, and 75 years, the 75-year measure receives the most attention in policy debates. The 2005 Trustees Report projects a 75-year actuarial deficit of 1.92 percent of taxable payrolls. This deficit has a commonly applied policy interpretation:

> When the actuarial balance is negative, the actuarial deficit can be interpreted as the percentage that would have to be added to the current law income rate in each of the next 75 years, or subtracted from the cost rate in each year, to bring the funds into actuarial balance.[4]

Under this interpretation, the actuarial deficit indicates the size of an immediate and permanent payroll tax increase – 1.92 percentage points, from 12.40 percent to 14.32 percent of wages up to the taxable limit – that would be sufficient to restore the program to actuarial balance over 75 years, though not necessarily thereafter.[5]

Given how past wages enter into the calculation of Social Security benefits, it is easy to understand why many people believe that faster economic growth would improve the system's financial outlook. Benefits paid to current retirees are indexed only to inflation, rather than to nominal wage growth (which generally exceeds inflation by the growth rate of real labor productivity). Thus, faster growth in real productivity and wages would cause an immediate increase in the tax base and, therefore, in revenues, but would increase benefit payments only after a delay as working generations that experienced faster wage growth retire and claim benefits in the future. If the increase in wage growth were permanent, the annual cost rate – projected benefits as a percent of the projected tax base through the calculation horizon – would permanently decline relative to a lower wage growth scenario. Thus, cash balances relative to the payroll base would improve in every following year.

The Trustees' Annual Report for 2005 shows that over a 75-year horizon, this improvement in annual balances would carry over to an improvement in Social Security's actuarial balance. Assuming an increase in real wage growth from a baseline of 1.1 percent per year to 1.6 percent, the 75-year actuarial balance would improve by 0.53 percentage points, from a deficit of 1.92 percent of payroll to a deficit of 1.39 percent. This analysis lends credence to the widely shared view that faster economic growth would significantly *reduce* Social Security's projected actuarial deficit. Moreover, this view is reinforced under other standard measures of Social Security's finances such as annual balance ratios, the cross-over date (when noninterest receipts begin falling short of program outlays), the date of trust-fund exhaustion, and summarized actuarial balances calculated over truncated horizons of 25, 50, or 75 years. This is labeled as the "traditional" view.[6]

In recent years Social Security analysts have increasingly focused on very long term financing with the policy goal being solvency that can be sustained well beyond the traditional 75-year scoring period – often termed "sustainable solvency."[7] The Trustees note that

> Even a 75-year period is not long enough to provide a complete picture of Social Security's financial condition .... Overemphasis on summary measures for a 75-year period can lead to incorrect perceptions and to policy prescriptions that do not move toward a sustainable system. Thus, careful consideration of the trends in annual deficits and unfunded obligations toward the end of the 75-year period is important. In order to provide a more complete description of Social Security's very long-run financial condition, this report also includes summary measures for a time period that extends to the infinite horizon.[8]

Proponents of longer-term measures argue that focusing on 75-year solvency alone can distort policy decisions; the 1999 Technical Panel, for instance, argued that "When reformers aim only for 75-year balance, ... they usually end up in a situation where their reforms only last a year before being shown out of 75-year balance again."[9] For that reason, analysts have begun to calculate the Social Security program's finances beyond 75 years.[10] Beginning with the 2003 Report, Social Security's Trustees have published data on system financing measured over the infinite term. The main rationale for the infinite horizon measure is that it gives the fullest view of the total assets and obligations of the Social Security program. The Department of the Treasury notes that

> a 75-year projection is incomplete. For example, when calculating unfunded obligations, a 75-year horizon includes revenue from some future workers but only a fraction of their future benefits. In order to

provide a complete estimate of the long-run unfunded obligations of the programs, estimates should be extended to the infinite horizon[11]

Since then, measures of very long-term financing, both for social insurance programs and the federal budget in general, have gained increasing prominence in policy discussions.[12]

Calculations of long-term financing measures suggest that the traditional view may be an artifact of calculating Social Security's actuarial balance under a truncated projection horizon of 75-years. In particular, such limited-horizon measures reduce the effect of a projected decline in the worker-to-beneficiary ratio over the very long-term. Under perpetuity calculations, the conclusion that faster wage growth improves Social Security's actuarial balance could be reversed when the decline in the worker-to-beneficiary ratio is assumed to continue beyond the next 75 years. This result arises because a declining worker-to-beneficiary ratio magnifies the future impact of faster wage growth on Social Security's cost rate and widens the gap between the present value of its outlays and revenues to yield a *larger* actuarial deficit.

Exploring the sensitivity of Social Security's actuarial balance to individual economic assumptions involves examining its response to changes in one (economic or demographic) parameter at a time. However, altering the real wage growth assumption raises the question of "model consistency." Faster real wage growth could not occur isolated from changes in other relevant economic variables. For example, faster wage growth may be the result of technological progress, which increases the productivity of both capital and labor, and could be associated with higher interest rates. In that case, Social Security's (risk free) rate of interest could also be higher with accompanying effects on the system's actuarial balance.

If the increase in the government's interest rate associated with faster real wage growth were sufficiently large, bigger future Social Security outlays would receive a smaller weight in present value calculations, potentially confirming the traditional view. However, because interaction of faster wage growth with a declining worker-to-beneficiary ratio worsens Social Security's long-term actuarial balance under a constant discount rate, such a worsening may persist despite a simultaneous increase in the government's interest rate – up to a limit. With the actuarial balance calculation calibrated to US demographics and real wage growth, it can be shown that faster wage growth would generate smaller actuarial balances for a range of government interest rates.

This chapter analyzes the effect of increased economic growth on Social Security solvency measured in perpetuity.[13] Using a simple stylized model of pay-as-you-go Social Security, it can be shown analytically that faster wage growth would reduce the system's actuarial balance if the ratio of workers to beneficiaries declines sufficiently rapidly. These results are examined under a variety of demographic and interest rate assumptions. Next, the Social Security and Accounts Simulator (SSASIM) actuarial model is used to show that such a decline in Social Security's infinite-term actuarial balance is plausible under demographic and economic conditions projected for the United States even though the program's 75-year actuarial balance would improve under those conditions.

The chapter closes with a discussion of the results' meaning for Social Security financing and for the measures of solvency commonly applied to it. The discussion reconciles a seeming contradiction where wage growth improves cash balance ratios in each year but can worsen actuarial balance over the period.

11.2 A simple model of Social Security financing

This section builds a stylized model of a pay-as-you-go Social Security program. The initial specification is deliberately simplified for the purpose of better communicating the core insights, with increasing complexity and realism added as the model is developed.

Consider a program in which each beneficiary is paid a benefit equal to a constant percentage of the average wage in that year. The actuarial balance (AB) for such a program is defined as the present value of taxes minus the present value of benefits, expressed as a percentage of the present value of future payrolls.

$$AB = \frac{PVTaxes - PVBenefits}{PVPayroll} \tag{1}$$

This is the familiar equation in which the summarized cost rate is subtracted from the summarized income rate.[14]

Measured in perpetuity, the present value of taxes can be expressed as

$$PVTaxes = \tau w_0 \sum_{t=0}^{\infty} N_t G^t R^{-t}, \tag{2}$$

where τ = the payroll tax rate; w_0 = the average wage at time zero; N_t = the population of workers at time t; G = a growth factor $(1 + g)$, where g equals the annual real wage growth rate; and R = an interest factor $(1+r)$, where r equals the government annual interest rate; The present value of benefits equals

$$PVBenefits = w_0 \beta_0^{-1} \rho \sum_{t=0}^{\infty} N_t G^t B^{-t} R^{-t}, \tag{3}$$

where ρ = a constant replacement rate of the average current wage; β_0 = the worker-to-beneficiary ratio at time zero; and B = a factor $(1-b)$ where

b equals the annual rate of decline in the worker-to-beneficiary ratio. The present value of payrolls can be expressed as follows:

$$PVPayrolls = w_0 \sum_{t=0}^{\infty} N_t G^t R^{-t}. \tag{4}$$

Equation (3) shows that the present value of total benefits paid at time t is a function of a constant replacement rate, the initial values of wages, (the inverse of) the worker-to-beneficiary ratio, and changes in the worker population, wages, worker-to-beneficiary ratio, and accumulated interest between time zero and time t.

Note that the values of G^t and B^{-t} would be greater than 1 so long as real wages are rising ($g > 0$) and the worker-to-beneficiary ratio is declining ($b > 0$); the value of R^{-t} would be less than 1 so long as the real interest rate is positive ($r > 0$). Also note that equation (3) assumes that current benefits are a function of *current* wages. That is, there is no lag between realizing higher wages and higher Social Security benefits. This relationship would be obtained if Social Security benefits were indexed to wages throughout a retiree's lifetime. Although this is not true for Social Security in reality, examining its implications is helpful for developing intuition about results when this assumption is dropped.

The variables in equation (3) affect *PVBenefits* in the following ways: a higher value of g means that wages would be higher in each future period. Because benefits depend on contemporaneous wages by assumption, *PVBenefits* would be larger. Note that if g were larger, each term under the summation in equation (3) and, hence, the entire summation term, would also be larger. The same is true for *PVTaxes* in equation (2). Furthermore, if the tth term in *PVBenefits* increases by x percent as a result of an increase in g, so would the tth term in *PVTaxes*. Both taxes and benefits would, therefore, increase in the same proportion under a higher value of g.

Likewise, if the worker-to-beneficiary ratio declines (that is, if b were larger), there would be more beneficiaries per worker in the future, implying a larger *PVBenefits* relative to *PVTaxes* at each given value of g. In contrast, increases in the real interest rate (r) means that future benefit payments, taxes, and wages are all discounted more heavily – implying proportionate reductions in *PVBenefits*, *PVTaxes*, and *PVPayrolls*. These relationships are stated as:

Proposition 1: *Assuming (1) that the replacement rate is constant and (2) that current benefits depend on current wages:*

1. An increase in real wage growth (g) leads to proportionate increases in PVBenefits, PVTaxes, and PVPayrolls.
2. An increase in the real interest rate (r) leads to proportionate reductions in PVBenefits, PVTaxes, and PVPayrolls.
3. A faster decline in the worker-to-beneficiary ratio (increase in b), increases PVBenefits relative to both PVTaxes and PVPayrolls.

Using equations (2), (3), and (4), the actuarial balance defined in equation (1) can be expressed as

$$AB = \frac{\tau N_0 w_0 \sum_{t=0}^{\infty} G^t R^{-t} - N_0 w_0 \rho \beta_0^{-1} \sum_{t=0}^{\infty} B^{-t} G^t R^{-t}}{N_0 w_0 \sum_{t=0}^{\infty} G^t R^{-t}}.$$

Assuming, for simplicity, that the total worker population remains constant over time at N_0, the expression for AB can be expressed as

$$AB = \tau - \frac{\rho \beta_0^{-1} \sum_{t=0}^{\infty} B^{-t} G^t R^{-t}}{\sum_{t=0}^{\infty} G^t R^{-t}} = \tau - \Omega. \tag{5}$$

Equation (5) says that the actuarial balance is equal to the tax rate minus the summarized cost rate (Ω), where both revenues and costs are expressed as percentages of payrolls. The assumption of a constant worker population but a declining worker-to-beneficiary ratio obviously implies a growing total population.

Next, the impact of faster wage growth on the actuarial balance is explored under alternative parametric assumptions, progressively making the model more realistic.

Case A: Constant worker-to-beneficiary ratio

This case assumes $b = 0$, which implies that the age structure of the population remains constant over time. Then, $B^{-t} = 1$ for all future periods t, eliminating it from equation (5) and allowing a simplified expression for the actuarial balance

$$AB = \tau - \rho \beta_0^{-1}. \tag{6}$$

Equation (6) is intuitively easy to understand: For a system that receives τ cents per worker to be balanced, that amount must be sufficient to pay benefits to the number of beneficiaries per worker (β_0^{-1}).[15] Note that the compound wage growth term G^t is also eliminated from the expression for AB, implying that in this simplified model (a change in) wage growth does not influence the actuarial balance.

Proposition 2: *With an unchanging population structure ($b = 0$) and with current benefits being proportional to current wages, the Social Security system's actuarial balance is unchanged in response to a change in the rate of real wage growth.*

In this simplified setting, a Social Security system that is initially in (out of) balance will remain in (out of) balance to the same degree regardless of the rate of real wage growth.

Case B: Declining worker-to-beneficiary ratio

Now consider the case where $b > 0$ – that is, where the worker-to-beneficiary ratio declines over time. First, all other things equal, this will reduce the actuarial balance of the system. With $b > 0$, $B^{-t}\,[= 1/(1-b)^t]$ must be larger than 1.[16] Compared to the cost rate under Case A, a positive b increases the numerator in the second term of equation (5) and makes the system's costs as a percentage of payrolls larger, thereby reducing actuarial balance.

Proposition 3: *Other things equal, a faster rate of decline, b, in the worker-to-beneficiary ratio is associated with a smaller actuarial balance.*

Moreover, when the worker-to-beneficiary ratio is declining (that is, when $b > 0$), the actuarial balance is not neutral with regard to changes in wage growth (g) because $B^{-t} > 1$ in each future period t. In this case, a larger value of g causes a disproportionately large increase in the numerator of the second term in equation (5) compared to its denominator, causing a change in the actuarial balance.

Proposition 4: *When the worker-retiree ratio is declining (b > 0), increased economic growth reduces the actuarial balance.*

Although the proof of Proposition 4 is intuitively clear (as described above) a formal proof is provided in Appendix A. Essentially, if the population of retirees is growing, the population of workers is constant, and retirement benefits are determined by current wages, faster wage growth would cause benefit outlays to grow faster than payrolls.

Figure 11.1 illustrates Propositions 3 and 4 by calculating actuarial balance for a range of values of the parameters b and g. The system is calibrated to have a zero actuarial balance in perpetuity when annual wage growth is 1 percent and the rate of annual decline in the worker-to-beneficiary ratio is

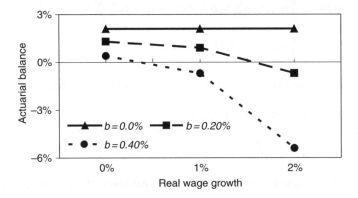

Figure 11.1 Effect of faster real wage growth on actuarial balance under a constant versus a declining worker-to-beneficiary ratio

0.3 percent, roughly the long-term rate projected for the current Social Security program.[17] From this base, the rate of decline of the worker-to-beneficiary ratio is varied in steps (from a low of zero percent to a high of 0.4 percent) and the rate of real wage growth is varied (from zero percent through 2 percent).

When the worker-to-beneficiary ratio is stable ($b = 0$), changing the assumed rate of real wage growth has no effect on the actuarial balance. Figure 11.1 shows that, consistent with Proposition 3, AB is smaller at each given level of g when $b > 0$. In addition, consistent with Proposition 4, when $b > 0$, an increase in g reduces AB, whereas a reduction in g increases AB. Furthermore, AB becomes more sensitive to changes in g at larger values of b. Thus, in a pure pay-as-you-go program in which benefits are based on current average wages, increased economic growth reduces actuarial balance calculated in perpetuity so long as the worker-retiree ratio is declining.

Case C: Benefits dependent on current wages and wages lagged one period

Equation (3) for *PVBenefits* bears an important distinction from the current Social Security program in that it pays benefits as a percentage of *current* average wages alone, whereas the Social Security program's benefits depend upon *past*, or lagged, wages. As a result, an immediate increase in wages, and thus tax revenues, would not lead to an immediate increase in benefits. This lag in translating wage growth to benefit growth underlies the common belief that system financing unequivocally improves in response to faster economic growth.

Equation (3) is rewritten below to express the current benefit as an equally weighted function of current wages and wages 1 period ago. This makes benefits at time t a function of wages at time t and $t-1$.

$$PVBenefits = \frac{1}{2} w_0 \rho \beta_0^{-1} \sum_{t=0}^{\infty} N_t B^{-t} G^t R^{-t} + \frac{1}{2} w_0 \rho \beta_0^{-1} \sum_{t=0}^{\infty} N_t B^{-t} G^{t-1} R^{-t}$$

$$= \frac{1}{2} w_0 \rho \beta_0^{-1} \sum_{t=0}^{\infty} N_t (1 + G^{-1}) B^{-t} G^t R^{-t}. \quad (3a)$$

Given (3a), equation (5) for actuarial balance can be rewritten as

$$AB = \tau - \frac{\rho \beta_0^{-1} \sum_{t=0}^{\infty} B^{-t}(1 + G^{-1}) G^t R^{-t}}{2 \sum_{t=0}^{\infty} G^t R^{-t}} = \tau - \frac{1}{2}(1 + G^{-1}) \Omega. \quad (5a)$$

With a stable worker-retiree ratio ($b = 0$), equation (6) can be simplified to

$$AB = \tau - \frac{1}{2} \rho \beta_0^{-1}(1 + G^{-1}). \quad (6a)$$

This expression of the actuarial balance clarifies why many people believe that increased economic growth will improve system financing. Because G^{-1} declines as wage growth increases, higher wage growth reduces the cost rate, $(1/2)\rho\beta_0^{-1}(1 + G^{-1})$, relative to the revenue rate, τ, and improves the system's financing. This leads to the following:

Proposition 5: *Assuming (1) a stable worker-to-beneficiary ratio ($b = 0$) and (2) dependence of benefits on lagged wages, faster wage growth reduces the cost rate and improves the system's actuarial balance.*

The above discussion clarifies that when benefits are a function of lagged wages, faster wage growth has a differential impact on *PVBenefits* and *PVTaxes*. This becomes clear by comparing equations (5) and (5a).

The obvious next question concerns the impact of faster wage growth (g) on the actuarial balance when the worker-to-beneficiary ratio is declining – that is, the sign of the derivative dAB/dG when $b > 0$.

Appendix B shows that the expression for dAB/dG for the case of $b > 0$ can be written as

$$\frac{dAB}{dG} = -\omega(1 + G^{-1})G^{-1}\Omega\left[Z - \frac{G^{-1}}{1+G^{-1}}\right] \tag{7}$$

where Ω is the summarized cost rate as defined in equation (5) above and Z equals the net increase in Ω arising from a change in G. As discussed earlier, an increase in G would lead to a larger increase in the numerator of the second term of equation (5) compared to the increase in the denominator because each B^{-t} term in the numerator exceeds 1. The term Z in equation (7) [defined in equation A6 in Appendix A] equals the net increase in the numerator of the second term in equation (5) compared to the denominator due to an increase in G. The term Z is a function of b, $Z(b)$, with the properties: (1) that $Z \geq 0$ when $b \geq 0$, with equality holding when $b = 0$; and (2) that Z increases monotonically with b. Thus, Z in equation (7) captures the impact of the worker-to-retiree ratio on the change in the actuarial balance due to a change in the growth rate (dAB/dG).

What is equation 7 telling us? It is simply a combination of Propositions 4 and 5. Proposition 4 revealed that with retirees forming a larger fraction of the population over time, faster wage growth increases Social Security's cost rate and *worsens* the system's actuarial balance. Proposition 5 shows that under dependence of benefits on lagged wages, faster wage growth *improves* the system's actuarial balance. Equation 7 shows that change in the actuarial balance arising from faster wage growth depends on the balance of these opposing forces. Appendix B shows that setting $b = Z = 0$ in equation (7) yields the result of Proposition 5, namely that

$$\frac{dAB}{dG} = \frac{1}{2}G^{-2}\Omega > 0. \tag{8}$$

Equation (7) also clarifies that setting $b > 0$ (which implies $Z > 0$) could change the sign of dAB/dG from positive to negative – by flipping the sign of the term in the square brackets. That is, a sufficiently rapid decline in the worker-to-beneficiary ratio could result in Proposition 4's effect dominating that of Proposition 5. That would cause the system's actuarial balance to become smaller (more negative) in response to a change in the wage growth rate, contrary to the popular belief that higher wage growth improves Social Security's finances.

Case D: Benefits dependent on wages in several earlier periods

In practice, current Social Security benefit outlays are not just a function of wages one period ago but of wages often as many as 40 periods earlier. That is because although the benefits of those retiring today are wage indexed – that is, depend on current wages – the benefits of today's older retirees are based on wages from several periods ago (that prevailed in the years when they entered retirement) and now grow only with prices rather than wages. For example, Social Security benefits of those aged 92 today who retired when they were aged 62 are determined by the wage level from 30 periods ago whereas the benefits of retirees aged 67 today who retired when they were aged 62 depend on the wage level from just 5 years ago. Appendix C shows that if past wages entering the actuarial balance formula are equally weighted, the actuarial balance can be expressed as

$$AB = -\frac{1}{N+1}\gamma(G)G^{-1}\Omega\left[Z + \frac{(N+1)G^{-(N+1)}}{1-G^{-(N+1)}} - \frac{G^{-1}}{1-G^{-1}}\right] \quad (9)$$

where $\gamma(G)$ summarizes the dependence of benefits on past wages. Again, as Appendix C shows, the basic conclusions of Case C above would be preserved. That is, whether $dAB/dG \lessgtr 0$ depends on the balance of two opposing forces. For values of g and b where the two forces are exactly balanced, $dAB/dG = 0$. For other combinations of g and b, $dAB/dG \neq 0$, meaning it would be either negative or positive. This yields the following:

Proposition 6: *When current benefits are an equally weighted function of wages in the current period and N earlier periods, for each given value of g, there exists a value of $b^* = b(g)$ where $dAB/dG = 0$, with $dAB/dG > 0$ when $b < b^*$ and $dAB/dG < 0$ when $b > b^*$.*[18]

It is obvious that equally weighting past wages in the actuarial balance formula is inappropriate because mortality reduces the sizes of older cohorts whose benefits are determined by wages further back in the past. Hence, actuarial balance should be calculated using declining weights calibrated to the age distribution of cohort sizes over time. Applying smaller rather than equal weights to wage levels further back in the past implies that the force of

Proposition 5 (whereby actuarial balance improves in response to faster wage growth) diminishes relative to that of Proposition 4 in determining the change in actuarial balances with respect to a change in real wage growth. Because a larger share of total benefits would be paid to relatively younger retirees, faster wage growth would result in larger benefit outlays more quickly. Consequently, the combinations of g and b values at which $dAB/dG = 0$ would be different compared to the case of equal weighting.

Figure 11.2 shows locus (that is, combinations of the wage growth rate g, and the rate of decline in the worker-to-beneficiary ratio, $b(g)$) for which $dAB/dG = 0$. The calculations assume: τ (payroll tax rate) = 12.4 percent; w_0 (initial real wage) = 1; $N_t = N_0$ (population of workers at time t) = 1; r (interest rate) = 3 percent; ρ (benefit replacement rate) = 35 percent; β_0 (initial worker-to-beneficiary ratio) = 3.33; and N (the number of past wage periods that enter into the benefit formula) = 35.

In Figure 11.2, the locus is calculated under the assumption of declining weights for wages further back in the past. The weights are calculated on the basis of population shares of those aged 65 and older that would arise under age-specific conditional mortality rates for those aged 65 and older.[19] The derivative of actuarial balance with respect to G, dAB/dG, is negative for combinations of b and g that lie in the north-east direction relative to the locus. That is, higher wage growth would reduce actuarial balance under these circumstances. For wage growth rates approximating current rates in the United States – about 1 percent per year – values of $b^* = b(g^*)$ are very small – about 0.2 percent – making it quite likely that $dAB/dG < 0$ when b values are calibrated to US demographics.

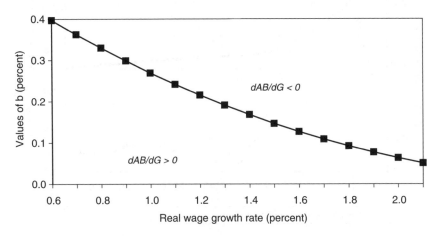

Figure 11.2 Locus of $dAB/dG = 0$ when current benefits depend on current wages and wages in 35 past periods – declining weights

Case E: Calibration to US demographic projections

Figure 11.3 shows projected values of the worker-to-beneficiary ratio for the United States.[20] It shows that the ratio is expected to decline sharply during the next three decades followed by a much more gradual decline after the baby-boom generation transitions into retirement and passes away.

Figure 11.3 also shows the corresponding projected time-varying rate of decline (b) in the worker-to-beneficiary ratio. The values of b are generally quite large compared to the values in Figure 11.2 at which $dAB/dG = 0$ when real wage growth equals 1 percent.

Note that while the worker-to-beneficiary ratio is projected to decline, this decline would take place alongside a *growing* projected population in the United States. Figure 11.4 shows the Social Security Administration's projection of the population of workers and that of workers plus retirees, both normalized to their population sizes in 2005. It indicates that a projected decline in the worker-to-beneficiary ratio does not involve a stagnant worker population as assumed earlier. Rather, both populations are projected to grow in absolute size in the United States. A declining worker-to-beneficiary ratio means just that the fraction of the total (and growing) population that would be in the workforce is expected to decline over the next 75 years.

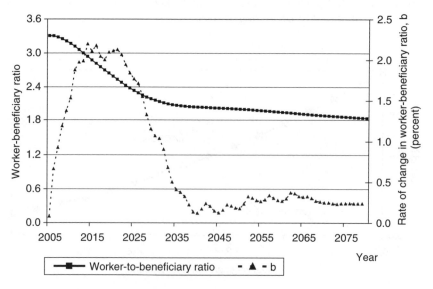

Figure 11.3 Projected worker-beneficiary ratio and its rate of change (b) in the United States

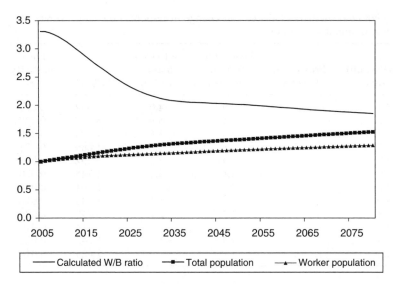

Figure 11.4 Projected US worker-beneficiary ratio, worker population, and total population

11.3 Response of actuarial balance under full calibration to US demographics

11.3.1 Main results

Incorporating US demographic projections into the actuarial balance calculation and assuming that the rate of decline in the worker-to-beneficiary ratio beyond the year 2080 remains constant at its 2080 value yields values for dAB/dG of 0.29 when $g = 1.1$ percent and -1.75 when $g = 1.6$ percent. The values of AB at those two values of g are -3.2 percent and -4.1 percent respectively.[21] That is, although at $g = 1.1$ percent the immediate marginal contribution of faster growth is positive, the marginal contribution becomes negative rapidly as g is increased and cumulatively results in a smaller (more negative) actuarial balance when $g = 1.6$ percent.

As Table 11.1 shows, restricting actuarial balance calculations to just 75 years would suggest the opposite conclusion: A larger value of real wage growth (g) produces an (algebraically) larger actuarial balance and positive values of dAB/dG. For example, using the baseline discount rate of 3 percent and real wage growth rate of 1.1 percent, the 75-year horizon yields an actuarial balance of just -1.5 percent, a much smaller deficit than the -3.2 percent obtained under the calculation in perpetuity. In addition, increasing the growth rate to 1.6 percent per year, the 75-year actuarial balance becomes algebraically larger (less negative): -1.1 percent.

Table 11.1 Actuarial balance and change in response to change in real wage growth and discount rates

Discount rate (%)	Projection horizon	Real wage growth rate (%)	Actuarial balance, AB (%)	dAB/dG	Local elasticity, $|\varepsilon|$
2.7	∞	1.1	−4.0	−0.582	0.023
2.7	∞	1.6	−5.9	−5.657	0.327
2.7	75	1.1	−1.6	1.783	0.028
2.7	75	1.6	1.2	1.669	0.021
3.0	∞	1.1	−3.2	0.292	0.009
3.0	∞	1.6	−4.1	−1.748	0.070
3.0	75	1.1	−1.5	1.761	0.026
3.0	75	1.6	−1.1	1.645	0.018
3.3	∞	1.1	−2.7	0.749	0.020
3.3	∞	1.6	−3.1	−0.314	0.010
3.3	75	1.1	−1.3	1.742	0.023
3.3	75	1.6	−1.0	1.624	0.016

11.3.2 Sensivity analysis: discount rate

Table 11.1 also shows that under perpetuity calculations, the (negative) response of actuarial balance to increases in wage growth rates is very large when present values are calculated using smaller discount rates. This is as expected because smaller discount rates increase the weight on dollar flows in the distant future relative to weights on dollar flows in the immediate future, making future benefit obligations larger in present value relative to earlier payroll tax-payments. The opposite result holds when the assumed discount rate is larger – as Table 11.1 shows.

11.3.3 Sensitivity analysis: rate of decline in b

The next step is to investigate the impact on actuarial balance of a slightly faster or slower decline in the US worker-to-beneficiary ratio when the calculation horizon is infinite. Figure 11.5 shows the actuarial balance for different values of a parameter, γ (gamma), applied to the time-varying values of b shown in Figure 11.3. For example, $\gamma = 0.9$ would imply a slower decline in the worker-to-beneficiary ratio over time whereas $\gamma = 1.1$ would imply a faster rate of decline in that ratio. Figure 11.5 shows the values of AB for values of γ ranging from 0.9 to 1.1 and values of wage growth (g) between 0.6 percent and 1.6 percent (that is, values of G ranging from 1.006 to 1.016). Figure 11.5 shows that at all levels of wage growth within this range, the actuarial balance is smaller (more negative) when γ is increased (the worker-to-beneficiary ratio declines faster). Moreover, Figure 11.5 shows that for each rate of decline in the worker-to-beneficiary ratio, there is a rate of productivity/wage growth at which the actuarial balance is maximized.

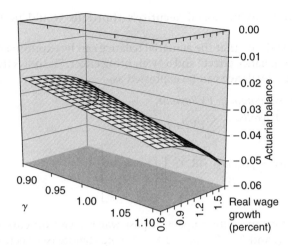

Figure 11.5 Actuarial balance for alternative rates of decline in the worker-beneficiary ratio and real wage growth

At $\gamma = 1$, the rate of real wage growth that maximizes the actuarial balance is much smaller, only around 0.5 percent – closer to that under the Social Security Trustees' "high-cost" assumptions. Under calculations in perpetuity, increasing real wage growth would, according to the figure, reduce Social Security's actuarial balance given projected demographic changes in the United States.[22]

11.4 Actuarial balance and annual balances under faster wage growth – a conundrum?

The previous section showed that under stylized calculations calibrated to features of the US Social Security system, faster growth would reduce the infinite horizon actuarial balance. Appendix D shows, however, that with benefits dependent on past wages, annual balance ratios (total payroll taxes minus total benefits as a ratio of total payrolls in any given year) would be *larger* in all future years.

This result seemingly creates a policy conundrum: The infinite-horizon actuarial balance is usually interpreted as the immediate and a permanent payroll tax hike required to balance the system's intertemporal budget constraint. A reduction in the actuarial balance under faster wage growth means that such a tax increase must be larger. However, an increase in each future year's annual balance ratios under faster wage growth implies that the "pay-as-you-go" tax rate increase that must be levied in each future year would be smaller. It is tempting to conclude, therefore, that the pay-as-you-go approach to resolving Social Security's shortfalls would be better than pre-funding.

Appendix D shows that the actuarial balance can be expressed as a product of an "annual-balance effect" and a "weighting effect." It shows that equation for the actuarial balance can be expressed as

$$AB = \sum_{t=0}^{\infty} \frac{Cash\ Balance_t}{Payrolls_t} \frac{PVPayrolls_t}{\sum_{t=0}^{\infty} PVPayroll_t}$$

$$= \sum_{t=0}^{\infty} \left[\frac{\tau G^t - \rho \beta_0^{-1} \omega \gamma(G) B^{-t} G^t}{G^t} \right] \cdot \left[\frac{G^t R^{-t}}{\sum_{t=0}^{\infty} G^t R^{-t}} \right], \tag{10}$$

where $\omega\,\gamma(G)$ captures the impact of past wages levels on current benefits, and $G = 1 + g$, and $B = 1 - b$, and $R = 1 + r$ as before (see Section 11.2).

In equation (10), the first term in square brackets equals the annual balance ratio in period t and the second term in square brackets is the present valued weight applied to year-t's annual balance ratio. According to equation (10), the weighted sum of all future annual balance ratios equals the actuarial balance. Appendix D clarifies that annual balance ratios unambiguously increase in each future year under faster real wage growth.

Figure 11.6 shows unweighted annual balance ratios when the stylized model of the earlier section is calibrated to features of the US Social Security system (corresponding to the cases shown in Table 11.1 with real wage growth rates of 1.1 and 1.6 percent and a discount rate of 3 percent). It shows that projected annual balance ratios are negative and declining over time. Increasing the real wage growth rate from 1.1 percent to 1.6 percent per year increases annual balance ratios (makes them less negative) in each future year but the ratios still decline over time.

Figure 11.7 indicates the present valued weights applicable each year according to equation (10) for the same two cases as shown in Figure 11.6. Figure 11.7 indicates (as explained in Appendix D) that under faster wage growth the weights applicable to the earlier annual balance ratios would be smaller. Those applicable to later annual balance ratios would be larger. Under a pay-as-you-go approach to resolving Social Security's future shortfalls, each year's weight can be interpreted as share of future payrolls (in present value terms) that would bear a pay-as-you-go tax rate hike equal to that year's annual balance ratio.

With this information, the policy conundrum mentioned earlier can be resolved. In Table 11.1, the infinite horizon actuarial balance was –3.2 percent under a wage growth rate of 1.1 percent and discount rate of 3.0 percent. Although increasing wage growth to 1.6 percent increases unweighted annual cash balance ratios in each future year, it also increases the share of

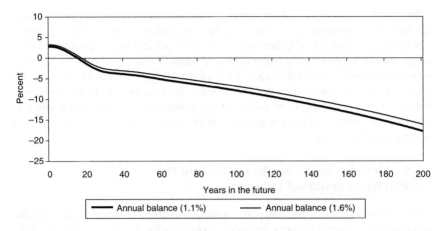

Figure 11.6 Annual balance ratios under alternative wage growth rates (1.1% and 1.6%) – stylized model under US calibration

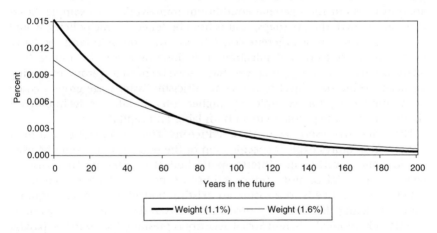

Figure 11.7 Present valued weights under alternative wage growth rates (1.1% and 1.6%) – stylized model under US calibration

present valued payrolls that would be subjected to pay-as-you-go tax rates larger than 3.2 percentage points and reduces the share of payrolls subject to a pay-as-you-go tax rate of less than 3.2 percentage points. Hence, under faster wage growth, present valued payrolls must, on average, bear a pay-as-you-go tax rate that is larger – 4.1 percentage points according to Table 11.1.

The conundrum mentioned earlier is resolved in the following sense: Although faster growth leads to smaller pay-as-you-go tax *rate hikes* in each future year, the share of future wages that is subject to larger tax pay-as-you-go tax *rates* (compared to the average rate under slower wage growth) increases. The latter (weighting effect) may be sufficiently large under faster wage growth to generate a larger actuarial balance – as appears to be the case when the model is calibrated to features of the US Social Security system. The choice between pay-as-you-go and pre-funding as methods for resolving future financial shortfalls is no longer unambiguous because under the former, a larger share of future wages would be subject to higher tax rates when wage growth is faster.

11.5 Model consistency in evaluating the sensitivity of actuarial balance

This section considers the issue of "model consistency" when exploring the response of actuarial balance to faster wage growth. The standard criticisms levied against the sensitivity analysis presented in the Social Security trustees' annual reports is that exploring the implications of changing a single factor while holding other inputs constant is inappropriate and the analysis cries out for a general equilibrium framework. For example, faster real wage growth that, perhaps, results from better economic policies, would be accompanied by a different constellation of economic (and, perhaps, demographic) outcomes. Replicating, as is done here, a static approach to analyzing Social Security's finances that is used by most government scoring agencies, would be subject to the same criticism: Faster wage growth could be accompanied, for example, by higher interest rates as technological shocks increase the productivity of both labor and capital.

There are two responses to these criticisms. First, a general equilibrium framework requires explicit specification of the policies that would be used to close the government's intertemporal budget constraint. The Trustees' analysis of Social Security finances imposes no such budget constraint. When the objective is to measure an existing budget gap, general equilibrium modeling is naturally precluded. A standard "budget measure" approach is adopted wherein Social Security is presumed to continue paying scheduled benefits even though revenues are inadequate.

Second, impending demographic change in the United States is likely to increase future capital intensity. A declining pool of workers relative to wealthier retirees would tend to dampen increases in interest rates arising from productivity enhancing technical progress. On the other hand, economic agents may demand higher returns on savings in an environment of higher growth but perhaps also greater economic volatility.

The standard approach to estimating the government's interest rate under uncertainty suggests equating it to the rate of time preference (say, 1 percent per year) plus the product of two items: the inverse of the degree of risk aversion and the standard deviation of productivity growth. However, there is no consensus in the economic growth literature on the size of the appropriate risk aversion parameter.

An inverse relationship between wage growth and Social Security's actuarial balance is supported under a range of interest rates. For example, calculations using the stylized model under Case E using a 3 percent discount rate show that when the real wage growth rate is increased from 0.6 percent per year to 1.6 percent per year, the actuarial balance declines from −3.0 percent to −4.1 percent. However, simultaneously increasing the government's interest rate from 3.0 percent to 3.3 percent would leave the actuarial balance unchanged at −3.0 percent.[23] That implies the actuarial balance could decline when faster wage growth is accompanied with higher interest rates over a limited but non-trivial range.

In addition to interest rate uncertainties, the calculations reported earlier assume that the decline in the worker-to-beneficiary ratio would continue indefinitely – implying that Social Security benefits would be financed by workers comprising an ever-smaller fraction of the population.[24] Although gradually increasing longevity and a gradual but continuing decline in fertility is not inconceivable for a number of decades beyond the next 75 years, the assumption of declining worker-retiree ratios in perpetuity is difficult to defend.

To explore how crucial this assumption is, the infinite-term actuarial balance is calculated under alternative ranges of years beyond the next 75 years during which the worker-to-retiree ratio declines, but stops declining thereafter. In other words, assume $b_t = b_{75}$ for $75 \leq t \leq S$ and $b_t = 0$ for $t > S$. Table 11.2 shows changes in the infinite term actuarial balance from increasing wage growth under alternative values of S. It shows that the infinite-term actuarial balance under wage growth of 1.6 percent per year is smaller (implying that the actuarial deficit is larger) than that under wage growth of 1.1 percent per year when the assumption of $b_t = b_{75}$ is maintained for just

Table 11.2 Infinite term actuarial balance under alternative horizons for continued decline in the worker-to-beneficiary ratio

S	Infinite term actuarial balance under alternative wage growth rate assumptions	
	1.1 percent	1.6 percent
85	−2.51	−2.47
95	−2.61	−2.61
105	−2.70	−2.74

Source: 2005 Social Security Trustees Report, Table VI.D.4.

20 additional years beyond the next 75 years (S > 95). Thus, although the negative impact of higher wage growth on the infinite-term actuarial balance requires the assumption of a continued decline in the worker-to-beneficiary ratio, it does not appear necessary to maintain that assumption for more than a few years beyond the conventional projection horizon of 75 years.

11.6 Simulations under a detailed model of Social Security – SSASIM

These stylized demonstrations of the impact of wage growth on Social Security's actuarial balance capture the essence of the current Social Security program – wherein current benefits are based on past wages – but do not capture the full details of Social Security financing.

This section reports results under the SSASIM model developed and maintained by the Policy Simulation Group. This model was developed during the 1994–1996 Advisory Council on Social Security under contract with a number of organizations, including the Social Security Administration, and has been regularly updated since then.[25] The SSASIM model has two modes of calculating system financing: a cell-based actuarial mode designed to replicate the results from the Social Security Administration's actuaries and a fully microsimulation-based mode similar to that utilized by the Congressional Budget Office (CBO). The results reported below were produced using SSASIM's cell-based mode, though simulations using the microsimulation-based mode produce qualitatively similar results. It should be noted, however, that results from the SSASIM model do not constitute official findings from the Social Security Administration's (SSAs) actuaries and official estimates may differ.

11.6.1 SSASIM performance relative to SSA estimates

The Social Security Trustees report results from sensitivity analyses conducted on a number of demographic and economic factors. These factors are shifted by a pre-set amount from their mid-point projections to examine how increasing or reducing their values affects Social Security's finances over the next 75 years. Table 11.3 reports the Trustees' findings on the sensitivity of the actuarial balance with respect to wage growth: Increasing the ultimate rate of real wage growth from 1.1 percent to 1.6 percent increases the 75-year actuarial balance by 0.53 percent of payroll. As expected, system solvency is improved through a decline in the summarized cost rate (the ratio of the present value of benefit outlays plus administrative expenses to the present value of taxable payrolls).[26]

Although the SSASIM model does not use real wage growth as a direct input, changes to assumed rates of productivity growth increase wage growth and impact system financing. The SSASIM baseline productivity

Table 11.3 Social Security trustees' sensitivity analysis of real wage growth on 75-year actuarial balance

	Assumed ultimate rate of real wage growth	
Percent of taxable payroll	1.1 percent	1.6 percent
Summarized income rate	13.87	13.74
Summarized cost rate	15.79	15.13
Actuarial balance	−1.92	−1.39

Source: 2005 Social Security Trustees Report, Table VI.D.4.

growth assumption of 1.6 percent is consistent with that assumed by Social Security's Trustees and the model produces a 75-year actuarial deficit of 1.92 percent of taxable payroll, also consistent with the Trustees' projections in their 2005 annual report. In the SSASIM model, increasing the assumed rate of annual productivity growth from 1.6 to 2.1 percent (which corresponds to an increase in the real wage growth rate from 1.1 percent to 1.6 percent), produces very similar results. The 75-year actuarial deficit is reduced from 1.92 to 1.42 percent of taxable payroll – an improvement of 0.50 percentage points – quite close to the 0.53 percentage point improvement reported by the Trustees.

Since 2003, the annual Social Security Trustees Report has published estimates of system financing in perpetuity. The 2005 Report estimated the program's actuarial deficit in perpetuity as 3.5 percent of taxable wages, meaning that an immediate and permanent payroll tax increase of 3.5 percentage points would be sufficient to maintain program sustainability under the Trustees' intermediate economic and demographic assumptions.[27] However, the Report does not conduct sensitivity analysis for changes in economic or demographic factors measured over an infinite horizon, as it does for solvency measured over the traditional 75-year horizon.

When the system's solvency is measured in perpetuity, the SSASIM model produces a revenue shortfall equal to 3.53 percent of the present value of payrolls – very close to the (rounded) 3.5 percent projected by the Trustees.[28]

11.6.2 SSASIM'S perpetuity estimate of sensitivity of actuarial balance to productivity growth

SSASIM model projections show that increasing the rate of productivity growth from 1.6 percent to 2.1 percent would *increase* Social Security's actuarial deficit from 3.5 percent to 3.7 percent of taxable payroll (that is, reduce its actuarial balance as defined in equation (5) in Section 11.2 from −3.5 percent to −3.7 percent). The reason for this is two-fold: economic growth increases costs by *more* than it increases payrolls, and increases income *less* than the increase in payrolls.

SSASIM model calculations show that the summarized cost rate increases from 17.25 percent of payroll in the base case to 17.29 percent of payroll in the high-growth scenario (see Table 11.4). Moreover, the program's income rate declines from 13.72 to 13.59 percent of payroll in response to faster wage growth.[29] The net impact of these two changes is a decline in the system's actuarial balance from −3.53 to −3.70 percent. Note that the actuarial balance would have declined even if the reduction in the income rate traceable to the existing trust fund were ignored.

The reason for the worsening of the actuarial balance can be traced to the opposing effects identified in Proposition 6 of Section 11.2: A direct actuarial-balance-increasing effect of the lagged dependence of benefits on wages versus the opposite effect due to a decline in the worker-to-beneficiary ratio. The SSASIM model's estimate of a worsening actuarial balance under faster productivity growth suggests that the latter effect dominates the former under an assessment of Social Security's finances in perpetuity.

Figure 11.8 shows the product of annual balance ratios and weights in each future year (as in equation (10) in Section 11.4), but utilizes SSASIM (rather than stylized model) results to illustrate the annual cash balances entering the actuarial balance calculation of equation (10).[30]

Recall that in equation (10), the actuarial balance is expressed as the weighted average of annual balance ratios, with weighting determined by the ratio of each year's discounted payroll to the present value of all payrolls over the measurement period.

Figure 11.8 illustrates that for roughly the next 115 years, the annual balance effect would dominate the weighting effect (see Appendix D) – that is, annual balance ratios weighted by present valued payroll shares in total present value of payrolls would be smaller under a 1.6 percent wage growth rate than under a 1.1 percent rate. After that period, however, annual improvements in annual cash balance ratios arising from faster wage growth would be insufficient and weighted cash balance ratios would become more negative under $g = 1.6$ percent compared to $g = 1.1$ percent. Hence, the

Table 11.4 Impact of productivity growth on infinite term income, cost, and payrolls

$ trillions present value (percent of payroll)	Productivity growth		percent change
	1.6 percent	2.1 percent	
Income	$44.52	$60.30	35.44%
	(13.72%)	(13.59%)	
Cost	$55.97	$76.80	37.21%
	(17.25%)	(17.29%)	
Payroll	$324.49	$444.00	36.83%

Source: Authors' calculations based on SSASIM model.

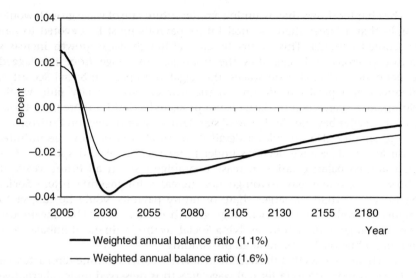

Figure 11.8 Weighted annual balance ratios under alternative wage growth rates (1.1% and 1.6%) (SSASIM model; $b > 0$; wage-price indexing)

infinite horizon actuarial balance is smaller under the faster wage growth assumption. Figure 11.8 also clarifies the seemingly contradictory result that faster wage growth improves actuarial balance over 75 years but reduces it in perpetuity.

11.7 Conclusion

Since 2003, the Social Security Trustees have begun to report the system's financial imbalance measured in perpetuity. Unfortunately, the Trustees' do not report the sensitivity of the perpetuity imbalance measure to alternative economic and demographic assumptions. Using a stylized model of Social Security finances and a detailed Social Security simulation model, both calibrated to the Social Security Administration's intermediate economic and demographic projections, this paper shows that faster real wage growth would substantially worsen Social Security's actuarial balance under the new perpetuity measure. This stands in sharp contrast to the conventional wisdom that faster wage growth would improve Social Security's financial status.

That wisdom has been reinforced under standard measures of Social Security's finances such as annual balance ratios, the cross-over date (when noninterest receipts begin falling short of program outlays), the date of trust-fund exhaustion, and summarized actuarial balances calculated over truncated horizons of 25, 50, or 75 years.[31] The chapter's analysis indicates that evaluating Social Security's financial status on the basis of standard measures would be hazardous.

The chapter shows that assuming a faster future rate of wage growth would imply that a larger share of total future payrolls must be devoted to pay scheduled benefits. This occurs because although wage growth increases future payrolls and magnifies the financial advantage from the lagged dependence of benefits on wages, the negative impact on Social Security's finances of a persistent decline in the worker-to-beneficiary ratio would dominate – even when the latter is not projected to last for more than a couple of decades beyond the Trustees' standard 75-year projection horizon.

The chapter also provides a detailed interpretation of why the infinite-term actuarial balance declines under faster wage growth despite the fact that annual balance ratios increase unambiguously in all future years. It shows, that under pay-as-you-go tax increases for meeting future Social Security's shortfalls, a larger share of future payrolls would be subject to higher payroll tax rates when wage growth occurs faster. That means the pay-as-you-go approach to resolving Social Security's financial imbalance is not unambiguously preferable to pre-funding.

The chapter shows that the decline in Social Security's infinite-term actuarial balance in response to faster real wage growth is preserved under alternative discount rate assumptions. It is also robust to simultaneous increases in wage growth and interest rates over limited ranges of those two variables.

Faster economic growth is obviously desirable because it would help increase living standards and provide additional resources for addressing growing entitlement costs in general. However, given that Social Security's revenues and benefits both depend on wages, faster wage growth would not necessarily improve, and may worsen, Social Security's finances when they are measured using the infinite-term actuarial balance.

Appendix A

Proof of proposition 4

Equation (5) in the text is

$$AB = \tau - \frac{\rho \beta_0^{-1} \sum_{t=0}^{\infty} B^{-t} G^t R^{-t}}{\sum_{t=0}^{\infty} G^t R^{-t}} = \tau - \frac{N}{D} = \tau - \Omega, \tag{A5}$$

where $R = (1 + r)$; $G = (1 + g)$; $B = (1 - b)$; and it is assumed that the numerator is well defined – that is $G/BR < 1$.

Note: $D = \sum_{t=0}^{\infty} G^t R^{-t}$;

$$dD = \sum_{t=0}^{\infty} t G^{t-1} R^{-t} dG = G^{-1} \sum_{t=0}^{\infty} t G^t R^{-t} dG;$$

$$N = \rho\beta_0^{-1}\sum_{t=0}^{\infty}B^{-t}G^tR^{-t};$$

and

$$dN = \rho\beta_0^{-1}\sum_{t=0}^{\infty}tB^{-t}G^{t-1}R^{-t}dG = G^{-1}\rho\beta_0^{-1}\sum_{t=0}^{\infty}tB^{-t}G^tR^{-t}dG.$$

Thus,

$$\frac{dAB}{DG} = -\frac{d\Omega}{dG} = -\frac{DdN - NdD}{D^2} = -\Omega\left[\frac{dN}{N} - \frac{dD}{D}\right]$$

$$= -\Omega\left[\frac{\left[G^{-1}\rho\beta_0^{-1}\sum_{t=0}^{\infty}tB^{-t}G^tR^{-t}\right]}{\rho\beta_0^{-1}\sum_{t=0}^{\infty}B^{-t}G^tR^{-t}} - \frac{\left[G^{-1}\sum_{t=0}^{\infty}tG^tR^{-t}\right]}{\left[\sum_{t=0}^{\infty}G^tR^{-t}\right]}\right]$$

$$= -G^{-1}\Omega\left[\frac{\left[\sum_{t=0}^{\infty}tB^{-t}G^tR^{-t}\right]}{\sum_{t=0}^{\infty}B^{-t}G^tR^{-t}} - \frac{\left[\sum_{t=0}^{\infty}tG^tR^{-t}\right]}{\left[\sum_{t=0}^{\infty}G^tR^{-t}\right]}\right] = -G^{-1}\Omega Z \quad (A6)$$

We know that $G^{-1} > 0$ and $\Omega > 0$ (cost is positive). In equation (A6), $Z > 0$ when $b > 0$ (see the Proof A below). That yields the result $[dAB/dG] < 0$ when $b > 0$.

Proof A:

To prove: $Z = \left[\dfrac{\left[\sum_{t=0}^{\infty}tB^{-t}G^tR^{-t}\right]}{\sum_{t=0}^{\infty}B^{-t}G^tR^{-t}} - \dfrac{\left[\sum_{t=0}^{\infty}tG^tR^{-t}\right]}{\left[\sum_{t=0}^{\infty}G^tR^{-t}\right]}\right] \geq 0$ when $b \geq 0$ (with equality

holding if $b = 0$). That is,

$$\left[\sum_{t=0}^{\infty}tB^{-t}G^tR^{-t}\right]\left[\sum_{t=0}^{\infty}G^tR^{-t}\right] \geq \left[\sum_{t=0}^{\infty}tG^tR^{-t}\right]\left[\sum_{t=0}^{\infty}B^{-t}G^tR^{-t}\right] \quad (A7)$$

Writing $G^tR^{-t} = x_t$, equation (A7) can be expressed as

$$\left[\sum_{t=0}^{\infty}tB^{-t}x_t^2\right] + \left.\sum_{i=0}^{\infty}iB^{-i}x_i\sum_{j=0}^{\infty}x_j\right|_{i\neq j} \geq \left[\sum_{t=0}^{\infty}tB^{-t}x_t^2\right] + \left.\sum_{i=0}^{\infty}ix_i\sum_{j=0}^{\infty}B^{-j}x_j\right|_{i\neq j}.$$

Eliminating the first terms on each side of the inequality yields

$$\sum_{i=0}^{\infty} iB^{-i}x_i \sum_{j=0}^{\infty} x_j \bigg|_{i \neq j} \geq \sum_{i=0}^{\infty} ix_i \sum_{j=0}^{\infty} B^{-j}x_j \bigg|_{i \neq j}.$$

To construct the proof, assume that the opposite (that is, replace $\geq$ with $<$) and show that doing so leads to a contradiction:

$$\text{Assume } \sum_{i=0}^{\infty} iB^{-i}x_i \sum_{j=0}^{\infty} x_j \bigg|_{i \neq j} < \sum_{i=0}^{\infty} ix_i \sum_{j=0}^{\infty} B^{-j}x_j \bigg|_{i \neq j}. \tag{A8}$$

Select any pair of terms in equation (A8) where, $I = n$ and $j = m$, in the first, and $I = m$ and $j = n$ in the second. Without loss of generality, assume $m < n$.

For this pair, the left-hand side of (A8) equals $nB^{-n}x_n x_m + mB^{-m}x_m x_n$, and the right-hand side equals $nx_n B^{-m}x_m + mx_m B^{-n}x_n$

Expression (A8) implies checking if $nB^{-n}x_n x_m + mB^{-m}x_m x_n < nx_n B^{-m}x_m + mx_m B^{-n}x_n$ for each such pair of terms.

That is, whether $nB^{-n} + mB^{-m} < nB^{-m} + mB^{-n}$;

Multiplying all terms by B^m, check whether $nB^{-(n-m)} + m < n + mB^{-(n-m)}$; or $B^{-(n-m)}(n-m) < n - m$.

However, given that $B^{-1} \geq 1$ when $b \geq 0$, this inequality cannot be true since $m < n$ by assumption. Because the contradiction applies to all pairs of terms i, j [(n,m) and (m,n) with $m < n$], it applies to equation (A8) in its entirety. Hence, $Z \geq 0$ when $b \geq 0$ (with equality holding when $b = 0$).

Moreover, Z is a monotonically increasing function of b. This follows from the fact that $B^{-1} = [1/(1 - b)]$ is a monotonically increasing function of b.

Appendix B

Proof of proposition 6

Suppose current benefits are determined by wages in two periods – the current period and 1 period ago. Assume that each period's wages receive the same weight, $\omega = 0.5$, in the benefit formula. Equation (A5) would be modified to

$$AB = \tau - \frac{\rho \beta_0^{-1} \omega (G^0 + G^{-1}) \sum_{t=0}^{\infty} B^{-t} G^t R^{-t}}{\sum_{t=0}^{\infty} G^t R^{-t}} = \tau$$

$$- \omega(1 + G^{-1})\Omega = \tau - \omega \left[\frac{1 - G^{-2}}{1 - G^{-1}} \right] \Omega, \tag{A9}$$

where $\omega = 0.5$, $G = (1 + g)$, and $B = (1 - b)$. Thus,

$$\frac{dAB}{dG} = -\omega\left[\left[\frac{1-G^{-2}}{1-G^{-1}}\right]\frac{d\Omega}{dG} + \Omega\left[\frac{1-G^{-2}}{1-G^{-1}}\right]\left[\frac{2G^{-3}}{1-G^{-2}} - \frac{G^{-2}}{1-G^{-1}}\right]\right] \quad (A10)$$

Using the result from equation (A6) that $\frac{d\Omega}{dG} = G^{-1}\Omega Z$ and simple algebraic manipulations yields

$$\frac{dAB}{dG} = -\omega(1 + G^{-1})G^{-1}\Omega\left[Z - \frac{G^{-1}}{1+G^{-1}}\right], \quad (A11)$$

where Z is as defined in Proof A above. Note that when $Z = 1$ when $b = 0$. Hence,

$$\lim_{b \to 0} \frac{dAB}{dG} = \omega G^{-2}\Omega > 0. \quad (A12)$$

When current benefits are a function of current wages and wages one period ago, for each given value of g there exists some value, $b^*(g)$, such that $[dAB / dG]|_{b=b^*}$. For $b > b^*(g)$, faster wage growth causes the actuarial balance to decline.

Appendix C

This Appendix generalizes the case of Appendix B by assuming that the current benefit level is based on the current wage and wages in N past periods. It is assumed that each period's wage receives an equal weight $\omega = 1/(N + 1)$. Then, the expression for AB becomes

$$AB = \tau - \frac{\rho\beta_0^{-1}\omega\left(\sum_{i=0}^{N}G^{-i}\right)\sum_{t=0}^{\infty}B^{-t}G^tR^{-t}}{\sum_{t=0}^{\infty}G^tR^{-t}} = \tau - \omega\left(\sum_{i=0}^{N}G^{-i}\right)\Omega = \tau - \omega\gamma(G)\Omega, \quad (A13)$$

where

$$\gamma(G) = \left[\frac{1 - G^{-(N+1)}}{1 - G^{-1}}\right].$$

Then,

$$\frac{dAB}{dG} = -\omega\Omega[\gamma(G)G^{-1}Z + \gamma'(G)]$$

$$= -\omega\gamma(G)G^{-1}\Omega\left[Z + \frac{(N+1)G^{-(N+1)}}{1 - G^{-(N+1)}} - \frac{G^{-1}}{1 - G^{-1}}\right] \quad (A14)$$

Equation (A14) (which is identical to equation (A11) when $N = 1$) shows that a result similar to that of Appendix B holds: When current benefits are a function of current and wages from N earlier periods, there exists a value $b = b^{**}(g)$ for which $[dAB/dG]|_{b\,=\,b^{**}} = 0$. For $b > b^{**}(g)$, higher growth causes the actuarial balance to decline.

Appendix D

Equation (A13) of Appendix C

$$AB = \tau - \frac{\rho\beta_0^{-1}\omega\left(\sum_{i=0}^{N}G^{-i}\right)\sum_{t=0}^{\infty}B^{-t}G^{t}R^{-t}}{\sum_{t=0}^{\infty}G^{t}R^{-t}} \quad (A13)$$

can also be expressed as

$$= \frac{\tau\sum_{t=0}^{\infty}G^{t}R^{-t}}{\sum_{t=0}^{\infty}G^{t}R^{-t}} - \frac{\rho\beta_0^{-1}\omega\left(\sum_{i=0}^{N}G^{-i}\right)\sum_{t=0}^{\infty}B^{-t}G^{t}R^{-t}}{\sum_{t=0}^{\infty}G^{t}R^{-t}}.$$

Letting $\gamma(G) = (\sum_{i=0}^{N}G^{-i})$, simple manipulation allows the actuarial balance to be expressed as

$$AB = \sum_{t=0}^{\infty}\left[\frac{\tau G^{t} - \rho\beta_0^{-1}\omega\gamma(G)B^{-t}G^{t}}{G^{t}}\right] \cdot \left[\frac{G^{t}R^{-t}}{\sum_{t=0}^{\infty}G^{t}R^{-t}}\right] \quad (A15)$$

Equation (A15) (which corresponds to equation (10) in the text) shows that the actuarial balance is a weighted sum of the ratio of annual net cash flows ($\tau G^{t} - \rho\beta_0^{-1}\omega\gamma(G)B^{-1}G^{t}$) to annual payrolls G^{t} (the "annual cash balance ratio"), where the weight equals $G^{t}R^{-t}/\sum_{t=0}^{\infty}G^{t}R^{-t}$. In annual-cash-balance-ratio term, the dependence of benefits on lagged wages is captured in the term $\gamma(G)$ and $\omega = 1/(N + 1)$, with N being number of past years' wages that factor into the benefit determination (Note: N depends on the age of the oldest cohort alive relative to the age of retirement).

The first term in equation (A15) represents the annual balance ratio. Rewriting it as $[\tau - \rho\beta_0^{-1}\omega\gamma(G)B^{-t}]$ clarifies that every future year's annual balance ratio would be unambiguously larger (that is, annual deficits would be smaller) under faster wage growth. That is because $\gamma(G) = (\sum_{i=0}^{N}G^{i})$ would be unambiguously smaller under faster wage growth. Call this the "annual balance effect."

However, another feature of equation (A15) is that faster wage growth implies larger weights on annual balances accruing in the more distant future. Note that the denominator in $G^t R^{-t} / \sum_{t=0}^{\infty} G^t R^{-t}$ also grows larger, but because it is an average over all future years, it grows at a slower rate than the numerator $G^t R^{-t}$ when t is large. Call this the "weighting effect."

Hence, if the out years are deficit years, (1) those deficits will be smaller because of the annual balance effect but (2) will become more important in the present value calculation because of the weighting effect. The net effect on the actuarial balance could be positive or negative. As Proposition 6 in the text shows, whether the actuarial balance is increased or reduced with faster wage growth depends on the rate at which the worker-to-beneficiary ratio declines over time and the way in which benefits depend on past wages.

Notes

* Andrew Biggs is Deputy Commissioner of the Social Security Administration and Jagadeesh Gokhale is a senior fellow at the Cato Institute. The authors thank Alan Auerbach, Michael Boskin, Jeffery Brown, Edward DeMarco, Stephen Goss, Stephanie Kelton, Liqun Liu, Joyce Manchester, Donald Marron, Scott Muller, David Pattison, Rudolph Penner, Andrew Rettenmaier, Thomas Saving, Kent Smetters, and seminar participants at the Social Security Administration and the Levy Institute at Bard College for helpful comments. The views expressed herein are the author's and do not necessarily represent the views of the Cato Institute.

1. See, for instance, Gordon (2003); Baker (1996); Weller and Rassell (2000); Baker and Weisbrot (1999); and Hall (2005). For contrasting views, see Penner (2003); Davis (2000); Biggs (2000). Note that this chapter does not comment on the appropriateness of the wage growth projections made by the Social Security Trustees or other agencies. For analysis of the Trustees' projections, see the 1999 and 2003 Technical Panel reports, as well as General Accounting Office (2000).
2. This is done to place past earnings on par with current ones by inflating the former at the rate of nominal wage growth during the intervening years. This accounts for both economy-wide general price inflation and real wage growth that occurred during those years. Disability benefits are calculated in a similar way, though with adjustments for decreased time in the labor force.
3. More specifically, the Trustees measure actuarial balance over a measurement period as the net value of the initial trust fund balance, the present value of income, the present value of costs, and the present value of scheduled benefits in the final year of the measurement period. This last amount is to satisfy the requirement that the ratio of trust fund assets to benefit payments in the final year equal 100 percent.
4. Board of Trustees (2005), p. 10.
5. The Trustees' 2006 report was not available at the time of writing this chapter. It should be noted that actuarial balance is not the sole "finite horizon" measure used to assess Social Security's finances. For example, the Social Security Trustees also report measures of "close actuarial balance." See the Board of Trustees (2005), p. 60. The Social Security Administration's Office of the Chief Actuary have suggested

additional measures, including cash balances and trust fund ratios in specific years and the direction of both at the close of a measurement period. See Goss (1999) and Chaplain and Wade (2005).
6. Although economic growth is a broader concept than real wage growth, the two are generally understood to occur concomitantly, at least in public debates about Social Security financing.
7. See 1994–1996 Advisory Council; 1999 Technical Panel; 2003 Technical Panel; Board of Trustees (2005).
8. Board of Trustees (2005), p. 12.
9. 1999 Technical Panel, p. 37.
10. For example, see Gokhale and Smetters (2003, 2006b), Auerbach (1994), and Auerbach, Gale, and Orszag (2004). In infinite horizon calculations, cash flows are projected into the future until the present value sums of future dollar flows (benefits, taxes, the tax base, and so on) become stable (asymptote to a finite value).
11. Department of the Treasury (2004), p. 88. See also Gokhale and Smetters (2006a).
12. Greenspan (2003) discusses the advantages of the related approach of accrual accounting for Social Security; Walker (2003) discussed "one possible approach would be to calculate the estimated discounted present value of major spending and tax proposals as a supplement to, not a substitute for, the CBO's current 10-year cash flow projections." Senator Joseph Lieberman (D-Conn.) has introduced legislation (S. 1915, The Honest Government Accounting Act of 2004) that would calculate 75-year and infinite horizon net present value measures on a government-wide basis. The Social Security Advisory Board's 2003 Technical Panel on Assumptions and Methods praised the Trustees' inclusion of measures of system financing in perpetuity and recommended that they be given greater prominence in the Report.
13. Admittedly, a change in economic growth over the long term would be associated with changes in other variables involved in measuring Social Security's financial status – such as wage growth, demographic change, capital returns, and discount rates. This chapter does not attempt to capture the interrelationships between these variables in a dynamic general equilibrium setting. Rather, it is limited to examining the impact of higher productivity and real wage growth on "static" measures of the program's financial condition that are traditionally used by the Social Security Administration and the program's Trustees.
14. Actuarial balance as measured by the Social Security Trustees also includes trust fund assets and a requirement that the final-year trust fund balance be equal to 100 percent of outlays in that year. To keep the derivations as simple as possible, the formulation of the actuarial balance [equation (1)] in the text assumes those amounts to be zero.
15. For instance, if the replacement rate were 32 percent and the worker-to-retiree ratio were 2, the tax rate required for a zero actuarial balance would be 16 (32×2^{-1}).
16. For instance, if b were 2% and t were 5 years, then β^{-t} would be equal to $1/(1 - .02)^5$, or 1.11.
17. The steady-state decline at the end of the 75-year period is roughly 0.24 percent annually; the rate of decline in the early part of the 75-year period, which has a disproportionate value in actuarial balance calculations, is significantly higher.
18. To keep the development of these propositions simple, current and past wages are weighted equally (see Appendix C). However, sub-section E below shows the

results obtained from assuming declining population weights for wage terms occurring earlier in the past.
19. Mortality rates provided by the Social Security Administration are used in calculating the weights.
20. All demographic projections are taken from the Social Security Administration. See http://www.ssa.gov/OACT/TR/TR05/lrIndex.html (noted as of 6 January 2005).
21. This stylized model of Social Security financing excludes many details of the actual Social Security program, including the income taxation of benefits, scheduled increases in the normal retirement age (NRA), survivor and disability benefits and actuarial reductions for early retirement. Its actuarial balance estimate should not, therefore, be expected to closely approximate the official estimate of the Social Security's Board of Trustees based on much more detailed calculations. The estimate of a 3.2 percent actuarial deficit under Social Security's intermediate growth and interest rate assumptions appears quite reasonable in comparison with the official estimate of 3.5 percent.
22. Again, remember that measurement of Social Security's finances is conducted under a "static" framework (see Note 13).
23. Under the steady state relationship $r = \rho + (x/\theta)$, where the rate of time preference (ρ) is assumed to equal 1 percent, productivity growth rate alternatives (x) ranging between 0.6 percent and 1.6 percent per year and interest rate alternatives (r) ranging between 2.6 and 3.2 percent per year are consistent with intertemporal elasticities of substitution (θ) between 0.27 and 1.0. These values of θ span the range of values estimated in the economics literature. However, note that this relationship characterizes a steady state whereas the US economy is undergoing a sizable transition.
24. Note that a declining share of the worker population in the total population is consistent with both populations growing over time.
25. For details, see Holmer (2005); www.polsim.com.
26. This improvement emerges despite a *decline* in the summarized income rate (defined as the value of the trust fund plus the present value of tax revenues expressed as a percentage of the present value of taxable payrolls). The decline in the summarized income rate occurs primarily because the initial value of the trust fund, while unchanged in dollar terms, falls relative to the larger present value of taxable payrolls under the high growth scenario. Another minor reason for the decline in the summarized income rate is that part of the program's revenue is derived from income taxes levied on benefit payments. Because benefits increase with a lag, so do those income tax revenues.
27. Board of Trustees, 2005, Section IV.B.5.
28. Note that the infinite horizon simulation in SSASIM was conducted using slightly different mortality assumptions than the 75-year forecast. The baseline 75-year projection in SSASIM assumes annual mortality reductions of 0.83 percent, versus 0.71 percent assumed by the Trustees, due to differences in how the SSASIM model incorporates changes to mortality. For the infinite horizon simulations, mortality reduction was returned to the 0.71 percent ultimate rate assumed by the Trustees. However, using consistent mortality assumptions between the 75-year and infinite horizon simulations does not change the outcome of altering the productivity assumption.
29. As outlined earlier, much of this is because of the decline in the fixed initial value of the trust fund relative to the larger tax base. SSASIM uses an initial trust fund balance of $1.553 trillion (differing slightly from the $1.501 value in the 2005

Trustees Report). This amount is equal to 0.48 percent of payroll under the baseline scenario, but only 0.35 percent of payroll when productivity growth is increased from 1.6 percent to 2.1 percent.
30. The actual profiles of annual cash balance ratios are different in Figure 11.7 compared to Figure 11.6 because the SSASIM model incorporates tax, benefit, and demographic features relevant for the Social Security program in much greater detail than the stylized model of Section 11.2.
31. The Social Security Administration's Office of the Chief Actuary also uses the reduction in the cash deficit in the final year of the 75-year period as a proxy measure for a reform proposal's improvement to the program's cash flows. See, for instance, Chaplain and Wade (2005).

References

1994–1996 Advisory Council on Social Security (1997) Final Report (Washington, DC).

Auerbach, A. (1994) "The US Fiscal Problem: Where We are, How We Got Here, and Where We are Going," in Stanley Fischer and Julio Rotemberg (eds) *NBER Macroeconomics Annual* (Cambridge, MA: National Bureau of Economic Research) pp. 141–175.

Auerbach, A., W. Gale and P. Orszag (2004) "Sources of the Long-Term Fiscal Gap," *Tax Notes* 103: 1049–1059.

Baker, D., 1996. "Privatizing Social Security: The Wall Street Fix," Economic Policy Institute *Issue Brief* #112, available at http://www.epinet.org/content.cfm/issuebriefs_ib112.

Baker, D. and M. Weisbrot (1999) *Social Security: The Phony Crisis* (Chicago: University of Chicago Press).

Biggs, A. G. (2000) "Social Security: Is It 'A Crisis That Doesn't Exist'?" Social Security Paper No. 21 (Washington, DC: Cato Institute).

Board of Trustees, Federal Old-Age and Survivors Insurance and Disability Insurance Trust Funds (2005) *2005 Annual Report* (Washington, DC: US Government Printing Office).

Chaplain, C. and A. W. Wade (2005) "Estimated OASDI Long-Range Financial Effects of Several Provisions Requested by the Social Security Advisory Board," memorandum, Office of the Chief Actuary, Social Security Administration, 10 August.

Davis, G. G. (2000) "Faster Economic Growth Will Not Solve the Social Security Crisis," The Heritage Foundation, 2 February.

General Accounting Office (2000) "Social Security Actuarial Projections," containing PricewaterhouseCoopers' "Report on the Actuarial Projection of the Social Security Trust Funds" (Washington, DC: US Government Printing Office) 14 January.

Gokhale, J. and K. Smetters (2006a) "Measuring Social Security's Financial Outlook Within An Aging Society," *Daedalus* (Winter): 91–104.

Gokhale, J. and K. Smetters (2006b) "Fiscal and Generational Imbalances: An Update," *Tax Policy and the Economy* (Cambridge, MA: National Bureau of Economic Research).

Gordon, R. J. (2003) "Exploding Productivity Growth: Context, Causes, and Implications," *Brookings Papers on Economic Activity*, 2 (Washington, DC: The Brookings Institution).

Goss, S. (1999) "Measuring Solvency in the Social Security System," in Olivia S. Mitchell, Robert J. Meyers, Howard Young and Robert Julius Myers (eds) *Prospects for Social Security Reform* (Philadelphia, PA: University of Pennsylvania Press) pp.16–36.

Greenspan, A. (2003) "Testimony before the Committee on Banking, Housing and Urban Affairs," US Senate, 11 February.
Hall, K. G. (2005) "Social Security Warnings Based on Pessimistic Assumptions, Experts Say," *Knight Ridder Newspapers*, 2 February.
Holmer, M. R. (2005) *Introductory Guide to SSASIM* (Washington, DC: Policy Simulation Group) September. http://www.polsim.com/guide.pdf
Penner, R. G. (2003) "Can Faster Growth Save Social Security?" Social Security Brief 15 (Chestnut Hill, MA: Center for Retirement Research).
Stiglitz, J. E. (2005) "Progressive Dementia," *The Atlantic Monthly* (November).
Technical Panel on Assumptions and Methods (1999) Report to the Social Security Advisory Board (Washington, DC).
Technical Panel on Assumptions and Methods (2003) Report to the Social Security Advisory Board (Washington, DC).
US Department of the Treasury (2004) *2004 Financial Report of the United States Government* (Washington, DC) available at www.fms.treas.gov/fr
Walker, D. (2003) Speech before the National Press Club, 17 September.
Weller, C. and E. Rassell (2000) "Getting better All the Time: Social Security's Ever-Improving Future," Issue Brief 140 (Washington, DC: Economic Policy Institute).

Comments to Chapter 11
Stephanie A. Kelton

Virtually everyone who has written or commented on the status (and future) of the Social Security system has offered a commentary that implicitly or explicitly advances the proposition that the government's ability to meet its obligations to future retirees is in jeopardy.[1] Though the actual balance-sheet operations are never discussed, it is typically argued that the Trust Funds are becoming insolvent (some even claim they are going "bankrupt") because projected receipts will not be sufficient to cover projected obligations to the disabled, the elderly and their survivors. About this, there is little (if any) political debate.

When it comes to the issue of political action, however, there has been little agreement about the kinds of changes that should be made or the urgency with which any reforms should be enacted. Democrats emphasize that the Trust Funds are solidly in the black and that deficits are not even projected for another 12 years.[2] And even then, they stress that the shortfall can be covered for another 24 to 34 years, as Social Security draws down its massive surplus – projected to stand at $3.7 trillion by that time. Thus, with the current system projected to honor its benefit commitments in full and on time until somewhere between 2042 and 2052,[3] Democrats deny that immediate changes are needed. They believe there is plenty of time to devise solutions to address the long range problems facing Social Security. They even argue that we might avoid the need to reform the system at all, if the economy performs better than the Trustees' forecast.

Republicans, in contrast, insist that the long-range problems require a short-range solution.[4] To make their case, they emphasize the $3.7 trillion shortfall[5] the Trustees have projected over the next 75 years, arguing that we must change the system today, so that we do not pass the burden of tackling tough problems on to our children and grandchildren. In their view, waiting is not only irresponsible but, ultimately, more costly, since an additional $600 billion is added each year if the problem is not addressed.

Though they make no use of political labels, Biggs and Gokhale set out to strengthen the Republican position, arguing that the government may not be able to grow its way out of the problem, even if the economy performs better than the Trustees' anticipate. It is a clever argument, for it eliminates the possibility that things might turn out alright, as long as future conditions are slightly more favorable than the Trustees' currently anticipate.

Specifically, the chapter argues that faster economic growth may not forestall Social Security's financial problems, because faster wage growth also implies faster growth of future benefit payments (since benefits are wage-indexed). In an interesting twist on the conventional wisdom, Biggs and Gokhale suggest that faster wage growth will actually *worsen* the System's infinite-term actuarial balance, when the ratio of workers/retirees is projected to continue to rise beyond the 75-year horizon. Again, it is a clever argument. Indeed, if one accepts the analysis for what it is and does not take issue with the assumptions that underlie the model, there are few grounds on which to quibble with their findings. But it is the job of a commentator to quibble, so let me begin with a minor squabble or two.

First, while the Trustee's have begun to estimate the program's finances in perpetuity, there are good reasons to question the usefulness of forecasts that purport to look into the indefinite future.[6] For their projections to be at all useful, the Trustees must fairly accurately predict the growth of GDP, immigration rates, inflation rates, wage growth, birth/death rates, the incidence of disability, and so on. It is obviously impossible to *precisely* forecast the behavior of economic and human variables such as these, and very small estimate errors make very significant differences when it comes to the issue of solvency.

Indeed, it has been argued that the current "crisis" is in no small part due to the increasingly pessimistic nature of the Trustees' assumptions. Consider, for example, the Trustees' projection for economic growth during the next 75 years (Figure 11.C.1).

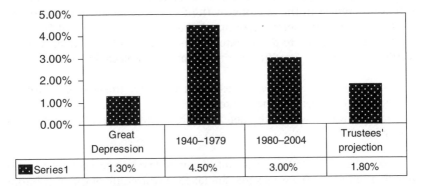

Figure 11.C.1   Historic and projected growth of US economy

Source: National Income and Product Accounts, Table 1.1.1. Percent Change From Preceding Period in Real Gross Domestic Product, Revised February 25, 2005, arithmetic averages.

According to their best-guess estimate (the Trustees' "Alternative II"), the US economy will grow at an average rate of just 1.8 percent per year *over the next 75 years*. Many economists consider this an exceedingly pessimistic (and unrealistic) assumption. In fact, some scholars maintain that the "problem" facing Social Security today, is in no small part due to the increasingly pessimistic nature of the assumptions that underlie the Trustees' forecasts (McGovern and Skidmore, 2006). Eliminate the pessimism, they maintain, and you eliminate the crisis too.

But this chapter rejects the notion that the problem disappears if the economy actually grows *more rapidly* than the Trustees' predict. The problem with the authors' analysis, however, is that it is carried out in a *static* setting. And here, it seems, there is further reason to squabble. This is because the chapter posits a change in long term growth, which impacts productivity and real wage growth, but it does not allow other variables (for example, demographic, capital returns, discount rates, and so on) to change. Now these variables will obviously not remain fixed, but Biggs and Gokhale make no attempt to determine the impact of faster growth in a *dynamic* setting.

Moreover, there are problems with the notion that economic growth and real wage growth occur concomitantly. We know, for example, that most of the working population suffered a decline in real wages throughout the period from 1973 until the mid-1990s, while real GDP growth was positive throughout most of this period. Thus, it is problematic to use "faster economic growth" and "faster wage growth" interchangeably.

Now let me turn to what I think are the more substantive problems with the chapter. First, the chapter concludes that under certain assumptions, faster wage growth would cause benefit outlays to grow faster than payrolls. But faster wage growth for whom?

The authors construct a model that is designed to assess the impact of faster wage growth on the actuarial balance, but it relies on *average* real wages so that differences in the rate of growth of low- vs. high-income earners are not a factor. But numerous economists have argued that Social Security's finances are projected to deteriorate because of worsening inequality in the *distribution of income*. Specifically, they blame the projected shortfall on

- rising wages of workers whose earnings are above the ceiling, relative to the wages of lower-income workers.
- rising nonwage income (dividends, interest, and capital gains), relative to wage income.

Since Social Security is financed exclusively by taxation of wages, and since there is a ceiling on the wages that are taxed, a worsening of the distribution of income results in large projected shortfalls in the financing of the program.

Figure 11.C.2 shows how these trends have affected the income subject to FICA withholdings.

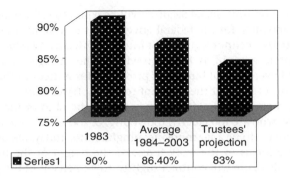

Figure 11.C.2 Percent of wages subject to Social Security tax
Source: 2005 Annual Statistical Supplement, Table 4.B1, and 2004 Trustees Report, p. 105.

In 1983, 90 percent of total wage income was below the ceiling. In the subsequent two decades, this figure had declined to 86.4 percent, and the Trustees predict that only 83 percent of total wage income will be subject to these withholdings in the future (Wolfson, 2006).

The bottom line is that the percent of taxable wage income is declining due to a worsening of the distribution of income.[7] Specifically, the decline in Social Security tax revenue is the result of sluggishness in the growth of earnings by those *near the cap* relative to other wage earners.

Having said that, one could argue that this chapter's main conclusion is correct: faster wage growth *is* a problem, but only because the wages of those above the cap are growing more rapidly than the incomes of those near the cap.

So what is the solution? This chapter makes no specific policy recommendation. Instead, it simply makes the case against relying on faster growth to eliminate the shortfall, since faster wage growth is presumed to *exacerbate* the system's financial difficulties in the super-long-run.

And here I must raise an additional objection, for there is something quite strange about the conclusion that faster wage growth worsens the super-long-run status of the system. Indeed, it must follow that the solution to the problem is *slower* wage growth (since this would improve the super-long-run actuarial balance), a point that makes little practical sense to this reader. Surely it will be less costly to provide for retirees when their wages have been high during their working years.

I am also reluctant to sympathize with proposals that call for overhauling the system today. Social Security is the only part of the federal government *not running at a deficit today*. It returns more than 99 cents for every dollar it takes in, making it the most efficient program around (public or private), and it is projected to run huge surpluses for years to come. Yet this is the part of the government's budget that is in crisis?

The time to "reform" Social Security will be when the shortfalls arrive, not now. It is impossible for the federal government to save for the future, and today's politicians cannot legislate for future politicians. We should strive for faster economic growth, as faster growth implies a bigger economic pie, which must lower the real burden of providing for retirees in the future.

It also seems to me that the constant refrain of fewer workers per retiree is a digression. I consider the dependency ratio – the ratio of the active work force to those who are too elderly, too young, or too disabled to be economically productive – to be a far more meaningful ratio. Today, about 46 percent of the population is in the work force. At the height of the baby-boomer retirement, this figure will contract slightly, to 44 percent of the population. The question is: can we continue to adequately provide for the dependent population even as the population of those in the work force contracts? If not, we will surely have a "crisis" on our hands.

But of course we have already proven that we can produce in sufficient quantities while maintaining Social Security with a much smaller work force – in 1965, the work force included only about 37 percent of the population. Surely a work force of 44 percent will be able to accomplish what a work force of 37 percent once did.

Finally, I would like to mention a few actions that might be taken, should the system eventually encounter the kind of financial difficulties that have been predicted.

One of my colleagues in Kansas City – a political scientist who has written extensively on Social Security – has proposed an interesting scheme in which the first $20,000 of earnings would be exempt from Federal Insurance Contributions Act (FICA) taxes on the worker. This would reverse the regressive way in which Social Security is currently financed and boost the economy by providing nearly every worker with an additional $1,240 to spend. According to him, such a plan would represent the "broadest, most general, tax reduction in history" (McGovern and Skidmore, 2006).[8]

The late Robert Eisner – a former President of the American Economics Association – also proposed ways in which to increase credits to the Trust Funds without resorting to privatization, means testing, increases in the retirement age or other reductions in retirees' benefits (1998a, 1998b). I have always appreciated Eisner's scholarship and still consider his work on Social Security to be the most honest and clear-headed appraisal I have yet come across. At the end of the day, he understood that the federal government's ability to meet its obligation to future retirees is in no way contingent on the balance in the Trust Funds.

Government spending on the elderly (like government spending on anything else) is constrained only by the government's willingness to make the appropriate payments. Biggs and Gokhale miss this point entirely and, consequently, present an argument that is mired in inaccuracies about the "solvency" and "affordability" of this most important program.

Notes

1. A handful of notable exceptions include (Eisner, 1998a; Bell and Wray, 2000; Mitchell and Mosler, 2005). The conventional wisdom is rejected in each of these papers, as the authors' argue that the government can "afford" Social Security, now and in the future, since the ability to pay benefits is not tied to the balance in the Trust Fund.
2. It should be noted that Social Security has run deficits – that is, paid out more in benefits than the government collected in payroll taxes – in 14 of the past 47 years, including 1975–1983.
3. The Social Security Trustees forecast solvency through 2042, while the CBO forecasts an additional decade of solvency. By either measure, the system is in better financial shape than at almost any time in its history.
4. Obviously, not every member of the Republican Party supports the president's agenda to act sooner rather than later, just as Democrats are not entirely united in their opposition to such reform. In the main, however, the line in the sand has been drawn along fairly obvious party lines.
5. President Bush likes to call it an $11 trillion shortfall, which he arrives at by rounding (up) the $10.4 trillion shortfall the Trustees project over an *infinite* time horizon.
6. My own view is that they are probably about as useful as the overlapping-generations models that scores of us were forced to endure in our graduate programs.
7. Some economists have estimated that if 90 percent of income had remained subject to taxation, about half of the current projected shortfall would disappear (Weller and Wolff, 2005).
8. To compensate for this reduction in payroll taxes, they recommend eliminating the cap on the amount of earnings subject to FICA and then dedicating an estate tax to the Trust Funds.

References

Bell, S. and L. R. Wray (2000) "Financial Aspects of the Social Security 'Problem'," *Journal of Economic Issues* (34) 2.

Eisner, R. (1998a) "Save Social Security from its Saviors," *Journal of Post Keynesian Economics* (21) 1: 77–92.

Eisner, R. (1998b) *Social Security: More, not Less* (New York: Century Foundation Press).

Biggs, A. G. and Gokhale, J. (2006) "Wage Growth and the Measurement of Social Security's Financial Condition," Chapter 11 this book.

McGovern, G. and M. Skidmore (2006) "Blowing Away the Smokescreen: A Real Plan for Social Security," draft manuscript.

Mitchell, W. and W. Mosler (2005) "Essential Elements of a Modern Monetary Economy with Applications to Social Security Privatization and the Intergenerational Debate," Working Paper 05–01 (Australia: Center of Full Employment and Equity) available at http://www.mosler.org/docs/docs/February Workshop.htm/

Weller, C. and E. N. Wolff (2005) *Retirement Income: The Crucial Role of Social Security* (Washington, DC: Economic Policy Institute).

Wolfson, M. H. (2006) "Neoliberalism and Social Security," *Review of Radical Political Economics* (38) 3: 319–326.

Part VI
Retirement Security: Problems and Prospects

Part VI

12
The Adequacy of Retirement Resources among the Soon-to-Retire, 1983–2001

Edward N. Wolff

12.1 Introduction

A central issue confronting the soon-to-retire workers (that is, in the age group 47–64) is whether they will have command over enough resources (both private and public) to maintain a decent standard of living in retirement. Typically, the adequacy of projected retirement income is judged in relation to some absolute standard (for example, poverty threshold) and pre-retirement income ("replacement rate"). In a previous study, utilizing data up to 1998 (Wolff, 2002b), I found that among the households headed by a soon-to-retire worker, the proportion expected to be in poverty or unable to replace at least half their pre-retirement income rose from 1989 to 1998. Since 1998 until 2001 at least, the economy boomed, the stock market surged, and the unemployment rate fell sharply. The principal focus of this chapter is to update the findings of the earlier study utilizing the 2001 Survey of Consumer Finances in order to shed light on the retirement income security of the soon-to-retire. Particular attention will be paid to the adequacy of pensions, Social Security, and financial wealth in relation to pre-retirement income.

I find that retirement income adequacy did indeed improve from 1989 to 2001. For instance, the share of households between 47 and 64 that could expect to have retirement incomes that were less than twice the poverty line declined from 40 percent in 1989 to 35 percent in 2001. Also, the share of households that could hope to replace at least half of their projected pre-retirement income at age 65 in retirement rose from 49 to 53 percent.

Despite these improvements, there were still large gaps in retirement preparedness for many households. First and foremost, it appears that improvements in pension coverage may have leveled off. By 2001, still 24 percent of households in this age group could expect to retire without a private pension plan, either a traditional defined benefit plan (DB) or a defined contribution (DC) plan.

Further, retirement wealth (RW) was unequally distributed. The level of RW – private pensions plus Social Security wealth – was substantially higher on average than for the median household, suggesting large inequities in the wealth distribution. These inequities are the result of an unequal distribution of private pension assets rather than of Social Security wealth.

Because Social Security offered almost universal coverage and because Social Security wealth grew on average at a respectable pace, it actually had a relatively larger effect on the retirement preparedness of vulnerable groups than private pension wealth. Among African-Americans and single women, Social Security played a comparatively stronger role in retirement income adequacy than private pension wealth in comparison to their respective counterparts.

Although there were important gains in retirement income adequacy, many households were still inadequately prepared for retirement in 2001. Taking a generally accepted replacement ratio of 75 percent of retirement income relative to pre-retirement income as a threshold, the data show that still two thirds of households between the ages of 47 to 64 would fall below this threshold. The shortfalls are larger for African-American or Hispanic households and for single women.

Seeing how well prepared for retirement today's near elderly are and how this preparedness has changed in the 1990s sheds some light on important policy conclusions. For instance, the fact that many households are still inadequately prepared for retirement is closely linked to the fact that they have little or no private pension wealth. This is especially true for African-American and Hispanic households and for single women. Hence, policies that could help to improve private pension coverage and wealth accumulation for these groups should be considered more seriously. Further, private pension wealth plays an important role for retirement income adequacy for those that have it. Thus, public policy should focus on securing private pension wealth to ensure that the accumulated savings are available when people retire. And finally, Social Security appears to be at the heart of improving retirement income security for many groups. Consequently, public policy should focus on securing Social Security for the long-term as an important step to improving retirement income adequacy.

The remainder of the chapter is organized as follows. The next section of the chapter (Section 12.2) provides a review of the pertinent literature on RW and retirement adequacy. Section 12.3 describes the data sources and develops the accounting framework used in the analysis. Section 12.4 shows time trends in standard measures of household wealth over the 1983–2001 period. Section 12.5 investigates changes in RW and total (augmented) household wealth. In Section 12.6, I present measures of retirement adequacy for age group 47–64. Concluding remarks are made in Section 12.7.

12.2 Literature review

Previous work has focused on just one or a few of the aspects of the adequacy of retirement income or wealth. For instance, a number of papers have presented estimates of Social Security and/or pension wealth. The seminal paper on this topic is Feldstein (1974), who introduced the concept of Social Security wealth and developed its methodology. In a follow-up paper, Feldstein (1976), using the Federal Reserve Board's 1962 Survey of Financial Characteristics of Consumers (SFCC), found that the inclusion of Social Security wealth had a major effect on lowering the overall inequality of (total) household wealth.

Wolff followed up this work by examining the distributional implications of both Social Security and private pension wealth. Wolff (1987) used the 1969 Measurement of Economic and Social Performance (MESP) database and showed that while Social Security wealth had a pronounced equalizing effect on the distribution of "augmented wealth" (defined as the sum of marketable wealth and RW), pension wealth had a disequalizing effect. The sum of Social Security and pension wealth had, on net, an equalizing effect on the distribution of augmented wealth. Wolff (2002a) re-examined the distributional effects of RW based on the Survey of Consumer Finances (SCF) from 1983 to 1998 and found that Social Security continued to have a mitigating distributional effect. With respect to DC wealth, though, Wolff (2007) found that the rise in DC wealth has led to greater wealth inequality. Kennickell and Sunden (1999), who based their study on the 1989 and 1992 SCF, also found a net equalizing effect from the inclusion of pension and net Social Security wealth in calculating total household wealth.

Several papers have used the Health and Retirement Survey (HRS). Gustman et al. (1997) found that, in 1992 pensions, Social Security, and health insurance accounted for half of the wealth for those aged 51–61; for 60 percent of total wealth for those in wealth percentiles 45–55; and for 48 percent of wealth for those in wealth percentiles 90–95. In a follow-up study Gustman and Steinmeier (1998) found that for 51- to 61-year-olds pensions were held by two-thirds of households and accounted for one-quarter of accumulated wealth on average. Social Security benefits accounted for another quarter of total wealth.

Several studies have documented changes in pension coverage, particularly the decline in DB pension coverage among workers over the last two decades. Bloom and Freeman (1992), using Current Population Surveys (CPS) for 1979 and 1988, were among the first to call attention to the decline in DB pension coverage. They reported that the percentage of all workers aged 25–64 covered by these plans fell from 63 percent to 57 percent over this period. Even and Macpherson (1994) showed a particularly pronounced drop in DB pension coverage among workers with low levels of education.

A related topic of interest is whether DC plans have substituted for DB plans. Popke (1999), using employer data (5500 filings) for 1992, found that, indeed, 401(k) and other DC plans have substituted for terminated DB plans and that the offering of a DC plan raises the chance of a termination in DB coverage. On the other hand, Poterba, Venti, and Wise (1998), using HRS data for 1993, found that the growth of 401(k) plans did not substitute for other forms of household wealth and, in fact, raised household net worth relative to what it would have been without these plans.

A Department of Labor report issued in 2000 found that a large proportion of workers, especially low-wage, part-time, and minority workers, were not covered by private pensions (see US Department of Labor, Pension, and Welfare Benefits Administration, 2000). The coverage rate of all private-sector wage-and-salary workers was 44 percent in 1997. The low coverage for part-time, temporary, and low-wage workers appeared to be ascribable to the proliferation of 401(k) plans and the frequent requirement for employee contributions to such plans. The report also found important racial differences, with 47 percent of white workers participating but only 27 percent of Hispanics. Another important distinction was union membership, with 70 percent of unionized workers covered by a pension plan but only 41 percent of nonunionized workers. Moreover, pension participation was found to be highly correlated with wages. While only 6 percent of workers earnings less than $200 per week were involved in a pension plan, 76 percent of workers earning more than $1,000 per week participated.

12.2.1 Retirement income adequacy

Calculations of retirement income adequacy typically relate retirement consumption to pre-retirement consumption in three possible ways. First, a household may be considered adequately prepared for retirement if it can maintain a similar real level of consumption as during its working years. Usually, 80 percent of pre-retirement income is thus considered adequate since the income needs of retirees are likely to be lower than those of workers (Aon, 2001). Households no longer need to save for retirement, taxes are lower, work related expenses disappear, the family size of retirees is smaller than that of workers, and households eventually pay off their debt (McGill et al., 1996). Second, retirement income adequacy may be defined as a constant nominal level of consumption during retirement as during working years. This means that consumption needs are expected to decline during retirement over time, but in a somewhat arbitrary fashion. Third, real consumption may decline if the marginal utility of consumption is held constant and uncertainty about income and life expectancy are introduced (Engen, Gale, and Uccello, 1999). As households must consider an uncertain future, their marginal utility of certain consumption today is higher than the marginal utility of uncertain consumption in the future.

A number of studies have analyzed retirement savings adequacy, with differing results. For instance, Gustman and Steinmeier (1998) found using the HRS that the average household could replace 60 percent of pre-retirement income in real terms, and 86 percent of pre-retirement income in nominal terms. The finding for the nominal replacement ratio led the authors to conclude that households on average were adequately prepared for retirement. Engen, Gale, and Uccello (1999) found, using the Survey of Income and Program Participation (SIPP) and the SCF estimated that 40–50 percent of households fell short of what they needed for adequate retirement income. But as their calculations are based on a stochastic model, only 50 percent of households should be expected to meet the target retirement savings. The average replacement ratio for the median income quintile household calculated by Engen Gale, and Uccello (1999) is still 72 percent, leading the authors to conclude that households are close to being adequately prepared for retirement. In an updated study, Engen Gale, and Uccello (2002) found that the upswing in stock prices from 1995 to 1998 did not substantially alter their earlier findings on retirement income. This suggests that much of the increase in RW was concentrated among households who were already adequately prepared for retirement. Further, Haveman et al. (2003) using Social Security's New Beneficiary Data System (NBDS) found that retired beneficiaries had a median replacement ratio of about 80 percent, and that only 30 percent of households had a replacement ratio of less than 70 percent in 1982.

By contrast, several studies concluded that households were inadequately prepared for retirement. For instance, Moore and Mitchell (2000) found, using the 1992 HRS, that the median wealth household would have to save an additional 16 percent annually of earnings if it were to retire at age 62 and an additional 7 percent annually for retirement at age 65 to finance an adequate real replacement ratio. Their estimate of a savings rate of 7.3 percent for households wishing to retire at age 65 was three times as much as what households actually saved (Mitchell andMoore, 1998). This meant that households had on average between 75 percent and 88 percent – depending on marital status – of what it needed when retiring at 65 in 1992 (Mitchell and Moore, 1998). Also, Gustman and Steinmeier's (1999) figures show that, based on real replacement ratios, the average household had 28 percent less than adequate retirement savings. Lastly, Wolff (2002b) concluded that 61 percent of households could not replace 75 percent of their pre-retirement income in retirement based on data from 1998, up from 56 percent of households in 1989.

One issue to consider, though, is what a shortfall relative to adequate savings means. In some cases, a shortfall will still allow households to finance most of their expected consumption. Engen, Gale, and Uccello (1999) point out that the households used in Moore and Mitchell (1998) could still finance more than 90 percent of the consumption prescribed by their model with no additional savings. Similarly, Haveman et al.'s (2003) study shows that about 20 percent of households have a replacement ratio between 70 percent and 80 percent. That is, one-fifth of households have more than 90 percent, but less than 100 percent, of what is generally assumed for retirement income adequacy – 80 percent of pre-retirement earnings.

As wealth is unequally distributed, there may be a large share of households for which the shortfalls are larger. Engen, Gale, and Uccello (1999) calculated that households in the 75th percentile – the closest income percentile for *average* (not median) income – had 121 percent to 172 percent of what they needed for retirement. For the median household, the same ratios ranged from 47 percent to 124 percent. Thus, the median household reached only 62 percent of the preparedness of the average household in 1992. Moreover, Wolff (2002a) documented that the gap between average wealth and median wealth to income ratios increased further by 1998. Following the unequal distribution of wealth, a large share of households is likely to experience retirement consumption shortfalls.[1] Gustman and Steinmeier (1999) found that households in the bottom quartile had nominal replacement ratios of 50 percent and real replacement rates of 33 percent, compared to nominal replacements of 121 percent and real replacement rates of 81 percent for the top quartile. Also, Wolff (2002b) found that 16 percent of households could replace less than 25 percent of their pre-retirement income and that 43 percent of households could replace less than half of their pre-retirement income during retirement in 1998.[2] Lastly, Haveman et al. (2003) found that single men were more likely be inadequately prepared than single women, who were in turn less likely than married couples to be adequately prepared for retirement.

To make ends meet in retirement, when facing an income shortfall, households will have to curtail their retirement consumption. In fact, one of the distinguishing features between studies that conclude that households are adequately prepared for retirement and those that do not is the consumption pattern in retirement. For instance, Engen, Gale, and Uccello (1999) and Gustman and Steinmeier (1999) conclude that households are adequately prepared for retirement based on the fact that real retirement consumption declines with age in their models. Similarly, Haveman et al. (2003) base their conclusions on the assumption of declining consumption in retirement, albeit at a slower pace than Gustman and Steinmeier (1999) In the past few years, a number of studies have looked at the changes of retirement income adequacy over time. Wolff (2002b) found that the share of households between the ages of 47 and 64 that could replace less than 75 percent of their current income in retirement rose from 56.1 percent in 1989 to 61.2 percent in 1998. In comparison, Engen, Gale, and Uccello (2002) found that retirement income adequacy by their stochastic definition had changed little from 1995 to 1998. Lastly, Smith (2003) found using data from the Panel Study of Income Dynamics (PSID) and the CPS that median after-tax income replacement ratios in retirement showed an increasing trend, particularly since the early 1990s.

12.3 Data sources and accounting framework

The principal data sources used for this study are the 1983, 1989, and 2001 SCFs conducted by the Federal Reserve Board. Each survey consists of a core representative sample combined with a high-income supplement. The SCF provides considerable detail on both pension plans and Social Security contributions. The SCF also gives detailed information on expected pension and Social Security benefits for both husband and wife. For 1983, the Federal Reserve Board also made its own calculations of the wealth equivalent value of both expected pension benefits and Social Security benefits. I use these estimates in this chapter. However, this has not been done for other years.[3]

The basic wealth concept used here is marketable wealth (or net worth, NW), which is defined as the current value of all marketable or fungible assets minus the current value of debts. Total assets are the sum of: (1) the gross value of owner-occupied housing (2) other real estate (3) cash and demand deposits; (4) time and savings deposits, certificates of deposit, and money market accounts; (5) bonds and other financial securities; (6) the cash surrender value of life insurance plans; (7) the current market value of DC pension plans, including Individual Retirement Accounts (IRAs), Keogh, and 401(k) plans; (8) corporate stock and mutual funds; (9) net equity in unincorporated businesses; and (10) equity in trust funds. Total liabilities are the sum of: (1) mortgage debt, (2) consumer debt, including auto loans, and (3) other debt. It should be stressed that the standard definition of net worth includes the market value of DC pension plans.[4]

A word should be said on why I use the SCF instead of the newer HRS, which has much more complete data on earnings histories and has employer-provided information on individual DB pension plans. There are three reasons. First, the SCF provides much better data on the assets and liabilities that constitute marketable net worth. Second, the SCF data date from 1983, whereas the HRS data start only in 1992. Third, the age coverage of the HRS is limited whereas the SCF covers the whole population.

The imputation of both pension and Social Security wealth involves a large number of steps, which are summarized below.

12.3.1 Pension wealth

For retirees (r) the procedure is straightforward. Let PB be the pension benefit currently being received by the retiree. The SCF questionnaire indicates how many pension plans each spouse is involved in and what the expected (or current) pension benefit is. The SCF questionnaire also indicates whether the pension benefits remain fixed in nominal terms over time for a particular beneficiary or is indexed for inflation. In the case of the former, the (gross) DB pension wealth is given by

$$DB_r = \int_0^\infty PB(1-m_t)e^{-\delta t}dt \qquad (1)$$

where m_t is the mortality rate at time t conditional on age, gender, and race;[5] δ the discount rate which is set at 5 percent (2 percent when PB is indexed for inflation), and the integration runs from the person's current age to age 109.[6]

Among current workers (w) the procedure is somewhat more complex. The SCF provides detailed information on pension coverage among current workers, including the type of plan, the expected benefit at retirement or the formula used to determine the benefit amount (for example, a fixed percentage of the average of the last five year's earnings), the expected retirement age when the benefits are effective, the likely retirement age of the worker, and vesting requirements. Information is provided not only for the current job (or jobs) of each spouse but for up to five past jobs as well. On the basis of the information provided in the SCF and on projected future earnings, future expected pension benefits (EPB_w) are then projected to the year of retirement or the first year of eligibility for the pension. Then the present value of pension wealth for current workers (w) is given by

$$DB_w = \int_{LR} EPB(1 - m_t)e^{-\delta t} dt \qquad (2)$$

where RA is the expected age of retirement and $LR = A - RA$ is the number of years to retirement. As above, and the integration runs from the expected age of retirement to age 109.[7]

It should be noted that the calculations of DB pension wealth for current workers are based on employee response, including his or her stated expected age of retirement, *not* on employer-provided pension plans. A couple of studies have looked at the reliability of employee-provided estimates of pension wealth by comparing self-reported pension benefits with estimates based on provider data. Using, data from the 1992 wave of the HRS, both Gustman and Steinmeier (1999) and Johnson, Sambamoorthi, and Crystal (2000) found that individual reports of pension benefits varied widely from those based on provider information. However, the latter also calculated that the median values of DB plans from the two sources were quite close (about a 6 percent difference).

12.3.2 Social Security Wealth (SSW)

For current Social Security beneficiaries (r), the procedure is again straightforward. Let SSB be the Social Security benefit currently being received by the retiree. Again, the SCF provides information for both husband and wife. Since Social Security benefits are indexed for inflation, (gross) SSW is given by:

$$SSW_r = \int_0^\infty SSB(1 - m_t)e^{-\delta t} dt \qquad (3)$$

where it is assumed that the current Social Security rules remain in effect indefinitely.[8]

The imputation of Social Security wealth among current workers is based on the worker's projected earnings history estimated by regression equation. The steps are briefly as follows, First, coverage is assigned based on whether the individual expects to receive Social Security benefits and on whether the individual was salaried or self-employed. Second, on the basis of the person's earnings history, the person's Average Indexed Monthly Earnings (AIME) is computed. Third, on the basis of existing rules, the person's Primary Insurance Amount (PIA) is derived from AIME. Then,

$$SSW_w = \int_{LR} PIA(1 - m_t)e^{-\delta^* t} dt. \tag{4}$$

As with pension wealth, the integration runs from the expected age of retirement to age 109.[9]

Here, too, it should be noted that estimates of Social Security wealth are based on reported earnings at a single point in time. These estimates are likely to be inferior to those based on longitudinal work histories of individual workers (see, for example, Smith, Toder, and Iams, 2001, whose estimates are based on actual Social Security work histories.) In fact, actual work histories do show much more variance in earnings over time than one based on a human capital earnings function projection. Moreover, they also show many periods of work disruption that I cannot adequately capture here. However, I do have some *retrospective* information on work history provided by the respondent. In particular, each individual is asked to provide data on the total number of years worked full-time since age 18, the number of years worked part-time since age 18, and the expected age of retirement (both from full-time and part-time work). On the basis of this information, it is possible to approximate the total number of full-time and part-time years worked over the individual's lifetime and use these figures in the estimate of the individual's AIME.

Nonetheless, since my estimates of SSW assume a continuous work life, I am likely to be overstating the value of SSW for many workers. This is likely to bias upward my estimates of mean and median SSW, as well as a downward bias in the variability of Social Security wealth. It may also lead to an understatement of the correlation between net worth and SSW.

12.3.3 Employer Contributions to DC Plans

So far I have treated DB and DC pension wealth as well as SSW as comparable concepts. However, there are important differences in their estimation. Most notably, the calculation of DB wealth is estimated on the basis of the future stream of pension benefits on the assumption that the employee remains at his or her firm of employment until the person's expected retirement date.

The computation of SSW is also based on the assumption that the worker remains at work until the person's expected retirement date. On the other hand, the DC valuation is based on the current market value of DC plans.

To put DB (and SSW) and DC wealth on an "equal footing," I project forward the employer contribution to DC plans, like 401(k)s. If we assume, as in the case of DB pensions, that workers remain at their company until retirement and that the terms of their DC contract with their employer stays the same, then it is possible to do this. In most cases, the employer contribution is a fixed percentage of the employee's salary. On the basis of the estimated human capital earnings functions for each worker, it is possible to calculate the annual stream of future employer contributions to the DC plan until retirement (which I call DC2).[10] The addition of DC2 to household wealth puts the treatment of DC pension wealth roughly on a par with that of DB pension wealth since both represent future additions to household wealth from the *employer*.

The SCF questionnaire indicates how many DC pension plans each spouse has (up to three per spouse).[11] Information on the employer contribution to DC pensions plans is recorded in two ways. First, in some cases, the contribution is given as a flat dollar amount. Though it is not indicated in the survey data whether the dollar contribution is indexed to inflation over time, I assume that it is indexed to the CPI, which seems the more likely arrangement.[12] Let EMPAMT be the dollar amount of the employer contribution to the DC plan. Then, the present value of the stream of future employer contributions, $DC2_a$, is given by:

$$DC2_a = {_0}\!\int^{LR} EMPAMT(1 - m_t)e^{-\delta t}dt \tag{5}$$

where m_t is the mortality rate at time t conditional on age, gender, and race; and the discount rate δ is set at 2 percent.[13] The integration runs from the current year to LR, where RA is the expected age of retirement and LR = A−RA is the number of years to retirement.

Second, in most cases, the employer contribution is given as a percent of earnings. If we assume that the proportion, EMPPER, is fixed over time, then $DC2_b$, is given by

$$DC2_b = {_0}\!\int^{LR} EMPPER \cdot E^*_t(1 - m_t)e^{-\delta t}dt \tag{6}$$

where E^*_t is the predicted earnings of the worker at time t in constant dollars.

Estimates are provided for the following components of household wealth:

$$DC = DC1 + DC2 \tag{7}$$

where DC1 is the current market value of households' DC accounts.

NW = NWX + DC (8)

where NWX is marketable household wealth excluding DC. Total pension wealth PW is given by

PW = DB + DC (9)

RW is then given as the sum of pension and Social Security wealth:

RW = PW + SSW (10)

Finally, augmented household wealth, AW, is given by

AW = NWX + RW (11)

12.4 Time trends in standard measures of net worth

Table 12.1 documents a robust growth in wealth during the 1990s. After rising by 7 percent between 1983 and 1989, real median wealth among all households was 16 percent greater in 2001 than in 1989.[14] As a result, median wealth grew slightly faster between 1989 and 2001, 1.32 percent per year, than between 1983 and 1989, at 1.13 percent per year. Mean net worth was 65 percent higher in 2001 than in 1983 and 44 percent larger than in 1989. Mean wealth grew quite a bit faster between 1989 and 2001, at 3.02 percent per year, than from 1983 to 1989, at 2.27 percent per year. Moreover, mean wealth grew almost three times as fast as the median, suggesting widening inequality of wealth over these years.

The robust performance of median net worth over the 1990s contrasts sharply to trends in median income. Median household income, based on the SCF data, after gaining 3.0 percent between 1983 and 1989, grew by

Table 12.1 Mean and median household wealth and income, 1983, 1989, and 2001 (in thousands of 2001 dollars)

	1983	1989	2001	Percentage change		
				1983–1989	1989–2001	1983–2001
Net worth						
1. Median	59.3	63.5	73.5	7.0	15.8	23.9
2. Mean	231.0	264.6	380.1	14.6	43.7	64.6
Income						
1. Median	34.7	35.7	39.0	3.0	9.2	12.5
2. Mean	49.5	53.3	67.2	7.8	26.2	36.0

Source: Author's computations from the 1983, 1989, and 2001 Survey of Consumer Finances.

9.2 percent from 1989 to 2001 – slower than median net worth in both periods. The net change over the whole period was 12.5 percent. In contrast, mean income rose by 8 percent from 1983 to 1989 and by another 26 percent from 1989 to 2001, for a total change of 36 percent.[15]

The wealth picture changes as households grow older (Table 12.2). For one, average wealth was substantially higher for older households. Households between the ages of 47 and 64 had on average $598,300 in total wealth in 2001, 57 percent higher than for the population at large. The growth in mean net worth over the 1983–2001 period was a little lower than average for age group 47–64, while the growth in median net worth was a little higher. The growth in both mean and median income, on the other hand, was above average for age group 47–64.

The average wealth to income ratio increased from 5.0 to 5.6 – a more than 10 percent gain over this period for all households. In comparison, the wealth to income ratio for households nearing retirement grew by 11 percent from 5.9 to 6.5. In other words, older households had a slightly higher wealth to income levels and increased those somewhat more than the population at large.

12.5 Retirement and Augmented Wealth (AW)

The only form of RW that is almost universally held is Social Security wealth (see Table 12.3). By 2001, 98 percent of households between the ages of 47 and 64 were covered by Social Security, up from 92 percent in 1983. In comparison, private pension coverage continues to show large holes that are only very slowly being filled. For instance, the share of households between 47 and 64 with a DC or DB plan was 76 percent, compared to 98 percent with Social Security coverage. However, pension coverage among this age group rose from 70 percent in 1983 to 76 percent in 2001. The increase in overall pension coverage came about from the very rapid expansion of the

Table 12.2 Household net worth and income, ages 47–64, 1983, 1989, and 2001 (in thousands of 2001 dollars)

	1983	1989	2001	Percentage change		
				1983–1989	1989–2001	1983–2001
1. Mean net worth (NW)	373.3	407.4	598.3	9.2	46.9	60.3
2. Median net worth (NW)	108.3	133.2	137.6	23.0	3.3	27.0
3. Mean income	63.3	68.1	91.5	7.6	34.3	44.5
4. Median income	41.9	42.8	49.0	2.3	14.4	17.0

Note: Households are classified by the age of the head of household.
Source: Authors' computations from the 1983, 1989, and 2001 Survey of Consumer finances.

Table 12.3 Percentage of households with retirement wealth ages 47–64, 1983, 1989, and 2001 (in percentage points)

	1983	1989	2001	Percentage change 1983–1989	Percentage change 1989–2001	Percentage change 1983–2001
1. DC pensions	11.9	28.3	62.4	16.4	34.1	50.5
2. DB pension wealth	68.9	56.8	45.3	−12.1	−11.5	−23.6
3. Pension wealth (PW)	70.1	67.6	76.3	−2.5	8.7	6.2
4. Social Security wealth (SSW)	92.1	96.2	97.9	4.1	1.7	5.8
5. Retirement wealth (RW)	97.0	97.1	98.1	0.1	1.1	1.1

Note: Households are classified by the age of the head of household.
Key: Pension Wealth PW = DB + DC. Retirement Wealth RW = PW + SSW.
Source: Authors' computations from the 1983, 1989, and 2001 Survey of Consumer Finances.

DC system, with the share with DC coverage ballooning from 12 percent to 62 percent over these 18 years. In contrast, DB coverage fell rather rapidly as well.

In 2001, 98 percent of all households in the pre-retirement age groups (47–64) had some form of RW. The share covered by some form of RW was up slightly, from 97 percent in 1983.

From 1983 to 2001, different forms of wealth have shown different increases (see Table 12.4). With respect to RW, Social Security wealth took up the largest share in 1983, accounting for 60 percent of the RW of age group 47–64. However, by 2001, pension wealth was the larger component, comprising 52 percent of RW. DC wealth by itself comprised 33 percent of RW in comparison to 19 percent for DB wealth. In 1983, in contrast, DB made up 37 percent of RW and DC virtually nothing. In terms of growth rates, mean PW almost doubled over the 1983–2001 period, while mean SSW gained only 21 percent.[16]

The wealth distribution differs across RW categories. This means that separate groups of households will rely on different forms of RW to varying degrees. Specifically, Social Security wealth was more equally distributed than other forms of RW. The average Social Security wealth for households between the ages of 47 and 64 was $184,500 in 2001, or only 4.6 percent higher than the median Social Security wealth for this age group. In comparison, average private pension wealth for this age group was almost three times the median private pension wealth, Hence, the wealth distribution reflects the less than universal coverage of private pension plans as well as a more unequal distribution of private pension wealth.

Mean RW also grew robustly over the years 1983 to 2001, advancing by more than half, while median RW increased by a respectable 22 percent. Results are difference for total (augmented) household wealth. Over the

Table 12.4 Mean retirement and augmented wealth, ages 47–64, 1983, 1989, and 2001 (in thousands of 2001 dollars)

	1983	1989	2001	Percentage change		
				1983–1989	1989–2001	1983–2001
1. DC pensions	8.0	28.9	127.3	260.9	340.2	1488.8
2. DB pension wealth	94.6	85.6	74.3	−9.5	−13.3	−21.5
3. Pension wealth (PW)	102.6	114.6	201.6	11.7	76.0	96.5
4. Social Security wealth (SSW)	152.7	147.8	184.5	−3.2	24.8	20.8
5. Retirement wealth (RW)	255.3	262.3	386.1	2.8	47.2	51.2
6. Augmented wealth (AW)	589.9	632.9	782.8	7.3	23.7	32.7
Memo						
6. Median pension wealth (PW)	42.4	41.4	69.0	−2.3	66.5	62.8
7. Median Social Security wealth (SSW)	144.7	142.8	176.3	−1.3	23.5	21.9
8. Median retirement wealth (RW)	212.7	207.1	259.6	−2.7	25.4	22.0
9. Median augmented wealth (AW)	376.4	367.8	389.2	−2.3	5.8	3.4

Note: Households are classified by the age of the head of household.
Key: Pension Wealth PW = DB + DC. Retirement Wealth RW = PW + SSW. Augmented Wealth AW = NWX + RW.
Source: Authors' computations from the 1983, 1989, and 2001 Survey of Consumer Finances.

years 1983 to 2001, mean AW gained 32 percent, while median AW was up by a meager 3.4 percent. Thus, most of the gains in AW accrued to richer households.

For middle class households, those in the middle three income quintiles, the importance of Social Security becomes even more apparent (Table 12.5). In 2001, SSW comprised 57 percent of their RW, as compared to 48 percent for all households in this age group. Since 1989, it declined as a share of RW by a mere 0.4 percentage points, much less than the 8.6 percentage point decline for all households in the age group.

Both pension wealth and Social Security wealth grew robustly for middle income families nearing retirement. As a result, mean RW gained 47 percent for age group 47–64 between 1989 and 2001, about the same as for all households in the age group, and AW was up by 38 percent, somewhat more than for all households in the age bracket.

12.5.1 Retirement wealth (RW) by race

As the distribution of RW has become more unequal, the question is whether certain demographic groups are more likely than others to have seen below

Table 12.5 Mean income and wealth, middle three income quintiles, ages 47–64, 1989 and 2001 (in thousands of 2001 dollars)

	1989	2001	Percent change 1989–2001
1. Mean income	44.7	52.7	18.0
2. Mean net worth (NW)	199.1	255.5	28.3
3. Mean pension wealth (PW)	94.5	137.5	45.6
4. Mean Social Security wealth (SSW)	122.6	181.6	48.2
5. Mean retirement wealth (RW)	217.0	319.1	47.1
6. Mean augmented wealth (AW)	416.1	574.6	38.1

Note: Households are classified by the age of the head of household.
Key: Pension Wealth PW = DB + DC. Retirement Wealth RW = PW + SSW. Augmented Wealth AW = NWX + RW.
Source: Authors' computations from the 1983 and 2001 SCF.

or above average increases in RW and retirement income adequacy. We analyze RW and retirement income adequacy by two demographic characteristics: race and family status.

Despite improvements, minority households (defined here as African-Americans and Hispanics)[17] still had considerably less wealth accumulated than nonminority households as they approached retirement in 2001. For households between the ages of 47 and 64, the mean RW of nonHispanic whites was almost two and a half times larger than for minorities in 2001 (Table 12.6). The ratio of median RW was very similar.

Differences are even more extreme for net worth. In the age group 47 to 64, whites had 5.5 the net worth of nonwhites in 2001 (Table 12.7). Differences are less pronounced for total (augmented) wealth. The ratio of average total (augmented) wealth of non-Hispanic whites to the average wealth of minorities in 2001 was 3.6 for households between the ages of 47 and 64 (Table 12.7) and the ratio of median AW was 2.9. These results once again highlight the equalizing effect of Social Security. In fact, in 2001, the ratio of mean SSW between the two groups was (only) 2.0.

African-American and Hispanic households made no progress in closing the large gap with respect to white households in terms of RW or total wealth. In fact, the gaps widened between 1983 and 2001. While mean RW gained 84 percent for whites, it actually lost 1 percent for minorities (Table 12.6). Even more extreme differences are apparent for median RW. There was a *huge* gap in the growth rates of mean pension wealth between the two races, with the ratio of mean PW between minorities and whites slipping from 0.66 to 0.35 over this period. The switchover from the traditional DB system to the newer DC pension system hurt minorities much more than white households.

Table 12.6 Retirement wealth by race/ethnicity, ages 47–64, 1983, 1989, and 2001 (in thousands, 2001 dollars)

Category	Mean value			Percentage change		
	1983	1989	2001	1983–1989	1989–2001	1983–2001
A. Non-Hispanic White						
Mean Pension Wealth (PW)	110.1	134.1	229.5	21.8	71.2	108.5
Mean Social Security Wealth (SSW)	161.1	140.4	204.3	−12.8	45.5	26.8
Mean Retirement Wealth (RW)	271.2	274.5	433.8	1.2	58.0	60.0
Median Retirement Wealth (RW)	224.9	196.3	301.8	−12.7	53.8	34.2
B. African-American or Hispanic						
Mean Pension Wealth (PW)	72.5	56.1	80.0	−22.6	42.6	10.3
Mean Social Security Wealth (SSW)	112.5	110.4	103.2	−1.9	−6.5	−8.3
Mean Retirement Wealth (RW)	185.0	166.5	183.2	−10.0	10.0	−1.0
Median Retirement Wealth (RW)	146.4	124.6	124.3	−14.9	−0.3	−15.1

Notes: Households are classified by the age of the head of household. Asians and other races are excluded from the table because of small sample sizes.
Source: Author's computations from the 1983, 1989, and 2001 SCF.

Table 12.7 Income and wealth by race/ethnicity, ages 47–64, 1983, 1989, and 2001 (in thousands, 2001 dollars)

Category	Mean value			Percentage change		
	1983	1989	2001	1983–1989	1989–2001	1983–2001
A. Non-Hispanic White						
Mean Income	69.3	78.1	103.7	12.7	32.7	49.5
Mean Net Worth (NW)	433.3	485.8	710.7	12.1	46.3	64.0
Mean Augmented Wealth (AW)	695.4	724.6	996.5	4.2	37.5	43.3
Median Augmented Wealth (AW)	412.1	390.3	469.9	−5.3	20.4	14.0
B. African-American or Hispanic						
Mean Income	34.4	30.6	44.1	−11.0	44.2	28.3
Mean Net Worth (NW)	74.4	100.6	130.1	35.1	29.3	74.7
Mean Augmented Wealth (AW)	256.1	260.4	278.2	1.7	6.8	8.6
Median Augmented Wealth (AW)	194.5	182.1	161.9	−6.4	−11.1	−16.8

Notes: Households are classified by the age of the head of household. Asians and other races are excluded from the table because of small sample sizes.
Key: Augmented Wealth AW = NWX + RW.
Source: Author's computations from the 1983, 1989, and 2001 SCF.

As a result of the growing cleavage in RW, the gap in augmented wealth also widened over the period. This was the case despite the fact that the (large) net worth gap actually narrowed somewhat over the 1983–2001 period (from a ratio of 5.8 to 5.5). The ratio of mean augmented wealth grew from 2.7 to 3.6 over the period and the ratio of median AW from 2.1 to 2.9.

12.5.2 Retirement Wealth (RW) by marital status

Another important demographic distinction is based on marital status. We analyze levels and trends of RW and total wealth for married couples, single females, and single males. Our results show that married couples had substantially more RW and total wealth than single households, and that single male headed households had more wealth than single female headed households in 2001. Further, the analysis also shows that single women fell further behind single men and married couples from 1983 to 2001.

Total accumulated wealth still differed widely by marital status in 2001. Single women typically had less than single men, who had less than married couples. Single women had only 31 percent of the mean RW that couples had in 2001 (Table 12.8) and between 29 and 32 percent of their median RW.

Table 12.8 Retirement wealth by family status, ages 47–64, 1983, 1989, and 2001 (in thousands, 2001 dollars)

Category	Mean value			Percentage change		
	1983	1989	2001	1983–1989	1989–2001	1983–2001
A. Married couple						
Mean Pension Wealth (PW)	119.2	147.9	271.0	24.1	83.2	127.3
Mean Social Security Wealth (SSW)	198.3	189.1	239.2	−4.6	26.5	20.6
Mean Retirement Wealth (RW)	317.5	337.1	510.1	6.2	51.3	60.7
Median Retirement Wealth (RW)	276.0	266.3	355.5	−3.5	53.5	28.8
B. Single male						
Mean Pension Wealth (PW)	47.8	59.4	148.0	24.4	149.0	209.8
Mean Social Security Wealth (SSW)	72.8	76.5	127.1	5.0	66.1	74.5
Mean Retirement Wealth (RW)	120.6	135.9	275.1	12.7	102.3	128.1
Median Retirement Wealth (RW)	96.3	97.0	185.9	0.7	91.7	93.0
C. Single female						
Mean Pension Wealth (PW)	73.3	56.3	68.8	−23.2	22.2	−6.2
Mean Social Security Wealth (SSW)	61.3	70.6	90.0	15.3	27.4	46.8
Mean Retirement Wealth (RW)	134.6	127.0	158.8	−5.7	25.1	17.9
Median Retirement Wealth (RW)	111.1	103.9	113.3	−6.4	9.0	2.0

Note: Households are classified by the age of the head.
Key: Retirement Wealth RW = PW + SSW.
Source: Author's computations from the 1983, 1989, and 2001 SCF.

Single women had 58 percent of the mean RW that single men had (and 61 percent of their median RW). Further, the ratio of mean RW for single men to that of married couples in 2001 was 54 percent and the ratio of median RW was 52 percent.

Single women were better off relative to married couples in terms of Social Security than in terms of pensions. In 2001, single women held 38 percent of the Social Security wealth of married couples and only 25 percent of the pension wealth of couples. On the other hand, single males in age group 47 to 64 had 55 percent of the pension wealth of married couples in 2001, compared to 53 percent of their Social Security wealth.

Single women were at about the same level relative to married couples in terms of net worth and total augmented wealth as in terms of RW (Table 12.9). In 2001, the ratio of mean AW between the two groups was 29 percent, compared to 28 percent for net worth and 31 percent for RW. The ratio of median AW was 28 percent. The ratio of mean AW between single males and couples in 2001 was 36 percent, while the ratio of median AW was 47 percent.

Single women not only had less wealth than married couples or single men in 2001 but they also generally fell further behind over the period from 1983

Table 12.9 Income and wealth by family status, ages 47–64, 1983, 1989, and 2001 (in thousands, 2001 dollars)

Category	Mean value			Percentage change		
	1983	1989	2001	1983–1989	1989–2001	1983–2001
A. Married couple						
Mean Income	79.2	88.5	117.5	11.8	32.8	48.5
Mean Net Worth (NW)	493.3	546.0	824.2	10.7	51.0	67.1
Mean Augmented Wealth (AW)	810.8	883.0	1334.4	8.9	51.1	64.6
Median Augmented Wealth (AW)	473.9	473.3	556.9	−0.1	17.7	17.5
B. Single male						
Mean Income	35.5	46.9	77.6	32.0	65.4	118.5
Mean Net Worth (NW)	183.2	227.4	333.2	24.1	46.5	81.9
Mean Augmented Wealth (AW)	294.5	342.4	478.3	16.3	39.7	62.4
Median Augmented Wealth (AW)	165.4	195.4	261.5	18.2	33.8	58.1
C. Single female						
Mean Income	31.4	26.7	37.1	−15.0	38.9	18.1
Mean Net Worth (NW)	129.3	143.2	227.7	10.8	59.0	76.1
Mean Augmented Wealth (AW)	263.9	270.2	386.4	2.4	43.0	46.4
Median Augmented Wealth (AW)	182.8	163.2	158.2	−10.7	−3.1	−13.5

Note: Households are classified by the age of the head.
Key: Augmented Wealth AW = NWX + RW.
Source: Author's computations from the 1983, 1989, and 2001 SCF.

to 2001. With respect to average RW, single men saw by far the largest gains from 1983 to 2001 at 128 percent, whereas single women saw much smaller gains than either single men or married couples. The same pattern held for median RW. Single women did make a substantial gain in terms of mean Social Security wealth but experienced an absolute decline in their pension wealth.

With respect to mean and median AW, single men and married couples had much larger gains than single women. The ratio of mean AW between single females and married couples fell from 33 to 29 percent between 1983 and 2001 and that of median AW plunged from 39 to 28 percent. Indeed, median AW actually declined in absolute terms for single females.

12.6 Retirement income adequacy

I now turn to the primary topic of the chapter, changes in retirement income adequacy. Retirement income is based on four components: (1) standard wealth holdings, (2) DC pension holdings, (3) DB pensions, and (4) Social Security. Standard net worth excluding DC pensions (NWX) is first projected forward to year of retirement using a 3 percent real rate of return. This rate was chosen because it is approximately the average real rate of return on the average household portfolio from 1960 to 2000 (see Wolff, Zacharias, and Caner, 2003, for details). An income flow equal to a seven percent real rate of return on projected wealth at retirement is then used to estimate income from wealth at retirement.[18] It should be stressed that I am *not* attempting to fully model the savings behavior of households nearing retirement, as one can do in a microsimulation model. As a result, my estimates of retirement income (and replacement rates) should be viewed as lower bounds. However, they are useful for comparing retirement preparedness of an age group at *two points in time*, such as 1989 and 2001, to determine whether there is improvement or deterioration.

The second component, DC pensions, is treated in exactly the same way as NWX. For the third component, I use either the respondent's estimates of his (or her) annual pension benefit at retirement or my estimated value (see Section 12.3). The fourth component, annual Social Security benefits, is based on my estimated value of PIA (see Section 12.3).

I then measure retirement adequacy in three ways. The first is the annual projected retirement income. The second is the percentage of households whose projected retirement income is greater than twice the poverty threshold.[19] The third is the income replacement rate. This is based on projected retirement income and projected income up to the year of retirement. For the latter, I use a 2.045 percent annual growth rate of real income, an estimate based on the growth of real income for age group 47 to 64 over the period 1983 to 2001. Because the underlying data in the 1983 SCF do not permit an estimate of either Social Security or DB benefits at retirement, I show results only for 1989 and 2001.

12.6.1 Mean retirement income

The mean retirement income for all households in age group 47–64 in 2001 was estimated to be $74,800 (see Table 12.10). This compares to the actual mean income of this group in 2001 of $91,500. In 2001, 59.4 percent of total retirement income was projected to come from this group's net worth, down from 64.8 percent in 1989; 23.3 percent from pensions, up from 16.5 percent in 1989; and the remaining 17.3 from Social Security, down slightly from 18.6 percent in 1989. The biggest change was the portion from DC pensions, which was estimated to grow by 11.0 percentage points, from 5.4 to 16.4 percent of total retirement income.

Projected retirement income was also estimated to have grown very strongly between 1989 and 2001. Among all households in age group 47–64, expected mean retirement income increased by 38 percent, for age group 47–55 by 31 percent and for age group 56–64 by 48 percent. The biggest growth was in DC pensions, more than tripling in real terms between 1989 and 2001, while annual benefits from DB plans were expected to decline by 13 percent in absolute terms.

Because of the widening racial gap in both RW and total AW, minorities were expected to fall behind non-Hispanic whites in retirement income – a 14 percent increase between 1989 and 2001 versus a 45 percent gain. By 2001, the mean retirement income of minorities was expected to be *about one fourth* that of white households. (This compares to an actual income ratio among 47–64 year olds between the two groups of 42 percent in 2001.) In fact, the ratio of minority to white retirement income was projected to fall from 0.329 in 1989 to 0.259 in 2001. Minorities were to obtain a much higher share of their retirement income from Social Security – 0.305 versus 0.156 in 2001 – and a higher share from pensions – 0.318 versus 0.266 – and a correspondingly much smaller share from standard wealth holdings – 0.377 versus 0.578.

Despite the fact that the RW and total AW of single females declined relative to married couples between 1989 and 2001, their actual retirement prospects showed a slight relative improvement. Their expected retirement income gained 53 percent between 1989 and 2001, compared to a 47 percent increase for married couples (and a 57 percent increase for single males). Still, in 2001, the mean expected retirement income of single females was only 29.4 percent of that of married couples, though up from 28.3 percent in 1989. Single females in 2001 obtained a higher percent of their retirement income from Social Security than married couples – 20.1 versus 15.7 percent – but a lower fraction from pensions – 21.7 versus 27.1 percent.

12.6.2 Twice the poverty threshold

In 2001, 34.6 percent of households in age group 47–64 were projected to have retirement income less than twice the poverty line for their family size (Table 12.11). The percentage was smaller for older age groups, falling from

Table 12.10 Expected mean retirement income based on wealth holdings and expected retirement benefits, 1989 and 2001 (in thousands, 2001 dollars)

Category	Mean retirement income by source, 1989					Mean retirement income by source, 2001						% change by source, 1989–2001				
	NWX	PW	a) DC	b) DB	SSW	Total	NWX	PW	a) DC	b) DB	SSW	Total	NWX	PW	a) DC	b) DB	SSW	Total
All ages 47–64	35.1	8.9	2.9	6.0	10.1	54.1	44.4	17.4	12.3	5.2	12.9	74.8	27	95	316	-13	28	38
Age: 47–55	37.8	9.3	4.4	4.9	8.2	55.3	42.6	18.0	13.0	5.1	11.9	72.5	13	93	192	4	44	31
Age: 56–64	32.2	8.5	1.4	7.2	12.1	52.8	47.2	16.6	11.2	5.4	14.5	78.3	47	94	720	-25	20	48
A. By race/ethnicity[a]																		
1. Non-Hispanic white, 47–64	41.7	10.5	3.6	6.9	11.0	63.1	53.0	24.4	14.2	10.2	14.3	91.7	27	131	289	48	31	45
2. African-American or Hispanic, 47–64	8.4	5.0	0.6	4.4	7.3	20.8	8.9	7.5	3.7	3.9	7.2	23.7	7	49	475	-12	-2	14
B. By family status																		
1. Married couple, 47–64	47.4	11.6	3.9	7.7	13.3	72.3	60.8	28.8	16.8	12.0	16.7	106.4	28	148	333	55	26	47
2. Single male, 47–64	19.9	4.5	1.2	3.3	5.9	30.3	24.0	14.6	8.2	6.5	8.9	47.5	20	225	597	94	51	57
3. Single female, 47–64	11.3	4.3	1.4	2.9	4.9	20.5	18.2	6.8	3.8	3.0	6.3	31.3	62	57	173	2	28	53

Notes: Households are classified by the age of the head of household.
Net worth and DC pensions are projected forward to year of retirement using a three percent real rate of return.
A seven percent annuity is assumed for net worth and DC pension accounts at time of retirement.
Pension Wealth PW = DB + DC.
[a] Asian and other races are excluded from the table because of small sample sizes.

Source: Author's computations from the 1989 and 2001 SCF.

Table 12.11 Percent of households with expected retirement income less than twice the poverty line, 1989 and 2001

	From marketable wealth (NWX) holdings only			From marketable wealth and expected retirement benefits		
	1989	2001	Change 1989–2001	1989	2001	Change 1989–2001
All ages 47–64	69.6	70.6	1.0	39.5	34.6	−4.9
Age: 47–55	67.4	71.5	4.1	37.7	37.3	−0.4
Age: 56–64	71.9	69.2	−2.7	41.4	30.5	−10.9
A. By race/ethnicity[a]						
1. Non-Hispanic white, 47–64	64.2	65.8	1.6	28.9	27.5	−1.4
2. African-American or Hispanic, 47–64	91.8	91.5	−0.2	76.0	64.4	−11.6
B. By family status						
1. Married couple, 47–64	64.5	63.8	−0.8	24.1	20.0	−4.0
2. Single male, 47–64	71.3	77.4	6.1	56.2	42.6	−13.6
3. Single female, 47–64	81.3	82.5	1.2	70.3	64.6	−5.7

Notes: Households are classified by the age of the head.
Net worth and DC pensions are projected forward to year of retirement using a three percent real rate of return.
A seven percent annuity is assumed for net worth and DC pension accounts at time of retirement.
[a] Asian and other races are excluded from the table because of small sample sizes.
Source: Author's computations from the 1989 and 2001 SCF.

37.3 percent for ages 47–55 to 30.5 percent for ages 56–64. Only 27.5 percent of white households were projected to fall below twice the poverty standard, compared to *almost two-thirds* (64.4 percent) of minorities. Differences were also marked by marital status, with only 20.0 percent of married couples compared to 64.6 percent of single females falling below twice the poverty line.

A comparison of the two sets of columns reveals the importance of retirement assets for retirement income. In 2001, 70.6 percent of households in ages 47–64 were projected to have retirement income below twice the poverty line on the basis of their net worth alone (excluding DC pensions), compared to 34.6 percent on the basis of both net worth and retirement assets – a difference of 36.0 percentage points. Differences were greater for the older age group than the younger one (38.7 versus 34.2 percentage points), for whites than for minorities (38.3 versus 27.1 percentage points), and for married couples than single men or single women (43.7 versus 34.8 and 17.9 percentage points).

All groups saw a reduction in the share with expected retirement income less than twice the poverty line between 1989 and 2001. Overall, there was a 4.9 percentage point decline. Percentage points decline were much greater for age group 56–64 than for 47–55. Minority households experienced a much greater decline than white households – 11.6 versus 1.4 percentage points. Single males also saw a large decline – 13.6 percentage points – especially compared to married couples (4.0 percentage point decline) and single females (5.7 percentage point decline). All groups saw a bigger reduction in the share with expected retirement income less than twice the poverty line from increases in the sum of net worth plus retirement income than from increases in net worth alone. These results reflect the growing importance of DC pension wealth over time.

12.6.3 Replacement rates

Changes in the share of households with expected retirement income greater than one half of projected income at retirement were much smaller than changes in the share that would fall short of twice the poverty standard. The reason is that the former is a relative standard whereas the latter is an absolute standard. Changes in the replacement rate reflect changes in both expected retirement income and pre-retirement income itself (which is projected to grow at about 2 percent per year).

In 2001, only 53.4 percent of all households in age group 47 to 64 are expected to have replacement rates more than 50 percent (Table 12.12). The share with at least a 50 percent replacement rate increased by 4.5 percentage points between 1989 and 2001. The share also rises with age, from 42.2 percent for age group 47–55 to 70.5 percent for age group 56–64. Moreover, the older group experienced the greater increase in the proportion meeting this standard between 1989 and 2001 (9.5 percentage points versus 4.6 percentage points for the younger group).

Despite the higher pre-retirement income of whites, the share with replacement rates over half was 58.2 percent in 2001, compared to 32.2 percent for minorities. Moreover, the share of minority households that could replace less than 50 percent of their pre-retirement income remained almost unchanged between 1989 and 2001, while the share of white household increased by 4.2 percentage points.

Likewise, despite the lower pre-retirement income of single females, the share with a replacement rate over 50 percent was much lower for single females, 42.5 percent, than for married couples, 59.4 percent, or single men, 47.9 percent. Moreover, single women saw a smaller improvement in retirement income adequacy, at least if a replacement standard is used, than married couples between 1989 and 2001 (1.8 versus 7.7 percentage points), while single men saw an absolute decline.

It is also of note that the share of households aged 47–64 that could replace at least half their income on the basis of net worth alone (excluding DC pensions) was only 8.6 percent in 2001, compared to 53.4 percent on the basis of the sum of net worth and retirement income (a difference of 44.8 percentage points). As with twice the poverty threshold standard, differences are greater for the older than younger age group (44.6 versus 29.0

Table 12.12 Percent of households with expected replacement income more than one half of projected income at retirement, 1989 and 2001

	From marketable wealth (NWX) holdings only			From marketable wealth and expected retirement benefits		
	1989	2001	Change 1989–2001	1989	2001	Change 1989–2001
All ages 47–64	10.3	8.6	−1.8	48.9	53.4	4.5
Age: 47–55	11.4	13.2	1.8	37.5	42.2	4.6
Age: 56–64	21.3	25.9	4.6	61.0	70.5	9.5
A. By race/ethnicity[a]						
1. Non-Hispanic white, 47–64	24.4	20.9	−3.4	53.9	58.2	4.3
2. African-American or Hispanic, 47–64	8.8	6.5	−2.3	31.3	32.3	0.9
B. By family status						
1. Married couple, 47–64	22.0	19.7	−2.3	51.7	59.4	7.7
2. Single male, 47–64	26.7	13.3	−13.4	51.4	47.9	−3.5
3. Single female, 47–64	18.1	18.3	0.2	40.7	42.5	1.8

Notes: Households are classified by the age of the head.
Net worth and DC pensions are projected forward to year of retirement using a three percent real rate of return.
A seven percent annuity is assumed for net worth and DC pension accounts at time of retirement.
[a] Asian and other races are excluded from the table because of small sample sizes.
Source: Author's computations from the 1989 and 2001 SCF.

percentage points), for whites than for minorities (37.3 versus 25.8 percentage points), and for married couples than single men or single women (39.7 versus 34.6 and 24.1 percentage points). It is also of note that the increases in replacement rates that occurred from 1989 to 2001 emanated largely from accumulations of retirement assets rather than increases in net worth.

Similar patterns exist when we look at different cut-off points for replacement rates (Table 12.13). Declines in the proportion of households that fall below each of the four replacement rate standards are almost across the board (the notable exception being single males). Using a 75 percent replacement standard, the share of all households in age group 47–64 falling below this standard declined by 2.9 percentage points from 1989 to 2001. The decline was even larger among age group 56–64 (6.3 percentage points) and married couples (4.7 percentage points).

12.7 Conclusion

Retirement income adequacy has gained in importance over the decades as the share of the population nearing retirement has grown. The starting point

Table 12.13 Distribution of households in age group 47–64 by expected replacement rates, based on wealth holdings and expected pension and Social Security benefits, 1989 and 2001 (in percentage points)

	Income replacement rates, 1989				Income replacement rates, 2001			
	<25%	<50%	<75%	<100%	<25%	<50%	<75%	<100%
All ages 47–64	17.4	51.1	70.7	82.2	15.6	46.6	67.8	79.2
Age: 47–55	23.3	62.5	79.7	88.2	22.2	57.8	76.3	85.7
Age: 56–64	11.0	39.0	61.0	75.7	5.6	29.5	54.7	69.4
1. Non-Hispanic white	12.8	46.1	66.1	79.8	11.9	41.8	64.3	77.1
2. African-American or Hispanic	34.1	68.7	86.5	91.2	31.5	67.7	83.2	89.5
3. Married couple	10.9	48.3	70.0	84.1	10.6	40.6	65.3	77.6
4. Single male	16.9	48.6	64.9	74.1	20.2	52.1	70.4	82.4
5. Single female	33.7	59.3	74.8	81.0	24.6	57.5	72.0	81.2

Notes: Households are classified by the age of the head.
Net worth and DC pensions are projected forward to year of retirement using a three percent real rate of return.
A seven percent annuity is assumed for net worth and DC pension accounts at time of retirement.
Source: Author's computations from the 1989 and 2001 SCF.

for retirement income adequacy is an assessment of how much wealth households have accumulated by the time they are about to retire.

The analysis here focuses on the wealth accumulation of households nearing retirement, between ages 47 and 64. The data show that still many households have to rely solely on Social Security for their retirement income. Almost one quarter of all households nearing retirement had no private pension plans in 2001.

Also, RW is very unevenly distributed. Whites and married couples and men had substantially larger wealth accumulations than their respective counterparts. However, expected retirement income grew robustly from 1989 to 2001 (by 38 percent in real terms) and the share with expected retirement income less than twice the poverty line fell by 5 percentage points. The percentage point decline was even greater for minority households (11.6) and single females (5.7). The change in the share with replacement rates over 50 percent was 4.5 percentage points, though in this case much lower for minorities (0.9 percentage points) and single females (1.8 percentage points). However, percentage point changes were much smaller at 75 percent and 100 percent replacement rates.

Notes

1. Shortfalls in retirement savings vary with household demographics. Mitchell et al. (2000) and Engen, Gale, and Uccello (1999) found that black and Hispanic married households experienced a larger shortfall in retirement income adequacy than

whites, and that less education resulted in a worsening of retirement income adequacy. Mitchell and Moore (1998) also found that single households were less adequately prepared than married ones.

2. In comparing these figures with findings of other studies, for example, Haveman et al. (2003), it needs to be kept in mind that, for instance, Haveman et al. (2003) only considered Social Security earnings for their replacement ratio calculations, thus understating the level of household income. Also, Wolff (2002b) considered the wealth of households nearing retirement, whereas Haveman et al. (2003) considered wealth for those who were retired. Obviously households can increase their savings before entering retirement and occasionally while in retirement.

3. The underlying data are not available for the 1983 SCF to re-do these estimates in exactly the same form as for 1989 and 2001, though I try to follow their method as much as possible for these two years. The difference in methodology may introduce compatibility problems between the 1983 estimates and those of the other two years. Moreover, pension and Social Security wealth imputations in the 1983 data are not available for households under the age of 40.

4. Only assets that can be readily converted to cash (that is, "fungible" ones) are included. As a result, consumer durables, such as automobiles, televisions, furniture, household appliances, and the like, are excluded here since these items are not easily marketed or their resale value typically far understates the value of their consumption services to the household.

5. The mortality rate data are from the US Bureau of the Census, *Statistical Abstract of the United States, 1985, 1991 and 2003*, Washington, DC, US Government Printing Office.

6. I also used as alternatives real discount rates of 1.5, 2.5, and 3.0 percent. The results of the analysis are not materially altered (and not shown in the chapter).

7. Technically speaking, the mortality rate m_t associated with the year of retirement is the probability of surviving from the current age to the age of retirement. The discount rate is again set at 5 percent (2 percent if PB is indexed).

8. Separate imputations are performed for husband and wife and an adjustment in the Social Security benefit is made for the surviving spouse. The discount rate is again set at 2 percent.

9. As with pension wealth, the mortality rate m_t associated with the year of retirement is the probability of surviving from the current age to the age of retirement and the discount rate is set at 2 percent.

10. Moreover, the 1983 data do not present a problem, since DC wealth was a trivial amount, so that we can again safely ignore this in the wealth comparison between 1983 on the one hand and 1989 and 2001 on the other hand.

11. The SCF records DC plans only for the main job of each respondent. No information on DC plans is provided for secondary employment. This does not appear to be a significant problem because in 2001, 99.4 percent of the total labor earnings of the head and 98.8 percent of that of the spouse came from the person's primary job.

12. This will, if anything, bias upward the estimated employer contribution to the DC pension plan.

13. This calculation assumes that the real rate of return on DC assets equals the discount rate δ. It should also be noted that past employer contributions to DC plans are already included in the current market value of DC wealth.

14. The CPI-U is used as the deflator for both income and wealth.

15. The Current Population Survey (CPS) data show somewhat different time trends, with median income rising by 11 percent between 1983 and 1989 and then only

2.3 percent from 1989 to 2001, and mean income growing by 16 and 12 percent, respectively.
16. Both mean and median SSW declined slightly from 1983 to 1989. This change mainly reflects the increase in the normal retirement age (NRA) for Social Security benefits which came into effect in the early 1980s. The age at full Social Security benefits advances from 65 and 2 months for those born in 1938 to 67 for those born in 1960 or later.
17. Because of small sample sizes, I have combined these two groups. Moreover, I have excluded the group "Asians and other races" for the same reason.
18. It should be noted that I am using net worth including houses in computing the annuity flow here and treating the net equity in homes as an asset value like stocks or bonds.
19. I assume that the family's marital status remains unchanged over time.

References

Aon Consulting (2001) *Replacement Ratio Study* (Chicago, IL: Aon Consulting).
Bloom, D. E. and R. B. Freeman (1992) "The Fall in Private Pension Coverage in the United States," *American Economic Review Papers and Proceedings* 82(2): 539–558.
Engen, E. M., W. G. Gale, and C. E. Uccello (1999) "The Adequacy of Household Saving," *Brookings Papers on Economic Activity*, 2 (Washington, DC: The Brookings Institution) pp. 65–165.
Engen, E., W. Gale and C. E. Uccello (2002) "Effects of Stock Market Fluctuations on the Adequacy of Retirement Wealth Accumulation," paper presented at the American Economics Association meeting, Washington, DC, January 2003.
Even, W. E. and D. A. Macpherson (1994) "Why Has the Decline in Pension Coverage Accelerated among Less Educated Workers?," *Industrial and Labor Relations Review* 47: 439–453.
Feldstein, M. S. (1974) "Social Security, Induced Retirement and Aggregate Capital Accumulation," *Journal of Political Economy* 82: 905–926.
Feldstein, M. S. (1976) "Social Security and the Distribution of Wealth," *Journal of the American Statistical Association* 71: 800–807.
Gustman, A. L., O. S. Mitchell, A. A. Samwick, and T. L. Steinmeier (1997) "Pension and Social Security Wealth in the Health and Retirement Study," Working Paper W5912 (Cambridge, MA: National Bureau of Economic Research).
Gustman, A. L. and T. L. Steinmeier (1998) "Effects of Pensions on Saving: Analysis with Data from the Health and Retirement Study," Working Paper W6681 (Cambridge, MA: National Bureau of Economic Research).
Gustman, A. L., and T. L. Steinmeier (1999), "What People Don't Know About Their Pensions and Social Security: An Analysis Using Linked Data from the Health and Retirement Study," Working Paper W7368 (Cambridge, MA: National Bureau of Economic Research).
Haveman, R., K. Holden, B. Wolfe, and S. Sherlund (2003) "Have Newly Retired Workers in the US Saved Enough to Maintain Well-Being through Retirement Years?," paper presented at the annual meetings of the Association of Policy Analysis and Management (APPAM) (Washington, DC) November.
Johnson, R. W., U. Sambamoorthi, and S. Crystal (2000), "Pension Wealth at Midlife: Comparing Self-Reports with Provider Data," *Review of Income and Wealth* 46(1): 59–83.
Kennickell, A. B. and A. E. Sunden (1999) "Pensions, Social Security, and the Distribution of Wealth," mimeo (Washington, DC: Federal Reserve Board).

McGill, D. M., K. N. Brown, J. J. Haley, and S. Schieber (1996) *Fundamentals of Private Pensions*, 7th Edition (Philadelphia, PA: University of Pennsylvania Press).

Mitchell, O. S. and J. Moore (1998), "Can Americans Afford to Retire? New Evidence on Retirement Saving Adequacy," *Journal of Risk and Insurance* 65(3): 371–400.

Mitchell, O. S., J. Moore, and J. Phillips (2000), "Explaining Retirement Saving Shortfalls," in O. S. Mitchell, B. Hammond, and A. Rappaport (eds) *Forecasting Retirement Needs and Retirement Wealth* (Philadelphia, PA: University of Pennsylvania Press) pp. 139–166.

Moore, J. F. and O. S. Mitchell (2000) "Projected Retirement Wealth and Saving Adequacy," in O. Mitchell, B. Hammond, and A. Rappaport (eds) *Forecasting Retirement Needs and Retirement Wealth* (Philadelphia, PA: University of Pennsylvania Press) pp. 68–94.

Popke, L. E. (1999) "Are 401(k) Plans Replacing Other Employer-Provided Pensions?," *Journal of Human Resources* 34(2): 346–368.

Poterba, J. M., S. F. Venti, and D. A. Wise (1998) "401(k) Plans and Future Patterns of Retirement Saving," *American Economic Review Papers and Proceedings* 88(2): 179–184.

Smith, J. P. (2003) "Trends and Projections in Income Replacement during Retirement," *Journal of Labor Economics* 21(4): 755–781.

Smith, K., E. Toder, and H. Iams (2001), "Lifetime Redistribution of Social Security Retirement Benefits" (Washington, DC: Social Security Administration).

US Bureau of the Census (various years) *Statistical Abstract of the United States: 2002* (Washington, DC: US Government Printing Office).

US Department of Labor, Pension and Welfare Benefits Administration (2000) "Coverage Status of Workers Under Employer Provided Pension Plans: Findings from the Contingent Work Supplement to the February 1999 Current Population Survey" (Washington, DC: Department of Labor).

Wolff, E. N. (1987) "The Effects of Pensions and Social Security on the Distribution of Wealth in the US," in E. Wolff (ed.) *International Comparisons of Household Wealth Distribution* (Oxford, UK: Oxford University Press) pp. 208–247.

Wolff, E. N. (2002a) "Is the Equalizing Effect of Retirement Wealth Wearing Off?," unpublished working paper, Department of Economics (New York, NY: New York University).

Wolff, E. N. (2002b) *Retirement Insecurity: The Income Shortfalls Awaiting the Soon-to-Retire*. (Washington, DC: Economic Policy Institute).

Wolff, E. N. (2007) "The Transformation of the American Pension System," in T. Ghilarducci and J. Turner (eds) *Work Options for Older Americans* (Notre Dame, IN: University of Notre Dame Press) pp. 175–211.

Wolff, E. N., A. Zacharias, and A. Caner (2003) *The Levy Institute Measure of Economic Well-Being* (Levy Institute) (December).

Comments to Chapter 12
Brooke Harrington

> Inequality comes largely from the solutions that elite and non-elite actors improvise in the face of recurrent organizational problems – challenges centering around control over symbolic, positional or emotional resources.
>
> – Pierre Bourdieu

Edward Wolff's chapter raises a number of provocative questions about the sources and distribution of retirement resources in the United States. A major theme of the chapter is the growing fragility of the three-legged stool framework for retirement funding, which includes private pension wealth (from employer-based plans), individual wealth (savings, home equity, and investments), and Social Security. Wolff's findings indicate that the first two legs of the stool are becoming increasingly shaky, leaving Social Security to bear increasing weight for Americans facing retirement.

Wolff's chapter has particularly interesting implications for two issues currently at the center of public debate about retirement: economic inequality and the purpose of Social Security. The chapter documents the result of 20 years' worth of American policy makers' responses to the recurrent organization problems – as the late French sociologist Pierre Bourdieu (1984) would put it – of ensuring adequate economic resources for retired persons. The provision and distribution of these resources have been freighted with tremendous symbolic importance, clouding the policy discourse; this foregrounds the contribution of Wolff's chapter, since it offers an empirically-grounded state of the union report on Americans' preparedness for retirement. His work invites us to revisit basic questions about what we as a society hope to achieve through public policies focused on the economic position of retirees and the soon-to-retire.

What is social about Social Security?

A recurrent underlying motif in Wolff's chapter is the linkage between the funding and the politics of retirement. In reading the chapter, one is constantly reminded that the ways in which retirement wealth (RW) gets distributed, particularly by the government, has significant predictive power for the development of political movements and alliances. Particularly noteworthy in this regard are Wolff's data showing the increasing reliance on Social Security by the middle class. The chapter indicates that Social Security accounts for 55 percent of RW for middle class families between the ages of 47 and 55, compared to the average of 46.6 percent for that age group as a whole. The gap persists and even widens slightly for the 56- to 64-age group: among the middle class, Social Security provides 59.3 percent of RW, compared to an average 49.3 percent for all households nearing retirement.

Is this bad news or good news? Wolff's data invites reconsideration of such questions, and the answers are not at all self-evident. On the one hand, some policy makers might see reason for alarm in the increasing reliance of the middle class on a program often stigmatized as a safety net for economically vulnerable groups. If middle-class Americans perceive themselves as losing ground compared to those of lower socio-economic status that could galvanize a significant and destabilizing political response.

However, readers acquainted with political theory might read Wolff's findings in an entirely different light, as an indicator of potentially positive developments on the civic front. At the very least, the increasingly common lot of middle-class and economically vulnerable groups in retirement provides a foundation for inter-class solidarity (Habermas, 1984). If that leads to political mobilization, so much the better for deepening political engagement and the development of the participatory publics (Avritzer, 2002) crucial to a healthy civil society.

Social Security, from its inception, has always had a Tocquevillian element, building the associational foundations of society not only through the widespread economic participation of citizens (both as contributors to and beneficiaries of the program), but by creating the opportunity for broad-based public debate and decision-making about public resources. Because Social Security and retirement planning affect virtually everyone, they are among the very few issues that engage both the pocketbooks and political interests of citizens otherwise divided by class, racio-ethnicity, and other group affiliations (Harrington, 2004). For this reason, Social Security is laden with intense symbolic meaning as well as economic consequence. Further, Wolff's data suggest that this link may be growing stronger.

What is secure about Social Security?

Wolff's data also suggest that Social Security is meeting its broad commitment to limiting economic inequality among Americans. His chapter alludes to the increasing importance of this safety net in light of broad changes within labor markets and the composition of household wealth. This is particularly important in light of claims by the Bush administration that

Americans would enjoy greater benefits from Social Security if a portion of the program's funds were turned into private accounts that could be invested in the stock market. In contrast, Wolff's data show that the main virtue of Social Security for Americans nearing retirement is precisely its detachment from the vagaries of the market, while the other two sources of retirement wealth (private pensions and personal wealth) are increasingly exposed to those risks.

For example, as American firms rely on temporary and part-time labor to a greater and greater extent, fewer individuals have access to private pension programs. Less than half of those who *do* have access to such pensions participate. As Wolff notes, only 44 percent of private sector wage-and-salary workers were eligible for private pensions, and participation was very low for non-white and nonunionized workers. More than 20 percent of all households nearing retirement, he writes, have no private pension plan wealth at all. The most economically vulnerable groups – such as women, people of color, and renters – are particularly affected by these trends, and thus increasingly reliant on Social Security.

In addition, Wolff documents that privately held wealth among Americans is increasingly subject to the vagaries of the market. From 1989 through 2001, he shows, most increases in household wealth derived from stock holdings; however, his preliminary analysis of more recent data (2001–2004) indicates that a much larger portion of household wealth now comes from home value. In other words, personal wealth was tied first to the stock market bubble, and has now shifted to the real estate bubble. Combined with low levels of personal savings, and high rates of credit card debt and personal bankruptcy filings, personal wealth would appear to provide an uncertain foundation for retirement funding.

Thus, both middle-class homeowners and the less privileged find themselves in an economic position that intensifies their reliance on Social Security for retirement funding. In keeping with the original intent of the program, Social Security provides a much-needed buffer against instability in employment and in sources of personal weath; what's new about the recent past, as Wolff's data suggest, is the increasingly large segment of American society in need of such a buffer. Thus, despite the regressiveness of the taxation which funds it, the program sets some of the few remaining limits on the growth of economic inequality among Americans.

An appreciation

Among the many things to like about Wolff's chapter is the factual basis it provides for assessing the status of Americans' preparedness for retirement. With a refreshing absence of ideological inflections, Wolff presents data that suggest reason for optimism, particularly about Social Security – in striking contrast to recent claims that the program has failed and is doomed to collapse within a generation. Wolff's chapter suggests that reports of Social Security's imminent demise have been greatly exaggerated.

On the contrary, it would appear from the evidence Wolff presents that Social Security is proving increasingly valuable in fostering social solidarity and economic security in the United States at a time when both are in short supply. On the social side, Social Security continues to play its traditional Tocquevillian role of providing a policy space in which the interests of rich, the poor, and other social groups converge. While this is by no means a guarantee of either solidarity or civic engagement, it provides one of the few opportunities for bridging categorical inequalities among citizens. The creation of a political commons on which a broad-based public discourse can be constructed is of incalculable value in sustaining democracy, especially amidst the fragmentation of Red States versus Blue States, immigrants versus natives, and other factions that serve the divide-and-conquer strategy that has come to characterize American civic life.

References

Avritzer, L. (2002) *Democracy and the Public Space in Latin America* (Princeton, NJ: Princeton University Press).
Bourdieu, P. (1984) *Distinction: A Social Critique of the Judgment of Taste*, Richard Nice (Transcription) (Cambridge, MA: Harvard University Press).
Habermas, J. (1984) *The Theory of Communicative Action, Volume 1: Reason and the Rationalization of Society* (Boston, MA: Beacon Press).
Harrington, B. (2004) "Can Small Investors Survive Social Security Privatization?," in D. Canon, J. Coleman, and K. Mayer (eds) *Faultlines: Debating the Issues in American Politics*, 2nd Edition (New York: W. W. Norton) pp. 308–313.

13
Minimum Benefits in Social Security

Melissa M. Favreault, Gordon B. T. Mermin, and
C. Eugene Steuerle*

13.1 Introduction

In 1998, the bipartisan National Commission on Retirement Policy advanced a reform proposal that contained a minimum benefit within Social Security. Since then, numerous congressional proposals have included minimum benefits as part of a package of reforms, and a commission President George W. Bush set up during his first term also recommended one. Little effort, however, has been made to develop the rationale for a minimum benefit or to examine alternative designs.[1] As a consequence, the design of a minimum benefit – or, for that matter, of almost all redistributive formulas within Social Security – has seldom been based on any theoretical or empirical notion of exactly what goals are sought and what types of formulaic adjustments would best achieve them.

This study attempts to fill that gap. It has three main sections. In the first, we examine Social Security's redistributive purpose and how it relates to the program's other purposes. We discuss the current system's redistributive features, and consider whether a minimum benefit might improve program adequacy in a more equitable or efficient way. We also consider an alternative: increasing the basic means-tested program that provides an income floor for the aged and disabled.

With this theoretical context in mind, we turn to the second section, in which we design a few minimum benefits on the basis of years of work and the poverty threshold. In this section, we consider how Social Security currently treats low-wage workers, review literature on minimum benefits, and examine benefit design elements. Our benefit design draws from the principles outlined above, as well as from empirical research about distributions of numbers of years in covered employment for men and women.

In the third section, we empirically examine how well different types of minimum benefits achieve various goals, such as reducing poverty. We compare the minimums with similar mechanisms (for example, changes to the benefit formula bend points). We use DYNASIM, the Urban Institute's dynamic microsimulation model of the US population (Favreault and Smith 2004), in these analyses. Our aim is not to reach a definitive conclusion about how minimum benefits should be designed but rather to show how certain Social Security purposes – particularly those associated with poverty relief – can be better achieved when they are solidly grounded in thoughtful analysis and empirical research.

We make roughly fiscally equivalent comparisons assuming a system that is reduced relative to scheduled benefits because of Social Security's long-term fiscal deficit (OASDI Board of Trustees 2005). We assume that increased contributions meet approximately half of Social Security's annual deficit in 2050, and benefit reductions meet the other half.[2] These estimated reductions, based on Social Security cost projections, are inherently uncertain. Social Security may require smaller or greater adjustments depending on how accurate these predictions turn out to be. Nonetheless, this is a reasonable starting place.

13.2 Progressivity and other goals of Social Security

Social Security's current design reflects compromises between the principles of progressivity and individual equity. It contains both redistributive features and features that relate benefits to workers' payments into the system. It differs from means-tested programs that are available to people only when their means/income are below some given amount. Almost all Social Security contributors – provided they have made deposits for at least 10 years – and their spouses are entitled to benefits when they reach retirement age.

13.2.1 Adequacy/progressivity

Providing adequate retirement income stands out as a clear goal for Social Security. At the program's outset, poverty rates among the aged were quite high. As late as 1959, over a third of the elderly lived in poverty. Today, the aged are less likely than prime-age workers or children to be poor.[3] Undoubtedly, one of Social Security's major goals – and accomplishments – has been to reduce aged poverty (Englehardt and Gruber, 2004). The Social Security Administration regularly estimates the extent to which Social Security payments might reduce poverty among the aged, recently suggesting that the program brought 12 million Americans out of poverty (derived from Koenig, 2002).

In addition to redistributing from younger to older generations, the system attempts to redistribute *within* each generation of the aged by providing higher replacement rates for those with lower lifetime earnings, even though higher earners pay the same rate (up to a taxable maximum, set at $94,200 in 2006[4]). Put another way, Social Security's benefit formula is progressive with respect to earnings, while the payroll tax is roughly proportionate (or regressive annually because of the maximum[5]). Other redistributive mechanisms are also part of the system.[6]

Recent US data on income of aged persons suggest that, despite Social Security's enormous impacts on adequacy, there is room for further poverty reduction. In 2004, almost 8 percent of Social Security beneficiaries of ages 65 and older had family income below the poverty line, and almost 15 percent had family income below 125 percent of poverty (Social Security Administration, 2006b). For certain groups, risk levels are more substantial. Almost 10 percent of women, for example, have income less than poverty, but this poverty rate jumps to 17 percent for nonmarried women, 28 percent of whom have family income below 125 percent of poverty. Race differences in poverty also reveal high-risk groups. In 2003, over a quarter (27.4 percent) of black women and a fifth (21.7 percent) of Hispanic women of ages 65 and older were poor (He et al., 2005). For older black and Hispanic women who live alone, rates reach 40 percent.

13.2.2 Equity

Social Security requires most workers to participate, thus sharing the burden for the retirement system as a whole. The system's design helps to prevent free riders – those who might avoid paying into a collective effort but still rely on it by consuming their income when they are younger and later becoming eligible for income-conditioned old-age assistance.

After paying taxes for a modest number of years, each taxpayer qualifies for a Social Security benefit. Relating benefits to taxes paid is consistent with the notion that those who pay for government benefits ought to receive something back (corresponding to the benefit principle of taxation, in which taxes are considered payment for goods/services received). This is associated with the broader notion of individual equity, which holds that people are entitled to the rewards from their own labors.

13.2.3 Evaluation

Little research in Social Security's early years determined just how much redistribution the program was accomplishing. The replacement wage for an "average wage" worker was set at about 40 percent, a figure imperfectly related to expenses of old age, taxes at younger ages, evolving family work patterns, or other considerations.[7] Moreover, because benefits related to earnings rather than to taxes paid, the amount of income the system redistributed varied enormously across generations, with substantially higher returns for earlier generations, which paid lower tax rates for similar replacement wages (Moffitt, 1984; Steuerle and Bakija, 1994).

Recent research reveals that, when measured by rates of return on taxes paid or lifetime benefits relative to lifetime taxes, Social Security redistributes less within generations than conventional wisdom may have suggested, despite its many redistributive features. Shorter life expectancy for lower-income persons partially offsets the system's mechanisms for redistributing to those with lower lifetime earnings.[8] (See, for instance, Steuerle and Bakija, 1994; Caldwell et al., 1999; Coronado, Fullerton, and Glass, 1999; Gustman and Steinmeier, 2000; Smith, Toder, and Iams, 2003/2004.) Results from these types of studies are sensitive to outcome measures (Leimer, 1995); to definition of lifetime earnings (for example, actual versus potential, individual versus couple); and to the program components (Old Age Insurance (OAI) worker benefits, Disability Insurance (DI) worker benefits, spouse/survivor benefits, children's benefits) one includes.

13.3 Tools for redistribution: existing provisions versus a minimum benefit

13.3.1 Existing provisions

Social Security has three primary provisions for redistributing to those with lower lifetime earnings: (1) a progressive formula of benefit rates; (2) a limited number of years counted in the benefit formula; and (3) spousal and survivor benefits.[9] Social Security includes a "special minimum PIA" under current law, but few receive benefits on this basis.[10]

13.3.1.1 *A progressive formula*

The progressive benefit formula provides those with lower lifetime earnings higher replacement rates (defined as benefits divided by average lifetime earnings subject to payroll tax). For instance, a worker with average indexed monthly earnings (AIME) of less than $656 in 2006 will receive a benefit equal to 90 percent of that average (assuming he/she claimed benefits at the normal retirement age (NRA)). As earnings increase, the benefit returns only 32 percent of the additional dollars of earnings, then eventually (above $3,995) only 15 percent of additional earnings. For someone with average monthly earnings of $2,000 in 2006, the combination of the 90, 32, and 15 percent replacement wage for different portions of earnings yields about 50 percent on net. At average earnings of $5,000, it yields about 36 percent on net.[11]

The benefit formula's progressive rate schedule may be Social Security's most effective mechanism for progressively redistributing benefits. Cohen, Steuerle, and Carasso (2004) break out the components of Old Age and Survivors Insurance (OASI) redistribution and show that none comes close to the formula in tilting benefits toward those with lower lifetime earnings. It is unique in the US social welfare structure in its dependence on *lifetime* rather than *annual* circumstances.

The progressive rate structure also redistributes to those whose incomes fall because they are out of the labor force for a variety of reasons, including unemployment, time off to raise children, part-time work, or residence abroad (for example, immigration). Just as additional dollars of earnings generate lower average replacement wages, reduced earnings generate higher average replacement wages. The progressive benefit formula does not differentiate one cause for lesser earnings from another.

13.3.1.2 A limited number of years counted in the benefit formula

In counting only the highest 35 years of earnings, the system provides some reprieve for those who are unemployed or out of the workforce for other reasons. However, this adjustment is fairly arbitrary in its application. Because of the way it interacts with the progressive benefit formula, it fails to reward lower-income workers who might work more years. For example, it provides higher benefits to those who have average indexed annual earnings of $40,000 for 30 years than to those with earnings of $30,000 for 40 years. All earnings count toward the benefit for the former workers, while for the latter just 35 years worth of earnings count. Penalizing workers who pay as much tax and work more years over a lifetime seems inequitable. Similarly, the formula tends to penalize workers who work half-time for 20 years of a 45-year career, who might get to count only half the earnings from those part-time years in the formula, compared with those who drop out entirely for 10 years but then can count every dollar earned over a 35-year career.

13.3.1.3 Spousal and survivor benefits

Spousal and survivor benefits represent another redistributive mechanism in OASDI. To compensate for the fact that two people have more expenses than one, Social Security provides spousal benefits of one half of the worker's benefit when both spouses are alive, and the full worker's benefit for survivors. If a family has two workers, the lower earner can take the higher of his/her own worker benefit or the spousal benefit. Social Security spousal and survivor benefits require no extra contribution by workers.[12]

Never married parents, single persons, and persons divorced before 10 years of marriage to a worker cannot access these benefits, leading to inequities. A single head of household can work more, pay more taxes, and raise more children than a spouse, yet receive lower Social Security benefits. Spouses who marry workers with high earnings get higher benefits than those who marry low-wage workers.[13] One worker can generate several spousal/survivor benefits through multiple marriages without paying additional tax.

OASDI spousal and survivor benefit structures also treat some households that pay the same amount of payroll tax (and presumably have equal needs) unequally. Two-earner couples in which one spouse earns much more than the other get more benefits than two-earner couples with more equal earnings, even though both pay the same amount of tax. The disparity between the couples rises significantly when one spouse dies, as the survivor then gets the benefit associated with the higher of the two earners. As an example, a typical couple with one spouse earning $30,000 and the other nothing will get around $100,000 more in lifetime benefits than a couple in which each earns $15,000.

13.3.2 Minimum benefit

A minimum benefit could redistribute more efficiently than these existing mechanisms – especially limited computation years and spousal/survivor benefits.[14] A minimum could take many forms. Some minimum benefit proposals require no years of work, thus ensuring a universal minimum support level for all aged persons; others require some minimum number of work years and/or ratchet up the minimum benefit as years of work increase. These latter types of minimums rely more on a backup welfare system (for example, Supplemental Security Income, or SSI) to cover those in need. Table 13.1 summarizes minimum benefit proposals that have appeared in a variety of legislative, advisory, and advocacy contexts.

The table suggests that minimums that require some work have been more common than universal ones in recent proposals. The National Commission on Retirement Policy (NCRP) minimum benefit recommendation (1998) offered workers a benefit equal to 60 percent of poverty with 20 years of work, increasing by 2 percent of poverty for each additional work year and reaching a maximum 100 percent of poverty with 40 years. The benefit was scheduled to take effect in 2010 and be wage-indexed thereafter.[15] The context for the NCRP plan's minimum was a package with carve-out personal accounts, retirement age increases, and other changes.

The President's Commission to Strengthen Social Security (CSSS) report (2001) contained two plans with minimum benefits and other changes. Its "model two" minimum would apply those with over 20 years of work, providing a benefit of 120 percent of poverty for minimum-wage workers with 30 or more years of earnings (prorated for those with 21 to 29 work years). It is combined with numerous changes, most notably carve-out personal accounts and price indexing (rather than wage indexing) of initial Social Security benefits. The "model three" minimum would provide a benefit of 100 percent of poverty for minimum-wage workers with 30 or more years of earnings (again, prorated for those with 21 to 29 years of earnings), and again in concert with carve-out personal accounts, but also with longevity-indexed benefits. In the model two case, the minimum benefit was price-indexed; in model three, it was indexed at a level between wages and prices. Liebman, MacGuineas, and Samwick (2005) develop a plan that includes, among other changes, the model two minimum benefit. Diamond and Orszag (2003) also propose a low-earner primary insurance amount (PIA) enhancement for workers with 21 or more years of earnings in their solvency plan. Senator Lindsey Graham (R-SC) (2003) proposed a minimum benefit that equals 120 percent of poverty with 35 years of work and phases out at 10 work years.

Smeeding and Weaver (2001) proposed a Senior Income Guarantee (SIG) that resembles a minimum benefit but essentially develops a third tier in the US retirement income system (that falls between SSI and OASDI). Their full guarantee requires 40 years of residence and 40 covered quarters, but can be

Table 13.1 Selected minimum benefit proposals for Social Security

Proposal name and source	Size of minimum (amount granted at NRA)	Minimum number of years required (and maximum if applicable)	Definition of a year (e.g., CQ, 20 hours/week at minimum wage, etc.)	Allow partial years?	Future treatment of initial level (default = price-indexed)	Empricial analyses
National Commission on Retirement Policy (1998) (similar in Kolbe-Stenholm [2002], Kolbe-Boyd [2005])	60% poverty at 20 years, up to 100% at 40 years	20 (up to 40)	4 CQs (2006 = $3,880)	yes in law, no in some cited studies	Wage-indexed	Herd (2005) "Privatization"; Sandell, Iams, Fanaras (1999); Favreault, Steuerle, Sammartino (2002); Zedlewski (2002)
Herd "Worker"	Poverty	10	4 CQs (2006 = $3,880)	no	Price-indexed	Herd (2005)
"Resident" (1979 SS Advisory Council)	$545 (72.5% of poverty): federal SSI level in 2002	0	n/a	n/a	Price-indexed	Herd (2005)
President's Commission to Strengthen Social Security Model 2 (2001)	120% poverty at 30 years	21 to 30 (no work after 60 assumed)	minimum wage worker (2000 hours per year at $5.15 in 2000, wage-indexed, or $10,300)	still counts CQs when < 4 in any year	Price-indexed	Goss and Wade (2002) (primarily aggregate)

Continued

Table 13.1 Continued

Proposal name and source	Size of minimum (amount granted at NRA)	Minimum number of years required (and maximum if applicable)	Definition of a year (e.g., CQ, 20 hours/week at minimum wage, etc.)	Allow partial years?	Future treatment of initial level (default = price-indexed)	Emprical analyses
President's Commission to Strengthen Social Security Model 3 (2001)	100% poverty at 30 years	21 to 30	as in CSSS Model 2	still counts CQs when < 4 in any year	Intermediate-indexed (projected CPI + 0.5)	Goss and Wade (2002) (primarily aggregate)
Diamond and Orszag (2003)	60% poverty at 20 years, up to 100% at 35 years	21 (up to 35)	minimum wage worker ("steadily rising to" 2000 hours per year at $5.15 in 2000, wage indexed, or $10,300)	still counts CQs when < 4 in any year	Wage-indexed	Goss (2003) (primarily aggregate)
Graham (2003)	120% poverty at 35 years, reduced by 1.2% for each	11(up to 35)	4 CQs (2006 = $3,880)	yes	Price-indexed	Chaplain and Wade (2003) (primarily aggregate)

Proposal	Details				Source
Fitzpatrick et al. (2003)	CQ under 140 (phased in); prorate for DI		no	No change	Fitzpatrick et al. (2003)
	1. Adjust special minimum: change years of service from 30 to 25				
	2. Adjust special minimum: lower amount necessary for a year of service	26 percent of average wage ($9,516 in 2005)	no	No change	
	3. Count partial years of service		yes	No change	
Senior Income Guarantee (Smeeding, Weaver 2001)	75% poverty at 40 years residence and 10 work years	10	4CQs (2006 = $3,880)	prorate	Unspecified, appears price-indexed	Simple estimates in Smeeding, Weaver (2001)

Abbreviations: CPI – Consumer Price Index; CQ – covered quarter; CSSS – President's Commission to Strengthen Social Security; NA – not applicable; NRA – Normal Retirement Age.

prorated for persons with shorter residency. The SIG would award a benefit of 75 percent of the poverty threshold at the NRA and allow persons to exclude $200/month of other income (including OASDI) when determining eligibility. The program would also impose an asset test that would be more liberal than current SSI asset tests. The SIG would not automatically confer Medicaid eligibility, as SSI does in most states.

13.3.3 Key design parameters in a minimum benefit

The preceding discussion reveals several key issues associated with the design of a minimum benefit for Social Security, including the following:

- The benefit level (often expressed as a percentage of poverty) and how it varies with years of service (steeper slopes encourage work but can reduce benefit adequacy).
- The number of years of service required (usually based on work, though this could be based on combinations of, for example, childrearing and work).
- The definition of a year of service (for example, four covered quarters, 1,000 hours at the minimum wage, care for a child under age five).
- Whether partial years of service are permitted (for example, people earning half the designated threshold receive half a credit).
- Whether and how disabled persons can qualify.
- Future treatment of the benefit level (for example, is it wage-indexed or price-indexed, or something in between)? If the benefit is indexed, when does indexing begin?
- Computation method (for example, is it attached to the PIA, or does it occur after actuarial adjustments?).
- Whether it confers an additional spousal right.
- Whether it unintentionally creates windfalls for groups without strong attachment to Social Security-covered work (for example, uncovered state and local workers, immigrants living in the United States for a short time) and whether prorating addresses such trajectories.[16]
- How well it coordinates with means-tested assistance (for example, does imposing the minimum remove people from – or move people onto – Medicaid and other programs?).

These issues interact in complex ways. Such interactions could lead a minimum benefit design to have extraordinarily high replacement rates, discontinuities (for example, cliffs at which benefits drop markedly), and strong or less strong work incentives/disincentives.

13.3.4 Is a minimum benefit needed?

Simple examples of workers with wages at certain levels for select numbers of years can help illustrate how minimum benefits could work and how some recent proposals for minimums would alter current law (Table 13.2). The table presents the workers in descending level of work effort, starting with a worker who has worked full-year, full-time (that is, 2,000 hours per year) at the federal minimum wage, then showing a worker who worked half as much (also at the minimum wage), and finishing with a worker who earned exactly the threshold for four quarters of coverage in a year (equivalent to $3,880 in 2006).[17] For each wage profile, we compute Social Security benefits for different numbers of years in the labor force (0 through 40)[18]. We examine benefits at ages 62 and 66 (the early eligibility age and NRA for members of this cohort). At NRA, we add SSI benefits (assuming eligibility) to the OASDI benefit, where applicable.

Table 13.2 Combined Social Security and SSI benefits as a percentage of poverty under current law for never married low-wage workers from the 1943 birth cohort

	Career earnings type	Number of work years	Combined annual benefit (OASI + SSI) as percentage of poverty for single person)						OASI replacement rate (current law)	
			Current law				NCRP-style minimum (ineligible)			
			SSI-ineligible		SSI-eligible					
	Claiming age		62	NRA	62	NRA	62	NRA	62	NRA
			1	2	3	4	5	6	7	8
1a	Federal minimum wage ($5.15 in 2005), full-year, full-time (2,000 hours/year)	0	0%	0%	NC	74%	NC	NC	NA	NA
1b		10	38%	50%	NC	76%	NC	NC	68	90
1c		20	61%	80%	NC	82%	NC	82%	68	90
1d		40	76%	99%	NC	100%	NC	100%	68	90
2a	Federal minimum wage, full-year, part-time or half-year full-time (1,000 hours/year)	0	0%	0%	NC	74%	NC	NC	NA	NA
2b		10	19%	25%	NC	76%	NC	NC	68	90
2c		20	36%	47%	NC	76%	45%	60%	68	90
2d		40	56%	73%	NC	76%	75%	100%	68	90
3a	Exactly 4 CQ threshold in all years ($3,880/year in 2006)	0	0%	0%	NC	74%	NC	NC	NA	NA
3b		10	3%	3%	NC	76%	NC	NC	68	90
3c		20	7%	9%	NC	76%	45%	60%	68	90
3d		40	20%	27%	NC	76%	75%	100%	68	90

Notes: Person claims benefits in 2005 (at age 62), does not qualify for spouse/survivor benefit. When reaching age 65, person would be eligible for monthly SSI benefits of up to $603 (2006) if his/her assets (excluding full value of a home) were less than $2,000. SSI calculations assume no earnings or other income besides OASDI and that the worker lives in a state without an SSI supplement. We assume work years commence at age 20 and continue without interruption (that is, a worker with 10 years of work earns at ages 20–29, a worker with 20 years of work earns at ages 20–39, and so on).

Abbreviations: NC – no change from current law; SSI-ineligible person; NA – not applicable (because of zero denominator); CQ – covered quarter; OASI – Old-Age and Survivors Insurance; SSI – Supplemental Security Income.

Source: Authors' calculations.

One striking finding from this table is that at age 62 a worker who had worked for 40 years at the minimum wage would be eligible for an OASDI benefit of significantly less than poverty – approximately 76 percent of the threshold (see row 1d, column 1). At NRA of age 66, the worker would earn a benefit that just reaches poverty (row 1d, column 2). When they turn to age 65, virtually all these workers would be eligible to receive SSI benefits in addition to OASDI if they met SSI's asset tests and had no other income sources (for example, an employer pension).[19] Indeed, except for the minimum wage, full-year, full-time workers, all recipients are only slightly better off on an annual basis with Social Security than they would be had they not worked at all and received only SSI (compare row 1d to 1a in the SSI eligible column 4, where benefits rise, and 2d to 2a and 3d to 3a in the same column, where benefits barely change). Of course, workers can receive benefits for three additional years – ages 62 through 64 – if they accrue Social Security rights, so they are clearly better off on a lifetime basis even if annual benefits do not change much. Also, while these workers' Social Security benefits do not exceed poverty, the replacement rates are high. All the workers have AIMEs that fall below the first bend point under current law, so OASDI replaces 90 percent of their preretirement earnings at the NRA, or 68 percent at age 62. So while these workers may have low retirement incomes, they are not much worse off than they were, on average, before retirement.

With the addition of a minimum benefit styled after the NCRP minimum, Social Security benefits increase significantly for workers in the latter two work categories (full-year half-time work and four covered quarters) in most instances. For example, at age 62 the worker who consistently worked four covered quarters for 20 years would see a benefit increase from 7 percent of poverty under scheduled benefits to 45 percent of poverty with the minimum (row 3c, columns 1 and 5). If that person waited until age 66 to claim, he/she would receive 9 percent of poverty under current law, but 60 percent under this option (row 3c, columns 2 and 6).

Social Security data on distributions of worker benefits (Table 13.3) reveal that these sample workers, while stylized, reflect an important reality: that nontrivial fractions of beneficiaries reach retirement with OASDI benefits of less than poverty. In December 2004, almost half of women Social Security retired worker beneficiaries received benefits of less than 99 percent of poverty, as did about a fifth of men worker beneficiaries.[20] Women's fractions with benefits lower than 99 percent of poverty decrease with age, due largely to many women converting (upon their spouses' deaths) from workers or dually entitled spouses to dually entitled survivors. For men, the age pattern is less clear.

Of course, Social Security benefits of less than poverty do not necessarily translate into incomes of less than poverty. About 20 percent of the aged in 2004 had OASDI as their sole income source, and these benefits made up

Table 13.3 Percentage of retired worker beneficiaries with OASDI benefits of less than 99 percent of poverty under current law, December 2004

Ages	Men	Women
All	19.2	47.4
62–64	21.5	64.7
65–69	17.9	52.3
70–74	19.6	52.1
75–79	19.0	46.9
80–84	20.3	39.6
85–89	18.6	29.3
90+	20.5	27.9

Notes: We use the Census Bureau's aged poverty threshold for all groups, even though Census classifies persons ages 62 to 64 using nonaged thresholds. This table reflects data on worker benefits, so it does not include all Social Security beneficiaries of age 62 and older; workers must have earned a minimum number of quarters of coverage.
Source: Authors' calculations from Social Security Administration (2006a), Table 5.B9.

more than 90 percent of total income for 31 percent (Social Security Administration, 2006b, Table 6.A1). The remaining recipients had other resources, sometimes quite substantial. Because of their strong relationship to lifetime earnings, OASDI benefits tend to be highly correlated with other forms of wealth and income. But individual circumstances vary, so taking other income sources into account when evaluating OASDI reforms can help target resources where they are most needed. (This is especially important for persons with substantial pensions earned in uncovered employment.)

13.3.5 Evaluating a minimum benefit

Relative to the benefit formula already in Social Security, a minimum benefit is similar to increasing the rate (now 90 percent) for the first dollars of average earnings. Under the benefit formula, one only has to work for 10 years (40 covered quarters), so differences arise depending on minimum design issues, especially the way that the formula counts years of work.

By concentrating redistribution on those with lesser lifetime earnings, a minimum benefit can avoid unintended inequities and work disincentives that result from failing to count earnings for years of work beyond 35 toward benefits. Such provisions could redistribute to those with higher earnings if they were more likely to take years out of the labor force. With minimum benefits, however, those with higher lifetime earnings would already be eligible for basic Social Security benefits that exceeded the minimum.

If we spent the same amount on a minimum benefit as we spend on auxiliary benefits, OASDI could more effectively reduce poverty and increase well-being for those aged persons with lower-than-average incomes (see, for example, Herd, 2005). Moreover, it would not leave out single parents and other divorced and never married persons who cannot access the current spousal and survivor benefit and are relatively vulnerable economically.

In sum, a carefully designed minimum benefit has the potential to achieve progressive goals in a more efficient, straightforward manner than do the current redistributive mechanisms in Social Security. We analyze this empirically below.

13.3.6 Expansion of means-tested programs

An alternative to using minimum benefits would be to means test benefits, so that only those with lower incomes/assets benefit from redistribution. Congress has thus far avoided means testing OASDI, and many program advocates oppose means testing, believing that it reduces program popularity.[21] A large amount of literature discusses the relative merits of targeting and universalism in social policy (on OASDI specifically, see Kingson and Schulz, 1997). Often, recipients view means-tested benefits as degrading, and many do not apply for them even when they are eligible. For example, recent estimates of Supplemental Security Income program participation by the eligible aged are typically less than two-thirds (for example, Davies et al., 2002).

Among the aged, a means-tested approach poses additional problems. Many people with significant capability to save for retirement choose not to save. By requiring almost everyone to pay into the system, Social Security minimizes low-saving problems (whether they are due to myopia or "free rider" issues). The flip side to this is that no one is denied benefits because her/his earnings are too high. Second, means tests are less effective at measuring well-being among the aged. While one can reasonably use annual income to identify those who are not well-off among workers, it is weaker at determining who has need (or ability to pay) among persons who can decide whether to work. Choosing not to work typically lowers one's income by tens of thousands of dollars annually, regardless of ability. Meanwhile, those who are relatively well-off can easily recognize little or no capital income (and, in many cases, income from retirement accounts) by holding onto stock that pays few dividends, avoiding realizing gains on appreciating stock, transferring assets into homes that yield no direct earnings (and may not count against program asset tests), or hiding income in foreign assets. Likewise, transferring money to one's children can make an aged person eligible for means-tested programs. Tracking down these types of transfers is difficult and costly. Finally, means tests often impose high tax rates and large marriage penalties on participants (see for example, Balkus and Wilschke, 2003).

Besides these philosophical and administrative issues, program interactions are important in the US social policy context. Simply expanding SSI could create technical issues that might significantly alter costs. For example, many states closely link SSI participation and other programs, such as Medicaid, food stamps, energy assistance, and other supports. Enhancements in SSI's generosity could increase Medicaid costs substantially, which in turn could erode support for reform.[22]

Another issue with minimum benefits is that if they depend on years of work, some people still might not benefit (or benefit enough) to pull themselves out of poverty. One example is partially disabled people with little work experience who do not qualify for DI.

In sum, expanding means testing could target transfers progressively to those with less income, but would raise significant enforcement and administration problems, could generate inequities and program interactions, and many people would consider it degrading. However, some features of a backup means-tested program may still be required, even if primary emphasis were placed on a minimum benefit, depending on its parameters (for example, work years).

13.4 Empirical evidence on designing a minimum benefit based on years worked

Because, as Table 13.1 shows, many minimum benefit proposals structure benefit eligibility and levels on the basis of the number of years one spends in Social Security – covered employment, it is helpful to examine distributions of years in the labor force for today's Americans. Tabulations of Social Security – covered employment from survey data matched to Social Security administrative data (Table 13.4) suggest that men's and women's employment histories differ greatly (Burtless, Ratcliffe, and Moskowitz, 2004). The data show that approximately 20 percent of women and 72 percent of men ages 60 to 64 in 2000 have worked 36 or more years under Social Security. A significant share (21 percent) of women entering retirement (for example, reaching the early eligibility age of 62) in 1998 through 2002 would not be eligible for a minimum benefit that required at least 10 years of earnings (though current law spousal/survivor benefits cover many of these women). However, younger cohorts have accumulated more years of covered earnings, so the group that a minimum based on work years would not cover is shrinking. About 84 percent of all women are fully insured as workers for Social Security, as are close to 90 percent in prime age (Social Security Administration, 2006a, Table 4.C5).[23]

More subtle aspects of covered employment histories impact minimum benefit design, including the issue of whether persons with low wages continue to have low wages for a long career. Over a full career (ages 22 to 61), those with low lifetime earnings are overwhelmingly women, and most have

Table 13.4 Years of Social Security – covered earnings in 2000 for the 1936–1940 cohort, by sex

Years of covered earnings	(Percentage distribution)	
	Women	Men
0	4	0
1–5	9	1
6–10	8	2
11–15	9	3
16–20	10	4
21–25	11	3
26–30	14	4
31–35	16	10
36+	20	72

Notes: Sample excludes immigrants and persons who became disabled or died before age 62. A year of earnings is defined as one having any earnings.

Source: Burtless, Ratcliffe, and Moskowitz 2004. Authors use pooled 1990–1993 panels of the Survey of Income and Program Participation matched to Summary Earnings Records.

low lifetime earnings because of years out of the labor force, not low wages for long periods (Hungerford, 2004). Over shorter periods, mobility is considerable, though less for workers with less education, and with some increase in low-wage work and sustained low-wage work from the early 1980s to the early 1990s (Ryscavage, 1996).

A second minimum benefit design issue is how to handle periods of covered and uncovered employment. Under current law, legislators attempt to avoid providing windfalls (because of Social Security's progressive benefit rate structure) to those with work outside of Social Security – covered employment. Windfall avoidance provisions would need to apply to minimum benefits as well. Similarly, work by immigrants raises similar issues.[24] Designers of a minimum may wish treat workers with substantial fractions of their working lives outside the United States in ways that reflect these complexities.

13.5 Previous studies on minimum benefits

While explorations of minimum benefit design and rationale have been sparse, several recent studies illustrate various minimums' effects. Herd (2005) considers three different minimum benefit types: (1) one that, like NCRP, offers long-career low-wage workers a poverty-level benefit that declines to 60 percent of poverty for workers with a 20-year work history; (2) one that provides poverty-level benefits to workers with at least 10 work years; and (3) a universal one that provides SSI-level benefits to all citizens or residents, regardless of whether their assets meet SSI tests. To offset costs for these latter two types, Herd eliminates spousal benefits. She simulates the alternatives using a simplified microsimulation model. She finds important differences in the minimums' redistributive properties: All have more progressive effects than current spousal benefits. The universal minimum and benefit that requires just 10 work years direct more benefits to the bottom (defined by asset quintiles) than does the minimum more closely tied to work.

Fitzpatrick, Hill, and Muller (2003) focus on Social Security's existing special minimum benefit provisions. They consider expanding it four ways: (1) lowering the number of required years; (2) lowering the level required for a year of earnings; (3) counting partial coverage years; and (4) counting quarters of coverage toward the minimum. The authors simulate effects using survey data matched to administrative records. They find that the changes could greatly increase the number of persons with below-median earnings qualifying for the special minimum, that effects by gender are similar across reforms, and that the special minimum population would become less skewed toward persons with less than a high school education under the reforms.

Favreault, Sammartino, and Steuerle (2002) and Favreault and Sammartino (2002) simulate minimum benefits resembling the NCRP version, both alone as an add-on to the system and combined with other provisions aimed at increasing the system's equity (for example, caps on spousal benefits). They simulate effects using an earlier version of DYNASIM. Their findings stress minimum benefits' efficacy in relieving poverty compared with alternatives (for example, survivor benefit increases). Davies and Favreault (2004) use The Modeling Income in the Near Term data system (MINT) to model a minimum benefit equal to 50 percent of poverty for workers with at least 15 years of work, with 2 percent added for each additional work year (reaching a maximum 100 percent of poverty for those with 40 years). They find that minimum benefits in OASDI tend to be more effective at reducing poverty than SSI reforms (liberalizing asset tests, increasing the general income exclusion, and increasing benefit levels).

Sandell, Iams, and Fanaras (1999) simulate the effects of a minimum similar to the NCRP version. They use longitudinal data matched to earnings records, focus on early baby-boomers, and project earnings on the basis of the administrative records. They find that substantial fractions of this population (21 percent of men and nearly half of women) could benefit from the minimum. The authors also combine a minimum with increasing the averaging period for AIME, and find that the minimum counteracts some effects of a computation years increase.

Zedlewski (2002) considers how minimum benefits (again, styled after NCRP's) might affect OASDI entitlement for women with welfare system experience. Zedlewski constructs representative workers for three groups (those with limited, moderate, and high public assistance usage) using longitudinal data and considers the late 1990s uptick in single mothers' work. She finds that single mothers with the most work (least welfare) experience almost reach poverty-level OASDI benefits at age 62, but this minimum does not help them much at that point. Women with more extensive public assistance experience earn benefits that are farther below poverty, so benefit more from the minimum (though more so at the NRA than at 62). Those in the highest welfare use group end up not much better off with Social Security and additional work than they would have been with SSI alone. In some cases, though, they no longer need to meet SSI's asset tests and can receive benefits for more years, no longer needing to wait until age 65 to collect.

Our study complements this literature. It differs from others (Herd 2005, Sandell, Iams, and Fanaras, 1999; Fitzpatrick, Hill, and Muller, 2003) in that our simulation model is more detailed with a broader population base (the full US noninstitutionalized population in 1992), and can thus focus on younger cohorts that are more likely to experience reform. This should enable us to capture important cohort changes, especially in women's work and marital patterns. It builds on the Favreault, Sammartino, and Steuerle, papers (2002), which use a similar method and focus on alternatives to spousal/survivor expansion, by implementing reforms in a reduced (rather than increased) system. (Of the studies we mention, only Davies and Favreault (2004) use a reduced system as a benchmark.) Finally, we use information on total income to help identify instances in which low OASDI benefits do not signify increased need.

13.6 Simulations

13.6.1 Description of options

In this section, we simulate eight alternative benefit options (plus two sensitivity tests) that target workers with relatively low incomes (Table 13.5). We compare current law benefits reduced due to OASDI's long-term fiscal imbalance with four distinct minimum benefits, one formula adjustment, and then one of the minimums combined with two other often-mentioned reforms. (The two sensitivity tests simulate changes to certain design details.) Like the current law baseline, all simulations are embedded in the context of a reduced Social Security system. We assume that an approximately equal combination of benefit reductions and tax increases will close the long-run fiscal deficit. We process these simulations in a roughly cost-neutral manner, defining cost neutrality as approximately equivalent costs at a point in time (2050).

Table 13.5 Options Simulated

Option	Minimum details (% of poverty by year, work year – 4 CQ)	Solvency mechanism(s)
Current Law with Feasible Benefits		
1 Reduced current law	None	Uniform cuts of 12.45%
Minimum Benefits		
2 Standard price-indexed minimum benefit	55% at 10, increment by 1.5% to reach 100% at 40	Uniform cuts of 12.81%
3 Standard wage-indexed minimum benefit	55% at 10, increment by 1.5% to reach 100% at 40	Uniform cuts of 14.27%
4 Generous price-indexed minimum benefit	80% at 10, increment by 2.0% to reach 100% at 20, increment by 1.0% to reach 120% at 40	Uniform cuts of 13.64%
5 Generous wage-indexed minimum benefit	80% at 10, increment by 2.0% to reach 100% at 20, increment by 1.0% to reach 120% at 40	Uniform cuts of 18.62%
Formula Adjustments		
6 Add a bend point to the benefit formula at the point where benefit equals the poverty threshold	N/A	Reduce upper two formula factors (to 23.6125% and 9.445%); first and new segments retain CL (90%, 32%) replacement rates
Minimum Benefits Combined with Other Well-Known Reforms		
7 Standard wage-indexed minimum benefit with chained CPI	As in 3	COLA cut of 0.50% plus uniform cuts of 7.67%
8 Standard wage-indexed minimum with increase in computation years	As in 3	Increase computation years (to 40) plus uniform cuts of10.22%
Sensitivity Analyses		
9 Standard wage-indexed minimum benefit, but lowest bracket shielded	As in 3	Reduce upper two formula factors by 24.0% (90% bracket is unchanged)
10 Standard wage-indexed minimum benefit, but DI years not prorated	As in 3, except for DI	Uniform cuts of 13.7%

Notes: All options take effect in 2007. Work years requirements are prorated for those on DI (except in option 10). Benefit reductions are across the board for new entitlees and target cost equivalence in 2050. Expenditure time paths of the reforms differ (see Table 13.10).

Abbreviations: CL – current law scheduled; COLA – Cost-of-Living Adjustment; CPI – Consumer Price Index; CQ – covered quarter; DI – Disability Insurance; N/A – Not Applicable

Turning to details of the minimums, we first examine two minimum benefits that are standard for the literature. Our "standard" minimum resembles those found in the NCRP plan (and related congressional proposals) but is more generous for persons who have worked between 10 and 20 years. Instead of offering 60 percent of poverty at 20 work years plus an extra 2 percent for each additional year up to 40, we offer 55 percent of poverty for 10 years of work and an additional 1.5 percent of poverty for each added year (again, up to 40).[25] The first version of this standard minimum is price-indexed, and the second wage-indexed, consistent with NCRP. We then consider two minimum benefits that are on the generous end of those from the literature. Our more generous minimum has some features that are consistent on the top end with Senator Graham's proposal. It starts at 80 percent of poverty for a worker with 10 years of work (more generous than Graham at the low end) and increases to 120 percent of poverty for 40 years (equivalent in generosity to Graham's proposal for a full career). Our minimums thus provide a spectrum of possibilities, although we do not consider minimum benefits that are not conditioned on years of work in some minimal way, as such plans have been rare in recent years.[26]

To implement cost neutrality, we simulated the first option, tabulated its 2050 costs, and determined that benefits needed to be reduced by 12.8 percent for all persons becoming entitled starting in the year the simulations take effect (2007) to meet our goal of resolving half the OASDI financing problem by 2050. When we wage-index the minimum, the size of the required cut is larger – about 14.3 percent. We construct the remaining simulations (the two generous minimums, adjusting the bend points/percentages under current law, and the combination options) so that we spend the same amount of money in 2050. When minimum benefits are larger and reach more people, we institute deeper across-the-board benefit cuts (for those entitled after 2007) in order to have equivalent costs.

By way of comparison, we then change the OASDI benefit formula to protect those with low incomes. Specifically, we add a third bend point (between the first and second) to the PIA formula at the point that results in a benefit equal to the poverty threshold (as defined for those aged 65 and older).[27] Figure 13.1 illustrates how the change works. The dotted line indicates the current law benefit formula's replacement levels, the line marked with triangles shows what current law would look like in the presence of scalar reductions that bring outlays and revenues closer to balance in 2050, and the solid line shows the alternative with the new bend point. Under this alternative, benefits remain identical to current law benefits through a poverty-level benefit and then are reduced progressively, with reductions of 26 percent (from 32 to 23.6 percent) at earnings between the new third and fourth bend points and 37 percent (from 15 to 9.4 percent) for earnings above the highest bend point. Compared with scalar-reduced current law, this formula generates higher benefits up to AIMEs of about $3,600

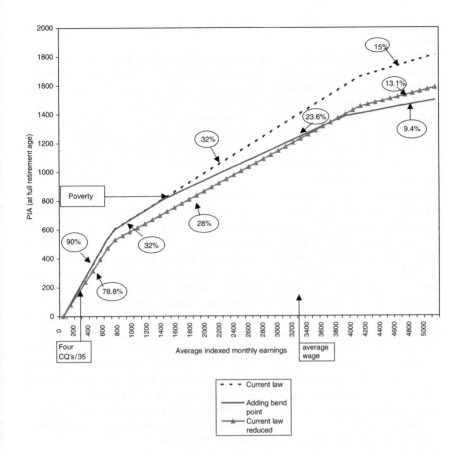

Figure 13.1 Design of simulation with additional bend point (in the context of reduced benefits), compared with current law and current law with scalar reductions

Note: Formula applies to a person first entitled in 2006.

(corresponding to average annual earnings over the 35 highest years of about $43,000) but then (depicted by the point at which the solid line and the line with the triangles cross) generates lower benefits.[28]

We next repeat the standard wage-indexed minimum benefit from above combined with two other frequently mentioned benefit reforms: a chained Consumer Price Index (CPI)[29] – assuming a 0.5 percentage point reduction in the OASDI cost-of-living adjustment (COLA) – and an increase in the number of computation years used for determining Social Security retirement benefits (to 40 from 35). Both of these parameter changes have received. Because the COLA cut and increase in computation years reduce system costs, the sizes of the scalar reductions required to keep these options in balance with the others are lower (7.7 percent for COLA, 10.2 percent for computation years).

Finally, the first sensitivity test again uses the wage-indexed standard minimum and alters the scalar adjustment that meets half the 2050 shortfall. We make the adjustment more progressive by explicitly shielding the bottom AIME bracket (the 90 percent replacement zone) from benefit cuts when making the benefit adjustments. The second sensitivity test considers what would happen if we did *not* prorate the work years requirements for people who are entitled to DI (that is, allow workers to qualify with years of service more proportionate to the length of their career prior to entitlement) for this same minimum benefit.

In all cases, the changes to OASDI (benefit reductions, minimums, and other adjustments) take place in 2007. For each alternative, we compare outcomes on the basis of lifetime earnings (calculated on both an individual and a couple basis for persons who have been married),[30] education, marital status, sex, race/origin, disability status, nativity (US or foreign-born), years of work, and other attributes. We aim to determine whether the alternatives perform better or worse than current law (reduced) on the basis of a set of adequacy, equity, and efficiency criteria. To evaluate performance on the adequacy criterion, we look at poverty rates, poverty reduction, and the fraction of benefits going toward beneficiaries with incomes of different multiples of poverty and in different earnings quintiles.[31] For the equity criterion, we consider fractions of benefits persons in different groups of years worked receive. We examine outcomes in 2025 and 2050 to understand how the effects of the minimums (and other changes) evolve over time: whether they shrink, grow, or stay relatively constant and whether they reach different types of people at the different points. The 2050 estimates, our focus, are ultimately more useful because of the cost neutrality that year.

13.6.2 Methods

Our method for simulating the effects of these minimum benefits is to integrate the proposed parameters into a dynamic microsimulation model of the US population, the Urban Institute's DYNASIM3 model.[32] DYNASIM relies on a starting sample of approximately 100,000 persons from the 1990 to 1993 panels of the Census Bureau's Survey of Income and Program Participation (SIPP). For each year, the model simulates birth, schooling, deaths, marriages, divorces, work, disability, and participation in Social Security. This aging procedure accounts for differentials in processes along important dimensions: age, gender, race, education, and earnings. We calibrate key assumptions about fertility, mortality, immigration, disability, work, and earnings to the assumptions of the OASDI Board of Trustees (2005). As earnings histories are vital for calculating Social Security benefits (and minimum benefits), the model includes a careful imputation of earnings histories based on earnings data from longitudinal sources and administrative records (Smith, Scheuren, and Berk, 2002).

In processing the options using DYNASIM, we assume that people do not substantially change their behavior in response to either the benefit reductions or the new minimum benefits. That is, we assume that they work, earn, and collect OASDI benefits no differently after the change than they did under current law. This allows us to focus on the policies' effects in a relatively simple environment. (Assumptions about behavioral change – especially behavioral change differentials – can be controversial given the absence of empirical data from which to estimate changes.) Because of this simplifying assumption, readers should interpret our results conservatively.

13.6.3 Results: comparing the minimums

Table 13.6 presents the fraction of beneficiaries age 62 and older who receive the minimum benefit under each scenario in 2025 and 2050.[33] All four minimum benefits have a fairly broad reach in 2025. The standard wage-indexed minimum reaches about 11.3 percent of beneficiaries, compared with 6.3 percent for the standard price-indexed minimum. The more generous minimum benefits more than double these impacts. In the wage-indexed case, nearly 3 in 10 persons who have Social Security income receive the minimum. Almost 19 percent receive the price-indexed generous benefit of up to 120 percent of poverty. Of course, in this cost-neutral context, the larger minimum benefits trigger larger benefit reductions than more standard minimums. This means that the benefit reduction qualifies more people for the minimum, in addition to the minimums' reaching farther into the distribution.

The story changes fairly dramatically for the price-indexed minimums when we reach 2050. At that point, the standard price-indexed minimum

Table 13.6 Percentage of OASDI beneficiaries age 62 and older receiving a minimum benefit under four alternative specifications, 2025 and 2050

		N	Standard wage-indexed	Standard price-indexed	Generous wage-indexed	Generous price-indexed
2025						
	All	25,336	11.3%	6.3%	29.3%	18.7%
	Men	11,215	8.7%	4.8%	24.4%	14.4%
	Women	14,121	13.4%	7.6%	33.2%	22.0%
2050						
	All	31,302	15.8%	4.6%	35.4%	12.1%
	Men	14,709	15.1%	4.3%	32.7%	11.0%
	Women	16,593	16.4%	4.8%	37.7%	13.0%

Source: Authors' tabulations from the Urban Institute's *DYNASIM3* (run ID 432).

has markedly declined in impact. Only 5 percent of beneficiaries receive on this basis. For the price-indexed generous minimum benefit, 12 percent receive the minimum. Interestingly, the wage-indexed standard minimum surpasses the price-indexed generous benefit in its reach by 2050. About 16 percent receive a benefit from this provision. The wage-indexed generous benefit still reaches well over a third of persons in 2050, documenting persistence in both need and in the minimums' ability to reach if it is wage-indexed. This does represent a flattening of benefits, and potentially lesser replacement for added effort despite the benefit's tie to work years.

In addition to these aggregate differences, the *types* of people that the minimums reach differ across the four options. Women are far more likely to receive a minimum than men in all four cases. This is even more true in 2025, when women's histories differ more significantly from men's, than in 2050, when the groups have more similar lifetime work experiences. For example, in 2025, the ratio of women to men receiving the standard wage-indexed minimum is about 1.5:1. This falls to 1.1:1 in 2050. Further, the price-indexed minimums reach proportionately more women than the wage-indexed versions in both years. Minimums with broader reach extend farther up the earnings scale, where women earners dominate the distribution less.

Whether people receive the minimum is a limited measure of its reach given our cost-neutral concept. We also need to know *how much* people receive from the minimum and how this compares with their current situation (assuming proportional benefit reductions that bring the system closer to long-term fiscal balance). Table 13.7 displays the *share* of total OASDI benefits that each group will receive in 2050. In terms of aggregate expenditures, the more generous minimums make the system more redistributive toward women. For example, under current law reduced 50.44 percent of total benefits to people aged 62 years and older go to women, while after incorporating the standard wage-indexed minimum directs 50.49 percent of benefits go toward them. The more generous wage-indexed minimum has the largest effect for women as a whole (50.71 percent of total benefits), especially for married women (18.77 percent, compared with 18.32 percent under current law reduced). All four minimums direct higher fractions of total OASDI to persons in the bottom quintile of the AIME distribution (measured both individually and sharing with spouses), those with income of less than twice the poverty threshold, and those with less than a college education. The minimum benefits further lead to greater fractions of benefits for non-Hispanic blacks and Hispanics than for non-Hispanic whites in 2050.

Age patterns in benefit payments under the minimums differ markedly across the various types. Not surprisingly, the wage-indexed minimums have deeper effects at younger ages (62 to 66) in 2050, while the price-indexed minimums are less patterned by age. Of course, the youngest age group is relatively select. Workers who collect benefits at age 62 should be disproportionately female (Munnell and Soto, 2005) and somewhat more likely to be

Table 13.7 Share of OASDI benefits received by different groups at age 62 and older under four alternative minimum benefit specifications, 2050

		N	Share of all persons	Current law reduced	Standard wage-indexed	Standard price-indexed	Generous wage-indexed	Generous price-indexed
All		31,302	100.00	100.00	100.00	100.00	100.00	100.00
Sex and 2050 marital status								
Men	All men	14,709	46.99	49.56	49.57	49.56	49.29	49.51
	Married	8,670	27.70	30.13	30.08	30.11	29.81	30.05
	Widowed	1,986	6.34	7.18	7.10	7.16	6.95	7.13
	Divorced	1,777	5.68	5.66	5.69	5.66	5.70	5.67
	Never married	2,276	7.27	6.59	6.69	6.62	6.82	6.66
Women	All women	16,593	53.01	50.44	50.43	50.44	50.71	50.49
	Married	6,694	21.39	18.32	18.37	18.31	18.77	18.33
	Widowed	5,350	17.09	18.50	18.31	18.46	17.99	18.42
	Divorced	2,637	8.42	8.33	8.33	8.33	8.36	8.33
	Never married	1,912	6.11	5.30	5.42	5.34	5.60	5.41
Age								
62–66		5,740	18.34	15.12	15.43	15.16	15.93	15.21
67–70		5,899	18.85	20.46	20.50	20.46	20.53	20.44
71–74		5,100	16.29	17.14	17.13	17.14	17.12	17.13
75–79		5,360	17.12	17.99	17.90	17.97	17.77	17.96
80–84		4,425	14.14	14.45	14.34	14.44	14.17	14.43
85+		4,778	15.26	14.84	14.70	14.83	14.48	14.84

Continued

Table 13.7 Continued

	N	Share of all persons	Current law reduced	Standard wage-indexed	Standard price-indexed	Generous wage-indexed	Generous price-indexed
Highest grade 2050							
HS dropout	3,381	10.80	7.72	7.91	7.77	8.50	7.93
HS graduate	16,299	52.07	48.12	48.31	48.14	48.77	48.21
College	11,622	37.13	44.16	43.78	44.08	42.73	43.86
Race/ethnicity							
White, Non-Hispanic	19,595	62.60	65.99	65.86	65.95	65.33	65.84
Black, Non-Hispanic	3,675	11.74	10.32	10.45	10.35	10.67	10.41
Hispanic	5,391	17.22	15.31	15.37	15.32	15.72	15.39
Other	2,641	8.44	8.38	8.33	8.37	8.28	8.36
Work years							
Less than 10	1,397	4.46	2.88	2.90	2.89	3.02	2.94
10–19	3,630	11.60	7.81	7.92	7.85	8.49	8.02
20–29	5,594	17.87	15.39	15.41	15.41	15.69	15.45
30–34	4,134	13.21	12.94	12.94	12.93	12.96	12.92
35+	16,547	52.86	60.99	60.84	60.92	59.85	60.67
Immigration status							
Born in US	24,468	78.17	80.94	81.03	80.95	80.68	80.91
Not born in US	6,834	21.83	19.06	18.97	19.05	19.32	19.09

AIE class							
Lowest quintile	6,260	20.00	12.56	13.43	12.80	14.83	13.41
Second quintile	6,261	20.00	15.02	15.29	14.98	16.32	14.96
Middle quintile	6,260	20.00	18.84	18.60	18.79	18.51	18.64
Fourth quintile	6,261	20.00	23.72	23.33	23.66	22.34	23.47
Highest quintile	6,260	20.00	29.86	29.35	29.77	28.00	29.52
Shared AIE class							
Lowest quintile	6,260	20.00	11.69	12.58	11.90	14.22	12.48
Second quintile	6,261	20.00	16.46	16.56	16.43	17.09	16.39
Middle quintile	6,260	20.00	20.15	19.96	20.10	19.71	19.97
Fourth quintile	6,261	20.00	23.62	23.28	23.56	22.51	23.38
Highest quintile	6,260	20.00	28.08	27.63	28.00	26.47	27.78
Poverty level							
< 99.99%	1,322	4.22	1.64	2.03	1.78	2.59	2.03
100%–149.99%	2,241	7.16	4.12	4.37	4.15	5.02	4.30
150%–199.99%	2,406	7.69	5.57	5.69	5.58	6.04	5.64
200%–249.99%	2,557	8.17	6.96	7.00	6.96	7.13	6.97
250%+	22,776	72.76	81.71	80.90	81.53	79.21	81.05

Note: AIE is defined as average indexed earnings (covered and uncovered) from ages 22 to 62.
Source: Authors' tabulations from the Urban Institute's *DYNASIM3* (run ID 432).

disabled. The other age ranges reflect broader, and thus more representative, fractions of the beneficiaries in a given cohort.

13.6.4 Results: Minimum benefits and other adjustments

A central question is whether formula adjustments can be as effective as minimum benefits at achieving certain objectives (for example, ensuring adequate income while encouraging and rewarding work). When we compare the minimums to changes to the benefit formula to add a bend point at a poverty-level benefit and make it more progressive by reducing the upper replacement rates (Table 13.8), we see that in 2050 the formula adjustment has redistributive properties with respect to lifetime earnings that are similar to those for some of the minimums. Here we focus on a comparison with the standard wage-indexed minimum, the most common minimum from the literature. Again, we consider benefit shares for particular groups.

The formula adjustment (in the column labeled "poverty bend point") is more redistributive toward women than the wage-indexed standard minimum benefit with an across-the-board benefit cut for post-2007 entitlees. In 2050, it grants 50.74 percent of total benefits to women, compared with 50.43 under the standard wage-indexed minimum option and 50.44 under current law reduced. It also grants the highest fraction of benefits to those with a high school education and the lowest to those with at least some college education.

However, some equity trade-offs accompany this redistribution. Higher fractions of benefits go to those with fewer years of work under the formula adjustment than under any other option. For example, in 2050, fractions of benefits going to people with less than 10, 10 to 19, and 20 to 29 years of work all increase with the poverty-level benefit bend point compared with all of the other options and current law reduced.

The increased computation years option (in tandem with the standard wage-indexed minimum benefit and reductions for new entitlees in 2007 onward), in contrast, has several desirable equity properties. The share of benefits going to persons with the most (35 or more) work years, as well as the share going to those with at least 20 work years, increases compared with current law reduced in 2050. The option also tends to reduce redistribution toward immigrants compared with the other options and current law reduced. At the same time, it is fairly redistributive toward those in lower parts of the earnings distribution, certainly compared with current law reduced.

Adjustments to Social Security's COLA to account for a shift to using a chained CPI (again, along with a wage-indexed standard minimum) have a substantially different redistributive character than the other simulations. Only this simulation leads to a substantially greater fraction of benefits going to men than to women (compared with current law reduced). To a large extent, this reflects differences in benefits by age, as women are overrepresented at the oldest ages where COLA cuts have the deepest reach. Like the

Table 13.8 Share of OASDI benefits received by different groups at age 62 and older under wage-indexed standard minimum benefit specification and three alternatives, 2050

	N	Share of all persons	Current law reduced	Standard wage-indexed	Poverty bend point	Comp years + standard wage	COLA + standard wage-indexed
All	31,302	100.00	100.00	100.00	100.00	100.00	100.00
Sex and 2050 Marital status							
Men All men	14,709	46.99	49.56	49.57	49.36	49.63	49.94
Married	8,670	27.70	30.13	30.08	29.88	30.16	30.49
Widowed	1,986	6.34	7.18	7.10	7.08	7.11	6.95
Divorced	1,777	5.68	5.66	5.69	5.67	5.70	5.75
Never married	2,276	7.27	6.59	6.69	6.73	6.66	6.74
Women All women	16,593	53.01	50.44	50.43	50.64	50.37	50.06
Married	6,694	21.39	18.32	18.37	18.56	18.30	18.66
Widowed	5,350	17.09	18.5	18.31	18.27	18.34	17.74
Divorced	2,637	8.42	8.33	8.33	8.36	8.33	8.29
Never married	1,912	6.11	5.3	5.42	5.45	5.40	5.38
Age							
62–66	5,740	18.34	15.12	15.43	15.49	15.30	16.17
67–70	5,899	18.85	20.46	20.50	20.47	20.52	21.14
71–74	5,100	16.29	17.14	17.13	17.12	17.16	17.34
75–79	5,360	17.12	17.99	17.90	17.88	17.95	17.76
80–84	4,425	14.14	14.45	14.34	14.34	14.37	13.9
85+	4,778	15.26	14.84	14.70	14.70	14.70	13.69

Continued

Table 13.8 Continued

	N	Share of all persons	Current law reduced	Standard wage-indexed	Poverty bend point	Comp years+ standard wage	COLA+ standard wage-indexed
Highest grade 2050							
HS dropout	3,381	10.80	7.72	7.91	8.10	7.84	7.82
HS graduate	16,299	52.07	48.12	48.31	48.72	48.21	48.15
College	11,622	37.13	44.16	43.78	43.18	43.95	44.03
Race/ethnicity							
White, Non-Hispanic	19,595	62.60	65.99	65.86	65.45	66.07	65.76
Black, Non-Hispanic	3,675	11.74	10.32	10.45	10.55	10.39	10.45
Hispanic	5,391	17.22	15.31	15.37	15.59	15.29	15.43
Other	2,641	8.44	8.38	8.33	8.41	8.25	8.36
Work years							
Less than 10	1,397	4.46	2.88	2.9	2.97	2.89	2.77
10–19	3,630	11.60	7.81	7.92	8.22	7.82	7.74
20–29	5,594	17.87	15.39	15.41	15.78	15.12	15.27
30–34	4,134	13.21	12.94	12.94	13.02	12.77	12.92
35+	16,547	52.86	60.99	60.84	60.01	61.41	61.29

Immigration status						
Born in US	24,468	78.17	80.94	81.03	80.50	81.27	80.97
Not born in US	6,834	21.83	19.06	18.97	19.50	18.73	19.03
AIE class						
Lowest quintile	6,260	20.00	12.56	13.43	13.04	13.41	12.73
Second quintile	6,261	20.00	15.02	15.29	15.75	15.19	14.89
Middle quintile	6,260	20.00	18.84	18.60	19.28	18.43	18.49
Fourth quintile	6,261	20.00	23.72	23.33	23.50	23.26	23.62
Highest quintile	6,260	20.00	29.86	29.35	28.42	29.73	30.26
Shared AIE class						
Lowest quintile	6,260	20.00	11.69	12.58	12.57	12.47	11.81
Second quintile	6,261	20.00	16.46	16.56	17.04	16.40	16.16
Middle quintile	6,260	20.00	20.15	19.96	20.26	19.87	19.86
Fourth quintile	6,261	20.00	23.62	23.28	23.25	23.32	23.61
Highest quintile	6,260	20.00	28.08	27.63	26.86	27.94	28.56
Poverty level						
< 99.99%	1,322	4.22	1.64	2.03	1.85	2.02	1.93
100%–149.99%	2,241	7.16	4.12	4.37	4.52	4.33	4.22
150%–199.99%	2,406	7.69	5.57	5.69	5.91	5.61	5.55
200%–249.99%	2,557	8.17	6.96	7.00	7.18	6.91	6.90
250%+	22,776	72.76	81.71	80.90	80.54	81.12	81.40

Note: AIE is defined as average indexed earnings (covered and uncovered) from ages 22 to 62.
Source: Authors' tabulations from the Urban Institute's *DYNASIM3* (run ID 432).

computation years option, the COLA option concentrates benefits among those with more years of work and, indeed, surpasses the computation years option on several work-years dimensions. Again, this likely reflects the strong age/cohort – gender component of a COLA reduction. Because it contains the standard wage-indexed minimum, this option still maintains redistribution toward those with less education and benefits of less than poverty compared with current law with a simple across-the-board reduction. This option also causes the greatest income loss among the oldest old, who experience the most years of COLA benefit cut.

13.6.5 Results: Impacts on poverty

Our final focus is on the alternatives' adequacy effects. Table 13.9 displays results for the poverty rates and poverty reduction (in percentage terms and number of people no longer in poverty) from the minimum benefits with reductions to Social Security and the three alternative methods for restructuring benefits (new bend point at poverty, COLA cut, and computation years increase). The table also includes results from the two sensitivity analyses. Again, the table population is restricted to Social Security beneficiaries of age 62 and older. Poverty reduction is tracked relative to current law reduced for solvency using the uniform benefit reduction (under which poverty rates are 4.3 percent in 2050[34]).

The more generous minimums, not surprisingly, are highly effective at reducing beneficiary poverty. The more generous wage-indexed benefit leads the pack, reducing poverty by about two-thirds (or over 2.2 million people). The second most effective option with respect to poverty alleviation is the standard wage-indexed minimum in which we do not reduce benefits in the 90 percent bracket. It increases the poverty alleviation impact by over half compared with the same minimum alone without shielding the lowest bracket. This illustrates the importance of the form that any necessary benefit reductions might take.

The poverty-level bend point comes in third in terms of poverty alleviation, with a reduction of about a quarter (or almost 850,000 people). It is followed closely by the generous price-indexed minimum, the wage-indexed standard minimum benefit, and the standard wage-indexed minimum in concert with an increase in computation years (all granting between 22 and 24 percent reduction in poverty).

The sensitivity test in which work requirements for the disabled are not prorated on the basis of the number of years elapsed prior to disability does worse with respect to poverty alleviation than the minimum alone (a difference of about 110,000 people in 2050). This underscores the vulnerability of many in the DI population and the need to be careful to take account of their needs in minimum benefit design.

The least effective option is the more modest price-indexed minimum benefit, which reduces poverty by about 6 percent. Even the COLA simulation,

Table 13.9 Share and number of Social Security beneficiaries in poverty under the options at age 62 and older, 2050

Year	Current law reduced	Poverty bend point	Standard wage-indexed	Standard price-indexed	Generous wage indexed	Generous price-indexed	Computation years plus standard wage-indexed	COLA Cut plus standard wage-indexed	Shield lowest formula factors plus standard wage-indexed	Standard wage-indexed with no DI prorating
N	31,302	31,297	31,284	31,296	31,274	31,285	31,293	31,331	31,287	31,288
Poverty rate	4.26	3.19	3.24	3.99	1.42	3.23	3.31	3.72	2.68	3.38
Change in poverty										
Number of people		−848,000	−806,000	−213,000	−2,240,000	−814,000	−749,000	−429,000	−1,244,000	−696,000
Percentage points		−1.08	−1.02	−0.27	−2.85	−1.03	−0.95	−0.54	−1.58	−0.88
% change		−25.25%	−24.02%	−6.35%	−66.76%	−24.25%	−22.32%	−12.75%	−37.08%	−20.73%

Note: Changes are expressed relative to current law reduction.
Source: Authors' tabulations from the Urban Institute's *DYNASIM3* (run ID 432).

the second least effective with respect to poverty reduction, does substantially better than the price-indexed minimum benefit, with a reduction of almost 13 percent.

13.6.6 Caveats

A few caveats to these analyses are appropriate. First, predicting the future along so many dimensions (work/earnings, mortality, marriage, and so on) is difficult and warrants conservative interpretation. Our assumptions about minimal behavioral response also call for caution. If OASDI benefit reductions lead older workers to work longer, they may enter retirement in stronger financial positions because of lower actuarial reductions to their OASDI benefits and additional savings. Conversely, the high replacement rates that certain minimum benefits impose might lead some low-wage workers to work until qualifying for the minimum but then reduce labor supply in the absence of strong incentives. This chapter has focused on retirees age 62 and older (including disabled workers ages 62 to 64 and formerly disabled workers who convert to retired worker benefits). Including younger disabled workers requires design considerations that we have not addressed. Our estimates have not focused on family structure issues. Designers of a minimum may want to cap couples' benefit from the minimum (for example, limiting minimum benefit payments to spouses of workers with high benefits) so that a minimum does not replicate or exacerbate certain less desirable equity features of spouse and survivor benefits. Finally, while all the proposals have similar costs in 2050, the time paths for these costs differ (Table 13.10).[35] Some simulations front-load benefits, while others back-load them, so that all reach 2050 with similar costs.

13.7 Conclusions

Given that Social Security does not guarantee many low-wage workers a poverty-level benefit, there may be a case for expanding the program's minimum benefits. This is especially true because the system's long-term fiscal deficit is likely to lead to some type of benefit (or benefit growth) reductions. The US retirement benefit system is less generous to those with low lifetime earnings than those of similar countries, and SSI fails to reach a sizable number of people who would be eligible for assistance because of incomplete take-up and asset tests that have not kept up with inflation.

We find that minimum benefits could help reduce aged poverty substantially in the context of a system with benefits reduced to improve the program's long-term fiscal deficit. Minimum benefits that have relatively high requirements for qualification (for example, large numbers of work years) tend to have relatively modest impacts. More generous minimums have broader reach, but sometimes raise issues of equity for long-term workers and inadequate work incentives.

Table 13.10 Time paths of the alternatives: expenditures as a percentage of current law benefits under each of the options, 2010–2050

	Percent of Current Law Benefits								
Year	Current law reduced	Poverty bend point	Standard wage-indexed	Standard price-indexed	Generous wage indexed	Generous price-indexed	Computation years plus standard wage-indexed	COLA Cut plus standard wage-indexed	Shield lowest formula factors plus standard wage-indexed	Standard wage-indexed with no DI prorating
2010	97.850%	98.211%	97.846%	98.040%	98.251%	98.749%	97.656%	97.799%	98.047%	97.864%
2020	91.688%	92.042%	91.331%	91.913%	91.615%	93.061%	91.081%	91.558%	91.562%	91.460%
2030	88.925%	89.105%	88.456%	89.023%	88.414%	89.768%	88.247%	88.711%	88.590%	88.588%
2040	87.986%	87.992%	87.697%	88.015%	87.541%	88.342%	87.612%	87.732%	87.710%	87.745%
2050	87.666%	87.674%	87.666%	87.639%	87.672%	87.648%	87.655%	87.634%	87.644%	87.661%

Source: Authors' tabulations from the Urban Institute's *DYNASIM3* (run ID 432).

Although our analyses are stylized, a few important lessons for designers of Social Security policy are clear:

- Without wage-indexed parameters, many minimum benefit designs would have decreasing relevance over time.
- Trade-offs between adequacy and horizontal equity are apparent. Approaches that do the most to alleviate poverty tend to do less in terms of rewarding extra work. The most generous versions of a minimum could lead to a flatter benefit distribution, reducing Social Security's relationship to earnings, a source of the program's political support.
- Formula adjustments can do about as well as minimums on improving adequacy but could result in less of a tie between benefits and work effort.
- Women benefit disproportionately from minimum benefits in the aggregate. However, when men receive minimums, their average benefit increments are larger than women's.
- The form that benefit reductions take can interact with minimum benefit design. Designs that protect the bottom of the AIME distribution from reductions can greatly enhance a minimum's ability to reduce poverty.
- Minimum benefit designs that do not take into account the truncated work histories of disabled workers will be less successful in alleviating poverty than those that do.

In sum, the most effective OASDI changes are likely to combine parameter changes that improve program adequacy and changes that enhance horizontal equity. Careful analysis will be required to understand interactions between these parameters.

Notes

* The opinions and conclusions expressed in this report are those of the authors and do not represent the views of the Urban Institute, its board, or sponsors. The authors thank Elizabeth Bell and Daniel Murphy for research assistance. Sheila Zedlewski, Robert Triest, David Weaver, and three anonymous reviewers provided many helpful comments. This project would not have been possible without generous support from AARP Public Policy Institute.

1. Exceptions from the literature include Herd (2005) and Fitzpatrick, Hill, and Muller, (2003).
2. We choose 2050 because it is the DYNASIM simulation horizon.
3. Poverty rates in 2004 were 9.8 percent for those of ages 65 and older, 11.3 percent for those of ages 18 to 64, and 17.8 percent for children (DeNavas-Walt, Proctor, and Lee, 2005).
4. In 2003, approximately 5.5 percent of workers (8.2 percent of men and 2.5 percent of women) had earnings above the maximum taxable level (Social Security Administration 2006: Table 4.B4).
5. A comprehensive, lifetime definition of progressivity combines taxes *and* benefits.

6. Friedman (1962) brought early attention to the question of offsetting effects in Social Security progressivity. Aaron (1977) was among the first researchers to examine OASDI redistribution empirically.
7. The average-wage worker calculation was limited because many workers, especially women, drop out of the workforce over their working years. Hence, the average lifetime earnings of a typical worker who earns the average wage are less than the average wages of a worker who works all years.
8. Differential marriage and divorce rates by socioeconomic status, as well as the payroll tax cap, also have impacts.
9. Other redistributive provisions in OASDI include, for example, income taxation of benefits above certain thresholds. This provision's significance is declining because benefit taxation thresholds are not inflation indexed.
10. In 2004, 113,200 persons (less than 0.25 percent of the OASDI caseload) received benefits based on the special minimum PIA (Social Security Administration 2006a: Table 5.A8). Special minimum coverage has declined largely because its parameters are indexed to prices rather than wages. Olsen and Hoffmeyer (2001/2002) and Fitzpatrick, Hill, and Muller (2003) provide detail on the special minimum. Analyses suggest the special minimum will be irrelevant for new beneficiaries by 2013 (Feinstein, 2000).
11. These calculations assume benefit claiming at the full retirement age (age 66 for those reaching age 62 in 2005–2016). Many beneficiaries claim Social Security earlier (with the majority claiming at age 62), and receive benefit reductions to compensate for the longer receipt period. This implies significantly lower replacement rates. For example, individuals reaching age 62 this year receive 75 percent of their full benefit at age 62, implying replacement rates of 38 and 27 percent in the previous examples (for $2,000 and $5,000 in AIME, respectively).
12. In private sector pensions, workers typically pay for spousal/survivor benefit out of their own benefits (for example, they receive lower annuity payments initially in order to pay the expected cost of survivors' benefits).
13. The philosophical underpinnings of this result rely on the notion of a family replacement rate in retirement.
14. Of course, a minimum benefit could be used in combination with, rather than instead of, these other mechanisms.
15. Legislation sponsored by representatives Jim Kolbe (R-AZ) and Charles Stenholm (D-TX) (2002) (H.R. 1793 – 106th Congress, H.R. 2771 – 107th Congress, and H.R. 3821 – 108th Congress), Senators Judd Gregg (R-NH) and John Breaux (D-LA) (S. 2313 – 105th Congress), and, more recently, by Kolbe and Allen Boyd (D-FL) (2005) (H.R. 440 – 109th Congress) included a minimum benefit of this nature. In subsequent legislation Gregg and Breaux substituted a benefit formula change for the minimum benefit (S. 1383 – 106th Congress).
16. These issues played an important role in earlier debates about the minimum Social Security benefit (General Accounting Office 1979).
17. We chose the four covered quarters threshold because, as Table 13.1 shows, several proposals use this value for determining minimum benefit eligibility.
18. These computations require many assumptions. We assume that workers are born in 1943, first collect OASI benefits at age 62 (in 2005), and do not qualify for disability, spouse, or survivor benefits. Work years occur beginning at age 20 in all cases, and last without interruption until the designated end age (29, 39, and 59). The poverty calculations use the Health and Human Services poverty threshold for the contiguous 48 states.

19. SSI's 2006 asset test standard is "countable resources" not exceeding $2,000 for an individual ($3,000 for a couple). In determining countable resources, the Social Security Administration excludes the value of a home and personal effects (within reasonable limits); the value of an auto (up to $4,500 or the vehicle's full value if used for medical purposes); the value of life insurance cash surrender and burial funds (both to $1,500).
20. We chose the 99 percent threshold (as opposed to 100 percent), as it is at a break point in the Social Security Administration (2006a) table (5.B9).
21. Congress did create a means-tested program for the aged and disabled, called Supplemental Security Income, in 1974 to provide a floor for those with low or no Social Security.
22. Similarly, OASDI minimum benefit increases would need to be coordinated with other means-tested programs. In particular, one might want to allow people to qualify for health insurance under SSI or SSI-type programs in cases where they might otherwise lose coverage. (Under current law, Medicaid is available immediately if one receives disability under SSI, but Medicare requires a two-year waiting period under Social Security Disability Insurance.)
23. Fully insured status is defined as quarters of coverage greater than or equal to the number of elapsed years.
24. Immigrants, about 12 percent of the US population, often have limited years of work, leading to lower OASDI benefits. Gustman and Steinmeier (1998) point out that Social Security's formula treats high-earning immigrants with short careers relatively well. Years spent out of the country are treated as zero earnings years, leading to relatively high replacement rates.
25. In defining poverty, we use Census Bureau thresholds for the aged.
26. In all cases, we determine minimum benefits at the point of PIA calculation, with three implications: (1) actuarial reductions and delayed retirement credits apply (so individuals below the normal retirement age when first taking benefits do not get the full poverty fraction the minimum designates); (2) individuals do not "age onto" the minimums (when wage indexing increases the minimums beyond the point at which one would be eligible if entitlement were redetermined); and (3) the minimum can generate spousal and survivor benefits (beyond the worker entitlement). Also, we prorate work years requirements for persons on DI so that they remain proportionate to possible work years (except in the second sensitivity analysis, option 10).
27. We use 2006 bend points of $656, $1,320, and $3,995, compared to $656 and $3,995 under current law. Our rates are 90, 32, 23.6125, and 9.445 percent, compared to 90, 32, and 15 percent under current law.
28. This benefit formula change resembles Pozen-style progressive price indexing (2005) in that it does not implement reductions below a certain point. The change differs from Pozen in that it occurs at a single point in time and does not grow over time. This implies stable (though reduced) replacement rates at middle and upper income ranges.
29. The rationale for a chained CPI is that persons can substitute various goods in the CPI basket as prices fluctuate.
30. We define lifetime earnings as average earnings between ages 22 and 62, where we divide each year's earnings by the average wage. This resembles AIME for Social Security purposes but differs because of the age range and lack of computation years (that is, we do not sort and drop the lowest years).

31. These poverty measures reflect most major retirement income sources. DYNASIM projects earnings, defined benefit and defined contribution pensions, income from assets, SSI, OASDI, and co-resident income. Excluded income sources that Census integrates into its poverty definition are transfer income other than OASDI or SSI (for example, benefits from Temporary Assistance for Needy Families, unemployment insurance, veterans' benefits, or workers' compensation). In 2004, about 3.2 percent of Americans 65 and older had income from veterans' benefits that averaged $8,800 annually, suggesting the size of this exclusion's potential bias (Whitman and Purcell 2005).
32. The specific DYNASIM release that we use is run number 432 (FEH data file date stamped October 26, 2005).
33. This measure is a complex one. For each formula change, it identifies the people who receive the minimum. This is not equivalent to the number of people receiving higher benefits than under our current law baseline, which is reduced to equate costs with revenues in 2050.
34. These rates are low relative to current rates. We expect this because wages (and thus OASDI benefits, which are initially indexed to wages) typically grow faster than prices (and thus poverty thresholds), all else equal.
35. When projecting the proposals' costs, we examine the OASDI program as modeled in DYNASIM. DYNASIM represents retired and disabled worker benefits (including spouses and survivors of retired and disabled workers) but does not currently include children's benefits of any type.

References

Aaron, H. J. with P. Spevak (1977) "Demographic Effects on the Equity of Social Security Benefits," in M. S. Feldstein and R. P. Inman (eds) *The Economics of Public Services: Proceedings of a Conference Held by the International Economic Association at Turin, Italy* (London: MacMillan) pp. 151–173.

Balkus, R. and S. Wilschke (2003) "Treatment of Married Couples in the SSI Program," Social Security Issue Paper No. 2003-01 (Washington, DC: Social Security Administration, Office of Policy).

Burtless, G., C. Ratcliffe, and D. Moskowitz (2004) "Evaluation of Polisim's Employment and Earnings Modules, Revised," letter report to the Social Security Administration (Washington, DC: The Urban Institute).

Caldwell, S. B., M. Favreault, A. Gantman, J. Gokhale, L. J. Kotlikoff, and T. Johnson (1999) "Social Security's Treatment of Postwar Americans," in J. M. Poterba (ed.) *Tax Policy and the Economy, 13* (Cambridge, MA: MIT Press and National Bureau of Economic Research) pp. 109–148.

Chaplain, C. and A. Wade (2003) "Estimated OASDI Financial Effects of 'Social Security Solvency and Modernization Act of 2003' introduced by Senator Lindsey Graham," memorandum to Stephen C. Goss, chief actuary, November 18 (Baltimore, MD: Social Security Administration, Office of the Chief Actuary). http://www.ssa.gov/OACT/solvency/index.html

Cohen, L., C. E. Steuerle, and A. Carasso (2004) "Redistribution under OASDI: How Much and to Whom?" in K. Buto, M. Priddy Patterson, W. E. Spriggs, and M. Rockeymoore (eds) *Strengthening Community: Social Security in a Diverse America* (Washington, DC: Brookings Institution Press) pp. 103–113.

Coronado, J. L., D. Fullerton, and T. Glass (1999) "Distributional Impacts of Proposed Changes to the Social Security System," in J. M. Poterba (ed.) *Tax Policy and the Economy* 13 (Cambridge, MA: MIT Press) pp. 149–186.

Davies, P. S. and M. M. Favreault (2004) "Interactions Between Social Security Reform and the Supplemental Security Income Program for the Aged," Working Paper #2004–02 (Chestnut Hill, MA: Center for Retirement Research).

Davies, P. S., M. Huynh, C. Newcomb, P. O'Leary, K. Rupp, and J. Sears (2002) "Modeling SSI Financial Eligibility and Simulating the Effect of Policy Options," *Social Security Bulletin* 64(2): 16–45.

DeNavas-Walt, C., B. D. Proctor and, C. H. Lee (2005) *Income, Poverty, and Health Insurance Coverage in the United States: 2004*, US Census Bureau, Current Population Reports, pp. 60–229 (Washington, DC: US Government Printing Office). Available at www.census.gov/prod/2004pubs/p60-229.pdf (accessed September 2005).

Diamond, P. and P. Orszag (2003) *Saving Social Security: A Balanced Approach* (Washington, DC: The Brookings Institution Press).

Englehardt, G. V. and J. Gruber (2004) "Social Security and the Evolution of Elderly Poverty," Working Paper 10466 (Cambridge, MA: National Bureau of Economic Research).

Favreault, M. M. and F. J. Sammartino (2002) "Impact of Social Security Reform on Low-Income and Older Women," Project Report for AARP Public Policy Institute, Number 2002–11 (Washington, DC: AARP).

Favreault, M. M., F. J. Sammartino, and C. E. Steuerle (2002) "Social Security Benefits for Spouses and Survivors: Options for Change," in M. M. Favreault, F. J. Sammartino and C. E. Steuerle (eds) *Social Security and the Family: Addressing Unmet Needs in an Underfunded System* (Washington, DC: Urban Institute Press) pp. 177–227.

Favreault, M. M. and K. E. Smith (2004) "A Primer on the Dynamic Simulation of Income Model (DYNASIM3)," Discussion Paper, the Retirement Project (Washington, DC: The Urban Institute). Available at www.urban.org/UploadedPDF/410961_Dynasim3Primer.pdf (accessed December 2004).

Feinstein, C. A. (2000) "Projected Demise of the Special Minimum PIA," Actuarial Note Number 143 (Baltimore, MD: Social Security Administration, Office of the Chief Actuary). Available at www.ssa.gov/OACT/NOTES/note2000s/note143.html (accessed October 2005).

Fitzpatrick, C. S., C. Hill, and L. Muller (2003) "Increasing Social Security Benefits for Women and Men with Long Careers and Low Earnings," paper prepared for Institute for Women's Policy Research Research Conference, 24 June.

Friedman, M. with the assistance of R. D. Friedman (1962) *Capitalism and Freedom* (Chicago, IL: University of Chicago Press).

General Accounting Office (United States) (1979) "Minimum Social Security Benefit: A Windfall That Should Be Eliminated," Report to the Congress, HRD 80–29.

Goss, S. C. (2003) "Estimates of Financial Effects for a Proposal to Restore Solvency to the Social Security Program," memorandum to Peter Diamond and Peter Orszag, October 8 (Baltimore, MD: Social Security Administration, Office of the Chief Actuary). http://www.ssa.gov/OACT/solvency/index.html

Goss, S. C. and A. Wade (2002) "Estimates of Financial Effects for Three Models Developed by the President's Commission to Strengthen Social Security," memorandum to Daniel Patrick Moynihan and Richard D. Parsons, January 21 (Baltimore, MD: Social Security Administration, Office of the Chief Actuary). http://www.ssa.gov/OACT/solvency/index.html

Graham, L. (2003) "Social Security Solvency and Modernization Act of 2003," S. 1878 of 108th Congress.

Gustman, A. L. and T. L. Steinmeier (2000) "How Effective Is Redistribution under the Social Security Benefit Formula?" Dartmouth College Working Paper. Available at www.dartmouth.edu/~agustman/Redistr6.pdf (accessed March 2004).

Gustman, A. L. and T. L. Steinmeier (1998) "Social Security Benefits of Immigrants and US Born," Working Paper 6478 (Cambridge, MA: National Bureau of Economic Research).

He, W., M. Sengupta, V. A. Velkoff, and K. A. DeBarros (2005) *65+ in the United States*. US Census Bureau. Current Population Reports Special Studies, pp. 23–209 (Washington DC: US Government Printing Office). Available at www.census.gov/prod/2006pubs/p23-209.pdf (accessed April 2006).

Herd, P. (2005) "Ensuring a Minimum: Social Security Reform and Women," *The Gerontologist* 45(1): 12–25.

Hungerford, T. (2004) "How Ignoring Earnings Fluctuation in Lifetime Earnings Affects Social Security," *Challenge* 47(2): 90–108.

Kingson, E. R. and J. H. Schulz (1997) "Should Social Security be Means Tested?" in E. R. Kingson and J. H. Schulz (eds) *Social Security in the 21st Century* (New York: Oxford University Press) pp. 41–61.

Koenig, M. (2002) *Income of the Population 55 or Older, 2000*, Social Security Administration, Office of Policy, Office of Research and Statistics (Washington, DC: US Government Printing Office).

Kolbe, J. and A. Boyd (2005) "Bipartisan Retirement Security Act of 2005," introduced as H.R. 440, 109th Congress.

Kolbe, J. and C. Stenholm (2002) "Twenty-first Century Retirement Security Act," original legislation introduced as H.R. 1793, 106th Congress, revised and reintroduced as H.R. 2771, 107th Congress.

Leimer, D. R. (1995) "A Guide to Social Security Money's Worth Issues," *Social Security Bulletin* 58(2): 3–20.

Liebman, J. B., M. MacGuineas, and A. Samwick (2005) "Nonpartisan Social Security Reform Plan," available at www.newamerica.net/Download_Docs/pdfs/Doc_File_2757_1.pdf (accessed March 2006).

Moffitt, R. A. (1984) "Trends in Social Security Wealth by Cohort," in M. Moon (ed.) *Economic Transfers in the United States* (Chicago, IL: University of Chicago Press).

Munnell, A. H. and M. Soto (2005) "Why Do Women Claim Social Security Benefits So Early?" Issue in Brief 35 (Chestnut Hill, MA: Center for Retirement Research). Available at www.bc.edu/centers/crr/issues/ib_35.pdf (accessed October 2005).

National Commission on Retirement Policy (1998) *The 21st Century Retirement Security Plan* (Washington, DC: Center for Strategic and International Studies).

OASDI Board of Trustees (2005) *2005 Annual Report of the Board of Trustees of the Federal Old-Age and Survivors Insurance and Disability Insurance Trust Funds* (Washington, DC: US Government Printing Office).

Olsen, K. A. and D. Hoffmeyer (2001/2002) "Social Security's Special Minimum Benefit," *Social Security Bulletin* 64(2): 1–15.

Pozen, R. (2005) "A 'Progressive' Solution to Social Security," *Wall Street Journal*, 15 March, A20.

President's Commission to Strengthen Social Security (CSSS) (2001) *Strengthening Social Security and Creating Personal Wealth for all Americans: Report of the President's Commission* (Washington, DC: US Government Printing Office). Available at http://csss.gov/reports/Final_report.pdf (accessed March 2003).

Ryscavage, P. (1996) "A Perspective on Low-Wage Workers," *Current Population Reports:* 70–57 (Washington, DC: US Census Bureau). Available at www.census.gov/prod/2/pop/p70/p70-57.pdf (accessed December 2004).

Sandell, S. H., H. M. Iams, and D. Fanaras (1999) "The Distributional Effects of Changing the Averaging Period and Minimum Benefit Provisions," *Social Security Bulletin* 62(2): 4–13.

Smeeding, T. M. and R. K. Weaver (2001) "The Senior Income Guarantee: A New Proposal to Reduce Poverty among the Elderly," Working Paper 2001–12 (Chestnut Hill, MA: Center for Retirement Research). Available at www.bc.edu/centers/crr/wp_2001- 12. shtml (accessed April 2006).

Smith, K. E., F. Scheuren, and J. Berk (2002) "Adding Historical Earnings to the Survey of Income and Program Participation (SIPP)," in *Proceedings of the 2001 Joint Statistical Meetings [CD-ROM]* (Alexandria, VA: American Statistical Association).

Smith, K., E. Toder, and H. Iams (2003/2004) "Lifetime Distributional Effects of Social Security Retirement Benefits," *Social Security Bulletin* 65(1): 33–61.

Social Security Administration (2006a) *Annual Statistical Supplement, 2005 to the Social Security Bulletin* (Washington, DC: US Government Printing Office). Available at www.ssa.gov/policy/docs/statcomps/supplement/2005/ (accessed October 2005).

Social Security Administration (2006b) *Income of the Population 55 or Older, 2004*, Office of Policy (Washington, DC: US Government Printing Office).

Steuerle, C. E. and J. M. Bakija (1994) *Retooling Social Security for the 21st Century: Right and Wrong Approaches to Reform* (Washington, DC: Urban Institute Press).

Whitman, D. and P. Purcell (2005) "Topics in Aging: Income and Poverty Among Older Americans in 2004," CRS Report for Congress, Order Code RL32697 (Washington, DC: Congressional Research Service).

Zedlewski, S. R. with R. Saha (2002) "Social Security and Single Mothers: Options for 'Making Work Pay' into Retirement," in M. M. Favreault, F. J. Sammartino, and C. E. Steuerle (eds) *Social Security and the Family: Addressing Unmet Needs in an Underfunded System* (Washington, DC: Urban Institute Press) pp. 89–121.

Comments to Chapter 13
Robert K. Triest*

Melissa Favreault, Gordon Mermin, and Gene Steuerle have provided a careful, thorough, and much needed, analysis of both the positive and normative aspects of proposals to incorporate a minimum benefit into the US Social Security program. As they point out, there is a strong normative case to be made for such a reform. Although Social Security has features which work toward income redistribution, especially the strongly progressive Primary Insurance Amount (PIA) formula, it does not fare well when its target-efficiency as a poverty-reduction program is evaluated. Favreault's, Mermin's, and Steuerle's simulations clearly show that incorporating a minimum benefit into Social Security has the potential to substantially decrease poverty among the aged.

The simulations are very carefully done, and I find the analysis convincing. In my comments here, I will expand on their discussion of the tradeoffs involved in establishing a minimum benefit. Social Security is an important policy tool for reducing poverty among the elderly, but it is not intended to be primarily an anti-poverty program. Any reform of Social Security must be evaluated not only in terms of how well it increases the target efficiency of Social Security in reducing poverty and near-poverty, but also in terms of how it affects the other objectives of Social Security.

Poverty alleviation versus compensating for incomplete markets

In the design of Social Security, there is a clear tension between the goal of providing near-universal minimally adequate benefits and Social Security's role of filling in a missing piece of the financial and insurance system. Social Security provides a portable defined benefit (DB) pension with real annuitization, a product hard to obtain from private market providers. Moreover, the redistributive benefit formula provides partial insurance against earnings loss prior to retirement – something not available at all in the private market. So, the welfare justification for Social Security extends well beyond that of alleviating poverty among the aged. Social Security helps to solve the problem of incomplete financial and insurance markets, and this aspect of Social Security is important to workers whose incomes are well above the poverty line. Even some of the redistributive aspects of Social Security have value in terms of addressing the incomplete markets problem, and so should not be evaluated only on the basis of their anti-poverty effectiveness.

It is perhaps ironic that Social Security's role in addressing the incomplete markets problem is, in part, the reason why it is so successful as an anti-poverty program. The fact that Social Security provides benefits to nearly all workers has led to its broad political support and the lack of stigma associated with receipt of benefits. The lack of stigma is an important and under-appreciated aspect of Social Security. It results in the take-up rate of Social Security benefits being higher than in virtually any other income transfer program, greatly adding to the program's effectiveness by enabling it to reach more beneficiaries. And the lack of stigma also increases the program's efficiency – there is no "leakage" of the money transferred to beneficiaries into the disutility associated with being perceived, or perceiving oneself, as being on the dole.

In evaluating the merits of the minimum benefit proposals, one must weigh the increased anti-poverty effectiveness achieved through implementing a minimum benefit with the reduction in benefits for workers higher up in the distribution of lifetime earnings. This requires that we undertake the formidable task of gauging the value that workers place on all of the insurance aspects of Social Security, including the limited earnings insurance and real annuitization at actuarially fair rates. It also requires that we consider the potential loss of political support and possible stigma associated with the receipt of benefits if a minimum benefit provision results in Social Security being increasingly viewed as a welfare program rather than as a mandatory pension scheme.

The reduction in benefits to higher income workers would be less of a concern if workers could voluntarily buy a close substitute for Social Security.[1] But close substitutes are not offered on the private market. Private DB pensions are arguably inferior to Social Security due to their lack of portability between jobs prior to retirement, their lack of indexation subsequent to retirement, and their lack of implicit earnings insurance, but are still arguably closer to Social Security than are defined contribution (DC) pensions. However, DB pensions are being gradually eclipsed by DC plans, and Social Security is increasingly the only DB pension available to most workers. The changing nature of private pensions may be increasing the value of the DB nature of Social Security to workers who are well above poverty levels, and argues for caution in moving Social Security toward being more of an anti-poverty program and less of a general social insurance program.

Design considerations

Equity considerations come into play in designing a minimum benefit provision. Most transfer schemes are based on current income, with some test for recipients' asset holdings. Social Security, in contrast, bases benefits on average earnings over a broad swath of one's working life. The minimum benefit proposals generally have a minimum number of years of work required for eligibility, with some minimum earnings threshold for each year or quarter counted for eligibility. We would ideally like to base the minimum benefit on the degree to which a worker utilizes his or her capacity to work, but the Social Security Administration (SSA) lacks sufficient information to actually implement this. The rationale for the minimum years of work requirement is to avoid skewing the minimum benefit's redistributive effect to those with relatively high income per year but few years of work. Some minimum level of earnings is required for a year to count for eligibility because there is a fine line between not working at all and working just a few hours per year. However, the lack of information available to the SSA makes it difficult to distinguish between a high wage individual working very few hours and a low wage full time worker. The higher the value of earnings required for a year to count toward the minimum, the less likely that a low wage worker will be able to qualify. But as the threshold is reduced, it becomes more likely that a high wage worker will qualify with scant work effort. There is no easy way to resolve this problem.

How generous should the minimum benefit be? I think there is a compelling case to be made for wage indexing rather than price indexing of the minimum benefit. Wage indexing would result in the minimum benefit increasing over time at roughly the same rate as the rise in living standards. In contrast, price indexing would fix the minimum benefit in real terms. Over time, it would then decrease relative to prevailing living standards. Expected future increases in Medicare parts B and D premiums also point to the need for a minimum benefit that grows faster than general price inflation.

How should a minimum benefit be financed? Favreault, Mermin, and Steuerle conduct the simulations under the assumption that a minimum benefit must be financed by restructuring of the existing benefit schedule, without an increase in the revenue accruing to the system. Overall, this is probably a wise decision. The prospect of massive fiscal deficits in the future makes it very unlikely that a minimum benefit provision could be introduced if it increased overall program expenditures. However, as discussed above, decreasing the benefits of individuals with relatively high lifetime earnings to pay for a minimum benefit provision may entail a substantial welfare cost. One of the options the authors investigate for freeing up resources to pay for minimum benefits is increasing the number of years of earnings used in the standard benefit formula. It would be interesting to also examine modifying spousal and survivor benefits. As the authors note, the current spousal and survivor benefit arrangements strike many as unfair and antiquated. Reform of this aspect of Social Security may be another promising way of freeing up resources to fund a minimum benefit provision.

Notes

* The views expressed here are those of the author and do not necessarily reflect those of the Federal Reserve Bank of Boston or the Federal Reserve System.

1. Workers can "buy" additional Social Security benefits by delaying their retirement and receipt of benefits up to age 70, but workers may not comprehend that this is the case. I thank Michael Hurd for pointing this out to me.

Author Index

Aaron, H.J., 383n.6
AARP, 5, 55, 56, 57
Aizcorbe, A.M., 4
Alho, J.M., 4, 254
Andersen-Ranberg, K., 36
Anderson, M., 254, 259, 261, 264
Andreski, P.M., 131, 134n.6
Annual Report of the Board of Trustees of the Federal Old-Age and Survivors Insurance and Stability Insurance Trust Funds, US Government Printing Office Washington, The (OASDI Board of Trustees) (2005), 62, 64, 66, 142, 166, 172nn.13, 17, 268, 274, 291, 301nn.3, 4, 5, 302nn.7–8, 13, 14, 303nn.21, 27–29, 307, 309, 348, 368
Annual Statistical Supplement (2005), 309
Antonopoulos, R., 10
Aon Consulting, 200, 214n.9, 318
Aro, A.R., 36
Auerbach, A., 302n.10
Avendano, M., 36
Avritzer, L., 344

Baker, D., 2, 301n.1
Bakija, J.M., 149, 349, 350
Balkus, R., 360
Barbaro, M., 204
Batini, N., 56, 57
Bayott, J., 4
Bell, E., 194
Bell, L., 196
Bell, S., 311n.1
Berk, J., 172n.18, 369
Bernanke, B.S., 1, 2, 9, 16n.1
Biggs, A.G., 14, 301n.1, 306, 307, 308, 310, 311
Blau, D.M., 229
Bloom, D.E., 57, 317
Boe, C., 250, 251, 254
Boersch-Supan, A., 7, 8, 40, 41, 42, 43, 48, 49, 51
Bongaarts, J., 252

Bonsang, E., 34
Booth, H., 251
Bosworth, B., 196
Bourdieu, P., 343
Boyd, A., 353
Brouard, A., 127
Brumberg, R., 178
Buchmueller, T.C., 229
Burdick, C., 14, 270, 271n.3
Bureau of Labor Statistics, 203
Burham, K., 214n.11
Burkhauser, R.V., 130
Burman, L.E., 165
Burns, S., 1, 16n.2
Burtless, G., 64, 65, 361
Butrica, B.A., 10, 131, 141, 143, 144, 171n.8, 209, 210

Cadette, W.M., 138
Caldwell, S., 5, 350
Callahan, J.J., Jr., 131
Callen, N., 56, 57
Caner, A., 7, 115n.1, 333
Canning, D., 57
Carasso, A., 5, 194, 350
Carter, L., 251
Centers for Medicare and Medicaid Services, 3
Chaplain, C., 302n.5, 304n.31, 354
Charles, K.K., 125
Choi, J., 214n.12
Clark, R.L., 130
Cleveland, R., 7, 114
Cobb-Clark, D.A., 229
Cohen, B., 172n.19
Cohen, L., 5, 350
Coile, C., 6, 143
Congressional Budget Office (CBO), 1, 57, 58, 59, 129, 130, 131, 134n.7, 172n.13, 194
Consumer Reports, 130
Copeland, C., 132
Coppock, S., 244
Coronado, J.L., 5, 350

Crystal, S., 322
CSSS, 63, 352, 354, 355
Cutler, D.M., 128

Danziger, S.D., 4
Davidoff, A.J., 6, 143, 241n.5
Davies, P.S., 360, 363, 364
Davis, G.G., 301n.1
DeBarros, K.A., 349
DeNavas-Walt, C., 7, 117, 382n.3
Department of the Treasury, 274, 302n.11
Diamond, P., 143, 352, 354
Disney, R., 250
Dowhan, D., 164
Duleep, H., 164

Easterlin, R.A., 253
Eaton, S.C., 10, 129, 138
Economist, The, 224
Eickelberg, H., 208
Eisner, R., 310, 311n.1
Employee Benefits Research Institute (EBRI), 209, 212n.6, 213, 214n.9
Engen, E.M., 318, 319, 320, 339n.1
Englehardt, G.V., 348
Epstein, L., 85
Esping-Andersen, G., 27, 45
Estes, C., 7
Eurobarometer, 52n.2
Eurostat Data Archive (2005), 26, 27, 28, 29, 30
Eurostat Online Data Archive April (2006), 36
Eurostat Yearbook (2005), 24
Even, W.E., 317

Favreault, A., 5, 15, 146, 161, 171n.8, 348, 350, 353, 363, 364, 389, 391
Federal Interagency Forum, 124, 128, 133, 134n.6
Feinstein, C.A., 128, 383n.10
Ferrucci, L., 128
Finkelstein, A., 6
Fitzpatrick, C.S., 355, 363, 364, 382n.1, 383n.10
Flippen, C., 125
Francis, V., 200
Freedman, V.A., 131, 134n.6
Freeman, R.B., 317

Fried, L.P., 128
Friedman, M., 3, 383n.6
Fronstin, P., 12, 221, 222, 223, 228, 232, 238
Fullerton, D., 5, 350

Gale, W.G., 165, 302n.10, 318, 319, 320, 339n.1
Gan, L., 11, 181, 182, 183, 184, 185, 186, 189
Gantman, A., 5, 350
Garsten, E., 17n.7
Gebhardtsbauer, R., 207, 208
General Accounting Office, 301n.1, 383n.16
Ghilarducci, T., 6, 11, 12, 201, 207, 218
Gilleskie, G.B., 229
Glass, T., 5, 350
Glasse, L., 7
Gokhale, J., 5, 14, 143, 302nn.10–11, 306, 307, 308, 310, 350
Goldwyn, J.H., 171n.8
Golub-Sass, F., 196, 200
Gong, G., 11, 181, 182, 183, 184, 185, 186, 189
Gordon, R.J., 67, 301n.1
Goss, S.C., 302n.5, 353, 354
Grace-Martin, K., 212
Graham, L., 352, 354, 366
Greenhouse, S., 204
Greenspan, A., 5, 302n.12
Gronchi, S., 52n.5
Gross, J., 126
Gruber, J., 5, 6, 43, 44, 143, 228, 229, 240n.2, 348
Guralnik, J.M., 128
Gustman, A., 5, 317, 318, 319, 320, 322, 350, 384n.24

Habermas, J., 344
Haider, S., 152, 153, 172n.11
Hall, K.G., 301n.1
Hamermesh, D.S., 238
Hansen, W.L., 82
Harrington, B., 15, 344
Harrington Meyer, M., 129
Haveman, R., 10, 319, 320, 340n.2
He, W., 349
Henderson, N., 5
Herd, P., 353, 360, 362, 363, 364, 382n.1

Hicks, U.K., 81
Hill, C., 132, 355, 363, 364, 382n.1, 383n.10
Hirsch, R., 128
Hoenig, H., 132
Hoffmeyer, D., 383n.10
Holden, K., 319, 320, 340n.2
Holmer, M.R., 172n.19, 303n.25
Holzmann, R., 52n.6
Hungerford, T., 10, 362
Hurd, M.D., 10, 11, 152, 153, 172n.11, 178, 180, 181, 182, 183, 184, 185, 186, 187, 188, 189, 190, 229, 392
Hutchens, R.M., 212
Huynh, M., 360
Hyndman, R.J., 251

Iams, M., 131, 209, 210, 323, 350, 353, 363, 364
immediateannuity.com, 214n.13
Ippolito, R.A., 214n.11

Janney, A., 172n.19
Jenks, E., 85
Johnson, R.W., 6, 126, 128, 130, 135n.8, 141, 143, 144, 171n.8, 204, 211, 241n.5, 322
Johnson, T., 5, 350
Joslin, D., 127

Kaiser-Hewitt Survey, 6
Kannisto, V., 250
Karoly, L.A., 228, 229, 233, 234, 237, 241n.5, 244, 245
Kelton, S.A., 14
Kennickell, A.B., 4, 317
Kingson, E.R., 360
Koenig, M., 348
Kolbe, J., 353
Kotlikoff, J., 1, 5, 16n.1, 143, 350
Krueger, A.B., 5
Krugman, P., 2
Kum, H., 9, 10
Kuznets, S.S., 85

Laibson, D., 214n.12
Lakin, C., 84
Landefeld, J.S., 85
Langer, D., 66

Lazear, E.P., 237
Lee, C.H., 382n.3
Lee, R.D., 13, 251, 253, 254, 259, 261, 264
Lee, S., 7, 129
Lefèbvre, M., 8
Lesthaege, R., 253
Leveille, S.G., 128
Li, N., 251, 256
Liebman, J.B., 5, 352
Loughran, D., 152, 153, 172n.11
Lumsdaine, R., 143

MacGuineas, M., 352
Mackenbach, J., 36
Macpherson, A., 317
Madrian, B.C., 214n.12, 228, 229, 240n.2
Maindonald, J., 251
Manchester, Joyce, 270, 271n.3
Martin, L.G., 131, 134n.6
Marton, J., 12, 13
McArdle, Frank, 244
McCaw, D., 208
McCulla, S.H., 85
McFadden, D., 181
McGarry, K., 130, 182, 229
McGovern, G., 308, 310
McKibbin, W., 56, 57
Mercer, 200, 208
Mermin, G.B.T., 15, 389, 391
Meseguer, Javier, 271
Metlife Mature Market Institute, 129
Miller, T., 251
Mitchell, O.S., 311n.1, 317, 319, 339n.1
Modigliani, F., 178
Moffitt, R.A., 349
Moon, M., 7, 130, 224
Moore, J.F., 319, 340n.1
Moore, K.B., 4
Moskowitz, D., 361, 362
Mosler, W., 311n.10
Muller, L., 355, 363, 364, 382n.1, 383n.10
Munnell, A.H., 196, 200, 203, 204, 209, 212n.2, 214n.12, 370

National Compensation Survey (NCS), 196, 197, 213n.4

National Income and Product Accounts, 82, 307
Newcomb, C., 360
Nisticò, S., 8, 52nn.3, 5
Norris, F., 63
Norton, E.C., 125
Nyce, S., 201

O'Higgins, M., 84
O'Leary, P., 360
OECD, 2, 4, 7, 63, 64, 126, 127, 132
OECD Factbook 2006, 23, 25, 26, 35
OECD Health Data 2005, 37
Olsen, K.A., 383n.10
Orszag, P., 302n.10, 352, 354

Panis, C.M., 152, 153, 172n.11
Papadimitriou, D.B., 2, 3, 9, 14, 65, 66, 69, 70
Papps, K.L., 212
Penner, R.G., 160, 301n.1
Perelman, S., 34
Perese, K., 6, 143, 241n.5
Perun, P., 160
Pestieau, P., 8
Phelan, C., 228
Phillips, J., 339n.1
Pigeon, M., 66, 67
Pischke, J.S., 5
Plan Sponsor, 208
Population Division, Department of Economic and Social Affairs, UN, 58, 60
Porter, E., 132
Poterba, J.M., 318
Proctor, B.D., 382n.3
Purcell, P., 196, 198, 214n.7, 385n.31

Quinn, J.F., 130

Radner, D.B., 81
Rassell, E., 301n.1
Ratcliffe, C., 361, 362
Rendall, M.S., 81
Rich, M., 132
Rodgers, W., 188n.2
Rogowski, J.A., 228, 229, 233, 234, 237, 241n.5, 244
Rohaly, J., 165
Rosen, S., 220
Ruggles, P., 84

Rupp, K., 360
Rust, J., 228
Ryscavage, P., 116n.16, 362

Saha, R., 353
St. Clair, P., 152, 153, 172n.11, 240n.3
Sambamoorthi, U., 322
Sammartino, F.J., 171n.8, 353, 363, 364
Samwick, A.A., 317, 352
Sandell, S.H., 353, 363, 364
Scheuren, F., 172n.18, 369
Schieber, S.J., 223
Schmidt, L., 11
Schoeni, R.F., 130, 131, 134n.6
Schulz, J.H., 360
Sears, J., 360
Sengupta, M., 349
Sevak, P., 125
Shaw, L.B., 7, 10, 129, 132, 137, 138
Sherlund, S., 319, 320, 340n.2
Short, K., 116n.5
Skidmore, M., 308, 310
Sloan, F.A., 132
Sluchynsky, A., 143
Smeeding, T.M., 7, 130, 352, 355
Smetters, K., 302nn.10–11
Smith, J.P., 187
Smith, K.E., 10, 131, 141, 143, 144, 146, 161, 171n.8, 172n.18, 209, 210, 212, 322, 323, 348, 350, 369
Smith, L., 251
Social Security Administration, 3, 66, 165, 171, 172n.18, 271, 272, 273, 284, 290, 291, 292, 293, 295, 301nn.1, 3, 5, 14, 302nn.5, 14, 303nn.13, 19, 20, 304n.31, 307, 309, 311n.3, 348, 349, 359, 361, 382n.4, 383n.10, 384nn.19–20
Soldo, B., 188n.2
Soto, M., 370
Speare, A. Jr., 81
Spencer, B.D., 254
Spevak, P., 383n.6
Startz, R., 9
Steinmeier, T.L., 5, 317, 318, 319, 320, 322, 350, 384n.24
Stenholm, C., 353
Steuerle, C.E., 5, 10, 16, 141, 143, 144, 160, 171n.8, 194, 212, 349, 350, 353, 363, 364, 389, 391
Stock, J.H., 143

Sun, W., 201
Sunden, A., 203, 204, 209, 214n.12, 317

Taylor, Jr., D.H., 132
Thatcher, A.R., 250
Thompson, L.H., 171n.8
Thornton, D.L., 11
Tienda, M., 125
Tilly, J., 129, 131
Toder, E., 323, 350
Triest, R.K., 16
Tuljapurkar, S., 13, 251, 253, 254, 256, 259, 261, 264, 266, 269
Turner, J.A., 200

Uccello, C.E., 129, 135n.8, 171n.8, 204, 318, 319, 320, 339n.1
UK Government Actuary, 251
UN population projections, 24
Urban Institute tabulations of DYNASIM3, The, 10, 16, 142, 144, 145, 149, 151, 153, 155, 156, 158, 159, 167–70, 175, 210, 347, 368, 369, 371–3, 375–7, 379, 381
US budget 2004, 195
US Census Bureau, 15, 61, 82, 83, 84, 85, 108, 115, 116n.5, 124, 131, 164, 196, 203, 214n.12, 228, 255, 259, 268, 317, 340nn.5, 15, 359, 368, 384n.25, 385n.31
US Chamber of Commerce, 198, 199, 214n.8
US Department of Labor, Pension, and Welfare Benefits Administration, 318
US Government Accountability Office (USGAO/GAO), 5, 207, 214n.10, 125, 131, 224, 383n.16

Valletta, R.G., 229
Van den Bosch, K., 34
VanDerhei, J., 132, 199, 200, 214n.9
Vanguard Group, 209
Van Houtven, H., 125

Vaupel, J.W., 250
Velkoff, V.A., 349
Venti, S.F., 318

Wade, A.W., 302n.5, 304n.31, 353, 354
Walker, D., 302n.12
Wallace, R., 188
Walsh, M.W., 200
Watkins, M., 208
Weaver, K., 352, 355
Webster, B.H. Jr., 7, 114
Weil, D., 74, 75, 76
Weinberg, D., 4
Weisbrod, B.A., 82
Weisbrot, M., 2, 301n.1
Weller, C., 207, 208, 209, 301n.1, 311n.7
Wellington, A.J., 229
Whitehouse, E., 5
Whitman, D., 385n.31
Wiatrowski, W.J., 202
Wiener, J.M., 126, 129, 131
Wilke, C.B., 33
Willems, P., 253
Wilschke, S., 360
Wise, D.A., 5, 143, 318
Wolf, D., 43, 44, 126, 127, 134n.7
Wolfe, B.L., 11, 13, 319, 320, 340n.2
Wolff, E.N., 4, 5, 7, 9, 10, 14, 15, 84, 115n.1, 195, 209, 311n.7, 315, 317, 319, 320, 333, 340n.2, 343, 344, 345, 346
Woodbury, S.A., 12, 13
Wray, L.R., 2, 3, 9, 14, 65, 66, 67, 69, 70, 73, 75, 76, 77, 78, 311n.1
www.ssa.gov/policy/docs/statcomps/ income_pop55/2002, 213n.3

Yaari, M., 178

Zacharias, A., 5, 9, 10, 84, 115n.1, 333
Zebrak, A., 244
Zedlewski, S.R., 353, 364
Zissimopoulos, J., 152, 153, 172n.11

Subject Index

activities of daily living (ADL), 126, 129
actuarial balance, 3, 14, 260–1, 272–6, 278–83, 290–6, 299, 300–2, 307–9
  and annual balances, under faster wage growth, 287–92
  response under full calibration, to US demographics, 285–7
  SSASIM, 293–5
adult day-care facilities, 127, 133
aged dependency ratio, 54, 57–9, 66, 67, 68, 71
aging, 1
  of baby-boom, 249, 257
  budgetary and macroeconomic implications of, 249, 266–71, 272, 306–10: actuarial balance, 285–92; demographic forecasts, 250–5; pension system and risk, 259–64; population projections, 255–9; public health care spending and policy, modeling, 264; Social Security financing, simple model, 276–85; SSASIM, 292–5
  burden of, 9, 53–6
  population, 2, 13, 16, 24, 45, 48, 53, 62–3, 71, 141, 160, 266, 268
  process, 23, 38, 368
  society, 50, 67, 71
  tracking, 57–8
annuity, 7, 81–3, 90, 108, 116, 147–9, 152–3, 161, 167–8, 171, 181, 184, 204–6, 218–19, 336, 338–9, 341, 383
Austria, 26–30, 32, 34–7, 42–3, 132
average indexed monthly earnings (AIME), 272, 323, 350, 358, 363, 382

baby-boom, 4, 7, 59, 68, 69, 209, 224, 249, 257, 284, 310, 363
Bayesian techniques, 271
bequeathable wealth, 11, 178–9, 180, 182–3, 185–6
base income, 82–3, 88–9, 109, 112, 114, 115, 119

Belgium, 26–30, 32, 35–7, 44

caregiver, 125–7, 137
  paid, 129
  spouse, 126, 128
  tax credits, 127
  unpaid, 123, 125–7, 130
childcare support systems, 9
Commission to Strengthen Social Security (CSSS), 352
Congressional Budget Office (CBO), 1, 134n.7, 311n.3
consumption, 34, 77, 84, 145, 148, 150, 159, 171n.2, 177, 178–9, 220, 268, 318, 320
  model, by singles, 179–87
  see also public consumption
Continuing Care Retirement Community (CCRC), 123, 130, 133
Current Population Survey (CPS), 15, 164, 196, 340

defined benefit (DB), 4, 6, 51, 165, 196, 198, 199–200, 204, 213n.5, 321–2, 323, 324
  argument against, 202
  versus 401 (K) simulations, 203–6
  policy implications, 206–8
defined contribution (DC), 6, 11, 51, 132, 145, 150, 152, 157, 164–5, 171, 193, 196, 207, 233, 315, 385, 390
dementia, 126, 128
demographic dividend, 57, 59
demographic forecasts
  fertility, 253–5
  migration, 255
  mortality, 250–3
demographic trends, 9, 13, 56–63, 69, 73, 137
  burden of aging, 53–6
  Social Security systems, implications for, 63–71

Subject Index 399

Denmark, 26–30, 32–8, 42–3, 45
dependents, 70, 228
   old, 73
   young, 73
disability, 3, 5, 27, 35, 38, 43, 45, 49, 64, 125, 127–8, 131, 138, 142, 148, 153, 162–4, 166, 179, 230, 259, 261, 271n.1, 301n.2, 303n.21, 307, 350, 368, 378, 383n.18
disability insurance prevalence, 5, 43, 45, 259, 271
disability pensions, 38
   generosity of, 43
disparities, 9, 10, 88, 92, 94, 100, 108, 116n.11, 351
   race/ethnicity, 90, 115
   sex/marital status, 87, 115
Dynamic Simulation of Income Model (DYNASIM), 10–11, 145–9, 152, 154, 161–2, 164–6, 171n.1, 8, 172n.13, 347, 363, 368–9, 382n.2, 385n.31, 32, 35

early-retirement incentives, 42–5
earnings, 7–9, 10, 14, 33, 82, 85, 116n.16, 141–6, 148–9, 150, 152, 156, 159, 160, 164, 166, 171n.1, 2, 6, 8, 18, 194–5, 208, 213, 214n.12, 272, 301n.2, 308–10, 311n.8, 318–19, 320–4, 340n.2, 348–50, 351–2, 358–9, 360–1, 363, 366–70, 374, 380, 382n.4, 385n.31, 389–91
   future, 3
   lifetime, 5, 8, 15–16, 18, 152–3, 160, 163, 172n.13, 350, 359, 361–2, 368, 374, 383n.7, 384n.24, 30, 390
   retirement, 145–7, 272
economic well-being of the elderly/nonelderly, 6, 7, 81, 118–22, 137–8
   base income, 88–9
   eldercare, in future, 130–3
   government expenditures and taxes, 92–100
   home and nonhome wealth income, 89–92
   household production, 100–1
   inequality, 108–14
   leisure, 127

LIMEW, 81–5, 100–7, 118–20
   old old-age and need for care, 128–30
   paid worker, working longer, 124–5
   unpaid work, caregiving responsibilities, 125–7
economy, 1, 4, 9, 14–15, 25, 38, 67, 70, 73, 77–8, 141–2, 154, 160, 245, 266, 301n.2, 303n.23, 306–8, 310, 315
effective demand, 66, 67, 70
eldercare, 126–8, 130–3, 137–8
emigrant health care sector workers, 56
employee benefits, 6, 13, 132, 154, 190, 201, 214n.9, 221, 243, 245
employer pension system, 11, 193, 207, 212n.3, 218–19
   coverage, shrinking, 196–8
   and DCs, 202–6
   government spending on elderly and tax expenditure, 194–5
   middle class retirement income and household saving, 195–6
   pension spending and pension security, disconnect between, 198–201
   policy implications, 206–8
employer-provided plans, 11
equity, 5, 7, 69, 89, 108, 132, 165, 219, 349, 363, 368, 374, 382, 391
EU15 countries, 8, 23, 27, 38
European Welfare states and generosity, 23
   causes: demography, 38–40; early retirement incentives, 42–5; political preferences, 40–2
   towards elderly, 27–8
   general generosity, welfare state size, 25–7
   old versus young, relative generosity and crowding out, 29–31
   policy outcomes, 31–8: health and longevity, 36–8; income, wealth and consumption distribution, 34; income levels, 33–4; youth and elderly unemployment, 35–6
   towards young, 28–9
   see also welfare state

Subject Index

Extended Care Career Ladder Initiative (ECCLI), 138
Extended Income (EI), 10, 108, 115, 119
  decomposition of, 111
  LIMEW, comparison with, 83
  Lorenz curve, 110

federal income taxes, 99–100, 143, 165
fertility, 2, 3, 8, 13, 23, 48, 54–5, 56, 57–9, 62, 63, 149, 249–50, 253–6, 258, 261, 264, 267–8, 271n.2, 291, 368
Financial Accounting Statement (FAS 106), 12, 223–4, 243
financial assets, 53, 69, 82
financial crisis, 2–3
financial provisioning, 3, 53, 69
fiscal balances, 4, 13, 370
fiscal imbalances, 6, 364
forecasting, 3, 13, 14, 175, 181, 249, 266–71, 307, 311n.3
  demographic forecasts, 250–5
  health expenditure and public policy, 264
  pension systems and risk, 259–64
  population projections, 255–9
formal long-term care, 129
formula adjustments, 365, 374, 382
401(k) plans, 12, 193, 194, 196, 198, 200–1, 203–6, 208–9, 218–19, 318, 321
France, 26–30, 32–7, 41–4, 63, 253

gender disparities and economic wellbeing, 10
  differing prospects, 123, 137–8
  net government expenditures, 81, 118–22
gender gaps, in earnings and working conditions, 10
generosity, 8, 43, 45–6, 55, 154, 224, 361, 366, 369–70, 378, 380, 382, 391
  towards the elderly, 2, 27–8, 29–32, 42
  size, of welfare states, 25–7
  towards the young, 25, 28–9, 29–32
Germany, 2, 16n.3, 26–30, 32–4, 36–7, 40–4, 63, 132
Gini ratios, 109–10, 114

global competitive pressure, 66
government cash transfers, 82, 84, 92–100
government expenditures, 16, 81–2, 84, 96–8, 103–7, 109, 112, 114–15, 130, 133
  and taxes, 92
Government spending, 1–16, 45, 50, 131, 132, 150, 310
  and tax expenditures, 194–5
government transfer programs, 75
gross money income, 7, 85, 88, 114

health and longevity, 8, 25, 33, 36–8
Health and Retirement Study (HRS), 6, 12, 125, 220–1, 227, 229, 233, 317
health care, 2, 12, 49, 55, 131, 212, 264
  cost, 1, 6, 17, 220, 243
  income, 56
health insurance (HI), 12, 82, 143, 220, 224, 228, 232, 243, 245, 317
health status, 36, 43, 177, 221, 229, 232, 233, 235
household characteristics, 8, 81, 89, 90, 92, 93, 94, 95–6, 97, 102, 126, 315–16, 319–20
  African Americans, 87
  Asians, 85–6
  elderly, 85–6
  Hispanics, 87
  non elderly, 85–6
household production, 9, 82–5, 100–1, 103, 107, 112, 116n.15, 119
household saving, 195–6, 318, 340n.2

immigration, 3, 9, 13, 55–6, 62, 131, 164, 249–50, 255–6, 267, 307, 350, 368, 372, 377
income, 4, 7, 9–10, 33–4, 81, 121, 149–54, 195–6, 315, 318–20, 326, 333–8
  base income, 88–9
  equality, 34
  from home wealth, 89–91, 107–8, 111–14, 116n.8, 119
  nonhome wealth, 89, 90–2, 103, 108–9, 111–15, 116n.14, 15, 16, 119

Subject Index 401

income distribution, 5, 11, 34, 195
India, 56, 75–6, 249
Individual Retirement Accounts (IRA's), 5, 166, 194, 219, 321
inequality, 4, 5, 7–9, 14–15, 16n.5, 23, 25, 31, 34, 46, 82, 115, 116n.16, 118–19, 131, 171n.8, 195, 298, 308, 317, 325, 343–5
  among elderly/non elderly, 108–14
  see also Gini ratios
Ireland, 25–30, 32, 36–8
Instrumental Activities of Daily Living (IADL), 126, 129, 134n.1
Intensive care, 126
investment, 4, 54, 68, 70, 77, 132, 166, 208, 218, 219, 268, 271n.2, 345
Italy, 2, 16n.3, 26–38, 40–4, 51–2, 56, 62–4, 67, 255

Japan, 2, 16n.2, 24, 35–8, 44, 56–7, 62, 67, 75–6, 132, 253

labor markets, 5, 9, 35, 54, 67, 208, 210, 220, 221, 233, 344
labor productivity, 66, 267
Lee-Carter method, 251–2
leisure, 23, 25, 50, 120, 124, 127, 142, 177, 210, 240
Levy Economics Institute, 5, 46
Levy Institute Measure of Economic Well-being (LIMEW), 9, 81, 103, 119
  components of the, 82
lifetime benefits, 5, 10, 16n.6, 141, 145, 154, 159, 349, 351
lifetime contributions, 5, 16n.6
liquidation, 69
Lisbon Target, 36
longevity, 3, 8, 25, 33, 36, 54, 62–3, 66, 68, 246, 291
long-term care insurance, 130, 138
  see also reverse mortgages

Maastricht process, 45, 48
Massachusetts Nursing Home Quality Care Initiative, 138
mean retirement income, 334–5
Measurement of Economic and Social Performance (MESP), 317

median age, 57
Medicaid, 1–4, 10, 94, 98–9, 120–1, 123, 125, 127, 129–34, 137–8, 212n.1, 356, 361, 384n.22
Medicare, 1–3, 5–7, 10, 12, 16n.1, 98–9, 120–1, 123, 128–9, 130–2, 134, 137, 145, 148, 160, 178, 194, 210, 212n.2, 220, 223–4, 227–8, 234, 238, 240n.1, 244–5, 384n.22, 391
migration, 250, 255
minimum benefit, 15–16, 160, 347, 350, 352–6, 365, 366, 367–71, 380, 382, 383nn.14, 15, 17, 384nn.22, 26, 389–92
  and other adjustments, 374–8
  empirical evidence, on designing, 361–2
  evaluating, 359–60
  key design parameters in, 356
  needfulness, 356–9
  previous studies, 362–4
  see also Social Security
minorities, 15, 124, 329, 334, 336, 337–8, 339
Modeling Income in the Near Term data system (MINT), 363
money income (MI), 7, 81, 84–5, 101, 103, 108, 114–15, 116n.11, 16, 118–19, 121, 213
Monte Carlo simulation, 260, 269–70
mortality, 7, 13, 56–7, 59, 62, 145, 152, 250–3, 282, 303n.19

National Income and Product Accounts (NIPA), 82, 84, 307
noncash transfers, 7, 81, 84, 92, 94, 98, 103, 108, 119, 120
Normal Retirement Age (NRA), 6, 14, 51, 63, 125, 145, 147, 150, 152, 160, 171n.4, 175, 176, 261, 303n.21, 341n.16, 350, 384n.26
Notional Defined Contribution (NDC) pension scheme, 51
Nursing home care, 125, 126, 127, 129, 132–3

Old Age and Survivors and Disability Insurance (OASDI), 5, 259, 271

old-age benefits, 11, 64
old-age dependency, 75, 76, 256–7
old-age pension, 2, 43, 65
Old Age Survivors Insurance (OASI), 350
Organization for Economic Co-operation and Development (OECD), 8, 63, 138

Panel Study of Income Dynamics (PSID), 5, 320
'paygo' benefit systems, 63–4
payroll tax, 2, 4, 70, 132, 142, 154, 296, 311n.8
revenue, 69
pension
coverage, 12, 163, 165, 193, 195–6, 198, 201, 213n.5, 214n.7, 218, 229–30, 237
plan, 165, 196, 198, 206–7, 214n.10, 230, 233, 315, 318, 340n.12, 345
spending, 2, 193, 198–9
systems and risks, 259
wealth, 4, 15, 120, 145, 147, 150, 160, 171n.6, 195, 316–17, 321–5, 327, 329, 332–3, 337, 340n.9, 343
Philippines, 56
policy
combinations, 264
implications, 6, 206, 221, 289
makers, 3, 7, 9, 206, 211, 272, 343–4
objectives, 264
outcomes, 8, 25, 31, 36, 266, 268–9, 270–1
political preferences, 40–2, 45
population bomb, 54
population projections, 24, 250, 255–9, 260
Portugal, 25–30, 32, 36–7
poverty, 15, 25, 31, 334–7, 348, 358–9, 363, 366, 372, 383n.18, 384n.25
impacts on, 378–80
reduction, 34, 349, 368, 378, 380, 389–90
Primary Insurance Amount (PIA), 323, 333, 350, 352, 384n.26, 389
private and public provisioning, interaction between
employer pension, changing role of, 193

retiree health benefit coverage and retirement, 220, 243–6
private pensions, 4, 5, 15, 65, 316, 318, 326, 345, 390
privatization, 63, 260, 310
probabilistic forecasts, 13, 249, 254
productive capacity, 4, 70
productivity growth, 3, 9, 53, 65–7, 71, 160, 194, 259, 272, 273, 290, 292–4, 303n.23, 304n.29
progressive formula, 15, 272, 350–1
public consumption, 9, 84, 94–8, 99, 100, 108–9, 120
educational expenditures, 94
public health care spending, 264
public pensions, 4, 33, 34, 43, 51, 65, 268

racial disparity, 90
real provisioning, for elderly, 3, 9, 53, 69
redistributive provisions, 15, 383n.9
reform proposals, 5, 8, 41, 304n.31, 347
regression, 30–1, 164, 323
based analysis, 244
fixed effects, 38
ordinary least squares (OLS), 38
replacement rates, 47, 143, 177, 320, 333, 337–9, 348, 350, 356, 358, 374, 380, 383n.11, 384n.24, 28
Retiree Health Benefit (RHB), 6, 12, 13, 220, 243–6
empirical findings, 234–8
empirical model and data, 229–34
existing research, 228–9
implications and extensions, 238–40
trends and changes, in health coverage, 221–8
retirement, 141, 175–7, 189–90
additional work effects: on general revenues, 157–9; on Social Security, 154–7
age, 6, 14, 40, 50, 63, 125, 142, 145–8, 153–4, 159–60, 175–6, 260–1, 265, 303n.21, 310, 322, 327, 341n.16, 348, 350, 352, 383n.11, 384n.26
and augmented wealth (AW), 326–33
benefits 11, 145, 161, 171n.8, 272, 279, 367
communities, 127, 132–3

Subject Index 403

retirement – *continued*
  credit, 6, 147
  DYNASIM, 145–9
  earnings and taxes, 144–5
  income adequacy, 15, 315–16, 318–20, 333–8
  income and wealth increase, for individuals, 149–54
  literature review, 143–4
  minimum benefits, in Social Security, 347, 389–2
  net intergenerational transfers, 178–87
  pension, 144–5
  policy, 16, 206, 347, 352
  savings adequacy, 318–19
  security, of workers, 11, 144–5
  soon-to-retire workers, 315, 343–6
  systems, 2
retirement wealth (RW), 316, 317, 319, 325, 326, 327–8, 334, 344
  by marital status, 331–3
  by race, 328–31
retrenchment, 25, 40–1, 45
reverse mortgage, 132

Scandinavian countries, 25, 28, 30
Senior Income Guarantee (SIG), 352, 356
single currency, 8, 45, 48
Slovak Republic, 35
social accounting, 84
social expenditures, 23, 25–8, 29, 32, 34, 38, 43, 45, 49
Social Security
  adequacy/progressivity, 348–9
  benefits, 5, 92, 124, 141–3, 145–7, 149, 152, 159–60, 165–6, 187–9, 171, 178, 183–4, 187, 189, 190, 195, 208
  caveats, 380
  contributions, 50, 194, 321
  equity, 349
  evaluation, 349–50
  existing provisions, 350–1
  financial status, 272, 295, 302n.13
  generosity of schemes, 8
  long-term funding imbalance, 272
  means-tested programs, expansion of, 360–1
  minimum benefit, 352–60, 361–4, 374–8
  poverty, impact on, 378–80
  provision, 360
  revenues, 16, 53
  shortfalls, 288, 296
  simulations, 364–74
Social Security Administration (SSA), 5, 171, 172n.18, 259, 260, 266, 284, 292, 295, 301n.5, 302n.13, 303nn.19, 20, 304n.31, 348, 384nn.19, 20, 391
Social Security and Accounts Simulator (SSASIM), 14, 276, 303n.28, 304n.30
  performance, relative to SSA estimates, 292–3
  perpetuity estimate of sensitivity, 293–5
  simulations under Social Security model, 292
social insurance programs, 7, 127, 275
Social Security Trust Funds, 3, 11, 14, 142, 144, 147, 271
  see also trust fund
Social Security wealth (SSW), 147, 150, 164, 166, 182, 183, 317, 322–4, 326
spousal and survivor benefits, 15, 351, 384n.26, 392
standard wage-indexed minimum, 367, 370, 374, 378
Statistical Office of the European Communities (EUROSTAT), 24
Stochastic population forecasts, 13, 249
Survey of Consumer Finances (SCF), 15, 121, 315, 317, 321–2, 324, 340n.11
Survey of Health, Aging and Retirement in Europe (SHARE), 8, 33, 34, 36–7, 38, 45
Survey of Income Program Participation (SIPP), 12, 166
Sweden, 2, 16n.3, 25–30, 32, 34–7, 43–4, 51, 64, 127, 253
Switzerland, 26, 37–8, 43

taxation, 2, 4, 149, 165, 303n.21, 308, 311n.7, 345, 349, 383n.9
  see also federal income taxes
taxes, 1, 3–4, 6, 9, 41, 48–9, 57, 63, 70, 81, 84, 92, 96, 100, 103, 108–9, 114, 119–21, 141–50, 152, 154, 157, 159,

taxes – *continued*
  161, 165, 171n.2, 6, 172n.13, 15, 212n.2, 249, 260, 262–3, 276–7, 287, 302n.10, 303n.26, 310, 311n.2, 8, 318, 349, 351, 382n.5
tax expenditure, 11, 193, 194–5, 196, 198, 206, 209
tax favoritism, 11, 193, 206
taxpayers, 50, 165, 249, 349
total dependency ratio, 58, 68, 268
trained professionals, 56
transfer payments, 4, 7, 75, 143, 194, 257
trust fund, 14, 63, 69–70, 71, 142, 166, 262, 301n.3, 306, 310
  see also Social Security Trust Funds
Turkey, 35

unemployment, 1, 8, 25, 31, 49–50, 52n.1, 54–5, 64, 66, 71, 125, 210, 212, 230, 268, 315, 350, 385n.31
  youth and elderly, 35–6
United Kingdom, 16n.3, 26–30, 32, 35–7, 44, 64, 127
United States, 1–4, 6, 9–10, 16n.3, 25, 35–8, 53–6, 58, 62–5, 67–9, 75, 77, 82, 126, 132, 138, 220, 250–4, 256, 259, 276, 283–4, 287, 290, 340n.5, 346, 356, 362
US Census Bureau, 11
US Social Security System, 250, 287, 288, 290
  solvency, 10

wealth, 7, 11, 15, 81, 82–4, 108–9, 112, 114, 147–8, 149–4, 178, 180–1, 182–7, 316–17, 321, 324–6, 337
  augmented wealth, 326–33
  distribution, 34
  income, from home and nonhome wealth, 89–92, 103, 119
  pension wealth, 321–2
  retirement wealth, 316, 317, 319, 325, 326, 327–34, 344, 345
  Social Security wealth, 322–3
welfare provisions, 48, 50
welfare state, 48–51, 73–8
  cautious optimism, 50–1
  generosity, 8, 34, 45–6
  global demographic trends and provisioning for future, 53: burden of aging, 53–6; demographic trends, 56–63; Social Security systems, implication for, 63–71
  young versus elderly people, 49–50
  see also European Welfare states and generosity
worker-to-beneficiary ratio, 275–7, 278–9, 280–6, 291–2, 294, 296, 301
working age population, 1, 58–9

youth dependency ratio, 54, 56, 57, 58–9, 68